Instructor's Manual with Test Bank for Spielvogel's

WESTERN CIVILIZATION

A Brief History

Third Edition

Eugene Larson

Los Angeles Pierce College

Australia • Canada • Mexico • Singapore • Spain • United Kingdom • United States

Printed in the United States of America
1 2 3 4 5 6 7 08 07 06 05 04

Printer: West Group

ISBN 0-534-62724-2

For more information about our products, contact us at:
Thomson Learning Academic Resource Center
1-800-423-0563
For permission to use material from this text or product, submit a request online at
http://www.thomsonrights.com
Any additional questions about permissions can be submitted by email to thomsonrights@thomson.com

Thomson Wadsworth
10 Davis Drive
Belmont, CA 94002-3098
USA

Asia
Thomson Learning
5 Shenton Way #01-01
UIC Building
Singapore 068808

Australia/New Zealand
Thomson Learning
102 Dodds Street
Southbank, Victoria 3006
Australia

Canada
Nelson
1120 Birchmount Road
Toronto, Ontario M1K 5G4
Canada

Europe/Middle East/South Africa
Thomson Learning
High Holborn House
50/51 Bedford Row
London WC1R 4LR
United Kingdom

Latin America
Thomson Learning
Seneca, 53
Colonia Polanco
11560 Mexico D.F.
Mexico

Spain/Portugal
Paraninfo
Calle/Magallanes, 25
28015 Madrid
Spain

Resource Integration Guide

For Spielvogel's

Western Civilization: A Brief History

Third Edition

Chapter 1—The Ancient Near East: The First Civilizations

Class Preparation and Lecture Tools

Instructor's Manual/ Test Bank
Includes suggestions for teaching Chapter 1, such as a chapter outline and summary, suggested student essay and research topics, discussion questions for the artwork and primary sources, detailed teaching resources, and Web links.

Book Companion Web Site http://history.wadsworth.com/spielvogelbrief03
Access to the Instructor's Manual and Test Bank, chapter outlines, InfoTrac College Edition exercises, and Internet activities for Chapter 1.

CNN® Today Video Western Civilization
Volume II: *Egyptian Art*
Volume III: *Origins of Modern Humans*

Full Color Map Acetate Package
1–9

Sights and Sounds of History Video
Ancient Egypt

World History Video Library
Ancient Britains
Ancient Egypt

Lecture Enrichment Slides, Set I
1–5

Testing Tools and Course Management

Instructor's Resource CD-ROM with ExamView®
Resources for Chapter 1.

WebTutor™ ToolBox
Text-specific online quizzing and student resources for Chapter 1, combined with course management functionality.

Instructor's Manual/ Test Bank
More than 100 questions, including multiple-choice, true/false, identification, short essay, and long essay questions for Chapter 1.

Study Aids, Tutorials, and Quizzing

History Interactive CD-ROM
Chapter 1: Organized by chapter, this study tool emphasizes key information to keep students focused on critical ideas and prepare them for tests.

Book Companion Web Site http://history.wadsworth.com/spielvogelbrief03
Chapter outlines, learning objectives, InfoTrac College Edition activities, relevant Web links and interactive quizzing for Chapter 1.

InfoTrac® College Edition
Keywords:
- antiquities
- Mesopotamia
- archeology
- Egypt

Map Exercise Workbook I
Part 1: The Ancient World: The First Civilizations: The Near East and Egypt

Document Exercise Workbook I
Chapter 1: The Nature of History
Chapter 2: Applying the Basics to Historical Sources
An Historical Artifact and the Code of Hammurabi

MapTutor CD-ROM
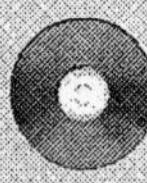
Part I: The Ancient World

Beyond the Book: Research, Writing, and Exploration

The Wadsworth Western Civilization Research Center http://history.wadsworth.com/western
Features Web links, interactive maps and timelines, and more for students to explore.

The Journey of Civilization CD-ROM
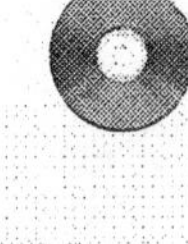
The Evolution of Writing
Hammurabi's Code
King Tut's Tomb

Magellan Atlas of Western Civilization
Maps 2, 3

Sources of World History, Volume I
Stories of Creation: 3
The Cradle of Civilization: 6, 8 and 9

ArtStudy CD-ROM
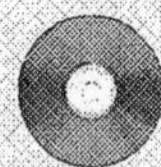
Chapters 1 and 3

HITS on the Web: History
Tips on using the Internet for assignments, studying, and research.

H-Connect: Interactive Explorations in Western Civilization

- The Origins of Western Civilization: Mesopotamia and Egypt, 3000–1200 B.C.

Chapter 2—The Ancient Near East: Peoples and Empires

Class Preparation and Lecture Tools

Instructor's Manual/ Test Bank
Includes suggestions for teaching Chapter 2, such as a chapter outline and summary, suggested student essay and research topics, discussion questions for the artwork and primary sources, detailed teaching resources, and Web links.

Book Companion Web Site http://history.wadsworth.com/spielvogelbrief03
Access to the Instructor's Manual and Test Bank, chapter outlines, InfoTrac College Edition exercises, and Internet activities for Chapter 2.

CNN® Today Video Western Civilization
Volume I: *Jerusalem*

Full Color Map Acetate Package
10–15

World History Video Library
Ancient Britons
Stonehenge
Back to the Bronze Age

Lecture Enrichment Slides, Set I
1–5

Testing Tools and Course Management

Instructor's Resource CD-ROM with ExamView®
Resources for Chapter 2.

WebTutor™ ToolBox
Text-specific online quizzing and student resources for Chapter 2, combined with course management functionality.

Instructor's Manual/ Test Bank
More than 100 questions, including multiple-choice, true/false, identification, short essay, and long essay questions for Chapter 2.

Study Aids, Tutorials, and Quizzing

History Interactive CD-ROM
Chapter 2: Organized by chapter, this study tool emphasizes key information to keep students focused on critical ideas and prepare them for tests.

Book Companion Web Site http://history.wadsworth.com/spielvogelbrief03
Chapter outlines, learning objectives, InfoTrac College Edition activities, relevant Web links and interactive quizzing for Chapter 2.

InfoTrac® College Edition
Keywords:
- Ancient Israel
- Assyrian
- Babylonian
- Phoenician
- Persian

Map Exercise Workbook I
Part 1: The Ancient World: The First Civilizations: The Near East and Egypt

MapTutor CD-ROM
Part I: The Ancient World

Beyond the Book: Research, Writing, and Exploration

The Wadsworth Western Civilization Research Center http://history.wadsworth.com/western
Features Web links, interactive maps and timelines, and more for students to explore.

Magellan Atlas of Western Civilization
Maps 3, 4

Sources of World History, Volume I
Stories of Creation: 4
The Cradle of Civilization: 10

ArtStudy CD-ROM
Chapter 2

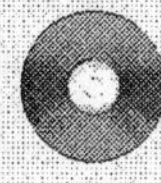

HITS on the Web: History
Tips on using the Internet for assignments, studying, and research.

Chapter 3—The Civilization of the Greeks

Class Preparation and Lecture Tools

Instructor's Manual/ Test Bank
Includes suggestions for teaching Chapter 3, such as a chapter outline and summary, suggested student essay and research topics, discussion questions for the artwork and primary sources, detailed teaching resources, and Web links.

Book Companion Web Site http://history.wadsworth.com/spielvogelbrief03
Access to the Instructor's Manual and Test Bank, chapter outlines, InfoTrac College Edition exercises, and Internet activities for Chapter 3.

CNN® Today Video Western Civilization
Volume II:
Ancient Greece
Ancient Messene
Elgin Marbles
Ancient Games
Music of Ancient Greece

Full-Color Map Acetate Package
17–23

Sights and Sounds of History Video
Ancient Greece

World History Video Library
Ancient Greece

Lecture Enrichment Slides, Set I
6–10

Testing Tools and Course Management

Instructor's Resource CD-ROM with ExamView®

Resources for Chapter 3.

WebTutor™ ToolBox
Text-specific online quizzing and student resources for Chapter 3, combined with course management functionality.

Instructor's Manual/ Test Bank
More than 100 questions, including multiple-choice, true/false, identification, short essay, and long essay questions for Chapter 3.

Study Aids, Tutorials, and Quizzing

History Interactive CD-ROM
Chapter 3: Organized by chapter, this study tool emphasizes key information to keep students focused on critical ideas and prepare them for tests.

Book Companion Web Site http://history.wadsworth.com/spielvogelbrief03
Chapter outlines, learning objectives, InfoTrac College Edition activities, relevant Web links and interactive quizzing for Chapter 3.

InfoTrac® College Edition
Keywords:
- ► Greek history
- ► Greek mythology
- ► Peloponnesian War

Map Exercise Workbook I
Part 1: The Ancient World: Colonialism and Imperialism: Greece

Document Exercise Workbook I
Chapter 3: A Basic Historical Skill-Selection: The Greeks

MapTutor CD-ROM

Part I: The Ancient World

Beyond the Book: Research, Writing, and Exploration

The Wadsworth Western Civilization Research Center http://history.wadsworth.com/western
Features Web links, interactive maps and timelines, and more for students to explore.

Magellan Atlas of Western Civilization
Maps 6, 7

Sources of World History, Volume I
Archaic and Classical Greece: 11–15

ArtStudy CD-ROM
Chapters 4 and 5

HITS on the Web: History
Tips on using the Internet for assignments, studying, and research.

H-Connect: Interactive Explorations in Western Civilization

- ► Ancient Greek and Roman Art and Architecture, c. 550 B.C.–330 A.D.

Chapter 4—The Hellenistic World

Class Preparation and Lecture Tools

Instructor's Manual/ Test Bank
Includes suggestions for teaching Chapter 4, such as a chapter outline and summary, suggested student essay and research topics, discussion questions for the artwork and primary sources, detailed teaching resources, and Web links.

Book Companion Web Site http://history.wadsworth.com/spielvogelbrief03
Access to the Instructor's Manual and Test Bank, chapter outlines, InfoTrac College Edition exercises, and Internet activities for Chapter 4.

CNN® Today Video Western Civilization
Volume I: *Alexander the Great*

Full-Color Map Acetate Package
24–25

Sights and Sounds of History Video
Macedonia and Hellenism

World History Video Library
Ancient Greece

Lecture Enrichment Slides, Set I
6–10

Testing Tools and Course Management

Instructor's Resource CD-ROM with ExamView®
Resources for Chapter 4.

WebTUTOR ToolBox

WebTutor™ ToolBox
Text-specific online quizzing and student resources for Chapter 4, combined with course management functionality.

Instructor's Manual/ Test Bank
More than 100 questions, including multiple-choice, true/false, identification, short essay, and long essay questions for Chapter 4.

Study Aids, Tutorials, and Quizzing

History Interactive CD-ROM
Chapter 4: Organized by chapter, this study tool emphasizes key information to keep students focused on critical ideas and prepare them for tests.

Book Companion Web Site http://history.wadsworth.com/spielvogelbrief03
Chapter outlines, learning objectives, InfoTrac College Edition activities, relevant Web links and interactive quizzing for Chapter 4.

InfoTrac® College Edition
Keywords:
- Greek history
- Alexander the Great
- Archimedes

Map Exercise Workbook I
Part 1: The Ancient World: Colonialism and Imperialism: Greece and Macedonia

Document Exercise Workbook I
Chapter 3: A Basic Historical Skill-Selection: The Greeks

MapTutor CD-ROM
Part I: The Ancient World

Beyond the Book: Research, Writing, and Exploration

The Wadsworth Western Civilization Research Center http://history.wadsworth.com/western
Features Web links, interactive maps and timelines, and more for students to explore.

Magellan Atlas of Western Civilization
Map 8

Sources of World History, Volume I
Archaic and Classical Greece: 14–15

ArtStudy CD-ROM
Chapter 5

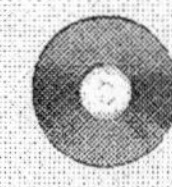

HITS on the Web: History
Tips on using the Internet for assignments, studying, and research.

Chapter 5—The Roman Republic

Class Preparation and Lecture Tools

Instructor's Manual/ Test Bank
Includes suggestions for teaching Chapter 5, such as a chapter outline and summary, suggested student essay and research topics, discussion questions for the artwork and primary sources, detailed teaching resources, and Web links.

Book Companion Web Site http://history.wadsworth.com/spielvogelbrief03
Access to the Instructor's Manual and Test Bank, chapter outlines, InfoTrac College Edition exercises, and Internet activities for Chapter 5.

CNN® Today Video Western Civilization
Volume I: *Puglia, Italy*
Volume II: *Roman Games*
Volume III: *History of European Currency*

Full Color Map Acetate Package
26–31

Sights and Sounds of History Video
Roman Culture and Life

World History Video Library
Ancient Rome

Lecture Enrichment Slides, Set I
11–15

Testing Tools and Course Management

Instructor's Resource CD-ROM with ExamView®
Resources for Chapter 5.

WebTUTOR ToolBox

WebTutor™ ToolBox
Text-specific online quizzing and student resources for Chapter 5, combined with course management functionality.

Instructor's Manual/ Test Bank
More than 100 questions, including multiple-choice, true/false, identification, short essay, and long essay questions for Chapter 5.

Study Aids, Tutorials, and Quizzing

History Interactive CD-ROM
Chapter 5: Organized by chapter, this study tool emphasizes key information to keep students focused on critical ideas and prepare them for tests.

Book Companion Web Site http://history.wadsworth.com/spielvogelbrief03
Chapter outlines, learning objectives, InfoTrac College Edition activities, relevant Web links and interactive quizzing for Chapter 5.

InfoTrac® College Edition
Keywords:
- Rome history
- Roman republic
- Roman mythology
- Roman law

Map Exercise Workbook I
Part 1: The Ancient World: Rome and Its Empire

Document Exercise Workbook I
Chapter 3: Change and Continuity in Similar Documents; The Roman Twelve Tables

MapTutor CD-ROM
Part I: The Ancient World

Beyond the Book: Research, Writing, and Exploration

The Wadsworth Western Civilization Research Center http://history.wadsworth.com/western
Features Web links, interactive maps and timelines, and more for students to explore.

The Journey of Civilization CD-ROM
Rome Wasn't Built in a Day

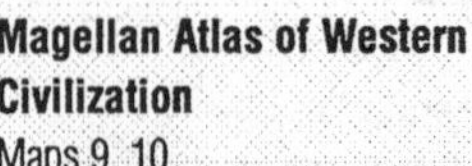

Magellan Atlas of Western Civilization
Maps 9, 10

Sources of World History, Volume I
Ancient Rome: 25

ArtStudy CD-ROM
Chapter 9

HITS on the Web: History
Tips on using the Internet for assignments, studying, and research.

H-Connect: Interactive Explorations in Western Civilization

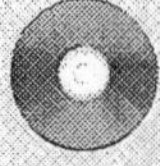

- Ancient Greek and Roman Art and Architecture, c. 550 B.C.–330 A.D.

Chapter 6—The Roman Empire

Class Preparation and Lecture Tools

Instructor's Manual/ Test Bank
Includes suggestions for teaching Chapter 6, such as a chapter outline and summary, suggested student essay and research topics, discussion questions for the artwork and primary sources, detailed teaching resources, and Web links.

Book Companion Web Site http://history.wadsworth.com/spielvogelbrief03
Access to the Instructor's Manual and Test Bank, chapter outlines, InfoTrac College Edition exercises, and Internet activities for Chapter 6.

CNN® Today Video Western Civilization
Volume I: *Puglia, Italy*
Volume II: *Roman Games*
Volume III: *History of European Currency*

Full-Color Map Acetate Package
32–38

Sights and Sounds of History Video
Roman Culture and Life

World History Video Library
Ancient Rome
The Celts

Lecture Enrichment Slides, Set I
11–15

Testing Tools and Course Management

Instructor's Resource CD-ROM with ExamView®
Resources for Chapter 6.

WebTUTOR ToolBox

WebTutor™ ToolBox
Text-specific online quizzing and student resources for Chapter 6, combined with course management functionality.

Instructor's Manual/ Test Bank
More than 100 questions, including multiple-choice, true/false, identification, short essay, and long essay questions for Chapter 6.

Study Aids, Tutorials, and Quizzing

History Interactive CD-ROM
Chapter 6: Organized by chapter, this study tool emphasizes key information to keep students focused on critical ideas and prepare them for tests.

Book Companion Web Site http://history.wadsworth.com/spielvogelbrief03
Chapter outlines, learning objectives, InfoTrac College Edition activities, relevant Web links and interactive quizzing for Chapter 6.

InfoTrac® College Edition
Keywords:
- Roman Empire
- Roman mythology
- Roman law
- Constantine

Map Exercise Workbook I
Part 1: The Ancient World: Rome and Its Empire

Document Exercise Workbook I
Chapter 5: Disagreeing with the Experts: St. Paul on Women

MapTutor CD-ROM
Part I: The Ancient World
Part II: Late Antiquity and the Middle Ages

Beyond the Book: Research, Writing, and Exploration

The Wadsworth Western Civilization Research Center http://history.wadsworth.com/western
Features Web links, interactive maps and timelines, and more for students to explore.

The Journey of Civilization CD-ROM
Rome Wasn't Built in a Day

Magellan Atlas of Western Civilization
Maps 10–12

Sources of World History, Volume I
Ancient Rome: 26–28

ArtStudy CD-ROM
Chapter 10

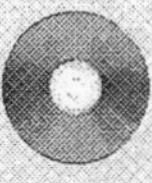

HITS on the Web: History
Tips on using the Internet for assignments, studying, and research.

H-Connect: Interactive Explorations in Western Civilization
- Ancient Greek and Roman Art and Architecture, c. 550 B.C.–330 A.D.

Chapter 7—The Passing of the Roman World and the Emergence of Medieval Civilization

Class Preparation and Lecture Tools

Instructor's Manual/ Test Bank
Includes suggestions for teaching Chapter 7, such as a chapter outline and summary, suggested student essay and research topics, discussion questions for the artwork and primary sources, detailed teaching resources, and Web links.

Book Companion Web Site http://history.wadsworth.com/spielvogelbrief03
Access to the Instructor's Manual and Test Bank, chapter outlines, InfoTrac College Edition exercises, and Internet activities for Chapter 7.

CNN® Today Video Western Civilization
Volume I: *Monastery Life*
Volume II: *Greek Music Resurrection*
Volume III: *History of Church Celibacy*

Full-Color Map Acetate Package
39–47

Sights and Sounds of History Video
The Byzantine Empire

World History Video Library
Ancient Rome
The Birth of the Middle Ages
Storm Over Europe

Lecture Enrichment Slides, Set I
16–18

Testing Tools and Course Management

Instructor's Resource CD-ROM with ExamView®
Resources for Chapter 7.

WebTUTOR ToolBox

WebTutor™ ToolBox
Text-specific online quizzing and student resources for Chapter 7, combined with course management functionality.

Instructor's Manual/ Test Bank
More than 100 questions, including multiple-choice, true/false, identification, short essay, and long essay questions for Chapter 7.

Study Aids, Tutorials, and Quizzing

History Interactive CD-ROM
Chapter 7: Organized by chapter, this study tool emphasizes key information to keep students focused on critical ideas and prepare them for tests.

Book Companion Web Site http://history.wadsworth.com/spielvogelbrief03
Chapter outlines, learning objectives, InfoTrac College Edition activities, relevant Web links and interactive quizzing for Chapter 7.

InfoTrac® College Edition
Keywords:
- Byzantium
- early Christianity
- Augustine
- Middle Ages

Map Exercise Workbook I:
Part 2: Late Antiquity and the Middle Ages:
Competing Empires: Byzantines and Carolingians
New People: Goths, Germans, and Slavs

Document Exercise Workbook I
Chapter 6: What Do You Believe?: The Emperor Justinian and His Court Historian Procopius

MapTutor CD-ROM

Part II: Late Antiquity and the Middle Ages

Beyond the Book: Research, Writing, and Exploration

The Wadsworth Western Civilization Research Center http://history.wadsworth.com/western

Features Web links, interactive maps and timelines, and more for students to explore.

The Journey of Civilization CD-ROM
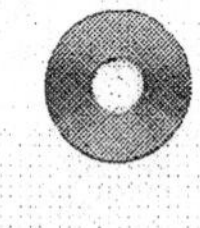
The Adventures of Ibn Battuta

Magellan Atlas of Western Civilization
Maps 12, 13

Sources of World History, Volume I
Africa and the Muslim World: 29–31
Europe After the Fall of Rome: 44–45
The Development of Christianity: 49 and 50

ArtStudy CD-ROM
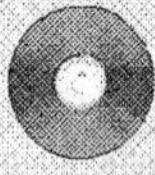
Chapters 11 and 12

HITS on the Web: History
Tips on using the Internet for assignments, studying, and research.

H-Connect: Interactive Explorations in Western Civilization
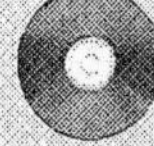
- Medieval Art and Architecture
- A Year in the Life of a Medieval Peasant
- Medieval Constantinople: The God-Guarded City

Chapter 8—European Civilization in the Early Middle Ages, 750–1000

Class Preparation and Lecture Tools

Instructor's Manual/ Test Bank
Includes suggestions for teaching Chapter 8, such as a chapter outline and summary, suggested student essay and research topics, discussion questions for the artwork and primary sources, detailed teaching resources, and Web links.

Book Companion Web Site http://history.wadsworth.com/spielvogelbrief03
Access to the Instructor's Manual and Test Bank, chapter outlines, InfoTrac College Edition exercises, and Internet activities for Chapter 8.

CNN® Today Video Western Civilization
Volume II: *Byzantine Art*
Greek Musical Resurrection

Full-Color Map Acetate Package
48–56

Sights and Sounds of History Video
Medieval Castles
Knights and Chivalry

World History Video Library
The Vikings
Charlemagne and the Holy Roman Empire
The Feudal System
Vikings and Normans

Lecture Enrichment Slides, Set I
19 and 20

Testing Tools and Course Management

Instructor's Resource CD-ROM with ExamView®
Resources for Chapter 8.

WebTUTOR ToolBox

WebTutor™ ToolBox
Text-specific online quizzing and student resources for Chapter 8, combined with course management functionality.

Instructor's Manual/ Test Bank
More than 100 questions, including multiple-choice, true/false, identification, short essay, and long essay questions for Chapter 8.

Study Aids, Tutorials, and Quizzing

History Interactive CD-ROM
Chapter 8: Organized by chapter, this study tool emphasizes key information to keep students focused on critical ideas and prepare them for tests.

Book Companion Web Site http://history.wadsworth.com/spielvogelbrief03
Chapter outlines, learning objectives, InfoTrac College Edition activities, relevant Web links and interactive quizzing for Chapter 8.

InfoTrac® College Edition
Keywords:
- Carolingian
- Charlemagne
- Vikings not Minnesota
- feudalism
- feudal

Map Exercise Workbook I
Part 2: Late Antiquity and the Middle Ages;
New Ideas: Christianity and Islam

Document Exercise Workbook I
Chapter 7: Historical Generalization: Judaism; Christianity; Islam
Chapter 8: Comparing and Contrasting Historical Documents: Germanic Law

MapTutor CD-ROM
Part II: Late Antiquity and the Middle Ages

Beyond the Book: Research, Writing, and Exploration

The Wadsworth Western Civilization Research Center http://history.wadsworth.com/western
Features Web links, interactive maps and timelines, and more for students to explore.

The Journey of Civilization CD-ROM
The Evolution of Writing
Hammurabi's Code
King Tut's Tomb

Magellan Atlas of Western Civilization
Maps 12, 13

Sources of World History, Volume I
Europe After the Fall of Rome: Chapters 46 and 48

ArtStudy CD-ROM
Chapters 12 and 13

HITS on the Web: History
Tips on using the Internet for assignments, studying, and research.

H-Connect: Interactive Explorations in Western Civilization
- A Year in the Life of a Medieval Peasant
- Constantinople: The God-Guarded City

Chapter 9—The Recovery and Growth of European Society in the High Middle Ages

Class Preparation and Lecture Tools

Instructor's Manual/ Test Bank
Includes suggestions for teaching Chapter 9, such as a chapter outline and summary, suggested student essay and research topics, discussion questions for the artwork and primary sources, detailed teaching resources, and Web links.

Book Companion Web Site http://history.wadsworth.com/spielvogelbrief03
Access to the Instructor's Manual and Test Bank, chapter outlines, InfoTrac College Edition exercises, and Internet activities for Chapter 9.

Full Color Map Acetate Package
57–60

Sights and Sounds of History Video
The Spiritual Visions of Hildegard of Bingen

World History Video Library
The Luttrell Psalter: Everyday Life in Medieval England
Medieval Manuscripts
World Inscribed: The Illuminated Manuscript

Lecture Enrichment Slides, Set I
21–25

Testing Tools and Course Management

Instructor's Resource CD-ROM with ExamView®
Resources for Chapter 9.

WebTUTOR ToolBox

WebTutor™ ToolBox
Text-specific online quizzing and student resources for Chapter 9, combined with course management functionality.

Instructor's Manual/ Test Bank
More than 100 questions, including multiple-choice, true/false, identification, short essay, and long essay questions for Chapter 9.

Study Aids, Tutorials, and Quizzing

History Interactive CD-ROM
Chapter 9: Organized by chapter, this study tool emphasizes key information to keep students focused on critical ideas and prepare them for tests.

Book Companion Web Site http://history.wadsworth.com/spielvogelbrief03
Chapter outlines, learning objectives, InfoTrac College Edition activities, relevant Web links and interactive quizzing for Chapter 9.

InfoTrac® College Edition
Keywords:
- peasantry
- cities and towns
- Middle Ages

Map Exercise Workbook I
Part 3: Late Middle Ages to the Reformation:
The Spread of New Ideas: Education

Document Exercise Workbook I
Chapter 9: Digging for Evidence: The Canterbury Tales and the Middle Ages

MapTutor CD-ROM

Part II: Late Antiquity and the Middle Ages

Beyond the Book: Research, Writing, and Exploration

The Wadsworth Western Civilization Research Center http://history.wadsworth.com/western
Features Web links, interactive maps and timelines, and more for students to explore.

Magellan Atlas of Western Civilization
Map 14

Sources of World History, Volume I
The Development of Christianity: 52

Wright Music CD-ROM

2-CD Set: 1/1
6-CD Set: 1/1–1/5

HITS on the Web: History
Tips on using the Internet for assignments, studying, and research.

H-Connect: Interactive Explorations in Western Civilization

- A Year in the Life of a Medieval Peasant Family

Chapter 10—The Rise of Kingdoms and the Growth of Church Power

Class Preparation and Lecture Tools

Instructor's Manual/ Test Bank
Includes suggestions for teaching Chapter 10, such as a chapter outline and summary, suggested student essay and research topics, discussion questions for the artwork and primary sources, detailed teaching resources, and Web links.

Book Companion Web Site http://history.wadsworth.com/spielvogelbrief03
Access to the Instructor's Manual and Test Bank, chapter outlines, InfoTrac College Edition exercises, and Internet activities for Chapter 10.

CNN® Today Video Western Civilization
Volume I: *Monastery Life*
Volume III: *The Crusades*

Full-Color Map Acetate Package
61–70

Sights and Sounds of History Video
Medieval Castles
Knights and Chivalry

World History Video Library
Battle of Hastings
Christians, Jews, and Moslems in Medieval Spain

Lecture Enrichment Slides, Set I
21–25

Testing Tools and Course Management

Instructor's Resource CD-ROM with ExamView®
Resources for Chapter 10.

WebTutor ToolBox

WebTutor™ ToolBox
Text-specific online quizzing and student resources for Chapter 10, combined with course management functionality.

Instructor's Manual/ Test Bank
More than 100 questions, including multiple-choice, true/false, identification, short essay, and long essay questions for Chapter 10.

Study Aids, Tutorials, and Quizzing

History Interactive CD-ROM
Chapter 10: Organized by chapter, this study tool emphasizes key information to keep students focused on critical ideas and prepare them for tests.

Book Companion Web Site http://history.wadsworth.com/spielvogelbrief03
Chapter outlines, learning objectives, InfoTrac College Edition activities, relevant Web links and interactive quizzing for Chapter 10.

InfoTrac® College Edition
Keywords:
- medieval Germany
- medieval England
- Saint Francis
- Crusades

Document Exercise Workbook I
Chapter 9: Digging for Evidence: The Canterbury Tales and the Middle Ages

MapTutor CD-ROM
Part II: Late Antiquity and the Middle Ages
Part III: Late Middle Ages and the Reformation

Beyond the Book: Research, Writing, and Exploration

The Wadsworth Western Civilization Research Center http://history.wadsworth.com/western
Features Web links, interactive maps and timelines, and more for students to explore.

Magellan Atlas of Western Civilization
Map 16

Sources of World History, Volume I
Europe After the Fall of Rome: 47
The Development of Christianity: 51
Cultures in Collision: 57–60

ArtStudy CD-ROM
Chapters 17 and 18

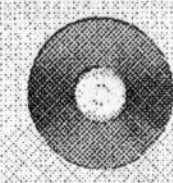

Wright Music CD-ROM
2-CD Set: 1/1
6-CD Set: 1/1–1/5

HITS on the Web: History
Tips on using the Internet for assignments, studying, and research.

H-Connect: Interactive Explorations in Western Civilization
- Medieval Constantinople: The God-Guarded City

Chapter 11—The Late Middle Ages: Crisis and Disintegration in the Fourteenth Century

Class Preparation and Lecture Tools

Instructor's Manual/ Test Bank
Includes suggestions for teaching Chapter 11, such as a chapter outline and summary, suggested student essay and research topics, discussion questions for the artwork and primary sources, detailed teaching resources, and Web links.

Book Companion Web Site http://history.wadsworth.com/spielvogelbrief03
Access to the Instructor's Manual and Test Bank, chapter outlines, InfoTrac College Edition exercises, and Internet activities for Chapter 11.

CNN® Today Video Western Civilization
Volume I: *Monastery Life*
Volume III: *History of Church Celibacy*

Full-Color Map Acetate Package
71–75

Sights and Sounds of History Video
Medieval Castles
Knights and Chivalry
The Spiritual Visions of Hildegard of Bingen

Testing Tools and Course Management

Instructor's Resource CD-ROM with ExamView®
Resources for Chapter 11.

WebTUTOR ToolBox

WebTutor™ ToolBox
Text-specific online quizzing and student resources for Chapter 11, combined with course management functionality.

Instructor's Manual/ Test Bank
More than 100 questions, including multiple-choice, true/false, identification, short essay, and long essay questions for Chapter 11.

Study Aids, Tutorials, and Quizzing

History Interactive CD-ROM
Chapter 11: Organized by chapter, this study tool emphasizes key information to keep students focused on critical ideas and prepare them for tests.

Book Companion Web Site http://history.wadsworth.com/spielvogelbrief03
Chapter outlines, learning objectives, InfoTrac College Edition activities, relevant Web links and interactive quizzing for Chapter 11.

InfoTrac® College Edition
Keywords:
- Black Death
- Edward III
- Hundred Years' War

Document Exercise Workbook I
Chapter 9: Digging for Evidence: The Canterbury Tales and the Middle Ages

MapTutor CD-ROM
Part III: Late Middle Ages and the Reformation

Beyond the Book: Research, Writing, and Exploration

The Wadsworth Western Civilization Research Center http://history.wadsworth.com/western
Features Web links, interactive maps and timelines, and more for students to explore.

The Journey of Civilization CD-ROM
World Trade and the Black Death

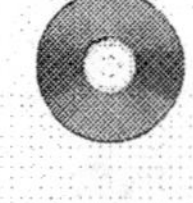

Magellan Atlas of Western Civilization
Maps 15–17

Sources of World History, Volume I
The Development of Christianity: 53

ArtStudy CD-ROM
Chapter 19

Wright Music CD-ROM
2-CD Set: 1/1
6-CD Set: 1/1-1/5

HITS on the Web: History
Tips on using the Internet for assignments, studying, and research.

Chapter 12—Recovery and Rebirth: The Age of the Renaissance

Class Preparation and Lecture Tools

Instructor's Manual/ Test Bank
Includes suggestions for teaching Chapter 12, such as a chapter outline and summary, suggested student essay and research topics, discussion questions for the artwork and primary sources, detailed teaching resources, and Web links.

Book Companion Web Site http://history.wadsworth.com/spielvogelbrief03
Access to the Instructor's Manual and Test Bank, chapter outlines, InfoTrac College Edition exercises, and Internet activities for Chapter 12.

CNN® Today Video Western Civilization
Volume I: *Puglia*
Leonardo's Horse
Volume II: *Dresden Orb*

Full-Color Map Acetate Package
76–78

Sights and Sounds of History Video
The Renaissance

World History Video Library
The Italian Renaissance

Lecture Enrichment Slides, Set I
26–43

Testing Tools and Course Management

Instructor's Resource CD-ROM with ExamView®
Resources for Chapter 12.

WebTUTOR ToolBox

WebTutor™ ToolBox
Text-specific online quizzing and student resources for Chapter 12, combined with course management functionality.

Instructor's Manual/ Test Bank
More than 100 questions, including multiple-choice, true/false, identification, short essay, and long essay questions for Chapter 12.

Study Aids, Tutorials, and Quizzing

History Interactive CD-ROM
Chapter 12: Organized by chapter, this study tool emphasizes key information to keep students focused on critical ideas and prepare them for tests.

Book Companion Web Site http://history.wadsworth.com/spielvogelbrief03
Chapter outlines, learning objectives, InfoTrac College Edition activities, relevant Web links and interactive quizzing for Chapter 12.

InfoTrac® College Edition
Keywords:
- Renaissance
- Machiavelli
- humanism
- Leonardo da Vinci

Map Exercise Workbook I
Part 3: Late Middle Ages to the Reformation;
Culture and Politics: Italy and the Renaissance

Document Exercise Workbook I
Chapter 10: Visual and Written Sources: Piecing Together the Evidence
Renaissance Humanism

MapTutor CD-ROM

Part III: Late Middle Ages and the Reformation

Beyond the Book: Research, Writing, and Exploration

The Wadsworth Western Civilization Research Center http://history.wadsworth.com/western
Features Web links, interactive maps and timelines, and more for students to explore.

Magellan Atlas of Western Civilization
Maps 17, 20

Sources of World History, Volume I
The Italian Renaissance: 54–56

ArtStudy CD-ROM
Chapters 19–22

Wright Music CD-ROM
2-CD Set: 1/2–1/3
6-CD Set: 1/6–1/7

HITS on the Web: History
Tips on using the Internet for assignments, studying, and research.

Chapter 13—Reformation and Religious Warfare in the Sixteenth Century

Class Preparation and Lecture Tools

Instructor's Manual/ Test Bank
Includes suggestions for teaching Chapter 13, such as a chapter outline and summary, suggested student essay and research topics, discussion questions for the artwork and primary sources, detailed teaching resources, and Web links.

Book Companion Web Site http://history.wadsworth.com/spielvogelbrief03
Access to the Instructor's Manual and Test Bank, chapter outlines, InfoTrac College Edition exercises, and Internet activities for Chapter 13.

CNN® Today Video Western Civilization
Volume I: *Monastery Life*
Volume II: *History of Church Celibacy*

Full-Color Map Acetate Package
79–84

World History Video Library
The Defeat of the Spanish Armada: Twelve Summer Days, 1588
The Spanish Armada

Lecture Enrichment Slides, Set I
26–43

Testing Tools and Course Management

Instructor's Resource CD-ROM with ExamView®
Resources for Chapter 13.

WebTutor ToolBox

WebTutor™ ToolBox
Text-specific online quizzing and student resources for Chapter 13, combined with course management functionality.

Instructor's Manual/ Test Bank
More than 100 questions, including multiple-choice, true/false, identification, short essay, and long essay questions for Chapter 13.

Study Aids, Tutorials, and Quizzing

History Interactive CD-ROM
Chapter 13: Organized by chapter, this study tool emphasizes key information to keep students focused on critical ideas and prepare them for tests.

Book Companion Web Site http://history.wadsworth.com/spielvogelbrief03
Chapter outlines, learning objectives, InfoTrac College Edition activities, relevant Web links and interactive quizzing for Chapter 13.

InfoTrac® College Edition
Keywords:
- Reformation
- Counter-Reformation
- Martin Luther not King
- John Calvin
- Elizabeth I

Map Exercise Workbook I
Part II: Late Middle Ages to the Reformation;
Politics and Religion: The Reformation

Document Exercise Workbook I
Chapter 12: Discovering Something New About Someone Well-Known: Martin Luther and the Reformation

MapTutor CD-ROM

Part III: Late Middle Ages and the Reformation

Beyond the Book: Research, Writing, and Exploration

The Wadsworth Western Civilization Research Center http://history.wadsworth.com/western
Features Web links, interactive maps and timelines, and more for students to explore.

Magellan Atlas of Western Civilization
Map 20

Sources of World History, Volume I
The Reform of Christianity: 81–84
Volume II
Monarchy and Revolution: 85

ArtStudy CD-ROM

Chapter 23

Wright Music CD-ROM

6-CD Set: 1/8–1/9

HITS on the Web: History
Tips on using the Internet for assignments, studying, and research.

Class Preparation and Lecture Tools

Instructor's Manual/ Test Bank
Includes suggestions for teaching Chapter 14, such as a chapter outline and summary, suggested student essay and research topics, discussion questions for the artwork and primary sources, detailed teaching resources, and Web links.

Book Companion Web Site http://history.wadsworth.com/spielvogelbrief03
Access to the Instructor's Manual and Test Bank, chapter outlines, InfoTrac College Edition exercises, and Internet activities for Chapter 14.

CNN® Today Video Western Civilization
Volume I: *Portugal*

Full-Color Map Acetate Package
85–94

Sights and Sounds of History Video
Spanish Invasions and Pueblo Revolts

World History Video Library
Masters in the Colonies
The Paths of Colonialism

Testing Tools and Course Management

Instructor's Resource CD-ROM with ExamView®
Resources for Chapter 14.

WebTUTOR ToolBox

WebTutor™ ToolBox
Text-specific online quizzing and student resources for Chapter 14, combined with course management functionality.

Instructor's Manual/ Test Bank
More than 100 questions, including multiple-choice, true/false, identification, short essay, and long essay questions for Chapter 14.

Study Aids, Tutorials, and Quizzing

History Interactive CD-ROM
Chapter 14: Organized by chapter, this study tool emphasizes key information to keep students focused on critical ideas and prepare them for tests.

Book Companion Web Site http://history.wadsworth.com/spielvogelbrief03
Chapter outlines, learning objectives, InfoTrac College Edition activities, relevant Web links and interactive quizzing for Chapter 14.

InfoTrac® College Edition
Keywords:
- Vasco da Gama
- Ferdinand Magellan
- Christopher Columbus
- mercantilism

Map Exercise Workbook I
Part 4: Early Modern Europe: Expansion, Crisis, Enlightenment East and West: Ottomans in Europe

Document Exercise Workbook I
Chapter 11: The Invaluable Helpmate–Maps; The Age of Discovery

MapTutor CD-ROM
Part IV: Early Modern Europe

Beyond the Book: Research, Writing, and Exploration

The Wadsworth Western Civilization Research Center http://history.wadsworth.com/western
Features Web links, interactive maps and timelines, and more for students to explore.

The Journey of Civilization CD-ROM
An Encounter with the Ancient Maya

Magellan Atlas of Western Civilization
Maps 19, 20, 22, 23

Sources of World History, Volume I
European Encounters: 66–74

ArtStudy CD-ROM
Chapter 22

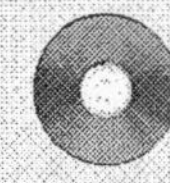

HITS on the Web: History
Tips on using the Internet for assignments, studying, and research.

H-Connect: Interactive Explorations in Western Civilization
- God, Gold, and Glory: Columbus and the Age of Exploration (1415–1776)

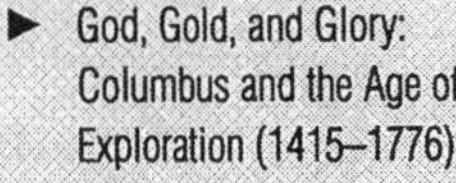

Chapter 15—State Building and the Search for Order in the Seventeenth Century

Class Preparation and Lecture Tools

Instructor's Manual/ Test Bank
Includes suggestions for teaching Chapter 15, such as a chapter outline and summary, suggested student essay and research topics, discussion questions for the artwork and primary sources, detailed teaching resources, and Web links.

Book Companion Web Site http://history.wadsworth.com/spielvogelbrief03
Access to the Instructor's Manual and Test Bank, chapter outlines, InfoTrac College Edition exercises, and Internet activities for Chapter 15.

CNN® Today Video Western Civilization
Volume II: *The Globe Theater*

Full-Color Map Acetate Package
95–103

Sights and Sounds of History Video
Absolutism in Western Europe

World History Video Library
Total War, 1644–1646
Daily Life at the Court of Versailles
Peter the Great

Lecture Enrichment Slides, Set I
44–50

Testing Tools and Course Management

Instructor's Resource CD-ROM with ExamView®

Resources for Chapter 15.

WebTutor™ ToolBox
Text-specific online quizzing and student resources for Chapter 15, combined with course management functionality.

Instructor's Manual/ Test Bank
More than 100 questions, including multiple-choice, true/false, identification, short essay, and long essay questions for Chapter 15.

Study Aids, Tutorials, and Quizzing

History Interactive CD-ROM
Chapter 15: Organized by chapter, this study tool emphasizes key information to keep students focused on critical ideas and prepare them for tests.

Book Companion Web Site http://history.wadsworth.com/spielvogelbrief03
Chapter outlines, learning objectives, InfoTrac College Edition activities, relevant Web links and interactive quizzing for Chapter 15.

InfoTrac® College Edition
Keywords:
- Thirty Years' War
- Peter the Great
- Oliver Cromwell
- Louis XIV

Map Exercise Workbook I
Part 4: Early Modern Europe: Expansion, Crises, and Enlightenment:
East and West: Ottomans in Europe

Document Exercise Workbook I
Chapter 13: Looking Twice and the Same Person: Louis XIV and Divine-Right Monarchy

MapTutor CD-ROM

Part IV: Early Modern Europe

Beyond the Book: Research, Writing, and Exploration

The Wadsworth Western Civilization Research Center http://history.wadsworth.com/western
Features Web links, interactive maps and timelines, and more for students to explore.

Magellan Atlas of Western Civilization
Maps 18, 20

Sources of World History, Volume I
European Politics and War: 85–86
Volume II
Monarchy and Revolution: 84, 86–87

ArtStudy CD-ROM

Chapter 24

Wright Music CD-ROM
2-CD Set: 1/4
6-CD Set: 1/9–1/13

HITS on the Web: History
Tips on using the Internet for assignments, studying, and research.

H-Connect: Interactive Explorations in Western Civilization

- Warfare in Early Modern Europe (1494–1648)
- Comparing Early Modern Art
- Comparing Early Modern Architecture
- Empires of Art: Comparing the Dutch Republic and the Spanish Empire (1500–1700)

Class Preparation and Lecture Tools

Instructor's Manual/ Test Bank
Includes suggestions for teaching Chapter 16, such as a chapter outline and summary, suggested student essay and research topics, discussion questions for the artwork and primary sources, detailed teaching resources, and Web links.

Book Companion Web Site http://history.wadsworth.com/spielvogelbrief03
Access to the Instructor's Manual and Test Bank, chapter outlines, InfoTrac College Edition exercises, and Internet activities for Chapter 16.

Testing Tools and Course Management

Instructor's Resource CD-ROM with ExamView®
Resources for Chapter 16.

WebTutor™ ToolBox
Text-specific online quizzing and student resources for Chapter 16, combined with course management functionality.

Instructor's Manual/ Test Bank
More than 100 questions, including multiple-choice, true/false, identification, short essay, and long essay questions for Chapter 16.

Study Aids, Tutorials, and Quizzing

History Interactive CD-ROM
Chapter 16: Organized by chapter, this study tool emphasizes key information to keep students focused on critical ideas and prepare them for tests.

Book Companion Web Site http://history.wadsworth.com/spielvogelbrief03
Chapter outlines, learning objectives, InfoTrac College Edition activities, relevant Web links and interactive quizzing for Chapter 16.

InfoTrac® College Edition

Keywords:
- Copernicus
- Galileo not Jupiter
- Isaac Newton
- Rene Descartes

Map Exercise Workbook II
Part 4: Early Modern Europe: Technology and Change: The Industrial Revolution

MapTutor CD-ROM
Part IV: Early Modern Europe

Beyond the Book: Research, Writing, and Exploration

The Wadsworth Western Civilization Research Center http://history.wadsworth.com/western
Features Web links, interactive maps and timelines, and more for students to explore.

The Journey of Civilization CD-ROM
Astronomy and the Scientific Revolution

Sources of World History, Volume II
The New Science: 88–89

Wright Music CD-ROM
2-CD Set: 1/4
6-CD Set: 1/9–1/13

HITS on the Web: History
Tips on using the Internet for assignments, studying, and research.

H-Connect: Interactive Explorations in Western Civilization
- The Scientific Revolution (1500–1750)

Chapter 17—The Eighteenth Century: An Age of Enlightenment

Class Preparation and Lecture Tools

Instructor's Manual/ Test Bank
Includes suggestions for teaching Chapter 17, such as a chapter outline and summary, suggested student essay and research topics, discussion questions for the artwork and primary sources, detailed teaching resources, and Web links.

Book Companion Web Site http://history.wadsworth.com/spielvogelbrief03
Access to the Instructor's Manual and Test Bank, chapter outlines, InfoTrac College Edition exercises, and Internet activities for Chapter 17.

Full Color Map Acetate Package
104–106

Lecture Enrichment Slides, Part II
1–5

Testing Tools and Course Management

Instructor's Resource CD-ROM with ExamView®
Resources for Chapter 17.

WebTutor™ ToolBox
Text-specific online quizzing and student resources for Chapter 17, combined with course management functionality.

Instructor's Manual/ Test Bank
More than 100 questions, including multiple-choice, true/false, identification, short essay, and long essay questions for Chapter 17.

Study Aids, Tutorials, and Quizzing

History Interactive CD-ROM
Chapter 17: Organized by chapter, this study tool emphasizes key information to keep students focused on critical ideas and prepare them for tests.

Book Companion Web Site http://history.wadsworth.com/spielvogelbrief03
Chapter outlines, learning objectives, InfoTrac College Edition activities, relevant Web links and interactive quizzing for Chapter 17.

InfoTrac® College Edition
Keywords:
- Copernicus
- Galileo not Jupiter
- Isaac Newton
- Rene Descartes

Map Exercise Workbook II
Part 4: Early Modern Europe: Technology and Change: The Industrial Revolution

MapTutor CD-ROM
Part IV: Early Modern Europe

Beyond the Book: Research, Writing, and Exploration

The Wadsworth Western Civilization Research Center http://history.wadsworth.com/western

Features Web links, interactive maps and timelines, and more for students to explore.

Sources of World History, Volume I
The European Enlightenment : 100–103

Wright Music CD-ROM
2-CD Set: 1/5–1/12
6-CD Set: 1/14–2/12

HITS on the Web: History
Tips on using the Internet for assignments, studying, and research.

Chapter 18—The Eighteenth Century: European States, International Wars, and Social Change

Class Preparation and Lecture Tools

Instructor's Manual/ Test Bank
Includes suggestions for teaching Chapter 18, such as a chapter outline and summary, suggested student essay and research topics, discussion questions for the artwork and primary sources, detailed teaching resources, and Web links.

Book Companion Web Site http://history.wadsworth.com/spielvogelbrief03
Access to the Instructor's Manual and Test Bank, chapter outlines, InfoTrac College Edition exercises, and Internet activities for Chapter 18.

Full Color Map Acetate Package
107–111

Lecture Enrichment Slides, Part II
1–5

Testing Tools and Course Management

Instructor's Resource CD-ROM with ExamView®
Resources for Chapter 18.

WebTutor™ ToolBox
Text-specific online quizzing and student resources for Chapter 18, combined with course management functionality.

Instructor's Manual/ Test Bank
More than 100 questions, including multiple-choice, true/false, identification, short essay, and long essay questions for Chapter 18.

Study Aids, Tutorials, and Quizzing

History Interactive CD-ROM
Chapter 18: Organized by chapter, this study tool emphasizes key information to keep students focused on critical ideas and prepare them for tests.

Book Companion Web Site http://history.wadsworth.com/spielvogelbrief03
Chapter outlines, learning objectives, InfoTrac College Edition activities, relevant Web links and interactive quizzing for Chapter 18.

InfoTrac® College Edition
Keywords:
- William Pitt
- Frederick II or Frederick the Great
- Joseph II
- Catherine the Great

Map Exercise Workbook II
Part 4: Early Modern Europe: Expansion, Crises, and Enlightenment

Document Exercise Workbook II
Chapter 14: The Difficult Art of Biography; Catherine II and Enlightened Despotism

MapTutor CD-ROM
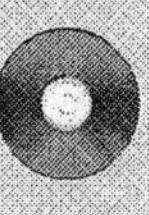
Part V: Europe in the Late 18th and 19th Centuries

Beyond the Book: Research, Writing, and Exploration

The Wadsworth Western Civilization Research Center http://history.wadsworth.com/western
Features Web links, interactive maps and timelines, and more for students to explore.

Magellan Atlas of Western Civilization
Maps 21, 22

Sources of World History, Volume II
The Balance of Power in Europe: 93–95

Wright Music CD-ROM

2-CD Set: 1/5–1/12
6-CD Set: 1/14–2/12

HITS on the Web: History
Tips on using the Internet for assignments, studying, and research.

Chapter 19—A Revolution in Politics: The Era of the French Revolution and Napoleon

Class Preparation and Lecture Tools

Instructor's Manual/ Test Bank
Includes suggestions for teaching Chapter 19, such as a chapter outline and summary, suggested student essay and research topics, discussion questions for the artwork and primary sources, detailed teaching resources, and Web links.

Book Companion Web Site http://history.wadsworth.com/spielvogelbrief03
Access to the Instructor's Manual and Test Bank, chapter outlines, InfoTrac College Edition exercises, and Internet activities for Chapter 19.

Full Color Map Acetate Package
112–116

Sights and Sounds of History Video
Revolutions

World History Video Library
The Battle of Austerlitz, 1805
The Battle of Trafalgar, 1805
The Battle of Waterloo, 1815
Napoleon's Last Great War
Napoleon Bonaparte

Lecture Enrichment Slides, Part II
8–12

Testing Tools and Course Management

Instructor's Resource CD-ROM with ExamView®
Resources for Chapter 19.

WebTUTOR ToolBox

WebTutor™ ToolBox
Text-specific online quizzing and student resources for Chapter 19, combined with course management functionality.

Instructor's Manual/ Test Bank
More than 100 questions, including multiple-choice, true/false, identification, short essay, and long essay questions for Chapter 19.

Study Aids, Tutorials, and Quizzing

History Interactive CD-ROM
Chapter 19: Organized by chapter, this study tool emphasizes key information to keep students focused on critical ideas and prepare them for tests.

Book Companion Web Site http://history.wadsworth.com/spielvogelbrief03
Chapter outlines, learning objectives, InfoTrac College Edition activities, relevant Web links and interactive quizzing for Chapter 19.

InfoTrac® College Edition
Keywords:
- French Revolution
- American Revolution
- Napoleon
- Napoleonic Wars

Map Exercise Workbook II
Part 5: Europe in the Late 18th and 19th Centuries: Revolutions and Ethnic Identities

Document Exercise Workbook II
Chapter 15: Music as an Historical Source: The French Revolution and Napoleon

MapTutor CD-ROM

Part V: Europe in the Late 18th and 19th Centuries

Beyond the Book: Research, Writing, and Exploration

The Wadsworth Western Civilization Research Center http://history.wadsworth.com/western
Features Web links, interactive maps and timelines, and more for students to explore.

Magellan Atlas of Western Civilization
Maps 24, 25

Sources of World History, Volume II
The Balance of Power in Europe: 95
The French Revolution: 104–106

Wright Music CD-ROM
2-CD Set: 1/5–1/2

HITS on the Web: History
Tips on using the Internet for assignments, studying, and research.

H-Connect: Interactive Explorations in Western Civilization
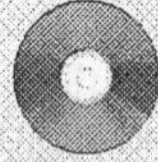
- The Summer of '89 and the Origins of the French Revolution
- The Order of the Day: Terror in the French Revolution (1792–1794)
- The Wars of the French Revolution (1792–1799)
- Napoleonic Europe

Chapter 20—The Industrial Revolution and Its Impact on European Society

Class Preparation and Lecture Tools

Instructor's Manual/ Test Bank
Includes suggestions for teaching Chapter 20, such as a chapter outline and summary, suggested student essay and research topics, discussion questions for the artwork and primary sources, detailed teaching resources, and Web links.

Book Companion Web Site http://history.wadsworth.com/spielvogelbrief03
Access to the Instructor's Manual and Test Bank, chapter outlines, InfoTrac College Edition exercises, and Internet activities for Chapter 20.

Full Color Map Acetate Package
117–119

Sights and Sounds of History Video
Industrial Revolution

World History Video Library
Early Victorian London

Lecture Enrichment Slides, Part II
21, 25, 26

Testing Tools and Course Management

Instructor's Resource CD-ROM with ExamView®
Resources for Chapter 20.

WebTUTOR ToolBox

WebTutor™ ToolBox
Text-specific online quizzing and student resources for Chapter 20, combined with course management functionality.

Instructor's Manual/ Test Bank
More than 100 questions, including multiple-choice, true/false, identification, short essay, and long essay questions for Chapter 20.

Study Aids, Tutorials, and Quizzing

History Interactive CD-ROM
Chapter 20: Organized by chapter, this study tool emphasizes key information to keep students focused on critical ideas and prepare them for tests.

Book Companion Web Site http://history.wadsworth.com/spielvogelbrief03
Chapter outlines, learning objectives, InfoTrac College Edition activities, relevant Web links and interactive quizzing for Chapter 20.

InfoTrac® College Edition
Keywords:
- Industrial revolution
- Industrial development
- Chartism

Map Exercise Workbook II
Part 4: Early Modern Europe: Technology and Change: The Industrial Revolution

Document Exercise Workbook II
Chapter 17: The Power of Numbers; The Industrial Revolution

MapTutor CD-ROM

Part V: Europe in the Late 18th and 19th Centuries

Beyond the Book: Research, Writing, and Exploration

The Wadsworth Western Civilization Research Center http://history.wadsworth.com/western
Features Web links, interactive maps and timelines, and more for students to explore.

Magellan Atlas of Western Civilization
Maps 26, 27

Sources of World History, Volume II
The Industrial Revolution in Britain: 114–117

Wright Music CD-ROM
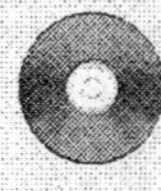
2-CD Set: 1/13–1/14
6-CD Set: 3/1–3/6

HITS on the Web: History
Tips on using the Internet for assignments, studying, and research.

H-Connect: Interactive Explorations in Western Civilization
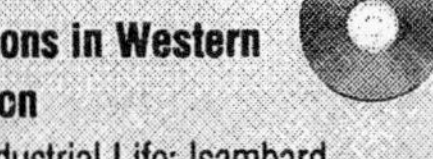
- An Industrial Life: Isambard Kingdom Brunel (1806–1859)

Chapter 21—Reaction, Revolution, and Romanticism, 1815–1850

Class Preparation and Lecture Tools

Instructor's Manual/ Test Bank
Includes suggestions for teaching Chapter 21, such as a chapter outline and summary, suggested student essay and research topics, discussion questions for the artwork and primary sources, detailed teaching resources, and Web links.

Book Companion Web Site http://history.wadsworth.com/spielvogelbrief03
Access to the Instructor's Manual and Test Bank, chapter outlines, InfoTrac College Edition exercises, and Internet activities for Chapter 21.

Full Color Map Acetate Package
120–124

World History Video Library
Ireland

Lecture Enrichment Slides, Part II
13–21, 26

Testing Tools and Course Management

Instructor's Resource CD-ROM with ExamView®
Resources for Chapter 21.

WebTUTOR ToolBox

WebTutor™ ToolBox
Text-specific online quizzing and student resources for Chapter 21, combined with course management functionality.

Instructor's Manual/ Test Bank
More than 100 questions, including multiple-choice, true/false, identification, short essay, and long essay questions for Chapter 21.

Study Aids, Tutorials, and Quizzing

History Interactive CD-ROM
Chapter 21: Organized by chapter, this study tool emphasizes key information to keep students focused on critical ideas and prepare them for tests.

Book Companion Web Site http://history.wadsworth.com/spielvogelbrief03
Chapter outlines, learning objectives, InfoTrac College Edition activities, relevant Web links and interactive quizzing for Chapter 21.

InfoTrac® College Edition
Keywords:
- Romanticism
- Habsburg/Hapsburg
- John Stuart Mill
- Goethe

Map Exercise Workbook II
Part 5: Europe in the Late 18th and 19th Centuries: Revolutions and Ethnic Identities

Document Exercise Workbook II
Chapter 16: The Influence of Ideas in History: Nationalism

MapTutor CD-ROM
Part V: Europe in the Late 18th and 19th Centuries

Beyond the Book: Research, Writing, and Exploration

The Wadsworth Western Civilization Research Center http://history.wadsworth.com/western
Features Web links, interactive maps and timelines, and more for students to explore.

Magellan Atlas of Western Civilization
Maps 25, 26

Sources of World History, Volume II
Critiquing Industrial Society: 118
Controlling Latin America: 124–125

ArtStudy CD-ROM
Chapter 28

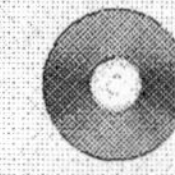

Wright Music CD-ROM
2-CD Set: 1/15–2/3, 2/5
6-CD Set: 3/7–4/5, 4/9

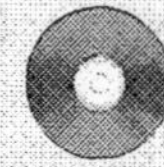

HITS on the Web: History
Tips on using the Internet for assignments, studying, and research.

H-Connect: Interactive Explorations in Western Civilization

- Revolutions of 1848

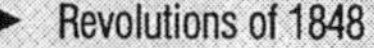

Chapter 22—An Age of Nationalism and Realism, 1850–1871

Class Preparation and Lecture Tools

Instructor's Manual/ Test Bank
Includes suggestions for teaching Chapter 22, such as a chapter outline and summary, suggested student essay and research topics, discussion questions for the artwork and primary sources, detailed teaching resources, and Web links.

Book Companion Web Site http://history.wadsworth.com/spielvogelbrief03
Access to the Instructor's Manual and Test Bank, chapter outlines, InfoTrac College Edition exercises, and Internet activities for Chapter 22.

CNN® Today Video Western Civilization
Volume I: *Italy*

Full Color Map Acetate Package
125–131

World History Video Library
Early Victorian London: 1837–1870
The Paris Commune
The Creation of Italy

Lecture Enrichment Slides, Part II
23, 25, 27

Testing Tools and Course Management

Instructor's Resource CD-ROM with ExamView®
Resources for Chapter 22.

WebTutor™ ToolBox
Text-specific online quizzing and student resources for Chapter 22, combined with course management functionality.

Instructor's Manual/ Test Bank
More than 100 questions, including multiple-choice, true/false, identification, short essay, and long essay questions for Chapter 22.

Study Aids, Tutorials, and Quizzing

History Interactive CD-ROM
Chapter 22: Organized by chapter, this study tool emphasizes key information to keep students focused on critical ideas and prepare them for tests.

Book Companion Web Site http://history.wadsworth.com/spielvogelbrief03
Chapter outlines, learning objectives, InfoTrac College Edition activities, relevant Web links and interactive quizzing for Chapter 22.

InfoTrac® College Edition
Keywords:
- Crimean War
- Victorian
- Karl Marx
- Charles Darwin

Map Exercise Workbook II
Part 5: Europe in the Late 18th and 19th Centuries: Revolutions and Ethnic Identities

Document Exercise Workbook II
Chapter 16: The Influence of Ideas in History: Nationalism

MapTutor CD-ROM
Part V: Europe in the Late 18th and 19th Centuries

Beyond the Book: Research, Writing, and Exploration

The Wadsworth Western Civilization Research Center http://history.wadsworth.com/western
Features Web links, interactive maps and timelines, and more for students to explore.

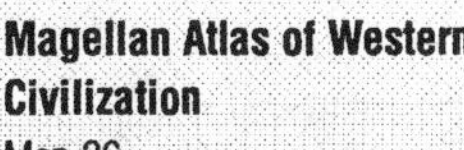

The Journey of Civilization CD-ROM
Building the Suez and Panama Canal

Magellan Atlas of Western Civilization
Map 26

Sources of World History, Volume II
Critiquing Industrial Society: 119, 121–122
Eastern Europe: 130–131

ArtStudy CD-ROM
Chapter 29

Wright Music CD-ROM
2-CD Set: 2/4
6-CD Set: 4/6–4/8

HITS on the Web: History
Tips on using the Internet for assignments, studying, and research.

H-Connect: Interactive Explorations in Western Civilization
- Nation Building (1848–1870): Italy, Germany and Comparative Examples
- Revolutions of 1848
- The Unification of Italy
- The Unification of Germany

Chapter 23—Mass Society in an "Age of Progress," 1871–1894

Class Preparation and Lecture Tools

Instructor's Manual/ Test Bank
Includes suggestions for teaching Chapter 23, such as a chapter outline and summary, suggested student essay and research topics, discussion questions for the artwork and primary sources, detailed teaching resources, and Web links.

Book Companion Web Site http://history.wadsworth.com/spielvogelbrief03
Access to the Instructor's Manual and Test Bank, chapter outlines, InfoTrac College Edition exercises, and Internet activities for Chapter 23.

CNN® Today Video Western Civilization
Volume I: *Queen Mary*

Full-Color Map Acetate Package
132–133

World History Video Library
The Paris Commune

Testing Tools and Course Management

Instructor's Resource CD-ROM with ExamView®
Resources for Chapter 23.

WebTutor™ ToolBox
Text-specific online quizzing and student resources for Chapter 23, combined with course management functionality.

Instructor's Manual/ Test Bank
More than 100 questions, including multiple-choice, true/false, identification, short essay, and long essay questions for Chapter 23.

Study Aids, Tutorials, and Quizzing

History Interactive CD-ROM
Chapter 23: Organized by chapter, this study tool emphasizes key information to keep students focused on critical ideas and prepare them for tests.

Book Companion Web Site http://history.wadsworth.com/spielvogelbrief03
Chapter outlines, learning objectives, InfoTrac College Edition activities, relevant Web links and interactive quizzing for Chapter 23.

InfoTrac® College Edition
Keywords:
- Marxism
- family nineteenth century
- socialism history

Map Exercise Workbook II
Part 5: Europe in the Late 18th and 19th Centuries: Population Growth

Document Exercise Workbook II
Chapter 17: The Power of Numbers: The Industrial Revolution

MapTutor CD-ROM

Part V: Europe in the Late 18th and 19th Centuries

Beyond the Book: Research, Writing, and Exploration

The Wadsworth Western Civilization Research Center http://history.wadsworth.com/western
Features Web links, interactive maps and timelines, and more for students to explore.

The Journey of Civilization CD-ROM
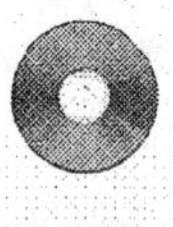
The Modern American Household

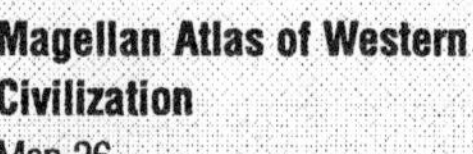

Magellan Atlas of Western Civilization
Map 26

Sources of World History, Volume II
Critiquing Industrial Society: 121

ArtStudy CD-ROM
Chapter 29

Wright Music CD-ROM
2-CD Set: 2/6
6-CD Set: 4/10–5/2

HITS on the Web: History
Tips on using the Internet for assignments, studying, and research.

H-Connect: Interactive Explorations in Western Civilization
- Journey into Darkest England: Jack the Ripper and Victorian London

Class Preparation and Lecture Tools

Instructor's Manual/ Test Bank
Includes suggestions for teaching Chapter 24, such as a chapter outline and summary, suggested student essay and research topics, discussion questions for the artwork and primary sources, detailed teaching resources, and Web links.

Book Companion Web Site http://history.wadsworth.com/spielvogelbrief03
Access to the Instructor's Manual and Test Bank, chapter outlines, InfoTrac College Edition exercises, and Internet activities for Chapter 24.

Full Color Map Acetate Package
134–143

World History Video Library
From Monarchy to Modernity

Lecture Enrichment Slides, Part II
27–36

Testing Tools and Course Management

Instructor's Resource CD-ROM with ExamView®
Resources for Chapter 24.

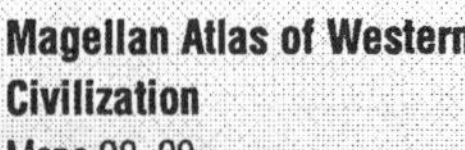

WebTutor™ ToolBox
Text-specific online quizzing and student resources for Chapter 24, combined with course management functionality.

Instructor's Manual/ Test Bank
More than 100 questions, including multiple-choice, true/false, identification, short essay, and long essay questions for Chapter 24.

Study Aids, Tutorials, and Quizzing

History Interactive CD-ROM
Chapter 24: Organized by chapter, this study tool emphasizes key information to keep students focused on critical ideas and prepare them for tests.

Book Companion Web Site http://history.wadsworth.com/spielvogelbrief03
Chapter outlines, learning objectives, InfoTrac College Edition activities, relevant Web links and interactive quizzing for Chapter 24.

InfoTrac® College Edition
Keywords:

- Nietzsche
- Sigmund Freud
- Social Darwinism
- imperialism

Map Exercise Workbook II
Part 5: Europe in the Late 18th and 19th Centuries:
Europe on the Eve of World War I

MapTutor CD-ROM
Part VI: Europe in the 20th Century

Beyond the Book: Research, Writing, and Exploration

The Wadsworth Western Civilization Research Center http://history.wadsworth.com/western
Features Web links, interactive maps and timelines, and more for students to explore.

Journey of Civilization CD-ROM
Building the Suez and Panama Canals
The New Imperialism

Magellan Atlas of Western Civilization
Maps 28, 29

Sources of World History, Volume II
Critiquing Industrial Society: 123
Imperialism: 137–140
India Under British Rule: 128–129

ArtStudy CD-ROM
Chapter 29

Wright Music CD-ROM
2-CD Set: 2/7
6-CD Set: 5/3–5/6

HITS on the Web: History
Tips on using the Internet for assignments, studying, and research.

H-Connect: Interactive Explorations in Western Civilization
- European Imperialism (1880–1900): Theory, Practice, Discourse
- Comparing Modern Art
- Identifying Modern Art Styles
- Aspects of Modernism: The Visual Arts (1863–1939)

Chapter 25—The Beginning of the Twentieth-Century Crisis: War and Revolution

Class Preparation and Lecture Tools

Instructor's Manual/ Test Bank
Includes suggestions for teaching Chapter 25, such as a chapter outline and summary, suggested student essay and research topics, discussion questions for the artwork and primary sources, detailed teaching resources, and Web links.

Book Companion Web Site
http://history.wadsworth.com/spielvogelbrief03
Access to the Instructor's Manual and Test Bank, chapter outlines, InfoTrac College Edition exercises, and Internet activities for Chapter 25.

CNN® Today Video Western Civilization
Volume I: *Trotsky Museum*

Map Acetates
144–153

Sights and Sounds of History
The United States Enters World War I
The Russian Revolution

World History Video Library
The Battle of the Marne
Aftermath of War
The Changing Face of War
Communism
The Peace Conference
Red Dawn
Stalin: The Red God

Testing Tools and Course Management

Instructor's Resource CD-ROM with ExamView®
Resources for Chapter 25.

WebTutor™ ToolBox
Text-specific online quizzing and student resources for Chapter 25, combined with course management functionality.

Instructor's Manual/ Test Bank
More than 100 questions, including multiple-choice, true/false, identification, short essay, and long essay questions for Chapter 25.

Study Aids, Tutorials, and Quizzing

History Interactive CD-ROM
Chapter 25: Organized by chapter, this study tool emphasizes key information to keep students focused on critical ideas and prepare them for tests.

Book Companion Web Site
http://history.wadsworth.com/spielvogelbrief03
Chapter outlines, learning objectives, InfoTrac College Edition activities, relevant Web links and interactive quizzing for Chapter 25.

InfoTrac® College Edition
Keywords:
- World War (1914–1918)
- Russian Revolution
- Bolshevik
- Versailles Treaty

Map Exercise Workbook II
Part 5: Europe in the Late 18th and 19th Centuries: Europe on the Eve of World War I
Part 6: Europe in the 20th Century: Europe to the Mid-Twentieth Century

Document Exercise Workbook II
Chapter 18: War Destroys Everything: World War I and Russia

MapTutor CD-ROM
Part VI: Europe in the 20th Century

Beyond the Book: Research, Writing, and Exploration

The Wadsworth Western Civilization Research Center
http://history.wadsworth.com/western
Features Web links, interactive maps and timelines, and more for students to explore.

Magellan Atlas of Western Civilization
Maps 29, 31

Sources of World History, Volume II
The First World War: 143–145

Wright Music CD-ROM
2-CD Set:: 2/8–2/10
6-CD Set: 5/7–5/15

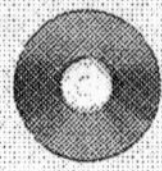

HITS on the Web: History
Tips on using the Internet for assignments, studying, and research.

H-Connect: Interactive Explorations in Western Civilization
- Origins of World War I

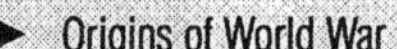

- "A New World Arisen": Russia's Revolutions (1900–1924)

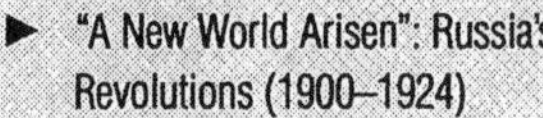

Chapter 26—The Futile Search for a New Stability: Europe Between the Wars, 1919–1939

Class Preparation and Lecture Tools

Instructor's Manual/ Test Bank
Includes suggestions for teaching Chapter 26, such as a chapter outline and summary, suggested student essay and research topics, discussion questions for the artwork and primary sources, detailed teaching resources, and Web links.

Book Companion Web Site http://history.wadsworth.com/spielvogelbrief03
Access to the Instructor's Manual and Test Bank, chapter outlines, InfoTrac College Edition exercises, and Internet activities for Chapter 26.

CNN® Today Video Western Civilization
Volume I: *Trotsky Museum*

Full-Color Map Acetate Package
154–157

World History Video Library
Fascism
The Peace Conference
Evil Rising
How the Nazis Came to Power
Stalin: The Red God
Caudillo: History of the Spanish Civil War

Lecture Enrichment Slides Part II
39, 40, 41–44

Testing Tools and Course Management

Instructor's Resource CD-ROM with ExamView®
Resources for Chapter 26.

WebTUTOR ToolBox

WebTutor™ ToolBox
Text-specific online quizzing and student resources for Chapter 26, combined with course management functionality.

Instructor's Manual/ Test Bank
More than 100 questions, including multiple-choice, true/false, identification, short essay, and long essay questions for Chapter 26.

Study Aids, Tutorials, and Quizzing

History Interactive CD-ROM
Chapter 26: Organized by chapter, this study tool emphasizes key information to keep students focused on critical ideas and prepare them for tests.

Book Companion Web Site http://history.wadsworth.com/spielvogelbrief03
Chapter outlines, learning objectives, InfoTrac College Edition activities, relevant Web links and interactive quizzing for Chapter 26.

InfoTrac® College Edition
Keywords:
- socialism history
- Great Depression
- Mussolini
- Hitler

Map Exercise Workbook II
Part 6: Europe in the 20th Century: Europe to the Mid-Twentieth Century

Document Exercise Workbook II
Chapter 18: War Destroys Everything: World War I and Russia

MapTutor CD-ROM
Part VI: Europe in the 20th Century

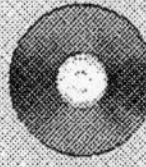

Beyond the Book: Research, Writing, and Exploration

The Wadsworth Western Civilization Research Center http://history.wadsworth.com/western
Features Web links, interactive maps and timelines, and more for students to explore.

Magellan Atlas of Western Civilization
Map 31

Sources of World History, Volume II
The Soviet Union: 150
Generations of Cultural Protest: 154

ArtStudy CD-ROM
Chapter 23

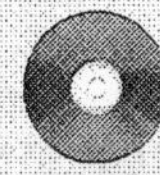

Wright Music CD-ROM
2-CD Set: 2/11–2/15
6-CD Set: 6/1–6/6, 6/10–6/13

HITS on the Web: History
Tips on using the Internet for assignments, studying, and research.

H-Connect: Interactive Explorations in Western Civilization
- Comparing Modern Art
- Identifying Modern Art Styles
- Aspects of Modernism: The Visual Arts (1863–1939)
- "A New World Arisen": Russia's Revolutions

Chapter 27—The Deepening of the European Crisis: World War II

Class Preparation and Lecture Tools

Instructor's Manual/ Test Bank
Includes suggestions for teaching Chapter 27, such as a chapter outline and summary, suggested student essay and research topics, discussion questions for the artwork and primary sources, detailed teaching resources, and Web links.

Book Companion Web Site http://history.wadsworth.com/spielvogelbrief03
Access to the Instructor's Manual and Test Bank, chapter outlines, InfoTrac College Edition exercises, and Internet activities for Chapter 27.

CNN® Today Video Western Civilization
Volume II: *Dresden*

Full-Color Map Acetate Package
160–164

Sights and Sounds of History Video
Diary of a German Soldier at Stalingrad
Hitler and the Holocaust
Truman and the Atomic Bomb
The Victims of Hiroshima

World History Video Library
Aftermath: The Remnants of War
Memoirs of Anne Frank
Schindler
How the Nazis Came to Power

Lecture Enrichment Slides, Part II
42–48

Testing Tools and Course Management

Instructor's Resource CD-ROM with ExamView®

Resources for Chapter 27.

WebTUTOR ToolBox

WebTutor™ ToolBox
Text-specific online quizzing and student resources for Chapter 27, combined with course management functionality.

Instructor's Manual/ Test Bank
More than 100 questions, including multiple-choice, true/false, identification, short essay, and long essay questions for Chapter 27.

Study Aids, Tutorials, and Quizzing

History Interactive CD-ROM
Chapter 27: Organized by chapter, this study tool emphasizes key information to keep students focused on critical ideas and prepare them for tests.

Book Companion Web Site http://history.wadsworth.com/spielvogelbrief03
Chapter outlines, learning objectives, InfoTrac College Edition activities, relevant Web links and interactive quizzing for Chapter 27.

InfoTrac® College Edition
Keywords:
- socialism history
- Holocaust
- Hitler

Map Exercise Workbook II
Part 6: Europe in the 20th Century: Europe to the Mid-Twentieth Century

Document Exercise Workbook II
Chapter 19: Morality and Historical Assessment: Hitler and World War II

MapTutor CD-ROM

Part VI: Europe in the 20th Century

Beyond the Book: Research, Writing, and Exploration

The Wadsworth Western Civilization Research Center http://history.wadsworth.com/western
Features Web links, interactive maps and timelines, and more for students to explore.

The Journey of Civilization CD-ROM
The Holocaust

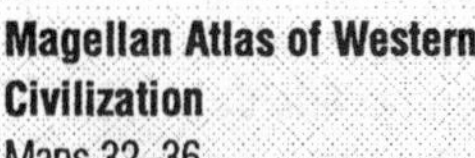

Magellan Atlas of Western Civilization
Maps 32–36

Sources of World History, Volume II
The Second World War: 158
The Soviet Union: 152

Wright Music CD-ROM
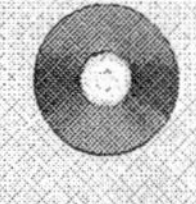
2-CD Set: 2/11–2/15
6-CD Set: 6/1–6/6, 6/10–6/13

HITS on the Web: History
Tips on using the Internet for assignments, studying, and research.

Chapter 28—Cold War and a New Western World, 1945–1970

Class Preparation and Lecture Tools

Instructor's Manual/ Test Bank
Includes suggestions for teaching Chapter 28, such as a chapter outline and summary, suggested student essay and research topics, discussion questions for the artwork and primary sources, detailed teaching resources, and Web links.

Book Companion Web Site http://history.wadsworth.com/spielvogelbrief03
Access to the Instructor's Manual and Test Bank, chapter outlines, InfoTrac College Edition exercises, and Internet activities for Chapter 28.

CNN® Today Video Western Civilization
Volume I: *Beatles Tour*
Volume II: *Yugoslavia's History*
Volume III: *Culture Clash of the 60s*

Full-Color Map Acetate Package
165–172

Sites and Sounds of History Video
The Cold War
The Chinese Revolution
Mohandas Gandhi

World History Video Library
Charles de Gaulle
The Origin and Development of NATO

Lecture Enrichment Slides, Part II
47–49

Testing Tools and Course Management

Instructor's Resource CD-ROM with ExamView®
Resources for Chapter 28.

WEBTUTOR ToolBox

WebTutor™ ToolBox
Text-specific online quizzing and student resources for Chapter 1, combined with course management functionality.

Instructor's Manual/ Test Bank
More than 100 questions, including multiple-choice, true/false, identification, short essay, and long essay questions for Chapter 28.

Study Aids, Tutorials, and Quizzing

History Interactive CD-ROM
Chapter 28: Organized by chapter, this study tool emphasizes key information to keep students focused on critical ideas and prepare them for tests.

Book Companion Web Site http://history.wadsworth.com/spielvogelbrief03
Chapter outlines, learning objectives, InfoTrac College Edition activities, relevant Web links and interactive quizzing for Chapter 28.

InfoTrac® College Edition
Keywords:
- Cold War
- Soviet Union relations with the United States
- decolonization
- Khrushchev

Map Exercise Workbook II
Part 6: Europe in the 20th Century: Post-Cold War Europe

Document Exercise Workbook II
Chapter 20: Everyone Their Own Historian: The Contemporary World

MapTutor CD-ROM
Part VI: Europe in the 20th Century

Beyond the Book: Research, Writing, and Exploration

The Wadsworth Western Civilization Research Center http://history.wadsworth.com/western
Features Web links, interactive maps and timelines, and more for students to explore.

The Journey of Civilization CD-ROM
Gandhi

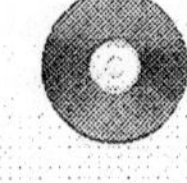

Magellan Atlas of Western Civilization
Maps 37–39

Sources of World History, Volume II
The Soviet Union: 151–153
Generations of Cultural Protest: 155–157
India and Independence: 162
Struggles for National Liberation: 164–165, 167

Wright Music CD-ROM
2-CD Set: 2/16
6-CD Set: 6/7-6/9, 6/14-6/18

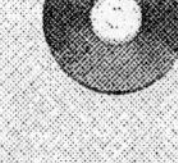

HITS on the Web: History
Tips on using the Internet for assignments, studying, and research.

Chapter 29—The Contemporary Western World (Since 1970)

Class Preparation and Lecture Tools

Instructor's Manual/ Test Bank
Includes suggestions for teaching Chapter 29, such as a chapter outline and summary, suggested student essay and research topics, discussion questions for the artwork and primary sources, detailed teaching resources, and Web links.

Book Companion Web Site http://history.wadsworth.com/spielvogelbrief03
Access to the Instructor's Manual and Test Bank, chapter outlines, InfoTrac College Edition exercises, and Internet activities for Chapter 29.

CNN® Today Video Western Civilization
Volume I: *Queen Mary*
Albania
Romania
Volume II: *Denmark*
European Families
Women and the Catholic Church
Yugoslavia's History
Religion in Kosovo
Gorbachev
Volume III: *Reagan's Conservatism*
Middle-East: How We Got Here
Clash of Civilizations

Map Acetates
173–176

World History Video Library
Royalty: The Surviving Monarchies

Lecture Enrichment Slides, Part II
49, 50

Testing Tools and Course Management

Instructor's Resource CD-ROM with ExamView®
Resources for Chapter 29.

WebTUTOR ToolBox

WebTutor™ ToolBox
Text-specific online quizzing and student resources for Chapter 29, combined with course management functionality.

Instructor's Manual/ Test Bank
More than 100 questions, including multiple-choice, true/false, identification, short essay, and long essay questions for Chapter 29.

Study Aids, Tutorials, and Quizzing

History Interactive CD-ROM
Chapter 29: Organized by chapter, this study tool emphasizes key information to keep students focused on critical ideas and prepare them for tests.

Book Companion Web Site http://history.wadsworth.com/spielvogelbrief03
Chapter outlines, learning objectives, InfoTrac College Edition activities, relevant Web links and interactive quizzing for Chapter 29.

InfoTrac® College Edition
Keywords:
- single European market
- Europe Communism
- perestroika
- Green parties

Map Exercise Workbook II
Part 6: Europe in the 20th Century:
Boundaries and Border: Changes in the Later 20th Century

Document Exercise Workbook II
Chapter 20: Everyone Their Own Historian: The Contemporary World

MapTutor CD-ROM
Part VI: Europe in the 20th Century

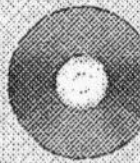

Beyond the Book: Research, Writing, and Exploration

The Wadsworth Western Civilization Research Center http://history.wadsworth.com/western
Features Web links, interactive maps and timelines, and more for students to explore.

Magellan Atlas of Western Civilization
Maps 40, 43–45

Sources of World History, Volume II
Struggles for National Liberation: 169–170

ArtStudy CD-ROM
Chapter 34

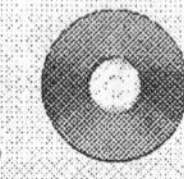

Wright Music CD-ROM
2-CD Set: 2/16
6-CD Set: 6/76/9, 6/146/18

HITS on the Web: History
Tips on using the Internet for assignments, studying, and research.

H-Connect: Interactive Explorations in Western Civilization
- Comparing Modern Art
- Identifying Modern Art Styles

PREFACE

Jackson J. Spielvogel's *Western Civilization: A Brief History* has long proved to be one of the most successful textbooks in the challenging task of teaching of the history of the West to college and university students. Its virtues are many, especially in making readily accessible to the student the many crucial issues and topics which have influenced the development and evolution of western civilization and which still impact the global world of today.

This current *Instructor's Manual* is a revision of earlier editions, reflecting the changes made in the third edition of *Western Civilization: A Brief History*. The manual includes chapter outlines and chapter summaries, suggested lecture topics, map exercises, discussion questions for the primary sources found in each chapter, student research and project topics, identifications, multiple choice questions, relevant web sites, videos, and musical selections, as well as student activity possibilities. There is also the Resource Integration Guide which references other print resources available from the publisher, as well as media and Internet resources relevant to the subjects of each chapter.

I want to thank Paul Massicotte of Wadsworth/Thomson Learning for his considerable assistance. We exchanged numerous telephone calls and e-mails over the several months it took to complete this new edition of the *Instructor's Manual*, and he was unfailingly supportive throughout.

In addition, I wish to acknowledge the support my colleagues at Los Angeles Pierce College gave to me during the course of the project. Last, but not least, my daughter Gillian deserves a word of thanks and praise for the toleration and love she showed me over of the many, many hours I spent downstairs with the computer, wrestling with the whys and wherefores of western civilization.

TABLE OF CONTENTS

CHAPTER 1
THE ANCIENT NEAR EAST: THE FIRST CIVILIZATIONS

CHAPTER OUTLINE

I. The First Humans
- A. The Hunter-Gatherers of the Old Stone Age
- B. The Neolithic Revolution (c. 10,000-4,000 B.C.)
  - 1. An Agricultural Revolution
  - 2. Consequences of the Neolithic Revolution
  - 3. New Developments

II. The Emergence of Civilization

III. Civilization in Mesopotamia
- A. The City-States of Ancient Mesopotamia
- B. Empires in Ancient Mesopotamia
- C. The Code of Hammurabi
- D. The Culture of Mesopotamia
  - 1. The Importance of Religion
  - 2. The Cultivation of New Arts and Sciences

IV. Egyptian Civilization: "The Gift of the Nile"
- A. The Old and Middle Kingdoms
- B. Society and Economy in Ancient Egypt
- C. The Culture of Egypt
  - 1. Spiritual Life in Egyptian Society
  - 2. The Pyramids
  - 3. Art and Writing
- D. Chaos and a New Order: The New Kingdom
- E. Daily Life in Ancient Egypt: Family and Marriage

V. Conclusion

CHAPTER SUMMARY

Africa was humanity's cradle, and humankind's beginnings were approximately four million years ago, according to the available archeological evidence. Through the many millennia early humans (hominids) began using stones, discovered fire, and in small bands they gathered wild plants and hunted wild animals. Modern humans, known as *Homo sapiens sapiens*, appeared first in Africa no later than 150,000 years ago, and eventually spread throughout the world by the end of the Paleolithic era, or the Old Stone Age.

A revolutionary event occurred beginning c. 10,000 B.C. Known as the Neolithic (New Stone Age) Revolution, its significance was in producing food through the domestication of plants and animals, an event which first occurred in the upland regions of the Middle East's Fertile Crescent. Permanent villages of up to a few thousand people replaced nomadic bands, pottery was made from clay, goods were accumulated and traded. A division of labor appeared, and eventually men became the dominant gender because of their labor in food production.

Increasing complexity led to the further development of what is called civilization, which can be defined as urban, with more formal institutions, the use of writing, monumental architecture, and the production of metal, bronze being the earliest. Civilizations developed elsewhere in the world, but in the West it was in the river valleys of Mesopotamia and Egypt where civilization first appeared.

Ancient Mesopotamia–the land between the Tigris and Euphrates Rivers–was a city-state civilization created by a people known as the Sumerians. The rivers were tamed, but remained unpredictable, affecting both religion and the arts (notably in the *Epic of Gilgamesh)*, priests and kings held a monopoly of power, temples (ziggurats) were constructed of brick, trade and commerce expanded, although most of the inhabitants were farmers. Writing on clay, known as cuneiform (wedge-shaped) began. Located on flat plains, the city-states were vulnerable to invasion. The result was the creation of a series of empires, beginning with the Akkadians c. 2340 B.C, later followed by the Babylonians, famous for Hammurabi's law code (c.1750).

Civilization also developed along Egypt's Nile River, a more predictable river than those in Mesopotamia, and Egyptian religion reflected its more benign nature. The Nile also served as a unifier of ancient Egypt, and surrounded by deserts, Egypt was less subject to invasion. Egyptian pharaohs were perceived as gods, unlike the rulers in Mesopotamia, and their tombs were the pyramids which were constructed during the Old Kingdom, c. 2600-2200 B.C. Religion was at the core, not least in the various divine manifestations of the ever-present sun. A quest for immortality developed, particularly around the cult of Osiris, and mummification became widespread during the Middle Kingdom (c.2050-1650 B.C.), whose end coincided with an invasion of a people known as the Hyksos. Native rule resumed during the New Kingdom (c. 1567-1085), an era of Egyptian imperialistic expansion throughout much of the Middle East.

LECTURE AND DISCUSSION TOPICS

1. Discuss the nature of historical study, including goals, subject matter, methodologies, terminology, etc.

2. Trace the emergence of "pre-history" through the Neolithic Revolution.

3. Consider the term "civilization," examining its meanings, locales, and significance.

4. Discuss, including comparisons and contrasts, religion in Mesopotamia and Egyptian civilizations.

5. Outline Mesopotamian development, including serial invasions, as well as change and continuity.

6. Discuss the legacy of the Ancient Near East and its contributions to Western Civilization.

7. Assess Egypt, the Nile, and geographical determinism in the context of ancient Egyptian civilization.

MAP EXERCISES

1. The Spread of *Homo sapiens sapiens*. MAP 1.1. Are there any questions and/or criticisms which could arise from the map as shown, both as to time and as to location and direction? (page 3)

2. The Ancient Near East. MAP 1.3. What are some of the geographical factors which can explain the development of civilization in the Near East? (page 6)

3. Ancient Egypt. MAP 1.4. From the map, discuss the concept that Egypt was the "gift of the Nile." Were there any other geographical factors which also played a role in the development and success of Egyptian civilization? (page 14)

DISCUSSION QUESTIONS FOR THE PRIMARY SOURCES (BOXED DOCUMENTS)

1. "The Code of Hammurabi": What do the 12 points of law from the Code of Hammurabi reveal about Mesopotamian society? How do they emphasize the principle of "an eye for an eye"? What legal rights do women receive from this code? (page 9)

2. "Significance of the Nile River and the Pharaoh": What do the two hymns reveal about the importance of the Nile River and the institution of the pharaoh to Egyptian civilization? Is there a possible connection between the geography of Egypt with its Nile focus and the emergence of a ruler who is considered to be divine? (page 13)

3. "The Great Flood": Analyze the flood story from *The Epic of Gilgamesh*. Read the biblical account to the class and ask the students to compare the two accounts. How does one account for both the similarities and differences? (page 12)

4. "A Father's Advice": According to this document, what social and political skills were prized by members of the Egyptian governing elite? What does the passage relate about Egyptian bureaucrats? Is there anything uniquely Egyptian about the advice, or was it applicable and universal to most ancient societies? (page 19)

STUDENT RESEARCH AND PROJECT TOPICS

1. Discuss the shift from a hunting and gathering economy to the production of food by systematic agriculture. Why do you think some historians call this transition the "greatest event of pre-history"?

2. Describe the basic elements of civilization and identify which element changed early human life and early human communities the most.

3. Some scholars refer to Mesopotamian and Egyptian civilizations as "hydraulic" cultures. Check the definition of "hydraulic," and write an essay justifying the application of this term to these cultures.

4. Compare and contrast the role of women and families in Mesopotamian and Egyptian societies.

5. Discuss the evolution of Egyptian religion; be sure to describe the roles of Amon-Re and Osiris.

6. Discuss some of the similarities and the differences between the religions and religious practices of the Mesopotamian region with those of Egyptian civilization.

7. The Code of Hammurabi was one of the first of all ancient legal codes. In what ways was it "modern"? How was it different from modern day Western legal codes? What do you think constituted “justice” for the inhabitants of Mesopotamian city-states?

8. Discuss the possible reasons why Mesopotamia saw so many different civilizations, from the Sumerians to the Persians, while civilization in the Nile Valley remained essentially unchanged for three millennium.

9. What do you think Western civilization has derived from the ancient civilizations of the Sumerians and the Egyptians?

10. What were the causes and the consequences of the migration of Indo-European speakers into the Near East during the second millennium B.C.?

IDENTIFICATIONS

1. Hominids
2. Australopithecine
3. *Homo erectus*
4. Neanderthals
5. *Homo sapiens sapiens*
6. Paleolithic Age
7. cave paintings
8. Neolithic Revolution
9. Çatal Huyuk
10. Mesopotamia
11. Sumerians
12. Tigris and Euphrates Rivers
13. Agricultural Revolution
14. Eridu, Ur, Uruk, and Lagash
15. Sargon of Akkad
16. Code of Hammurabi
17. ziggurat
18. cuneiform
19. *The Epic of Gilgamesh*
20. “The Gift of the Nile”
21. Menes
22. Old Kingdom
23. the pyramids
24. Middle Kingdom
25. polytheism
26. Amon-Re
27. hieroglyphs
28. Hyksos
29. New Kingdom
30. Akhenaten
31. Tutankhamon

32. Hatshepsut
33. Rameses II
34. Sea Peoples

MULTIPLE CHOICE QUESTIONS

1. The earliest human-like creatures, hominids, existed in Africa as early as
    a. 50,000 years ago.
    b. 1 million years ago.
    c. 2 million years ago.
    d. 3 to 4 million years ago.
        ANSWER: d (page 2)

2. Which of the following was not a society of the ancient Near East:
    a. Egyptian.
    b. Sumerian.
    c. Indus Valley.
    d. none of the above
        ANSWER: c (p. 5)

3. The first modern *homo sapiens*
    a. first appeared in Africa about 250,000 years ago.
    b. was a skilled hunter who had mastered the bow and arrow.
    c. lived mostly in small groups near the sea.
    d. a and c
        ANSWER: a (p. 2)

4. All of the following are believed to be developments of the Paleolithic Age <u>except</u>
    a. the utilization of tools.
    b. origins of religious and decorative art.
    c. a social system with rough equality between the sexes.
    d. the regular production of food through agriculture.
        ANSWER: d (p. 3)

5. In ancient civilizations, bronze would replace copper because
    a. bronze was stronger.
    b. it was prettier and therefore made prettier jewelry.
    c. bronze took less time to smelt.
    d. bronze ore was easier to find.
        ANSWER: a (p. 5)

6. The early Neolithic era saw
    a. a slow transition from hunting and gathering to an agricultural society.
    b. the rise of settled villages and towns.
    c. the gradual domestication of animals.
    d. all of the above
        ANSWER: d (pp. 4-5)

7. All of the following occurred during the agricultural revolutions except

a. domestication of animals.
b. development of tools stagnated.
c. agricultural villages grew in size.
d. men came to play a more dominant role in society.

ANSWER: b (pp. 4-5)

8. The early Neolithic revolution saw all of the following technical developments except

a. the invention of writing.
b. the use of metal tools.
c. the weaving of cloth.
d. the development of agricultural villages.

ANSWER: d (pp. 4-5)

9. The ancient city of Catal Huyuk was

a. a farming community located in Greece.
b. a Neolithic walled community sustained by food surpluses.
c. a large city with an elaborate water and sewer system.
d. an autocracy in which ruling religious elders exercise all political power.

ANSWER: b (p. 4)

10. The Sumerians

a. defeated the Hittites in 2600 B.C.
b. were plagued by incessant warfare between their many city-states.
c. had a complicated religion with a sophisticated belief in life after death.
d. were warriors who instituted totalitarian government.

ANSWER: b (p. 8)

11. The Sumerian government

a. eventually came to view kings as agents of their gods.
b. saw the various city-states erect different types of governments.
c. was a theocracy in which the priest ruled.
d. was a type of aristocracy where nobles were appointed by an assembly.

ANSWER: a (p. 7)

12. Sumerian politics of the Early Dynastic Age can best be characterized by

a. cooperation between city-states for mutual prosperity.
b. endemic warfare.
c. a movement towards smaller, more efficient governments.
d. democratic reform.

ANSWER: b (p. 8)

13. Sumerian kings derived their authority from

a. the will of the people.
b. the parliamentary councils of the city-states.
c. success in athletic tournaments.
d. the gods.

ANSWER: d (p. 7)

14. Which of the following is <u>not</u> true of Mesopotamian society:
  a. commerce and industry were important next to agriculture
  b. small villages, which were hard to defend, were the basic units of civilization
  c. several different social groups owned slaves
  d. the economy was divided into both public and private sectors
    ANSWER: b (p. 7)

15. The basic unit of early Mesopotamian civilization was
  a. the city-state.
  b. the village.
  c. the county.
  d. the land one man could plough in a day.
    ANSWER: a (p. 7)

16. The physical environment of the Mesopotamians generally led to
  a. an optimistic outlook emphasizing the secular life.
  b. a pessimistic outlook and loathing of religion.
  c. a pessimistic outlook with an emphasis on satisfying their angry gods.
  d. an optimistic outlook with a belief in providing for benevolent gods.
    ANSWER: c (p. 10)

17. The Sumerian economy
  a. although primarily agricultural, did include a mix of industry and commerce.
  b. included imported luxury items.
  c. went through cycles like modern economies.
  d. a and b
    ANSWER: d (p. 7)

18. Mesopotamian religion was
  a. monotheistic.
  b. very simple with few rules and tenets.
  c. severely critical of cultures that practiced divination.
  d. one in which no one god reigned supreme and deities were closely related to cities.
    ANSWER: d (p. 10)

19. Mesopotamian religious practices included all of the following <u>except</u>
  a. arts of divination.
  b. prayers to the gods.
  c. baptism of true believers.
  d. cultic spells.
    ANSWER: c (pp. 10-11)

20. Sumerian writing
  a. was originally pictographic but became cuneiform.
  b. could only be used for simple record keeping.
  c. could not express educational concepts.
  d. could not be used for epic poetry
    ANSWER: a (p. 11)

21. *The Epic of Gilgamesh* teaches that
   a. the gods are benevolent and care greatly for their people.
   b. a wish fulfilled is not always a good thing.
   c. human life is difficult and immortality is only for the gods.
   d. a periodic flood is necessary to cleanse the world.
      ANSWER: c (p. 10)

22. The Code of Hammurabi
   a. helped keep Babylonian society relative equal.
   b. was a harsh law code that afforded some justice for all social classes.
   c. had little to do with criminal laws as such.
   d. does not provide us with the value system in Mesopotamia.
      ANSWER: b (pp. 9-10)

23. Punishments for crimes under the Code of Hammurabi
   a. were more severe for the lower classes.
   b. did not apply to domestic family concern.
   c. stressed reform rather than retribution.
   d. were not for the upper class at all.
      ANSWER: a (p. 9)

24. Which of the following statements best applies to the status of women in Mesopotamian society?
   a. Women exclusively controlled roles in the priesthood.
   b. Divorce laws applied equally to men and women.
   c. Punishments for adultery were light compared to those for men.
   d. The woman's role was to be in the home and subservient to her husband.
      ANSWER: d (p. 10)

25. Mesopotamian mathematics included
   a. a number system based on 60.
   b. complex financial and engineering calculations.
   c. calculus.
   d. a and b
      ANSWER: d (p. 12)

26. The Nile River provided ancient Egyptians with
   a. an excellent artery of transportation.
   b. fertile soil due to annual floods.
   c. tropical plants which were used to make sweet smelling perfumes.
   d. a and b
      ANSWER: d (pp. 12-13)

27. The focal points and sources of life for the ancient Egyptians were
   a. the Nile River and the pharaohs.
   b. the herd animals and the temples.
   c. the Nile River and the military.
   d. the pharaoh and the stars.
      ANSWER: a (pp. 12-14)

28. In comparison to Mesopotamian society, Egyptian society was
a. more urban.
b. less dependent on rivers.
c. more rural.
d. without food surpluses.
ANSWER: c (p. 13)

29. Ancient Egyptian history is divided into ________ major periods.
a. two
b. seven
c. ten
d. three
ANSWER: d (p. 14)

30. According to Egyptian theology, the pharaoh derived his authority from
a. democratic elections.
b. the assent of local governors.
c. the fact that he was perceived as a divine instrument of order and harmony.
d. hereditary descent.
ANSWER: c (p. 14)

31. Egyptian pharaohs ruled and derived their authority from
a. the military.
b. the people.
c. the fundamental principle of *Ma'at*.
d. the elder male citizens.
ANSWER: c (pp. 14-15)

32. Egypt's Middle Kingdom
a. centered around the rule of the pharaoh Menes.
b. was a period of unsuccessful warfare against its neighbors.
c. saw the pharaohs provide more for the public welfare.
d. was preceded and followed by periods of stability.
ANSWER: c (p. 15)

33. For administrative purposes in the Old Kingdom, Egypt was
a. divided into provinces called nomes and governed by nomarchs.
b. practically ruled by the pharaoh in all facets of government.
c. divided into military districts directly responsible to an army commander.
d. a parliamentary government with representatives from each district.
ANSWER: a (p. 15)

34. Egypt's Middle Kingdom was portrayed by the Egyptians as
a. the democratic era.
b. a period of instability and warfare.
c. a golden age of Egyptian society.
d. the period of foreign domination.
ANSWER: c (p. 15)

35. The Hyksos
   a. were a Semitic people who infiltrated Egypt in the seventeenth century B.C.
   b. were Indo-European peoples who were recruited into the Egyptian military.
   c. were priests/astronomers in Egypt during the Old Kingdom.
   d. fought and defeated the Egyptians in the ninth century B.C.
      ANSWER: a (p. 18)

36. The economy of ancient Egypt relied most heavily on
   a. foreign trade.
   b. artisans and craftsmen.
   c. slavery.
   d. agriculture.
      ANSWER: d (p. 15)

37. Which of the following Egyptian gods was most closely associated with the mummification of the dead?
   a. Horus
   b. Re
   c. Osiris
   d. Isis
      ANSWER: c (p. 16)

38. Originally the Osiris cult was reserved for
   a. the wealthy who could afford preservation of the body.
   b. priests who knew religious secrets.
   c. the poor who lived by the Nile.
   d. the pharaohs alone.
      ANSWER: a (p. 17)

39. The Egyptian Pyramids
   a. were built during the period of the New Kingdom.
   b. were part of a large spiritual complex near Alexandria.
   c. were conceived and built as tombs for a city of the dead.
   d. were all dedicated to the god Aten.
      ANSWER: c (p. 17)

40. Which of the following is <u>not</u> true of Egyptian art?
   a. It was largely expressive and distinguished many great Egyptian artists.
   b. It was primarily functional and not intended to add beauty.
   c. It was highly stylized.
   d. It followed strict formulas governing form and presentation.
      ANSWER: a (p. 17)

41. Amenhotep IV is best known for
   a. the temporary installation of monotheism in Egyptian culture.
   b. expelling the Hyksos and leading Egypt along an imperialistic path.
   c. increasing the power of the Amon-Re priesthood.
   d. combating the invasion of the Sea Peoples.
      ANSWER: a (p. 18)

42. During the New Kingdom of Egyptian history, the Egyptians
a. became the most powerful state in the ancient near east.
b. developed a more professional and better equipped army.
c. defeated the Hyksos under the leadership of Ramses II.
d. a and b
ANSWER: d (p. 18)

43. Which of the following is <u>not</u> true of Egyptian social life?
a. Women had equal legal rights with men.
b. Marriages were based on love and personal attraction.
c. The upper classes devoted much time to entertainment.
d. The wife's primary role in the family was to produce children.
ANSWER: b (p. 19)

44. In general, during the imperialistic New Kingdom, Egyptian government changed by
a. a gradual lessening in the power of pharaohs over their neighbors.
b. a decrease in the size of the royal bureaucracy.
c. the growing poverty and powerlessness of priesthoods.
d. the growing weakness of army commanders.
ANSWER: a (p. 18)

45. Daily existence in Egypt was marked by all of the following <u>except</u>
a. acceptance of divorce as legal under the law.
b. no efforts by the people to enjoy life due to a harsh environment.
c. children were treated well and were valued.
d. music, games, and hunting were important.
ANSWER: b (pp. 18-20)

46. In the thirteenth century the Egyptians were driven out of Palestine and back to their original frontiers by the
a. Sumerians.
b. "Sea Peoples"
c. Babylonians
d. Hyksos.
ANSWER: b (p. 18)

47. Akhenaten
a. permanently converted the Egyptians to the worship of Aten.
b. murdered Tutankhamen to gain the throne.
c. established a new city called Akhetaten, 200 miles from Thebes.
d. greatly expanded the Egyptian empire.
ANSWER: c (p. 18)

48. One of the few female pharaohs was
a. Ramses.
b. Hatshepsut.
c. Menes.
d. Amenhotep.
ANSWER: b (p. 18)

49. In the first century B.C., Egypt became a colony of
a. Rome.
b. Persia.
c. Babylonia.
d. Mohenjo-Daro.
ANSWER: a (p. 18)

50. Egypt's pyramids were constructed during
a. the Old Kingdom
b. the First Intermediate Period.
c. the Middle Kingdom.
d. the Empire.
ANSWER: a (p. 17)

RELEVANT WORLD-WIDE WEB SITES/RESOURCES

1. Akhet Internet: The Cairo Museum:
http://www.akhet.freeserve.co.uk/cairo.htm
(Fine site on Egyptian arts and antiquities.)

2. Univ. of California, Riverside, Horus' History Links:
http://www.ucr.edu/h-gig/horuslinkswork.html
(Superb Egyptian texts and images.)

3. Univ. of Chicago, Oriental Institute Museum:
http://www-oi.uchicago.edu/OI/MUS/OI_Museum.html
(Vast Sumerian and Egyptian collections.)

4. Univ. of Chicago, Oriental Institute, Research Archives:
http://www-oi.uchicago.edu/OI/DEPT/RA/ABZU/ABZU.HTML
(Site gives hundreds of links to other resources.)

5. The Egyptian Museum, Cairo:
http://163.121.10.41/cult-net/museum.htm
(Egyptian State archaeological collections.)

6. Louvre Museum, Paris:
http://mistral.culture.fr/louvre/louvrea.htm
(Main site with access to all departments.)
Oriental Antiquities (in English):
http://mistral.culture.fr/louvre/anglais/musee/collec/ao.htm
Egyptian Antiquities (in English):
http://mistral.culture.fr/louvre/anglais/musee/collec/egypte.htm

7. Okeanos: Website for Biblical, Classical and Ancient Near Eastern Studies:
http://weber.u.washington.edu/~snoesel/okeanons12.html

8. Univ. of Pennsylvania Museum of Archaeology:
http://www.upenn.edu/museum/
(Excellent Middle-Eastern Collections on-line.)

9. The Scholars' Guide to the WWW:
http://members.aol.com/dann01/webguide.html
(Superb comprehensive website maintained by Dr. Richard Jensen, Professor of History, Emeritus, at the Univ. of Illinois, Chicago.
Site contains over 300 links to web resources relevant to Western Civilization, including humanities and literature pages, on-line maps, world museums, popular culture, and library manuscript collections. Ideal site for use with all chapters of this text.)

RELEVANT VIDEO COLLECTIONS

Egypt: The Sands of Time, Films for the Humanities and Sciences, (40 minutes).

Exploring the Egyptian Pyramids, Films for the Humanities and Sciences, (50 minutes).

Pyramid, PBS Home Video, (55 minutes). (In the David Macaulay Collection, using site visits and computer animation to explore the structure and funerary function of the edifice.)

Sumer, Babylon, Assyria: The Wolves, Films for the Humanities and Sciences, (26 minutes). Devoted to collections of British Museum.

The Western Tradition, Part I, Annenberg/CPB Collection/PBS Home Video, (26 programs, 30 minutes each), Program 1, "The Dawn of History," Program 2 "The Ancient Egyptians," and Program 3, "The Mesopotamians."

SUGGESTED STUDENT ACTIVITIES

1. Have students research the various *Homo sapiens* of the Paleolithic period, such as Java and Peking Man, Neanderthal Man, and Cro-Magnon Man.

2. Have students do a comparative study of the ancient Sumerian and Egyptian religions using World-Wide Web resources.

3. Students may research the complicated Egyptian belief in the afterlife, including discussions of the *Book of the Dead*, the Realm of the Dead, the Hall of Truth, and the Scales of Justice.

4. A study of the Pyramids, especially the Great Pyramid, would be of interest to most students.

5. The story of King Tutankhamon and the twentieth century discovery of the pharaoh's treasures would be of interest to most students. Have them do a report on Tut and his treasures. There are abundant Web and Video resources for this topic.

CHAPTER 2
THE ANCIENT NEAR EAST: PEOPLES AND EMPIRES

CHAPTER OUTLINE

I. On the Fringes of Civilization
- A. The Impact of the Indo-Europeans

II. The Hebrews: "The Children of Israel"
- A. The United Kingdom
- B. The Divided Kingdom
- C. The Spiritual Dimensions of Israel
  - 1. "I Am the Lord Your God": Ruler of the World
  - 2. "You Only Have I Chosen": Covenant, Law, and Prophets
- D. The Neighbors of the Israelites

III. The Assyrian Empire
- A. Assyrian Society and Culture

IV. The Persian Empire
- A. Governing the Empire
- B. Persian Religion

V. Conclusion

CHAPTER SUMMARY

Farming appeared in Europe's Balkans by 6500 B.C. and in central Europe by 4000 B.C. A characteristic of European societies during these millennia was the construction of large stone structures, or megaliths, the most famous being England's Stonehenge. Indo-European speakers migrated into Europe and the Middle East around 2000 B.C. One Indo-European group, the Hittites, established a kingdom in Asia Minor c. 1750. They were the first Indo-Europeans to use iron, but were destroyed by invaders known as Sea Peoples, who also attacked Egypt c.1200 B.C.

The Middle East was a complex and vibrant region during the first millennium B.C., with numerous peoples, sometimes as kingdoms and empires, contending with each other. Because of its later influence on the West and its other monotheistic religions of Christianity and Islam, one of the most significant peoples was the Semitic-speaking Hebrews. Much of their early history, from their nomadic beginnings to their sojourn in Egypt and the Exodus from that land under Moses, is found in the Hebrew Bible, which was written down only after 1000 B.C. Historians and archeologists disagree about the historical veracity of the early traditions, but by the end of the second millennium B.C. they had emerged as an identifiable people, with a united kingdom under Saul, David, and Solomon, which were followed by two smaller kingdoms–Judah and Israel. The latter succumbed to the power of the Assyrian Empire in the late eighth century B.C. and the former to the Chaldeans, or the Neo-Babylonians, in 586 B.C., which resulted in the so-called Babylonian Captivity which lasted for approximately fifty years.

It was not in political, military, or economic power that explains the importance of the Jews, but their religion of ethical monotheism. The single God of the Hebrews–Yahweh–was perceived as a universal and transcendent God who demanded morality and goodness from his worshipers. The Hebrews saw themselves as having a covenant, or a special relationship with Yahweh, and were expected to obey the laws of God, which included the requirement of practicing social justice. The theological and moral beliefs of the ancient Hebrews have affected the western world down to the present.

A Middle Eastern kingdom that had much greater political and military power was the Assyrian Empire, whose might at its height stretched from the Tigris and the Euphrates to the Nile. The Assyrian kings, who were considered to be absolute rulers, assembled a mighty army of well over 100,000, and was the first large army to make use of iron weapons. According to their many victims, the Assyrians resorted to terrorism to defeat and control their enemies: they had a fearsome reputation. Also a Semitic-people, their chief god was Ashur, and the Assyrians had assimilated much of the earlier Mesopotamian culture and religion. The Assyrian Empire reached its apogee under Ashurbanipal (d. 626 B.C.), but by the end of the seventh century it was destroyed and succeeded by a new imperial power, the Chaldeans, or Neo-Babylonians, headed by Nebuchadnezzar (d. 562 B.C.), with his capital of Babylon becoming one of the ancient world's great cities, which contained the famed Hanging Gardens.

However, the reign of the Chaldeans was brief and was followed by the Persians, an Indo-European speaking people, led by Cyrus the Great (d. 530 B.C.), from Persis in southern Iran. Under his leadership, the Persian Empire stretched from Asia Minor through the Middle East and Mesopotamia to western India. A politically astute or enlightened ruler, Cyrus conciliated the Babylonians and allowed the Jews, at least those who wished to, to return to their homeland. His successors, Cambyses and Darius, expanded and consolidated their rule, expanding into Egypt and, briefly, to Greece. Under Darius, Persia was the world's largest empire. An efficient bureaucracy and an integrated road system was established, along with a cosmopolitan army, and capitals were established at Susa and later at Persepolis. The most significant cultural contributions of the Persians was the religion of Zoroastrianism, a religion of the one god, Ahuramazda, who was opposed by an evil spirit, and which eventually resulted in a religion more dualistic than monotheistic in character.

LECTURE AND DISCUSSION TOPICS

1.Discuss the moral and spiritual legacy of the ancient Hebrews and their impact upon Western Civilization.

2. Explore the concept of "empire in the Ancient Near East, using Assyria and Persia as examples.

3. Examine the similarities and differences among the religious beliefs and practices of the peoples of the early Middle East, including a contrast between Hebrew monotheism and the region's more common polytheistic faiths.

4. Discuss the possible influences and interrelationship between Judaism and Zoroastrianism including the impact of both upon Christianity and Islam.

5. Explore the impact of geography in the context of Near Eastern imperial developments.

6. Compare and contrast the Assyrian Empire with the later Persian Empire.

7. Explore the fragility of "civilization," using the history of the Near East as a focus.

MAP EXERCISES

1. Palestine in the First Millennium B.C. MAP 2.1. Discuss the geographic vulnerability of the various Palestinian peoples during the first millennium. What impact did this have on the development of Israel's culture and history? (page 25)

2. The Assyrian and Neo-Babylonian Empires. MAP 2.2. Did either of the Assyrian and Neo-Babylonian empires extend their territories beyond earlier Mesopotamian empires? If so, where and why? (page 29)

3. The Persian Empire at the Time of Darius. MAP 2.3. What modern nations made up the ancient Persian Empire? What are the geographical elements, if any, which might explain why the Persian Empire was the largest in the world up to that time? (page 33)

DISCUSSION QUESTIONS FOR THE PRIMARY SOURCES (BOXED DOCUMENTS)

1. "The Covenant and the Law: The Book of Exodus": What was the nature of the covenant between Yahweh and the Hebrews? What was its moral significance for the Hebrew people? Could the covenant be considered a "contract"? Why and/or why not? (page 27)

2. "The Hebrew Prophets: Micah, Isaiah and Amos": What did the Hebrew prophets focus on as the transgressions of the Hebrew people? What do these selections reveal about the nature of the Hebrews as a "chosen" people? Are there any differences in either substance or emphasis between the three prophets? If so, what are they? (page 28)

3. "The Assyrian Military Machine": As seen in their own descriptions, what did Assyrian kings believe was important for military success? Do you think their accounts may be exaggerated? Why or why not? From the evidence presented in the documents, why were the Assyrians so feared in the eighth and seventh centuries? (page 30)

4. "A Dinner of the Persian King": What do we learn about the nature of Persian kingship from this description of a royal dinner? Does the description seem historically accurate? Why and/or why not? If possible compare the dinners of the Persian kings with those of Louis XIV at Versailles in the seventeenth century. (page 35)

STUDENT RESEARCH AND PROJECT TOPICS

1. What part did the Hebrew Bible, Hebrew law, and the prophets play in the development of Hebrew religion and society?

2. How did the Hebrew state and religion differ from earlier Near Eastern states and religions? How were they the same?

3. Discuss the role of the husband/father, wife/mother, and the sons and daughters in the Hebrew family.

4. Describe "the invention of history" for the Jewish people in the Hebrew Bible.

5. Discuss the contributions of the Jews, theological and non-theological, to later Western Civilization.

6. Compare and contrast the administrative structure and attitudes toward subject peoples of the Assyrian and Persian empires.

7. Discuss the military organization of the Assyrian and Persian empires. What were the reasons for each empire's success and failure?

8. Identify Zoroaster. How were his teachings unique? Relate his beliefs to the development of Persian religion.

9. What influence, if any, might Zoroastrianism have on later Judaism and Christianity?

10. Discuss the political and cultural achievements of Cyrus and Darius.

IDENTIFICATIONS

1. *megalith*
2. Indo-Europeans
3. Hittites
4. Hebrews
5. Monotheism
6. Moses
7. Hebrew Bible
8. The Exodus
9. Yahweh
10. David
11. Solomon
12. prophets
13. Torah
14. Jerusalem's Temple
15. the Divided Kingdom
16. Babylonian captivity of the Jews
17. covenant
18. Phoenicians
19. Byblos, Tyre, and Sidon
20. Assyrians
21. Ashurbanipal and Sennacherib
22. Nimrud and Nineveh
23. Chaldeans
24. Nebuchadnezzar
25. Hanging Gardens of Babylon
26. Persians
27. Archaemenid dynasty
28. Herodotus
29. Cambyses
30. Darius

31. Susa and Persepolis
32. satrapy
33. the Royal Road
34. Zoroastrianism and the *Zend Avesta*
35. Ahuramazda

MULTIPLE CHOICE QUESTIONS

1. The Hittites were
   a. an Indo-European speaking peoples.
   b. defeated and destroyed by the Egyptians.
   c. made iron weapons of war.
   d. a and c
   ANSWER: d (page 24)

2. Growing appreciation of astronomy among European peoples after 4000 B.C. is best seen in
   a. cuneiform star charts.
   b. wall paintings of galaxies.
   c. megalithic observatories.
   d. epic poems about the cosmos.
   ANSWER: c (p. 23)

3. The most famous of the megalithic constructions of Europe is
   a. Ziggurat.
   b. Woodhenge.
   c. Stonehenge.
   d. Lascaux.
   ANSWER: c (p. 23)

4. The original Indo-Europeans possibly came from
   a. Mesopotamia.
   b. the steppe region north of the Black Sea.
   c. the Indus Valley.
   d. the Aegean basin
   ANSWER: b (p. 24)

5. Which of the following is <u>not</u> an Indo-European language?
   a. Sanskrit
   b. Babylonian
   c. German
   d. Latin
   ANSWER: b (p. 24)

6. The Exodus in the Old Testament refers directly to
   a. battles between Hebrews and Philistines.
   b. the destruction of the Moabites by a vengeful God.
   c. the Hebrews' flight from Egypt under the guidance of Moses.
   d. King David's great congress of Jerusalem.
      ANSWER: c (p. 24)

7. King David's chief contribution in Hebrew history was
   a. the building of the temple in Jerusalem.
   b. the establishment of Hebrew control over all of Palestine.
   c. the strengthening of the Hebrew religion.
   d. the military defeat of the Egyptians.
      ANSWER: b (p. 24)

8. Solomon's most revered contribution to the Hebrew society was to
   a. centralize royal power along the lines of Mesopotamian despotism.
   b. divide the Hebrew tribes into two separate political kingdoms.
   c. decentralize royal power and spread it among the 12 Hebrew tribes.
   d. construct the Temple, the symbolic center of the Hebrew religion and society.
      ANSWER: d (p. 25)

9. The destruction of Jerusalem in 586 B.C. and the Babylonian Captivity of the Hebrews occurred at the hands of the
   a. Chaldeans.
   b. Assyrians.
   c. Philistines.
   d. Persians.
      ANSWER: a (p. 25)

10. All of the following are true of the Hebrew conception of God <u>except</u>
   a. he was the creator of but not an inherent part of nature.
   b. all peoples of the world were subject to him.
   c. that he would punish those not following his will.
   d. there was no room for personal relationships with him, as his word was law.
      ANSWER: d (p. 26)

11. The Hebrew religion
   a. believed in a created God–Yahweh.
   b. was an ethical religion centered around the Ten Commandments.
   c. taught there was covenant between the Hebrews and Ahurmazda.
   d. all the above
      ANSWER: b (pp. 26-27)

12. The Hebrew prophets
   a. were considered by the Hebrews to be the voice of Yahweh.
   b. often served as judges in the Hebrew courts.
   c. attempted to foretell the future for the Hebrew military leaders.
   d. were caretakers of the Ark of the Covenant.
      ANSWER: a (p. 27)

13. The Hebrew Bible
   a. differs fundamentally from the Torah and the Old Testament of the Christian Bible.
   b. focuses on the basic theme of the necessity of the Hebrews to obey their God.
   c. related only the words of the prophets and tells us little about Hebrew daily life.
   d. tells little about the history of the Hebrews before the Babylonian Captivity.
      ANSWER: b (p. 26)

14. The words of the Hebrew prophets
   a. promoted universalism by stating that all nations would one day worship the God of Israel.
   b. proclaimed that Israel would rise again from the ashes of conquest.
   c. advocated social justice by condemning the rich for mistreating the poor.
   d. all of the above
      ANSWER: d (pp. 27-28)

15. Many scholars today
   a. believe the Hebrew Bible is a completely accurate historical record.
   b. contend that the Hebrew Bible was originally written down in the fifth century A.D.
   c. doubt that the early books of the Hebrew Bible reflects the true history of the Israelites.
   d. argue that the Hebrew Bible was first written in Greek.
      ANSWER: c (p. 24)

16. Which of the following was <u>not</u> part of the Hebrew religious tradition?
   a. the law
   b. the revelation
   c. the covenant
   d. the prophets
      ANSWER: b (p. 26)

17. The greatest international sea traders of the ancient Near East were the
   a. Sea Peoples.
   b. Phoenicians.
   c. Carthaginians.
   d. Philistines.
      ANSWER: b (p. 28)

18. The Phoenicians' contributions to the ancient Near East included <u>all but</u>
   a. the founding of the colony of Carthage.
   b. a simplified alphabet and system of writing.
   c. the establishment of trading stations throughout the Mediterranean.
   d. their defeat and destruction of the Hebrew twelve tribes.
      ANSWER: d (p. 28)

19. All of the following are correct about Byblos <u>except</u>:
   a. It was an Egyptian commercial center.
   b. It was a Phoenician port city.
   c. It was a distribution center for Egyptian papyrus.
   d. The Greek work for book is derived from its name.
      ANSWER: a (p. 28)

20. All of the following were Assyrian kings <u>except</u> for
   a. Sennacherib.
   b. Shalmeneser III.
   c. Ashur.
   d. Ashurbanipal.
      ANSWER: c (pp. 29-30)

21. Which of the following statements <u>best</u> describes the Assyrian government?
   a. a limited monarchy, where the king's power was checked by an assembly
   b. a theocracy, where the priests of the temple had the real power
   c. an aristocracy, with the landed nobility possessing political power
   d. the king's power was absolute; they were vicars of the Assyrian god Ashur
      ANSWER: d (p. 31)

22. All of the following helped make Assyria an efficient military machine <u>except</u> for
   a. iron weapons.
   b. activities of terror.
   c. humane treatment of prisoners.
   d. superior, diversified tactics.
      ANSWER: c (pp. 30-31)

23. All of the following are true statements concerning the Assyrian military <u>except</u>
   a. It used intimidation as one of its chief tactics.
   b. It did not employ cavalry.
   c. The army was well trained and disciplined, and effectively used iron weapons.
   d. The army was known for its siege tactics, effectively using such machines as siege engines and battering rams.
      ANSWER: b (p. 30)

24. Assyrian kings organized their empire more effectively by
   a. increasing the power of local noble governors.
   b. reducing the numbers of royal officials.
   c. were middlemen in the international trade of the era.
   d. concentrating their resources on internal economic development rather than on military spending.
      ANSWER: c (p. 31)

25. At its height, the Assyrian Empire was ruled by
   a. the superintendent of the palace.
   b. the priesthood of the chief deity Ashur.
   c. a king whose power was absolute.
   d. a system of independent governorships.
      ANSWER: c (p. 31)

26. The Assyrian army was able to conquer and maintain an empire due to its
   a. ability to use diversified military tactics.
   b. avoidance of siege warfare.
   c. lenient treatment of rebellious subjects.
   d. Assyria's naturally protected boundaries.
      ANSWER: a (p. 30)

27. The Assyrians' use of terror tactics and atrocities
   a. were used universally on all captured prisoners.
   b. especially targeted inhabitants of the empire who rebelled against Assyrian rule.
   c. were used to make up for an absence of an intelligence network.
   d. prevented foreign cultures from mixing with the Assyrian population.
      ANSWER: b (p. 31)

28. Assyrian society was well known for its
   a. assimilation of other cultures and development of a polyglot society.
   b. manumission of slaves.
   c. monumental cities.
   d. monotheism.
      ANSWER: a (p. 31)

29. All of the following were unifying forces in Assyrian society <u>except</u>
   a. language.
   b. religious practices.
   c. economic and social equality.
   d. the king.
      ANSWER: c (p. 31)

30. The principal economic basis of Assyrian society was
   a. heavily irrigation-based farming.
   b. agriculture based on farming villages.
   c. international trade.
   d. sea-based commerce.
      ANSWER: b (p. 31)

31. Assyrian art was primarily concerned with
   a. outshining the remnants of Sumerian and Babylonian culture.
   b. illustrating the gods, especially Marduk.
   c. glorifying the king, hunting, and war.
   d. displaying the virtues of women and female priests.
      ANSWER: c (p. 31)

32. Nebuchadnezzar II accomplished all of the following <u>except</u>:
   a. the revision of the Persian law code.
   b. rebuilding Babylon.
   c. defeating the Assyrians.
   d. building the Hanging Gardens of Babylon.
      ANSWER: a (p. 32)

33. Which of the following statements is <u>not</u> true of the Chaldean Empire?
   a. Babylon was its great central city.
   b. It was the longest-lasting of the great Near Eastern empires.
   c. The Hanging Gardens was created in its time.
   d. The people of the empire welcomed its fall to the Persians.
      ANSWER: b (p. 32)

34. Cyrus the Great was perhaps best known for
   a. being a just and benevolent ruler.

b. conquering Egypt.
c. adopting the Babylonian law code.
d. defeating the Phoenicians at the Battle of Sidon.
ANSWER: a (p. 32)

35. The only region to escape Cyrus the Great's invasion and defeat was
a. Iran.
b. Egypt.
c. Asia Minor.
d. Mesopotamia.
ANSWER: b (p. 32)

36. The Persian Empire reached its largest territorial boundaries under
a. Cyrus.
b. Darius.
c. Xerxes.
d. Cambyses.
ANSWER: b (p. 33)

37. Cambyses' greatest achievement as king of the Persian Empire was
a. soothing over the hatred of subject peoples caused by Cyrus's policies of intolerance.
b. building a canal to link the Red Sea and the Mediterranean Sea.
c. bringing Egypt under Persian control.
d. causing a revolt of Ionian Greek cities in 499 B.C.
ANSWER: c (p. 32)

38. Darius accomplished all of the following <u>except</u>
a. building a canal that linked the Red Sea with the Mediterranean Sea.
b. conquering Egypt.
c. creating a Persian province in western India.
d. conquering Thrace.
ANSWER: b (p. 32)

39. The Persian Empire's system of satrapies allowed for
a. subject peoples to play a dominant role in civil administration.
b. a sensible system of collecting tribute based on an area's productive capacity.
c. noble offices to be filled by election rather than hereditary means.
d. widespread corruption by the satraps, who acted without the king's knowledge.
ANSWER: b (p. 33)

40. Which of the following statements concerning the Persian kings is false?
a. As he was considered a god, the king held the power of life and death over all subjects.
b. The Great Kings tended to become greedy and hoard their treasuries throughout the empire's duration.
c. Events like the "king's dinner" were meant to demonstrate the luxurious power of the king.
d. The king's palace demonstrated the international flavor and wealth of the empire.
ANSWER: a (pp. 33-35)

41. Which of the following was <u>not</u> a part of the Persian military?

a. cavalry
b. infantry
c. Praetorian Guard
d. Immortals

ANSWER: c (p. 34)

42. The weakening of the Persian Empire was largely attributed to

a. a corrupt system of satraps that was never closely monitored by the king.
b. the constant erosion of its standing army.
c. the kings' hoarding of wealth and over taxation of their subjects.
d. a lack of communication due to its vast size.

ANSWER: c (p. 34)

43. The Persian army

a. was very large compared to other ancient armies.
b. was a professional army that depended on mercenaries.
c. was plagued by corrupt and inept generals.
d. a and b

ANSWER: d (p. 34)

44. Which of the following statements concerning Zoroastrianism is false?

a. It was dualistic and monotheistic in nature.
b. It had few followers outside the Persian Empire.
c. It did not include a final judgment among its beliefs.
d. Its supreme deity was Ahuramazda.

ANSWER: c (p. 36)

45. Zoroastrianism

a. stressed the free will and power of humans to choose between good and evil.
b. became a powerful force in the Assyrian Empire.
c. ended the monotheistic religious practices previously carried out by Persians.
d. had no lasting impact on other future religious practices.

ANSWER: a (pp. 47-48)

46. The central, sacred text of Zoroastrianism is the

a. Talmud.
b. *Vedas*.
c. *Zend Avesta*.
d. prayers of Ashur.

ANSWER: c (p. 34)

47. In Zoroastrianism, the evil spirit was known as

a. Avesta
b. Ahriman.
c. Ahuramazda.
d. Mithra.

ANSWER: b (36)

48. The decline of the Hittites and Egyptians around 1200 B.C.
    a. brought an end to Near Eastern civilization.
    b. created a power vacuum which allowed several small states to emerge and temporarily flourish.
    c. allowed the Persians under Cyrus the Great to immediately establish an empire.
    d. was caused by Assyrian conquest.
        ANSWER: b (p. 36)

49. The most tolerant and efficient of the Near Eastern empires was the
    a. Egyptian.
    b. Assyrian.
    c. Chaldean.
    d. Persian.
        ANSWER: d (p. 36)

50. Hebrew monotheism had a spiritual legacy which included
    a. Christianity.
    b. Islam.
    c. Zoroastrianism.
    d. a and b
        ANSWER: d (p. 36)

RELEVANT WORLD-WIDE WEB SITES/RESOURCES

1. Ancient Scripts of the World:
http://alumni.eecs.berkeley.edu/~Lorentz/Ancient_Scripts/
(Excellent site for the study of historical linguistics and the development and use of writing in ancient cultures.)

2. University of Connecticut
WWW Virtual Library—Archaeology:
http://archnet.uconn.edu/
(Excellent site with extensive links to ancient and biblical archaeology collections on-line.)

3. Emory University, M.C. Carlos Museum:
http://www.emory.edu/CARLOS/carlos.html
(Fine permanent collections of ancient near-eastern art.)

4. Internet Jewish History Source Book:
http://www.fordham.edu/halsall/jewish/jewishsbook.html
(Excellent site with online original documents and fine links to other relevant web resources and museums.)

5. The Israel Museum, Jerusalem:
http://www.imj.org.il/main.html
(Virtual tour of museum's ancient masterworks with time lines of Jewish history and culture.)

6. Univ. of Michigan, Kelsey Museum of Archaeology:
http://www.umich.edu/~kelseydb/index.html
(Fine museum of archaeology and ethnography with good Semitic collections.)

RELEVANT VIDEO RESOURCES

From Jesus to Christ: The First Christians, PBS Home Video, (4 Programs, 55 minutes each). (Covers Hebrew sectarianism, formation of radical Jewish holy communities, and genesis of Christianity therein.)

Judaism: The Chosen People, Insight Media, (52 minutes). Overview of Jewish religious traditions and current religious practice.)

The Western Tradition, Part I, Annenberg/CPB Collection/ PBS Home Video, (30 minutes each program), Program 11, "Early Christianity."

RELEVANT MUSICAL PERFORMANCES

Music of the Bible Revealed, Harmonia Mundi France CD.

SUGGESTED STUDENT ACTIVITIES

1. Have students compare the Hebrew law code as found in the book of Leviticus with the Babylonian law code of Hammurabi.

2. Nebuchadnezzar's Hanging Gardens of Babylon are of interest to most students. Suggest that students do some Web research on this Wonder, as well as the other six ancient Wonders of the World.

3. It has been suggested that the Christian religion was influenced by Persian Zoroastrianism. Have students do a comparative study of the two religions.

4. Suggest to students that they compare the military systems of the Persians and the Assyrians as to size, organization, tactics, and overall effectiveness.

CHAPTER 3
THE CIVILIZATION OF THE GREEKS

CHAPTER OUTLINE

I. Early Greece
- A. Minoan Crete
- B. The First Greek State: The Mycenaeans

II. The Greeks in a Dark Age (c. 1100–c. 750 B.C.)
- A. Homer

III. The World of the Greek City-States (c. 750–c. 500 B.C.)
- A. The Polis
- B. Colonization and the Rise of Tyrants
- C. Sparta
- D. Athens

IV. The High Point of Greek Civilization: Classical Greece
- A. The Challenge of Persia
- B. The Growth of an Athenian Empire in the Age of Pericles
- C. The Great Peloponnesian War and the Decline of the Greek States
- D. The Culture of Classical Greece
    - 1. The Writing of History
    - 2. Greek Drama
    - 3. The Arts: The Classical Ideal
    - 4. The Greek Love of Wisdom
- F. Greek Religion
- G. Daily Life in Classical Athens

V. Conclusion

CHAPTER SUMMARY

Like the ancient Hebrews, the Greeks also had a profound influence on Western Civilization. Unlike the river valleys of the Middle East, Greece is mountainous land, with human occupation generally occurring in the narrow valleys. The soil was poor in most locations, and the peoples of Greece early turned to the sea, notably the Aegean Sea.

The first civilization in the region was a non-Greek society centered on the island of Crete. During the third millennium B.C. the Cretans, (or Minoans, from legendary King Minos), traded throughout the eastern Mediterranean. Commerce and art rather than military conquest governed the Minoans, practices reflected in the wall frescos at Knossos and elsewhere. However, c. 1450 B.C. its civilization was destroyed, perhaps by natural disaster, probably through military conquest by the Greek-speaking peoples of the mainland.

The earliest Greek-speakers (Indo-Europeans) migrated into Greece c. 1900 B.C., and by c. 1600 B.C. had established the first Greek, or Mycenaean, civilization (from one of its major cities, Mycenae). More war-like than the Minoans, the Mycenaeans dominated the Aegean world and beyond until they succumbed during the twelfth century B.C., possibly through invasions by new Greek-speakers from the north. A Dark Age resulted: civilization largely disappeared, an era covered by the stories of Homer's epic poems, which established the heroic values for later Greek society.

With the end of the Dark Age (c. 800 B.C.) the era of the polis, or city-state, began. Most numbered a few thousand persons, although Athens at its height reached 300,000. The polis was a community of citizens, and the citizens (at least the male citizens) ruled the polis. A military revolution also broadened polis participation. Farmers fighting as heavily armed infantrymen–hoplites–replaced the aristocrat cavalry, and consequently received, sometimes grudgingly, a say in the governing of the polis. Two of the most famous city-states were Sparta, a militarized polis ruled by an oligarchy, and where commerce and the arts were minimized, and Athens, which became noted for its democratic instructions in spite of the fact, like other poleis, the many slaves and women had no political rights.

War was endemic, with the poleis rarely uniting until Persians invaded Greece. The Persian War (499-479 B.C) temporarily unified the Greeks, who were victorious against the powerful Persian Empire. At the end of the war, Athens created the anti-Persian Delian League, but Athens converted the alliance into an empire. In reaction, Sparta created its own alliance, the Peloponnesian League. Eventually, war broke out, and in the resulting Peloponnesian War (431-404 B.C.), the Greek world suffered disastrously. In the fourth century Philip II of Macedonia took control of Greece.

The fifth and fourth centuries was the classical era in Greece, especially in Athens. Herodotus and Thucydides can be said to have invented history, Aeschylus, Sophocles, Euripides became the founders of tragic drama and Aristophanes the father of dramatic comedy. The ideals of Greek art and architecture (e.g. the Parthenon) have survived to the present. Rational and critical thought developed, and philosophers such as Socrates, Plato, and Aristotle posed questions about humanity and nature which are still being debated today. Religion and myth were important to most Greeks: the gods dwelt on Mt. Olympus, games and festivals were held in their honor, and oracles were consulted, notably at Delphi. Ancient Greece was no utopia, as slavery, poverty, repression of women, and violence was often the norm, but as the text notes, its civilization was the fountainhead of the culture of the West.

LECTURE AND DISCUSSION TOPICS

1. Discuss the growth of democracy in Ancient Greece---Athenian style.

2. Explore Greek history without Athens and Sparta---the other Greek *Poleis*.

3. Examine Greek history, focusing upon Greece's rural culture and its historical significance.

4. Discuss, perhaps pro and con, the claim that Greek civilization contributed more to Western Civilization than any other culture or civilization.

5. Analyze the ideal of ancient Greece as reflected in Greek vase painting and architecture. [a slide lecture]

6. Examine the central role, politically, socially, and religiously, that the Parthenon played in Athenian society. [a slide lecture]

7. Compare and contrast the natures of the Athenian and Spartan world views and the way each society dealt with internal and external events in the fifth century B.C.E.

8. Explore the several possible causes that led to the Golden Age of the fifth century B.C.E.

MAP EXERCISES

1. Classical Greece. MAP 3.1. How did the geography of Greece, both land and sea, influence the development and expansion of Greek culture and civilization? (page 40)

DISCUSSION QUESTIONS FOR THE PRIMARY SOURCES (BOXED DOCUMENTS)

1. "Homer's Ideal of Excellence": What important Greek ideals are revealed in this passage from the *Iliad*? What ideas and themes are there in the excerpt that could explain why Homer's writings remained the core text of the Greeks for centuries? (page 42)

2. "The Lycurgan Reforms": What does the passage from Plutarch's account of Lycurgus reveal about the nature of the Spartan state? What was the rationale for educating young Spartan males as revealed in the document? What might it mean "to be a Spartan"? (page 45)

3. "Athenian Democracy: The Funeral Oration of Pericles": According to Pericles, what are the ideals of Athenian democracy? Was Pericles correct in his assessment? Why or why not? How might Greeks from other city states, such as Sparta, have responded to Pericles' oration? Why? (page 48)

4. "Household Management and the Role of the Athenian Wife": What does the selection from Xenophon reveal about the role of a woman in the Athenian household? How did the Greeks conceive the "natural" attributes of men and women and how does the Greek view of the world shape Greek conceptions of gender and gender roles? (page 55)

STUDENT RESEARCH AND PROJECT TOPICS

1. What were the effects of Greek geography on Greek history?

2. Explain why Homer was used as the basis for Greek education. What did the Greeks learn from Homer?

3. What were the characteristics of the Greek city state? Compare it to the Sumerian city state.

4. Monarchy, democracy, oligarchy, aristocracy, and tyranny are all derived from the Greeks. What did each mean? Give a specific example of how each was practiced in and shaped Greek history.

5. Discuss the organization of the Athenian democratic system. Was it a democracy? In what ways is Athenian democracy similar to American democracy? In what ways is it different?

6. What do historians mean by the phrase "The Age of Pericles?" What were the characteristics of this period that made it distinct?

7. Discuss the causes and course of the Great Peloponnesian War. What impact did the war have on the Greeks?

8. The period of the classical age of Greece is known for its literary, artistic, and intellectual achievements. What basic characteristics of Greek culture are reflected in the major achievements of the Greeks in the writing of history, drama, the arts, and philosophy? What universal human concerns did these same achievements reflect?

9. What role did each of the following play in the life of Athens: male citizens, women, and slaves?

10. What were the causes, results, and the turning point of the Persian Wars?

11. How did Greek males regard Greek females and what opportunities did Greek society and culture offer to women for self-expression?

IDENTIFICATIONS

1. Pericles' Funeral Oration
2. mountains of Greece
3. Minoan Crete
4. Heinrich Schliemann
5. Knossos
6. Mycenaeans
7. Troy
8. Greek Dark Ages
9. Homer's *Iliad* and *Odyssey*
10. *arete*
11. *polis*
12. hoplites
13. phalanx
14. tyrant
15. Sparta
16. oligarchy
17. Lycurgus
18. *ephors*
19. helots
20. Attica
21. Solon
22. Cleisthenes
23. Darius and Xerxes
24. Marathon, Thermopylae, and Plataea
25. Delian League
26. Herodotus
27. Peloponnesian War
28. Thucydides
29. Aeschylus, Sophocles, and Euripides
30. Aristophanes
31. Parthenon
32. Sophists
33. Socrates
34. Plato's *Republic*

35. Aristotle
36. Olympian gods
37. oracle at Delphi

MULTIPLE CHOICE QUESTIONS

1. All of the following are prominent features of Greece's topography except
   a. extensive open plains.
   b. bays and harbors.
   c. mountains.
   d. valleys.
      ANSWER: a (page 39)

2. In general, separate early Greek communities
   a. developed close ties and cooperated with one another.
   b. exchanged diplomatic representatives only.
   c. avoided all contact to appease their city gods.
   d. became fierce rivals fighting so often as to threaten Greek civilization itself.
      ANSWER: d (p. 38)

3. The chief center of Minoan Crete was
   a. Athens.
   b. Sparta.
   c. Knossus.
   d. Thebes.
      ANSWER: c (p. 39)

4. Which of the following statements best describes the Mycenaeans.
   a. They were merchants who dominated Mediterranean trade in the fourth century B.C.
   b. They were a warrior people who achieved their apex between 1400 and 1200 B.C.
   c. They produced exotic articles of trade in the fifth century B.C.
   d. They were a people dominated by a theocracy, and were led into battle by their warrior priesthood.
      ANSWER: b (p. 40)

5. The civilization of Minoan Crete
   a. enjoyed great prosperity due to extensive sea trade and commerce.
   b. was poor and isolated.
   c. developed elaborate skills in art and architecture visible in defensive fortresses.
   d. flourished after 1450 B.C.
      ANSWER: a. (p. 39)

6. The group of people who succeeded the Mycenaeans in Greece around 1100 B.C. were the
   a. old Cretans.
   b. neo-Corinthians.
   c. Macedonians.
   d. new Greek-speaking barbarians..
      ANSWER: d (p. 41)

7. The period immediately following the collapse of the Mycenaean civilization is referred to as the
   a. Golden Age of Greece.
   b. Greek Dark Age.
   c. Age of Colonization.
   d. Age of Pericles.
      ANSWER: b (p. 41)

8. During the migrations of the Greek Dark Age, many Greeks
   a. occupied northern Greece.
   b. took control of the Peloponnesus.
   c. crossed the Aegean Sea to settle in Asia Minor.
   d. moved to Crete.
      ANSWER: c (p. 41)

9. What were the chief characteristics of the Greek Dark Age?
   a. It was a period of migrations and declining food production.
   b. It was a period of political anarchy and many foreign invasions.
   c. It was a period of intermittent warfare between highly developed city-states.
   d. It was the most economically productive period of Greek history due to the rapid development of Greek colonies.
      ANSWER: a (p. 41)

10. Homer's *Iliad* points out
   a. the honor and courage of Greek aristocratic heroes in battle.
   b. the exalted position of women in Greek society.
   c. the absolute abhorrence of violence by the Greeks.
   d. the Greeks' rejection of slavery.
      ANSWER: a (p. 42)

11. Which of the following is true of Greece from c. 750 to c. 500 B.C.?
   a. It was a period of social cohesion and great Greek empires.
   b. The Greeks' colonization efforts in the Aegean and Black Seas came to an end.
   c. The *polis* evolved into the central institution in Greek life.
   d. It was a period of incessant warfare.
      ANSWER: c (p. 43)

12. The *polis* was the Greek name for
   a. county.
   b. police.
   c. people.
   d. city-state.
      ANSWER: d (p. 43)

13. Which of the following was <u>not</u> a characteristic of the typical Greek *polis*?
   a. It contained an agora and acropolis within its fortifications.
   b. Each *polis* had a population of between 100,000 and 200,000 citizens.
   c. Each *polis* was autonomous from all other *poleis*.
   d. The strength of the community came through cooperation.
      ANSWER: b (p. 43)

14. The development of the *polis* had a negative impact on Greek society by
a. fostering a sense of disunity among commoners.
b. dividing Greece into fiercely competitive states.
c. discouraging the development of polytheistic religion.
d. retarding democracy in the organization of civic governments.
ANSWER: b (p. 43)

15. During the period of Greek history from 750-500 B.C.
a. the *polis* developed as the chief political institution.
b. trade and colonization increased greatly.
c. Athens became the dominant military force in all of Greece.
d. a and b
ANSWER: d (pp. 43-44)

16. The hoplite phalanx was
a. a new Greek military organization of heavily armed infantry.
b. a great Greek religious festival.
c. a system for organizing the administration of justice in cities.
d. a style of prized Greek vase painting.
ANSWER: a (p. 43)

17. The rise of tyrants in the *poleis* in the seventh and sixth centuries B.C.
a. had little to do with the development of the hoplite fighting force.
b. often encouraged the economic and cultural progress of the cities.
c. meant the increased oppression of the peasants.
d. crushed for good the power of the aristocratic oligarchies.
ANSWER: b (p. 44)

18. Tyranny in the Greek *polis* arose as
a. the people became complacent due to the egalitarian nature of Greek society.
b. the demand for strong leadership against the established aristocratic oligarchies.
c. the religious beliefs of the Greeks collapsed.
d. a consequences of aristocratic power and a widening gulf between the rich and the poor.
ANSWER: d (p. 44)

19. In Sparta
a. life resembled that of a military camp.
b. there was no class distinction.
c. helots (slaves) were treated well and could be expected to lead long lives.
d. the government was democratic.
ANSWER: a (pp. 43-44)

20. The Lycurgan reforms resulted in
a. the establishment of a permanent military state in Sparta.
b. more constitutional rights for Spartans.
c. outlawing religion in Sparta.
d. revolt among Spartan slaves.
ANSWER: a (p. 45)

21. In Sparta, the ephors
    a. led the armies into battle.
    b. were responsible for the education of the youth.
    c. decided upon the issues to be presented to the assembly
    d. were subject to the helot veto.
        ANSWER: b (p. 46)

22. Spartan helots
    a. were bound to the land and labored as farmers and servants.
    b. were forced to serve in the Spartan army.
    c. had achieved the right to hold land themselves by the sixth century B.C.
    d. a and b
        ANSWER: a (p. 45)

23. For the Greeks, the term *arete* described
    a. the moral failure of cowards.
    b. the essential virtues of ordinary women.
    c. the duties of a citizen.
    d. the striving for excellence.
        ANSWER: d (p. 42)

24. The early history of Athenian politics is marked by
    a. developments similar to the Spartan city-state.
    b. the rapid development of democracy.
    c. the quick elimination of all factions.
    d. the consistent desire of local aristocrats to avoid tyranny.
        ANSWER: d (p. 46)

25. Which of the following descriptions of Athenian leaders is <u>incorrect</u>?
    a. Pericles—statesman and orator
    b. Cleisthenes—created the ten tribes and Council of 500
    c. Solon—sole archon and political reformer
    d. Pisistratus—remodeled the Athenian constitution while neglecting his merchant supporters.
        ANSWER: d (pp. 46-48)

26. The political figure chiefly associated with the establishment of Athenian democratic institutions is
    a. Hippias.
    b. Solon.
    c. Cleisthenes.
    d. Draco.
        ANSWER: c (p. 46)

27. The immediate cause of the Persian Wars was
    a. a revolt of the Ionian Greek colonies in Asia Minor.
    b. the Ionian invasion of Persia.
    c. the capture of the Persian queen by Aristagoras of Miletus.
    d. the Persian defeat of Sparta.
        ANSWER: a (p. 47)

28. At the Battle of Marathon, the Greeks
   a. were routed, leading to a Persian invasion.
   b. were led by Sparta.
   c. won a decisive victory by aggressive attack against a stronger foe.
   d. learned to fear Persian military might.
      ANSWER: c (p. 47)

29. At the Battle of Thermopylae
   a. the Persian fleet was destroyed and the threat ended.
   b. the Greeks won a decisive victory in the Persian Wars.
   c. the Greek fleet was routed and forced to retreat.
   d. the Spartans fought a noble holding action to the last man.
      ANSWER: d (p. 47)

30. Which of the following phases best describes the Delian League?
   a. a trading league dominated by Sparta
   b. an alliance of city-states led by Athens against Persia
   c. a military alliance of kingdoms led by Persia
   d. a group of Greek city-states, led by Thebes, bent on imperialism
      ANSWER: b (p. 47)

31. During the Age of Pericles
   a. the power of the aristocrats was enhanced.
   b. Athenians became deeply attached to their democratic system.
   c. participation in government was encouraged of women.
   d. imperialism was dropped.
      ANSWER: b (p. 48)

32. Athenian government under Pericles
   a. grew more tyrannous.
   b. put more aristocrats in power.
   c. involved new councils and magistracies enabling ordinary citizens to hold public office.
   d. became chaotic and ineffective as his nepotism infuriated the public.
      ANSWER: c (p. 48)

33. The Peloponnesian War resulted in
   a. the consolidation of Pericles' power.
   b. the unification of the Greek city-states under Thebes.
   c. the defeat of Athens and the collapse of its empire.
   d. Athenian control of Sicily.
      ANSWER: c (p. 49)

34. One of the chief causes of the Peloponnesian War was
   a. Athens' fear of Spartan imperialism.
   b. Sparta's fear of the power of Athens and its maritime empire.
   c. Athens' entry into an alliance with the Persians.
   d. An attack by Corinth and Megara on Sparta.
      ANSWER: b (p. 49)

35. The Greek historian Thucydides differed from Herodotus in that the former
   a. was unconcerned with spiritual forces as a factor in history.
   b. exhibited a critical attitude toward his sources but Herodotus did not.
   c. devoted much of his writing to economic history.
   d. was unconcerned with teaching lessons based on history.
      ANSWER: a (p. 49)

36. The first real history of Western civilization was written by
   a. Thucydides.
   b. Plutarch.
   c. Herodotus.
   d. Solon.
      ANSWER: c (p. 49)

37. The Greek dramatist who was a realist and known for his portrayal of real life situations was
   a. Aeschylus.
   b. Sophocles.
   c. Euripides.
   d. Aristophanes.
      ANSWER: c (p. 50)

38. Greek comedy
   a. was developed before tragedy.
   b. was first organized in the festival of Cronos.
   c. was insignificant and not very popular.
   d. was used to express political views as evidenced by Aristophanes.
      ANSWER: d (p. 50)

39. The author of *Oedipus the King*
   a. Aeschylus.
   b. Sophocles.
   c. Euripides.
   d. Aristophanes.
      ANSWER: b (p. 50)

40. The Greek Parthenon
   a. was dedicated to Zeus, chief of the Greek gods.
   b. is considered the greatest example of classical Greek temple architecture.
   c. was designed by the Greek architect, Doryphoros.
   d. a and b
      ANSWER: b (p. 50)

41. Greek architecture
   a. was constructed according to mathematical ratios found in nature.
   b. was considered ornate and lavish when compared to other classical architecture.
   c. was dominated by the Doric, Ionic, and Corinthian columnar styles.
   d. was best exemplified in the cities of Sparta.
      ANSWER: c (p. 51)

42. Early Greek philosophy attempted to

a. eliminate divinity from the world.
b. explain the universe on the basis of rational thought.
c. undermine traditional Greek society.
d. turn all Greeks away from the world and toward contemplation.

ANSWER: b (p. 51)

43. The Sophists

a. were professional teachers who seemingly questioned the traditional values of their societies.
b. had as their chief spokesman Socrates.
c. were led by Plato and emphasized rote memory in education.
d. questioned traditional Greek religion and, instead, worshiped the Egyptian god Isis.

ANSWER: a (pp. 51-52)

44. Socrates was condemned to death for

a. corrupting the youth of Athens.
b. leading a political coup attempt.
c. killing one of his followers in a rage.
d. marrying his cousin and committing bigamy.

ANSWER: a (p. 52)

45. "The unexamined life is not worth living" is a cornerstone of the philosophy of

a. Socrates.
b. Aristotle.
c. Plato.
d. Pythagoras.

ANSWER: a (p. 52)

46. *The Republic* depicted

a. Socrates' idea about the "unexamined life."
b. Plato's idea of the ideal government and society.
c. Aristotle's response to Sophism.
d. Plato's idea of a return to nature.

ANSWER: b (p. 52)

47. Which of the following was <u>not</u> true of Greek religion?

a. It was polytheistic.
b. It involved ritual and sacrifice.
c. Festivals were held to honor the gods.
d. Myths served no particular social function.

ANSWER: d (p. 53)

48. Which of the following phrases best describes the social situation of Greek women?

a. Women were kept under strict control, cut off from formal education, and were always assigned a male guardian.
b. Women were afforded equal rights with men in city politics.
c. Women were often allowed to participate in public life, especially through jury service.
d. Women were not allowed to participate in any religious festivals.

ANSWER: a (p. 54)

49. In classical Athens, male homosexuality
  a. became an important subject in many tragic plays.
  b. was practiced and tolerated in part as a means by which mature men instructed young males about the masculine world of politics and patronage.
  c. after initial toleration became increasingly subject to moral and philosophical attack as a threat to the aristocratic family.
  d. was a practice only associated with actors and priests, never gaining public acceptance.
    ANSWER: b (p. 55)

50. The Greek tragedy was
  a. homosexuality, celibacy, and a declining birth rate.
  b. divisions and rivalries between the city states.
  c. being conquered by the Mycenaeans.
  d. never recovering from the Dark Age.
    ANSWER: b (p. 56)

RELEVANT WORLD-WIDE WEB SITES/RESOURCES

1. The Ancient City of Athens:
http://www.indiana.edu/~kglowack/athens/
(Fine multiple images of major Athenian buildings and monuments.)

2. The Ancient Greek World:
http://www.museum.upenn.edu/Greek_World/index.html
(One of the finest web sites available, covering many aspects of ancient Greek geography, economy, culture, and religion. Developed and maintained by museum staff at the University of Pennsylvania.)

3. Ancient World Web:
http://www.julen.net/aw/
(Massive index of relevant web sites with annotations on many, includes links to multiple illustrated sites on geography, cultural geography, and ethnography of ancient Mediterranean world.)

4. Classics and Mediterranean Archaeology:
http://rome.classics.lsa.umich.edu/welcome.html
(Massive Web clearing house of lists and links to hundreds of web sites pertinent to classical art, architecture, and culture.)

5. Images of Ancient Greece:
http://www.tulane.edu/lester/text/Western.Architect/
Greece/Greece.html
(Extensive images, drawings, and plans of classic Greek structures and design elements, images can be enlarged.)

6. Perseus Project:
http://www.perseus.tufts.edu
(Web site developed to accompany highly successful Perseus Project CD-ROM created for Mac, PC version soon to be available. Vast CD-ROM collection of images of Greek coins, vases, sculptures, and archaeological sites may eventually go fully on-line at this web site.)

7. www,pbs.org/empires/thegreeks/
(Site contains considerable information on ancient Greece, including interactive map and timelines, letter and word pronunciation, as well as information on people and events.)

RELEVANT VIDEO RESOURCES

The First World, Insight Media, (53 minutes). Program examines the mathematical and philosophical ideas of Pythagoras and Plato, drawing connections between Greek science and culture.
The Greeks, 4-part video series, Films for the Humanities and Sciences, (each part 58 minutes).

Greek Drama: Reconstructing a Greek Theatre, Films for the Humanities and Sciences (25 minutes).

Minoan Civilization, Films for the Humanities and Sciences, (53 minutes).
The Western Tradition, Part I, Annenberg/CPB Collection/
PBS Home Video, (30 minutes each program), Programs 5 and 6, "The Rise of Greek Civilization" and "Greek Thought."

RELEVANT MUSICAL PERFORMANCES

Music of Ancient Greece, Harmonia Mundi France CD.

SUGGESTED STUDENT ACTIVITIES

1. Have students read portions of Herodotus' account of the Persian Wars, having them look for instances of the historian's exaggeration and bias. Then students should read portions of Thucydides' account of the Peloponnesian Wars and determine why he was considered a better historian.

2. Have students investigate the trial and condemnation of Socrates. What does the man's conviction on charges of "corrupting youth" reveal about the culture and politics of Greek cities?

3. Students should realize how much the Greeks have influenced us politically and socially. Have pupils write a hypothetical essay describing the situation the United States and other western countries would be in had the Greeks been defeated by the Persians.

4. Most historians believe that the Persians had nearly all the advantages during the Persian Wars. Have pupils determine what were the advantages of the Greeks, especially military advantages.

5. Have students read and do oral reports on some of the writings of Plato and Aristotle, such as the former's *Last Days of Socrates* or *The Republic*; both books are small and present few reading difficulties.

6. Encourage students to use the World-Wide Web to obtain and report on a selection of images drawn from Greek vase painting evoking such themes as heroism, women's work, Greek entertainments, and Greek sexual mores.

CHAPTER 4
THE HELLENISTIC WORLD

CHAPTER OUTLINE

I. The Rise of Macedonia and the Conquests of Alexander the Great
- A. Alexander the Great
  - 1. The Conquests of Alexander
  - 2. The Legacy of Alexander

II. The World of the Hellenistic Kingdoms
- A. Hellenistic Cities
- B. Economic and Social Trends in the Hellenistic World
  - 1. New Opportunities for Women

III. Culture in the Hellenistic World
- A. New Directions in Literature and Art
- B. A Golden Age of Science
- C. Philosophy: New Schools of Thought
- D. Religion in the Hellenistic World
  - 1. The Jews in the Hellenistic World

IV. Conclusion

CHAPTER SUMMARY

The independence of the Greek poleis ended in the fourth century, and a new age, known as the Hellenistic era, came into being. Learning little from the disasters of the past, the city-states continued to war against each other. Meanwhile, to the north, the kingdom of Macedonia was waxing in power, thanks to extensive gold reserves and able rulers, most notably Philip II (d. 336 B.C.). Philip overcame the last Greek resistance at the battle of Chaeronea in 338 B.C. His next goal was to invade the Persian Empire, but he was assassinated in 336 B.C. and that task was left to his twenty-year old son, Alexander, known to history as Alexander the Great.

In 334 B.C. Alexander crossed into Asia Minor with an army of 37,000 soldiers. By 332 B.C. he captured Egypt, there building a new city on the Mediterranean, and naming it Alexandria. The Persian capitals of Susa and Persepolis fell by 330 B.C., and he reached India three years later. Alexander wanted to go on, but his troops rebelled. Still planning more campaigns, Alexander died in Babylon in 323 B.C. at age thirty-two, one of the ancient world's greatest heroes as well as one its most enigmatic figures. God in Egypt, autocrat in Persia, and king of Macedonia, but what motivated him?

The resulting society is known as Hellenistic, meaning Greek-like or to imitate Greeks. The Greek language became the international language, Greek ideas became influential, and Greek merchants, artists, philosophers, and soldiers found opportunities and rewards throughout the Near East, a world of kingdoms and empires rather than independent city-states. Alexander's new empire soon divided into several states, ruled by his generals and their descendants.

The great cities were also dominated by Greeks. Commerce increased, and women often played significant roles in economic activities. Slavery was extensive, with the slave market on the island of Delos selling as many as 10,000 slaves each day. Educational opportunities were broadened, with the state sometimes assuming a larger role, though most schools were established by wealthy individuals. As in the past, education was generally for boys, not girls.

Egypt's Alexandria was particularly significant in cultural matters: its library contained 500,000 volumes (or scrolls), and artists and intellectuals were attracted to the city. The era was rich in literature, and comedy and history both thrived. Sculptors and architects found many opportunities under the patronage of kings and other wealthy individuals. In a break from Greece's classic age, the art was more realistic and emotional. It was a golden age for science, with astronomers positing a heliocentric universe and accurately determining the circumference of the earth. Euclid's geometry and Archimedes' work on cylinders and spheres were revolutionary, and there were also advances in medicine.

There were new schools of philosophy, such as Epicureanism and Stoicism. Both asked how one could find happiness in a larger and more complex world than the earlier homogenous community of the polis. The former argued in favor of withdrawing from public concerns and finding happiness in private friendships while the latter claimed that happiness would come only through living a life of virtue in harmony with the divine or nature's laws. Religion remained central, but the worship of the Greek Olympian gods declined, and other religions came to the fore. Many were mystery religions which promised individual salvation, such as the Egyptian cult of Isis. Judaism remained the exception to the cults and civic religions, and worshiped Yahweh, whether in Judaea, which again achieved its independence in 164 B.C., or elsewhere.

The Hellenistic world was a Greek-like world, but there were many other influences in that cosmopolitan society, and much would have appeared foreign to the Greeks of sixth and fifth centuries.

LECTURE AND DISCUSSION TOPICS

1. Discuss the impact of Alexander the Great on his own era.

2. Consider the legacy of Alexander in the three centuries after his death.

3. Explore the failure of the Greek city states in the aftermath of the Peloponnesian War and the rise of Macedonia.

4. Compare and contrast the Hellenic world of the city state with Hellenistic civilization.

5. Discuss the several Hellenistic kingdoms and their "Greekness" or lack of it..

6. Analyze the Hellenistic world as a Golden Age of Science.

7. Compare and contrast urban life in Hellenic Greece to that of the cities of the Hellenistic era.

MAP EXERCISES

1. The Conquests of Alexander the Great. MAP 4.1. What were some of the geographical and political reasons which explain how Alexander was able to assemble such a vast empire in such a short time and why his successors were unable to hold it together. (page 62)

2. The World of the Hellenistic Kingdoms. MAP 4.2. What are the geographic factors, if any, which can explain the location of the several post-Alexander Hellenistic kingdoms? (page 64)

DISCUSSION QUESTIONS FOR PRIMARY SOURCES (BOXED DOCUMENTS)

1. “Alexander Meets an Indian King”: From the information in the text, does Alexander’s reaction to Porus seem historically valid? Why and/or why not? Why might Arian have praised the qualities of Porus but portray Darius III as weak and cowardly? Might Porus’ reactions and his character have given Alexander a justification for abandoning his Indian campaign, at least in retrospect? (page 61)

2. "A New Autonomy for Women": Judging by the content of these letters, what freedoms did Hellenistic women enjoy? How autonomous were they? Based upon your knowledge of gender and gender roles in shaping earlier cultures, how did Hellenistic civilization differ in its conceptions of what was "proper" for men and women? (page 66)

3. "The Stoic Ideal of Harmony with God": Based on Cleanthes' poem, what are some of the fundamental beliefs of the Stoics? Is Stoicism a religion? Why and/or why not? Does Stoicism reflect life in Hellenistic times? If so, how and why? (page 69)

STUDENT RESEARCH AND PROJECT TOPICS

1. Discuss the rise of Macedonia and its successful take-over of the Greek world, both in regards to Macedonian strengths and the weaknesses of the city-states in the south.

2. What were Alexander's goals and how successful was he in achieving them? What was his legacy to western civilization?

3. Why is Alexander the Great considered to be the first true super-hero of Western Civilization? Is that reputation justified? Why and or why not?

4. Discuss the political and military organization of the Hellenistic kingdoms. How did the new political systems differ from those of the Greek city-states? What impact did Philip and Alexander have on them?

5. What made Alexander such an outstanding general? Give examples from his military campaigns.

6. Discuss the major characteristics of Hellenistic cities. How did these urban centers differ from the Greek city-states of the classical era?

7. What were the major philosophies of the Hellenistic period? How did they differ from the philosophies of Classical Greece?

8. Compare and contrast the artistic, literary, and scientific achievements of the Hellenistic age with those of the classical age? How do you account for the differences?

9. Compare and contrast the situations of women during the classical era to the Hellenistic period.

10. How did Greek religious practices in the Hellenistic era differ from those in the classical era?

IDENTIFICATIONS

1. Macedonia
2. Philip II
3. Battle of Chaeronea
4. Hellenistic
5. Alexander the Great
6. a dagger and the *Iliad*
7. Alexandria
8. Battle of Gaugamela
9. Darius III
10. Porus
11. Seleucids
12. Battle of Issus
13. Attalids and Pergamum
14. Ptolemies
15. Seleucids
16. Antigonids
17. Arsinoe II and Ptolemy II
18. Theocritus
19. Menander
20. Polybius
21. Corinthian order
22. Aristarchus of Samos
23. Euclid
24. Archimedes
25. Epicurus and Epicureanism
26. Zeno and Stoicism
27. mystery cults
28. cult of Isis
20. Judas Maccabaeus
30. Hanukkah

MULTIPLE CHOICE QUESTIONS

1. Before Philip II, the Macedonians
   a. were greatly admired by the Greeks for their cultural achievements.
   b. spoke a language akin to Persian and unknown to the Greeks.
   c. were a rural people organized in tribes and considered backward by southern Greeks.
   d. forged a system of city-states marred by internal strife.
      ANSWER: c (page 59)

2. The orator who attacked Philip of Macedonia was
   a. Pericles.
   b. Isocrates.
   c. Demosthenes.
   d. Arrian.
      ANSWER: c (p. 59)

3. The battle which gave Philip the control of Greece was the battle of
   a. Chaeronea.
   b. Salamis.
   c. Thermopylae.
   d. the Milvian Bridge.
      ANSWER: a (p. 59)

4. All of the following were results of the battle of Chaeronea except for
   a. the formation of the Corinthian League, with Philip as head.
   b. the complete destruction of Athens for its leadership in the struggle against Macedonia.
   c. the establishment of Macedonian garrisons throughout Greece.
   d. Greek cooperation with Macedonia for a future war against Persia.
      ANSWER: b (p. 59)

5. The result of Macedonian incursions into Greece under Philip II was
   a. the waning and eventual collapse of Macedonian power.
   b. the creation of the Corinthian League under Philip.
   c. all Greek city-states allying themselves with the Persians.
   d. the complete destruction of Sparta as a center of Greek power.
      ANSWER: b (p. 59)

6. After the battle of Chaeronea, Philip
   a. gave the city-states freedom in foreign affairs but not in domestic matters.
   b. allowed the city-states economic freedom but not political nor social freedom.
   c. gave the city-states autonomy in domestic affairs, but not in foreign affairs.
   d. deprived the city-states of all freedom of action.
      ANSWER: c (p. 59)

7. Alexander's first military success after invading the Persian Empire was at the battle of
   a. Issus.
   b. Guagamela.
   c. Alexandria.
   d. the Granicus River.
      ANSWER: d (p. 60)

8. All of the following were conquered by Alexander except
   a. Syria.
   b. Babylon.
   c. Egypt.
   d. Arabia.
      ANSWER: d (p. 60)

9. Alexander claimed to be descended from the god
   a. Apollo.
   b. Zeus.
   c. Dionysus.
   d. Heracles.
      ANSWER: d (p. 59)

10. Alexander's military success against the Persians was partially attributable to
a. the chronic weakness of the Persian Empire.
b. numerically superior forces.
c. the role of Alexander's cavalry.
d. troop loyalty in all campaigns.
ANSWER: c (p. 60)

11. Alexander invaded the Persian Empire
a. with an army of 100,000 hoplite warriors.
b. by sea through Egypt.
c. but lacked a cavalry contingent.
d. with an army of 37,000 including 5,000 cavalry.
ANSWER: d (p. 60)

12. At the Battle of Gaugamela
a. Alexander was able to win a close victory by bringing up his war chariots at the last minute.
b. the Greeks under Alexander were able to break the center of the Persian line and with boldness turn the battle into a rout.
c. Alexander determined that the battle should be fought on a narrow plain, negating the numbers of the Persians.
d. Alexander struck the Persians at their weakest point.
ANSWER: b (p. 60)

13. By capturing the Persian capitals of Susa and Persepolis, Alexander
a. was able to gain possession of huge amounts of gold and silver.
b. was crowned king of the Medes and Assyrians.
c. was able to gain a trade route to India.
d. gained vast quantities of iron ore.
ANSWER: a (p. 60)

14. Alexander the Great's conquests in Asia occurred despite
a. his having no military expertise prior to his father's assassination.
b. the Persian king Darius III's refusal to make any peace settlements.
c. the lack of a strong cavalry and inability to capture Egypt.
d. his eventual difficulties in convincing his troops to fight so far from home.
ANSWER: d (p. 60)

15 The Indian ruler who resisted Alexander's invasion of northern India at the battle of the Hydaspes River, was
a. Changdragupta.
b. Seleucas.
c. Porus.
d. Kumar Barindra..
ANSWER: c (page 61)

16. Alexander the Great's troops rebelled when he made the decision to invade and capture
a. Arabia.
b. Pergamum.
c. India.
d. Cochin.
ANSWER: c (p. 60)

17. In establishing his empire, Alexander the Great
    a. saw himself as a descendant of Greek gods and heroes.
    b. combined Greek and Persian practices to allow its administration.
    c. demanded that the Greek city states "vote him a god."
    d. all of the above
        ANSWER: d (pp. 60-61)

18. "Hellenistic" refers to
    a. the era of the traditional polis.
    b. Helen of Troy, woman who caused of the Trojan War.
    c. "imitate Greeks".
    d. the take-over of the Eastern Mediterranean by Rome.
        ANSWER: c (page 61)

19. The Hellenistic era describes an age that saw
    a. the extension and imitation of Greek culture throughout the ancient Near East.
    b. the absence of autocratic power for nearly three centuries.
    c. the disappearance of a Greek cultural legacy until Roman times.
    d. Alexander's successors maintain a united empire until Roman times.
        ANSWER: a (p. 61)

20. During his numerous military campaigns, Alexander
    a. summoned an additional 60,000 soldiers from Greece.
    b. relied upon Persian warriors against his enemies.
    c. prayed to Zeus for assistance.
    d. relied upon elephants as his primary battlefield tactic.
        ANSWER: a (p. 61)

21. Upon the death of Alexander
    a. power was effectively passed to his young son.
    b. there was a period of tranquility under the leadership of his wife, Roxanne.
    c. his Macedonian generals became involved in successive power struggles.
    d. power was turned over immediately to his favorite general, Arrian.
        ANSWER: c (p. 62)

22. Which of the following was <u>not</u> a Hellenistic dynasty?
    a. Antigonid
    b. Ptolemaic
    c. Seleucid
    d. Abbasid
        ANSWER: d (p. 62)

23. The Hellenistic monarchies in the centuries after Alexander the Great
    a. became despotic monarchies.
    b. fought little amongst themselves.
    c. combined Greek-Macedonians and Near Eastern natives in administrative positions.
    d. showed little innovation in their armies.
        ANSWER: a (pp. 61-62)

24. Which of the following statements best describes Hellenistic cities?

a. small and governed by a military elite
b. important centers of administration, and which were dominated by Greeks and Greek culture.
c. urban centers, where the inhabitants spoke only their native tongue.
d. cities that had a population of under 10,000 which were dominated by a trading class

ANSWER: b (p. 63)

25. A clear trend of Hellenistic cities was

a. a decline in their importance as Hellenistic kings settled themselves in rural communities.
b. the successful importation and establishment of the *polis* as a way of life.
c. the close relationship between the Hellenistic rulers and the cities.
d. the continued success of social revolutions driven by the lower classes.

ANSWER: c (p. 63)

26. Improvements in trade and commerce in the Hellenistic world were greatly aided by all of the following <u>except</u>

a. growth of cities and the urban economy.
b. revolutionary innovations in agriculture.
c. the decline in the number political barriers..
d. the development of major trade routes.

ANSWER: b (p. 65)

27. The economic life of the Hellenistic world was characterized by

a. tremendous innovations in labor-saving machinery, as with the "Archimedean screw."
b. a significant shift in industry and manufacturing from Greece to the east.
c. little variety in products used for trading.
d. the virtual disappearance of slavery in manufacturing.

ANSWER: b (p. 64)

28. Which class of women achieved the most notable gains during the Hellenistic period?

a. lower class
b. middle class
c. upper class
d. trading class

ANSWER: c (p. 65)

29. Upper-class Hellenistic women achieved considerable progress and opportunity in all of the following areas <u>except</u>

a. legal equality.
b. economic opportunity.
c. educational possibilities.
d. literary and artistic recognition.

ANSWER: a (p. 65)

30. In the Hellenistic world cities

a. many Greeks were attracted to the numerous opportunities available.
b. Greek colonies played little role in politic and government.
c. the cities were independent of the kings's rule.
d. slavery disappeared and religion became irrelevant.

ANSWER: a (pp. 63-64)

31. Hellenistic education as embodied in the gymnasium
   a. was not supported through patronage by Hellenistic rulers who saw education as a threat to their power.
   b. was open to all classes of society except slaves.
   c. made no provision for physical education.
   d. closely and widely followed classical Greek ideas about proper education.
      ANSWER: d (p. 67)

32. An especially important cultural center with the largest library in ancient times was
   a. Thebes.
   b. Athens.
   c. Pergamum.
   d. Alexandria.
      ANSWER: d (p. 66)

33. Which of the following statements is <u>untrue</u> concerning Hellenistic culture?
   a. It was a great period of literature, especially in drama, history, and biography.
   b. It was a period that saw the need to preserve the writings of the classical Greeks.
   c. Sculptors and architects could very easily find work in the new Hellenistic cities.
   d. Artists remained social outcasts, and were rarely patronized by the rich who regarded artists as rebels.
      ANSWER: d (p. 67)

34. The theatrical center of the Hellenistic world and home of New Comedy was
   a. Athens.
   b. Alexandria.
   c. Rhodes.
   d. Sicily
      ANSWER: a (p. 67)

35. The New Comedy is best exemplified by the playwright
   a. Polybius.
   b. Menander.
   c. Aristophanes.
   d. Eratosthenes
      ANSWER: b (p. 67)

36. The surviving works of the Greek historian Polybius demonstrate
   a. his following of Thucydides in seeking rational motives for historical events.
   b. his focus on the growth of the Greek city-states from their origins to their collapse.
   c. the continued failure of ancient historians to find accurate, firsthand sources.
   d. his reliance on the models of Herodotus and willingness to ascribe historical change to the intervention of gods.
      ANSWER: a (p. 67)

37. Hellenistic sculpture and architecture
   a. moved away from realism toward more idealistic forms.
   b. showed remarkable diversity of forms throughout the Hellenistic world.
   c. flourished as monarchs were obsessed with beautifying their cities.
   d. rejected the Corinthian order in the construction of temples.
      ANSWER: c (p.67)

38. Hellenistic scientists were able to accomplish all of the following except
a. establishing the heliocentric theory of the universe.
b. estimating the circumference of the earth.
c. inventing the Archimedean screw.
d. inventing a crude telescope.
ANSWER: d (pp. 67-68)

39. The Alexandrian scholar Euclid's most famous achievement was
a. systematizing the study of geometry.
b. calculating the earth's circumference.
c. formulating and synthesizing the predominant elements in military science.
d. transferring the capital of Hellenistic science from Athens to Alexandria.
ANSWER: a (pp. 67-68)

40. The most famous scientist of his era, Archimedes of Syracuse, was responsible for all of the following except
a. uniting once more the disciplines of science and philosophy.
b. designing military devices to thwart siege attackers.
c. creating the science of hydrostatics.
d. establishing the value of the mathematical constant pi.
ANSWER: a (p. 68)

41. The philosophical school that stressed happiness through freeing oneself from a political life was
a. Hedonism.
b. Stoicism.
c. Platonism.
d. Epicureanism.
ANSWER: d (p. 68)

42. Stoicism
a. was formed by Epicurus.
b. later became very popular with the Romans.
c. maintained that people could gain inner peace by pursuing urban profession.
d. centered upon the quest for personal immortality.
ANSWER: b (pp. 68-69)

43. What was the primary difference between the philosophy of the Greek classical period and philosophy during the Hellenistic period?
a. Hellenistic philosophy dealt more with human happiness disassociated from the life of the polis.
b. Hellenistic philosophy was more political than classical philosophy.
c. Classical philosophy dealt primarily with ethics and human behavior.
d. Classical philosophy was centered in Athens; Hellenistic philosophy in Corinth.
ANSWER: a (p. 69)

44. The widespread popularity of Stoicism and Epicureanism in the Hellenistic world
a. demonstrated the renewed strength and belief in the *polis*.
b. occurred despite the continued growth of traditional Greek religious practices.
c. suggested a new openness to thoughts of universality.
d. amounted to proof of a growing homogenization of Greek thought.
ANSWER: c (p. 68)

45. How did religion in Greece change during the Hellenistic period?
   a. It changed to a various kinds of emperor worship.
   b. Fertility gods took the place of the classical Greek gods.
   c. The Greeks became very receptive to the eastern religious mystery cults.
   d. The Greeks reverted back to a form of animism.
      ANSWER: c (p. 69)

46. The mystery cults and religions of the Hellenistic world
   a. were completely foreign and thus unacceptable to the Greeks.
   b. helped pave the way for the success of Christianity.
   c. never achieved widespread popularity due to their inability to fulfill people's spiritual needs.
   d. lacked an emotional initiation experience, unlike the Greek civic cults.
      ANSWER: b (p. 70)

47. All of the following are true about the cult of Isis <u>except</u>
   a. it originated in the eastern Persian empire, an outgrowth of Zoroastrianism.
   b. it was one of the most popular of the mystery religions.
   c. she was associated with the giver of laws and letters to humankind.
   d. her cult promised an afterlife.
      ANSWER: a (p. 70)

48. The Jews of the Hellenistic cities
   a. were never fully integrated into Hellenistic culture.
   b. had no political and judicial rights, unlike other urban residents.
   c. were denied citizenship despite all their attempts.
   d. were harshly treated by the Seleucids after a failed rebellion in Jerusalem in 164 B.C.
      ANSWER: a (p. 100)

49. The Jewish rebellion against the Seleucid king Antiochus IV was led by
   a. Herod the Great.
   b. Amos the prophet.
   c. Judas Maccabaeus.
   d. Ptolemy II.
      ANSWER: c (p. 70)

50. Which of the following statements is correct about the Hellenistic civilization?
   a. It was an entirely stagnant civilization.
   b. There were few achievements in science and art.
   c. Signs of decline were apparent by the late third century B.C.
   d. In comparison to earlier Greek society, there was more equality between the rich and the poor.
      ANSWER: c (p. 71)

RELEVANT WORLD-WIDE WEB SITES/RESOURCES

1. Exploring Ancient World Cultures:
http://eawc.evansville.edu/index.htm
(Site with sections devoted to cultures of Mediterranean, Middle East, South Asia, etc. includes good introductory essays to each part and great links to relevant world museums.)

2. WWW Virtual Library for the History of Science, Technology, and Medicine: http://www.asap.unimelb.edu.au/hstm/hstm_society.htm
(Excellent site for all aspects of these topics, includes information on ancient scientists and physicians. Superb links to hundreds of other relevant sites.)

RELEVANT VIDEO RESOURCES

In the Footsteps of Alexander the Great, PBS Home Video,
4 programs on 2 cassettes, (55 minutes each).

The Spirit of Alexander the Great, Films for the Humanities and Sciences, (26 minutes).

SUGGESTED STUDENT ACTIVITIES

1. Have students examine closely the emplacement of new Greek colonies and cities in the regions captured by Alexander. How did the placement of these communities facilitate the projection of Greek values and cross-fertilizations between local cultures and mainland Greek societies?

2. Have students find traces of Hellenistic philosophies in modern day thought.

3. Scholars have said that Alexander inherited much of his father's military genius. Have students determine what Alexander did copy from his father, as well as what were Alexander's own ideas or innovations.

4. Have students write an essay substantiating one of the following statements:
a. Greek scientific gains were greater in the Hellenistic period than in the Classical period.
b. The Greek artistic achievement was greater in the Classical period than in the Hellenistic period.

CHAPTER 5
THE ROMAN REPUBLIC

CHAPTER OUTLINE

I. The Emergence of Rome
   A. The Greeks and the Etruscans
   B. Early Rome
II. The Roman Republic (c. 509–264 B.C.)
   A. The Roman State
      1. Political Institutions
      2. The Struggle of the Orders: Social Divisions in the Roman Republic
   B. The Roman Conquest of Italy
III. The Roman Conquest of the Mediterranean (264-133 B.C.)
   A. The Struggle with Carthage
   B. The Eastern Mediterranean
   C. The Nature of Roman Imperialism
IV. Society and Culture in the Roman Republic
   A. Roman Religion
   B. The Growth of Slavery
   C. The Roman Family
   D. The Evolution of Roman Law
   E. The Development of Literature and Art
   H. Values and Attitudes
V. The Decline and Fall of the Roman Republic (133-31 B.C.)
   A. A New Role for the Roman Army: Marius and Sulla
   B. The Collapse of the Republic
VI. Conclusion

CHAPTER SUMMARY

Italy, less mountainous and more fertile than Greece, almost bisects the Mediterranean, and was thus potentially positioned to dominate that inland sea, and under Rome it did so. The Greeks to the south and the Etruscans to the north were early influences, and the latter ruled Rome during the sixth century B.C. In 509 B.C. the Romans expelled the Etruscans establishing a republic. There were various magistrates, with two consuls at the apex. The Senate of 300 was not formally a legislature, but its advice came to have the force of law. The several assemblies were dominated by the rich few. Rome was a republic, but one ruled by an aristocratic oligarchy.

Roman citizens were divided into two groups, or orders, the few patricians and the many plebeians. At the beginning of the Republic the former had the power, but from the early fifth century the two orders struggled with each other. Over time, through the Roman genius for political compromise, the plebeian gained influence, including a plebeian assembly, the right to become magistrates, and intermarriage, but most of the advantages went to the richer plebeians.

Rome also struggled with its neighbors, but not so peacefully. By 264 B.C. Rome was the master of Italy. Roman diplomacy was as important as its armies, and its rule was softened by allowing local autonomy and gradually granting Roman citizenship to non-Romans. The next challenge was Carthage and its empire in Africa and Spain. Three wars were fought (the Punic Wars: 264-241, 218-202, and 149-146 B.C.), with Rome the victor. In the east, Rome conquered Macedonia in 148 B.C., taking over Greece. As the text states, there was no imperial master plan. Its empire resulted from a combination of factors, including sheer opportunism.

Religion and law permeated Roman life. Ritual was at the focus of religion, for ritual established the correct relationship with the gods, both for individuals (families had their household cults) and for the state. Roman law was among its most enduring accomplishments. The early laws, written in the Twelve Tables, was the civil law for Romans. As they expanded, a new body of law developed, the law of nations, for Romans and non-Romans alike. Finally, a system of natural law emerged, based upon reason and universal divine law. Late Republican Rome was influenced by Hellenistic Greece, particularly in literature, art, and Stoic philosophy.

In the second century the conservative and traditional values of Rome declined as affluence and individualism increased, and from 133 B.C. to 31 B.C. the Republic was in crisis. There were factional struggles within the governing oligarchy. The small farmer class, the backbone of Rome's armies, had largely lost their lands to the wealthy as a result of Rome's imperial ventures. Attempts were made to solve the problem of corrupted values and lack of an army by demanding lands be restored to the ex-farmers, recruiting an army by promising land to the landless, and dictatorship, but much Roman blood was shed in the process.

In 60 B.C., Pompey, Crassus, and Julius Caesar seized power. Caesar conquered Gaul (most of western Europe) during the 50s B.C., thus becoming a threat to Pompey and the Senate. War led the defeat of the Senate and the death of Pompey. Caesar became dictator, thus alienating the Senate oligarchy, who murdered him on March 15, 44 B.C. Mark Antony, Caesar's chief associate, and Caesar's young adopted heir, Octavian, then formed an alliance, but Antony's relations with the Egyptian ruler, Cleopatra, contributed to the breaking of the pact. At the battle of Actium (31 B.C.) Antony and Cleopatra were defeated, and Octavian became the sole ruler of the Roman world. The Republic had come to an end.

LECTURE AND DISCUSSION TOPICS

1. Discuss the Etruscans and their influence upon bringing about the establishment of the Roman Republic.

2. Analyze the political and social structure of the Roman Republic.

3. Explore the nature of Roman Imperialism, or how did Rome become an empire?

4. Examine the importance of the Punic Wars upon Roman society, then and later.

5. Discuss the various causes and interpretations of fall of the Roman Republic, and whether that event have any lessons for today.

6. Explore the breakdown of the Roman constitution or Republican consensus and the rise to power of the political-generals of the Late Republic.

7. Discuss the history of the Roman Republic as both a democracy and as an oligarchy.

8. Examine the role that "great men" play in history, or did Julius Caesar make history, or was he a product of his own society.

9. Discuss the proposition that Roman imperialism destroyed the Roman Republic.

MAP EXERCISES

1. Ancient Italy. MAP 5.1. What challenges did Rome have to overcome in uniting the Italian peninsula under its rule? What strategic advantages did Rome have because of its physical location in Italy? (page 74)

2. Roman Conquests in the Mediterranean, 264-133 B.C. MAP 5.2. What were the historical reasons which explain the development of Rome's Mediterranean empire in just over a single century? Geographically, who were Roman's most significant opponents and why? (page 80)

3. Roman Dominions in the Late Republic, 31. B.C. Where did Rome gain territory during the first century B.C., and why? What geographical factors explain those conquests? (page 90)

DISCUSSION QUESTIONS FOR THE PRIMARY SOURCES (BOXED DOCUMENTS)

1. "Cincinnatus Saves Rome: A Roman Morality Tale": What values did Livy emphasize in his account of Cincinnatus? How important were those values to Rome's success? Why was the story of Cincinnatus so important to many generations of Romans? (page 78)

2. "Cato the Elder on Women": What was Cato's attitude toward women? Compare and contrast this selection with the one by Xenophon in Chapter 3. Were Women in the late Roman Republic better off than most Greek women? (page 84)

3. "The Twelve Tables": What do the selections from the Twelve Tables reveal about Roman society and its conception of justice? How does this law code compare with earlier compilations of statutes and royal legal decrees marking the central evolution of law within western civilization? (page 85)

4. "The Assassination of Julius Caesar": What does the account of Caesar's assassination reveal about the character of Julius Caesar? Judging by this piece, what lessons did classical historians intend their readers to take away from retellings of great and dramatic political events? (page 89)

STUDENT RESEARCH AND PROJECT TOPICS

1. What was the impact of the Etruscans and Greeks on the early development of Roman civilization? How did Rome's contact with the Hellenistic world affect Roman civilization in the second and first centuries B.C.? In answering the latter questions, explain what the poet Horace meant when he wrote that "captive Greece took her barbarian conqueror captive."

2. The Greek historian Polybius described the Roman government in this fashion: "As for the Roman constitution, it had three elements, each of them possessing sovereign powers; and their respective share of power in the whole state had been regulated with such a scrupulous regard to equality and equilibrium, that no one could say for certain, not even a native, whether the constitution were an aristocracy or democracy or despotism." Is Polybius's description of the early Roman constitution an accurate one? Why or why not? Be specific.

3. In the "struggle of the orders," what did the plebeians want and what did they succeed in getting? Can it be said that Rome became a democracy because of this struggle? Why or why not?

4. Trace the steps by which Rome achieved its empire from 264 to 133 B.C. In the course of its expansion from 264 to 133 B.C., what happened to the political structure and the political values of the Roman Republic?

5. Compare and contrast Roman religion with the religion of the Greeks. How did its religion help Rome become such an important state?

6. Compare and contrast the Roman family of the Republic with the Greek family of Periclean Athens. Can it be said that women had more rights and freedom in one of these societies than the other? Why or why not?

7. It has been said that Roman culture was not very original, only a copy of the Greek. Prove or disprove this idea.

8. What were the causes and the results of the Punic Wars?

9. Discuss the role of the Senate, powerful generals, and politicians in the collapse of the Roman Republic.

10. "The fall of the Roman Republic was due to systemic institutional weaknesses rather than the personal ambitions generals and politicians." Discuss pro and con.

IDENTIFICATIONS

1. Etruscans
2. Latium
3. Tiber River
4. 753 B.C.
5. Romulus and Remus
6. praetors, quaestors, aediles, censors
7. *imperium*
8. consuls
9. *paterfamilias*
10. Roman Senate
11. patricians and plebeians
12. Struggle of the Orders
13. tribunes

14. Roman confederation
15. Roman citizenship
16. Carthage and the Punic Wars
17. Hannibal
18. Cannae
19. Scipio Africanus and Zama
20. Cato the Elder
21. Jupiter Optimus Maximus
22. Circus Maximus
23. *latifundia*
24. Twelve Tables
25. law of nations and law of nature
26. Plautus and Catullus
27. concrete
28. *nobiles*
29. *optimates* and *populares*
30. Tiberius and Gaius Gracchus
31. Marius and Sulla
32. Cicero
33. Crassus and Sparticus
34. Julius Caesar
35. First Triumvirate
36. Gaul
37. the Rubicon
38. Mark Antony and Cleopatra VII
39. Octavian
40. Battle of Actium

MULTIPLE CHOICE QUESTIONS

1. For the Romans, Italy's geography
   a. provided little productive land for agriculture.
   b. divided the peninsula into small isolated communities.
   c. made Rome a natural crossroads and an area easy to defend.
   d. made the conquering of the Mediterranean a difficult task.
      ANSWER: c (page 74)

2. Rome was established in the first millennium B.C. on the
   a. plain of Latium.
   b. river Danube.
   c. coast of the Aegean Sea.
   d. foothills of the Alps.
      ANSWER: a (p. 74)

3. The Etruscans were well known for
   a. the uncertainty of their origins.
   b. controlling most of Latium.
   c. conflicts with Greek colonists in southern Italy.
   d. all the above
      ANSWER: d (p. 75)

4. According to legend, Horatius
   a. defeated the Greeks at Cannae.
   b. defended the Tiber bridge against the Etruscans.
   c. led the Latins against the invasion by Rome
   d. wrote the Twelve Tables.
      ANSWER: b (pp. 73-74)

5. Livy's account of Cincinnatus
   a. was used to teach the Roman people the treachery of tyrant.
   b. was written as an act of defense against the government.
   c. tells the story of the founding of Rome.
   d. tells how the key virtues of duty and simplicity in the behavior of leaders enabled Rome to survive in difficult times.
      ANSWER: d (p. 78)

6. Rome set a precedent for treating its vanquished foes after forming the Roman Confederation by
   a. forcing slave labor on the populace of the defeated cities.
   b. offering the most favored "allied" full Roman citizenship, thus giving them a stake in successful Roman expansion.
   c. slaughtering the citizens wholesale and selling the rest to pirates.
   d. confiscating all the property of defeated peoples.
      ANSWER: b (p. 74)

7. Rome's conquest of the Italian peninsula by 264 B.C. can be attributed to
   a. superb diplomacy.
   b. a direct policy of expansion.
   c. the use of heavy cavalry.
   d. Rome's feeling of security.
      ANSWER: a (p. 78)

8. Executive authority or *imperium* during the Roman Republic
   a. was held by the consuls and praetors.
   b. could only be exercised with the approval of a majority of citizens.
   c. was abolished in favor of democracy.
   d. was embodied in one man, the emperor.
      ANSWER: a (p. 76)

9. In the Roman Republic, the praetor's first duty was
   a. a military command.
   b. control of taxation.
   c. administration of justice.
   d. management of colonial expansion.
      ANSWER: c (p. 76)

10. As Rome expanded, it became Roman policy to govern the provinces with officials known as
   a. consuls.
   b. quaestors.
   c. colonnae.
   d. proconsuls and propraetors.
      ANSWER: d (p. 76)

11. The *paterfamilias* in Roman society was
   a. a client to a patron or wealthy citizen.
   b. the male head of the household.
   c. an upper-class aristocrat.
   d. a common person.
      ANSWER: b (p. 83)

12. Originally the Roman Senate
   a. was the chief legislative body of the Republic.
   b. could only advise the magistrates in legal matters.
   c. was the most important popular assembly.
   d. saw its power wane by the third century B.C..
      ANSWER: b (p. 76)

13. The main achievement of the 287 B.C. law in Roman constitutional history was
   a. its removal of patricians from civic government.
   b. its establishment of the death penalty for treason against the state.
   c. its ruling that all *plebiscita* passed by the plebeian assembly had the force of law and were binding on the entire community, including patricians.
   d. its banishment of all Greeks law from the Roman legal system.
      ANSWER: c (p. 77)

14. In their struggle with the patricians, Roman plebeians employed which of the following tactics:
   a. a physical withdrawal from the state undercutting its military manpower
   b. the formation of popular councils to lobby for more political reforms
   c. open civil war
   d. a and b
      ANSWER: d (p. 76)

15. The Twelve Tables were
   a. the meeting place of the Roman Senate.
   b. used to record and inspire a new religious cult in Rome.
   c. art of the Roman festival celebrating spring's arrival
   d. the first formal codification of Roman law and customs
      ANSWER: d (p. 85)

16. The Carthaginians originated from
   a. Phoenician Tyre.
   b. northern Italy.
   c. the Greek city-state of Athens.
   d. Gaul.
      ANSWER: a (p. 79)

17. The immediate cause of the First Punic War was
    a. Carthaginian treachery in the Pyrrhic Wars.
    b. Roman colonization in North Africa.
    c. Carthaginian expansion along the Spanish and Italian coasts.
    d. Rome sending an army to Sicily.
        ANSWER: d (p. 79)

18. As a result of the First Punic War
    a. the Carthaginians were forced to withdraw from Spain.
    b. the Carthaginians were forced to withdraw from Sicily and pay an indemnity to Rome.
    c. Sicily gained its independence from both Rome and Carthage.
    d. Rome was forced to relinquish its Mediterranean claims.
        ANSWER: b (p. 79)

19. What was the significance of Scipio Africanus in the Second Punic War?
    a. He impeded Hannibal's advance in Italy through delaying tactics.
    b. He expelled the Carthaginians from Spain and later won the decisive Battle of Zama.
    c. He engineered a valuable alliance with the Gauls.
    d. He first utilized elephants as "living tanks."
        ANSWER: b (p. 80)

20. The Second Punic War saw Carthage
    a. try to force a naval war in the Mediterranean as a precursor to invasion of Italy.
    b. precipitate the war by encroaching on Roman Gaul.
    c. enlist the forces of Mongol allies.
    d. carry a land war to Rome by crossing the Alps.
        ANSWER: d (p. 79)

21. The Roman senator who led the movement for the complete destruction of Carthage was
    a. Cato.
    b. Scipio.
    c. Marius.
    d. Augustus.
        ANSWER: a (p. 80)

22. At the battle of Cannae the Romans
    a. suffered a devastating defeat by Hannibal.
    b. defeated the army of Hannibal.
    c. won a great victory, giving them control of the Straits of Messana.
    d. retreated to the walls of Sagantum.
        ANSWER: a (p. 79)

23. The result of the Third Punic War was
    a. an alliance between Rome and Carthage.
    b. the complete destruction and subjugation of Carthage.
    c. the loss of Rome's mastery of the Mediterranean Sea.
    d. the sacking of Rome.
        ANSWER: b (p. 80)

24. At about the same time that Rome destroyed Carthage, Rome also conquered
   a. Egypt.
   b. Greece and Macedonia.
   c. the Middle East.
   d. Perganum.
   ANSWER: b (p. 81)

25. It can best be said that Roman imperial expansion was
   a. carefully planned from the beginning and ruthless.
   b. driven solely by economic necessity.
   c. opposed by most senators as too costly and too dangerous.
   d. highly opportunistic as Romans responded to unanticipated military threats and new possibilities for glory.
   ANSWER: d (p. 81)

26. In Roman religion, a right relationship with the gods was achieved by
   a. exemplary personal morality.
   b. accurate performance of rituals and festivals.
   c. a reverence for Greek myths.
   d. occasional human sacrifice.
   ANSWER: b (p. 81)

27. Roman religious practices included
   a. a college of priests to carry out rituals correctly.
   b. the direct adoption of certain Etruscan gods like Apollo.
   c. clear separation of religion from politics.
   d. a ban on female participation in all religious rites.
   ANSWER: a (p. 81)

28. The peoples who had the greatest impact upon the Roman Republic by the fourth century B.C. were
   a. the Carthaginians.
   b. the Greeks.
   c. the Persians
   d. the Etruscans.
   ANSWER: b (p. 81)

29. Which of the following statements best applies to Roman schooling:
   a. Foreigners were not allowed to become teachers.
   b. Boys and girls were educated through a rigorous public school system borrowed from the Spartans.
   c. Education stressed training in Greek culture.
   d. Study of foreign languages was prohibited to purify the Latin language.
   ANSWER: c (p. 81)

30. Roman slaves
   a. often worked on the Roman *latifundia*.
   b. always received inhumane treatment from their owners.
   c. were often used as soldiers in the army.
   d. all the above
   ANSWER: a (p. 83)

31. Roman upper-class women typically
   a. had fewer freedoms than their Greek counterparts.
   b. married and bore children later in life.
   c. had some independent legal rights and property.
   d. were allowed to participate in public life.
      ANSWER: c (pp. 83-84)

32. From the time of the Twelve Tables until Justinian's Codification of Roman law in the sixth century
   a. Roman law was codified three times.
   b. law seldom changed and was considered to be outdated.
   c. was added to and corrected by the Roman Praetors.
   d. underwent a complete revision under Augustus.
      ANSWER: c (p. 84)

33. The Romans' most noticeable innovations in art and culture were found in
   a. sculpture.
   b. drama.
   c. architecture.
   d. wall painting.
      ANSWER: c (p. 86)

34. The most influential figure in oratory and the writing of philosophical treatises in the late Roman Republic was
   a. Catullus.
   b. Plautus.
   c. Clodia.
   d. Cicero.
      ANSWER: d (p. 86)

35. The *optimates* and *populares*
   a. were official political parties in the second century A.D.
   b. were political groups from the Roman aristocracy.
   c. were religious groups that followed different routes to achieve political ends.
   d. hoped to destroy the Roman Republic.
      ANSWER: b (p. 87)

36. Many Romans attributed the change of values in the Republic over time to
   a. affluence brought on by the addition of too much new territory.
   b. the lack of a dangerous enemy to threaten them after the destruction of Carthage.
   c. the emasculating influences of Greek culture and education.
   d. all the above
      ANSWER: d (p. 86)

37. Tiberius and Gaius Gracchus both
   a. were lower-class radical revolutionary leaders.
   b. successfully passed popular land reform bills.
   c. were killed by their political enemies.
   d. controlled the Senate which passed their reforms.
      ANSWER: c (p. 87)

38. The reforms of Gaius and Tiberius Gracchus
a. helped create a system of absolute political domination by the *optimates*.
b. eliminated the position of tribune of the plebs.
c. resulted in further instability and violence as they polarized various social groups.
d. were a total success, bringing some more egalitarian laws and customs.
ANSWER: c (p. 87)

39. The powerful families which dominated Rome during the second and first centuries B. C. were collectively known as the
a. *nobiles*.
b. *equites*.
c. *populares*.
d. *optimates*.
ANSWER: a (p. 97)

40. The first consul to attain full command of the army and supercede the Senate's right to conduct wars was
a. Marius.
b. Crassus.
c. Sulla.
d. Pompey.
ANSWER: a (p. 87)

41. Sulla's legacy and importance was that he
a. became the first non-Roman consul.
b. became the first Roman general to use siege engines.
c. prevented civil war by arbitrating disputes between Marius and Gaius.
d. employed his personal army in political disputes, paving the way toward Roman civil war.
ANSWER: d (pp. 87-88)

42. Among the dangerous military innovations of Marius threatening the Republic, one finds
a. he employed Greek mercenaries.
b. he recruited destitute volunteers who swore an oath of allegiance only to him.
c. he robbed the state treasury's tax revenues to buy weapons.
d. all the above
ANSWER: b (p. 87)

43. Julius Caesar
a. defeated Crassus at the Battle of Pharsalus in 48 B.C.
b. dissolved the Senate while he was dictator for life.
c. was assassinated for his strong beliefs in republican institutions.
d. led military commands in Gaul and Spain that enhanced his popularity.
ANSWER: d (p. 88)

44. The First Triumvirate included
a. Brutus, Crassus, and Pompey.
b. Caesar, Crassus, and Pompey.
c. Pompey, Caesar, and Brutus.
d. Cicero, Plautus, and Terence.
ANSWER: b (p. 88)

45. By crossing the Rubicon, Caesar showed that he
- a. was willing to disobey the direct orders of the Senate to advance his own bid for power.
- b. was willing to compromise with Pompey.
- c. had no will to fight his enemies in Rome.
- d. wished to retire peacefully to his rural estates.

ANSWER: a (p. 88)

46. All of the following were results of the Roman civil wars of 43-31 B.C. except
- a. the Second Triumvirate's defeat of Antony at the battle of Actium.
- b. the defeat of Caesar's assassins.
- c. the demise of republican institutions.
- d. the rule of Octavian.

ANSWER: a (pp. 89-90)

47. Which Roman writer is most closely associated with the development of a new poetry at the end of the Roman Republic?
- a. Sallust
- b. Cicero
- c. Catullus
- d. Plutarch

ANSWER: c (p. 86)

48. The military battle which symbolized the end of the Roman Republic was the battle of
- a. Chaeronea.
- b. Actium.
- c. Issus.
- d. Milvian Bridge.

ANSWER: b (pp. 89-90)

49. The sole survivor after the defeat of Antony and Cleopatra in 31 B.C. was
- a. Julius Caesar.
- b. Pompey the Great.
- c. Crassus.
- d. Octavian Caesar.

ANSWER: d (p. 90)

50. The individual most responsible for establishing a Roman imperial state was
- a. Julius Caesar.
- b. Antony.
- c. Octavian.
- d. Tiberius Gracchus.

ANSWER: c (91)

RELEVANT WORLD-WIDE WEB SITES/RESOURCES

1. Metropolitan Museum of Art, New York:
http://www.metmuseum.org
(Excellent on-line collection of Roman art objects.)

RELEVANT VIDEO RESOURCES

Cyber Rome, Films for the Humanities and Sciences, (38 minutes).
Superb virtual reality tour of great Roman structures and monuments, circa 200 A.D.

Intimate Details of Roman Life, Films for the Humanities and Sciences, (27 minutes).

Pompeii: Daily Life of the Ancient Romans, Films for the Humanities and Sciences, (45 minutes).

The Western Tradition, Part I, Annenberg/CPB Collection/
PBS Home Video, (30 minutes each program), Program 9, "The Rise of Rome."

SUGGESTED STUDENT ACTIVITIES

1. Have students do a comparative study of Greek and early Roman religion.

2. Have students do a study of Roman law, being sure to point out the ways that our American legal system has been influenced by the Romans.

3. Organize from the class two debate teams; have the teams take opposing sides on the phrase: "Julius Caesar: Politician or Autocrat?"

4. Give students the opportunity to do research on the Roman army, its organization, strategy, and tactics.

CHAPTER 6
THE ROMAN EMPIRE

CHAPTER OUTLINE

I. The Age of Augustus (31 B.C.–A.D. 14)
   A. The New Order
   B. Augustan Society
II. The Early Empire (14-180)
   A. The Five "Good Emperors" (96-180)
   B. The Roman Empire at its Height: Frontiers and Provinces
   C. Prosperity in the Early Empire
III. Roman Culture and Society in the Early Empire
   A. The Golden Age of Latin Literature
   B. The Silver Age of Latin Literature
   C. Roman Law
   D. The Upper-Class Roman Family
   E. Imperial Rome
   F. The Gladiatorial Shows
IV. Crisis and the Late Empire
   A. The Terrible Third Century
   B. The Reforms of Diocletian and Constantine
V. The Transformation of the Roman World: The Development of Christianity
   A. The Religious World of the Roman Empire
   B. The Jewish Background
   C. The Rise of Christianity
   D. The Growth of Christianity
VI. Conclusion

CHAPTER SUMMARY

Octavian, an astute politician, did not declare the Republic dead or himself emperor. In 27 B.C. he accepted the title of Augustus, and rather than emperor he called himself *princeps*, or chief citizen. He followed the prescribed legal forms, and the Senate had a role in governing, but most of the authority was in the hands of the *princeps*. Significantly, the army swore loyalty to him. Concerned about moral decline, he restored temples and shrines. The imperial cult was recognized: Julius Caesar had been deified at his death, as would be Augustus. Marriage and children were encouraged; extravagance was discouraged. It was a Golden Age in literature with works by Virgil, Horace, Ovid and Livy.

Augustus established the Julio-Claudian dynasty, which lasted until 68. In 69 Vespasian, a successful general but not a member of an old Senatorial family, founded the Flavian dynasty. His son, Domitian assumed the title of *imperator*, or emperor. What had been implicit with Augustus had become explicit. In the second century five "good emperors" maintained the *Pax Romana* (Roman peace). The empire, with its 50,000,000 inhabitants, was prosperous, but more so in the cities than the countryside. The age of expansion was over: the Rhine and Danube rivers served as the borders in Europe, and the Near East was governed by client rulers. Including auxiliaries, the army contained about 400,000 soldiers, ultimately too few to defend such a vast territory, as the events of the third century proved.

In the Early Empire Greek models were followed in the visual arts, as in medicine, but in architecture and engineering the Romans excelled, as exemplified in its 50,000 miles of roads and the Flavian amphitheater, or the Colosseum. Rome itself had a population of one million. The gulf between the rich and poor was enormous, and bread and circuses were provided: 200,000 received free grain, and the Colosseum held 50,000 spectators for gladiatorial games.

The third century was an era of decline. Generals fought each other in civil wars and German barbarian tribes and Persian armies invaded. There were plagues, population decline, and economic collapse. However, stability was restored in the Late Empire by Diocletian (r.284-305) and Constantine (r.306-337) by increasing the bureaucracy, establishing price controls, raising taxes, and making occupations hereditary.

The Late Empire saw Christianity triumph: Constantine, the first Christian emperor, legalized it, and Theodosius (r.378-395) proclaimed it the official religion. Christianity grew out of Judaism. Jesus (d. c.30 A.D) preached the love of God and one's neighbor instead of merely following religious laws. Some saw Jesus as a false messiah, others were disappointed that he did not lead a revolt against Rome, and the Romans, fearing he was a rebel, executed him. His followers believed that he rose from the dead and ascended into heaven, and that he would return and establish the Kingdom of God on earth. There were occasional persecutions because Christians refused to honor the state cults. Christianity, with its promise of salvation as a consolation to this life's trials, its similarity to many mystery religions, and its universality as a religion for all–rich and poor, men and women, Greek and Roman–slowly gained acceptance.

The fifth century saw the decline and fall of the Western Roman Empire (the empire was divided in 395). With fewer resources, the West was less able to repel the Huns and German. In 476 the last Western emperor was deposed, and numerous Germanic kingdoms replaced the Western Roman Empire, although the Eastern Empire survived for another thousand years.

LECTURE AND DISCUSSION TOPICS

1. Analyze the significance of the reign of Octavian/Augustus in the transition from the Roman Republic to the Roman Empire.

2. Consider Gibbon's claim that the second century C.E. was a "golden age."

3. Describe the cultural, religious, and socio-economic changes that transformed Roman society between the accession of Octavian/Augustus Caesar and the early third century C.E.

4. Trace and comment upon the various perceptions of the nature and causes of the decline and collapse of the Roman Empire after the early 200s C.E.

5. Explore the emergence and growth of Christianity as an anti-Roman radical, underground sect.

6. Examine the various theories and interpretations regarding the origins and evolution of Christianity.

7. Compare and contrast Judaism, Zoroastrianism, and Christianity in regards to historical and social origins, theological beliefs, as well as success and acceptance in the early centuries of their respective histories.

8. Discuss the major historical personalities of the Roman Empire from Augustus to the fall of the Western Empire.

9. Examine the various interpretations of the causes and consequences of "The Decline and Fall of the Roman Empire."

10. Analyze the radical nature of Jesus' challenge to Jewish and Roman authorities.

MAP EXERCISES

1. The Roman Empire from 14 to 117 (Augustus to Trajan). MAP 6.1. Examine expansion of Roman territorial control and the geopolitical implications of expanding Roman territories by comparing MAP 5.3 with MAP 6.1. Where did growth appear? Had Rome essentially reached its maximum geographical extent by the time of Augustus? Why or why not? (page 97)

2. Trade Routes and Products in the Roman Empire, c. 200. MAP 6.2. What does the map suggest about the importance of water transportation in the Roman Empire? From the map of the Silk Road on the previous page, which regions and which cities would benefit the most from the luxury trade from Asia? (page 99)

3. Imperial Rome. MAP 6.3. Compare the walls of the city of Rome in the fourth century B.C. with the later walls of the imperial period. Note the number of roads and gates entering Rome. What additional geographical information would be helpful in understanding the social, political, and economic elements in Roman life? (page 103)

4. Divisions of the Restored Roman Empire, c.300. MAP 6.4. What might have been the rationale for where the empire was divided? What might be the strengths and the weaknesses of both the East and West? (page 105)

DISCUSSION QUESTIONS FOR THE PRIMARY SOURCES (BOXED DOCUMENTS)

1. "The Achievements of Augustus": What were the achievements of Augustus? To what extent did these accomplishments create the "job" of being emperor? In what sense could this document be called a piece of propaganda? Was Augustus the greatest of the Roman Emperors? Why and/or why not? (page 95)

2. "The Daily Life of an Upper-Class Roman": What does Pliny's letter reveal about the life style of Rome's upper class? Could this life style be related to the decline of the Roman Empire, or does it reflect traditional and enduring Roman values? From this excerpt, did the Romans define a good life in material terms? Why and/or why not? (page 100)

3. "Ovid and the Art of Love": Why were Ovid's principles of love? Why do you think Augustus found *The Art of Love* so offensive? Do Ovid's principles and approach to love seem modern or uniquely Roman? Why? (page 101)

4. "Christian Ideals: The Sermon on the Mount": What are the ideals of early Christianity? How do they differ from the values and principles of Judaism and classical Greco-Roman civilization? What, if anything, was "new" about these Christian ideals? How would these words work as a clever public relations campaign by Jesus to increase the number of converts to his tiny radical sect? (page 108)

STUDENT RESEARCH AND PROJECT TOPICS

1. How did Octavian establish order and achieve control over the Roman world after the defeat of Antony? Why do historians refer to his reign as the Principate? Augustus has been called the first Roman Emperor. Why?

2. How does the literature of the late Republic, the Augustan Age, and the Early Empire reflect the political problems of each period?

3. Discuss the strengths and weaknesses of the Roman emperors from Augustus to Nero. How was the Empire able to survive the reigns of such emperors as Nero and Caligula?

4. It has been said of the Romans that two of their major contributions to Western civilization were in the areas of law and engineering. What exactly did the Romans achieve in each area?

5. Assume that you are a Roman citizen living in Rome in the second century A.D. Discuss both the potential good and bad points of your daily existence.

6. The history Edward Gibbon claimed that the Roman Empire in second century A.D. was a true Golden Age. What evidence could give credence to Gibbon's argument and what evidence could be given to refute it?

7. Explain the factors involved in the spread of Christianity in the Roman Empire. It has been said that Christian experience as outlaws and hunted fugitives was crucial to the successful development of the Christian church. Why is this true?

8. Discuss the efforts made by Diocletian and Constantine to restore the Roman Empire. Did they succeed or not?

9. One historian has said that the Romans became Christians and the Christians became Romans. Discuss. Be specific.

10. The historian Edward Gibbon believed that Christianity bore the ultimate responsibility for the fall of the Roman Empire. What argument do you think Gibbon would have made to support his position? What arguments can be made against Gibbon's thesis?

IDENTIFICATIONS

1. *princeps*
2. Augustus
4. *imperator*
5. legates
6. Varus and the Teutoburg Forest
7. Virgil's *Aeneid*
8. Horace
9. Ovid
10. Livy
11. Julio-Claudians
12. Nero
13. "the year of the four emperors"
14. Flavians
15. the "good emperors"
16. Marcus Aurelius' *Meditations*
17. Hadrian's Pantheon and Wall
18. Caracalla/212
19. Seneca
20. Tacitus
21. Colosseum
22. *insulae*
23. "Bread and Circuses"
24. gladiatorial games
25. Severan rulers
26. Sassanid Persia and Germanic tribes
27. Diocletian
28. Constantine
29. Byzantium/Constantinople
30. Sadducees, Pharisees, Essenes, and Zealots
31. Dead Sea Scrolls
32. the Messiah
33. Jesus
34. Christ
35. Paul of Tarsus
36. gospels/"good news"
37. bishops
38. Perpetua
39. Edict of Milan
40. Theodosius

MULTIPLE CHOICE QUESTIONS

1. The Roman Senate under Augustus was
    a. stripped of all but the most superficial of powers.
    b. a full and equal partner of the *princeps*.
    c. retained as the chief deliberative body of the Roman state.
    d. no longer a high court of justice nor allowed to control the public treasury.
        ANSWER: c (page 94)

2. The absolute monarchical powers of Augustus as *princeps* led to
    a. the ending of any Senate responsibilities.
    b. the abolishment of the army.
    c. his great popularity, as he followed proper legal forms for his power.
    d. all of the above
        ANSWER: c (pp. 94-95)

3. Which of the following important official powers did Augustus <u>not</u> hold:
    a. *imperator*
    b. consul
    c. tribune
    d. senator
        ANSWER: d (pp. 94-95)

4. The Augustan reorganization of the military involved all of the following <u>except</u>:
    a. maintained a standing army of 28 legions, or about 150,000 men.
    b. auxiliaries were used as cavalry and light cavalry.
    c. allowed Germans to serve as officers in the legions.
    d. created a new unit, the Praetorian Guard.
        ANSWER: c (p. 95)

5. The Roman praetorian guards
    a. were elite troops given the task of protecting the emperor.
    b. were mobile units meant to patrol the boundaries of the empire.
    c. were often used to train the gladiators.
    d. were cavalry used to spearhead military offensives.
        ANSWER: a (p. 95)

6. Under the rule of Augustus, the Roman Empire
    a. was a Principate, without Augustus acting as an equal co-ruler with the Senate.
    b. returned to its traditional republic institutions.
    c. turned towards an absolute monarchy with the princeps overshadowing the Senate.
    d. experienced a series of civil wars, making Augustus unpopular among the citizenry.
        ANSWER: c (pp. 94-95)

7. Roman provincial and frontier policy under Augustus was characterized by all of the following <u>except</u>

a. limitless expansion in central Europe.
b. the encouragement of self-government among provincial cities.
c. provincial rule by legates, appointed by Augustus.
d. minimum military force to the east.
ANSWER: a (p. 95)

8. The event that curtailed Augustus's expansionist policies was

a. the Senatorial rejection of imperialist policy in 20 B.C.
b. the defeat of Varus in the Teutoburg Forest.
c. the revolt of the Egyptians in 14 B.C.
d. the successful series of invasions by the Parthians in the east.
ANSWER: b (p. 96)

9. Among Augustus' key innovations in Roman provincial rule was his

a. abandonment of North Africa.
b. division of Roman provinces into those ruled directly by the princeps and those called senatorial provinces administered by the Senate.
c. use of military governors alone.
d. complete revision of provincial tax policies.
ANSWER: b (pp. 95-96)

10. Which of the following statements <u>best</u> describes the governing of Roman provinces under Augustus?

a. efficient, with the governor usually being a general
b. efficient under the rule of proconsuls and legates
c. poor, with Roman governors often being corrupt
d. efficient, with governors receiving one year of training before assuming their positions
ANSWER: b (pp. 95-96)

11. Which of the following statements was true of Augustan society?

a. Popular assemblies of the lower classes continually grew in importance.
b. Legislation was passed concerning the corruption of morals.
c. Equestrians gained the upper hand in the political sphere.
d. Religion was no longer considered important.
ANSWER: b (p. 96)

12. Concerning social classes during early Roman Empire,

a. provincials were allowed to hold certain high magisterial positions.
b. the power of the equestrian class was expanded.
c. the Senate was expanded to include 400 equestrians.
d. debt slavery was ended as a means to acquire slaves.
ANSWER: b (p. 96)

13. Among Augustus' most important actions in the area of Roman religion was his

a. destruction of the cults of Augustus and Roma.
b. claim to be a god in his own lifetime.
c. creation of an imperial cult.
d. outlawing all traditional female religious festivals.
ANSWER: c (p. 107)

14. Augustus' social legislation enacted to stop the decline of Roman morals
    a. meant a social revolution at every level of Roman society.
    b. made adultery a criminal offense and outlawed wasteful spending on frivolities.
    c. penalized couples for having too many children.
    d. all of the above
        ANSWER: b (p. 96)

15. Livy was best known in the Augustan Age for his
    a. *Aeneid.*
    b. *Metamophoses.*
    c. *Satires*.
    d. *History of Rome*.
        ANSWER: d (p. 101)

16. Identify the correct relationship between "golden age" author and his major work:
    a. Ovid–*The Art of Love*
    b. Virgil–*Amores*
    c. Ovid–*Aeneid*
    d. Horace–*History of Rome*
        ANSWER: a (p. 101)

17. The poems of Virgil, the most distinguished poet of the Augustan Age,
    a. led to his exile from Rome for their hostility toward Augustus.
    b. usually included satirical attacks against human weaknesses.
    c. ignored any connections between Greek and Roman civilization in his *Aeneid*.
    d. praised ideal Roman virtues.
        ANSWER: d (pp. 100-101)

18. Ovid's *The Art of Love*
    a. applauded the loose sexual morals of the Roman upper classes.
    b. caused great displeasure to Augustus and led to Ovid's eventual exile.
    c. was a guidebook for the seduction of women.
    d. all of the above
        ANSWER: d (p. 101)

19. The "golden age" historian Livy is well known for his
    a. rejection of Latin prose in favor of Greek poetic forms.
    b. perceiving history in terms of sharp moral lessons.
    c. factual accuracy and critical judgment toward his sources and Rome's past.
    d. *Epistles*, which portrayed Rome as a degenerate society in a state of collapse.
        ANSWER: b (p. 102)

20. The successor to Augustus and first of the Julio-Claudian rulers was
    a. Caligula.
    b. Nero.
    c. Tiberius.
    d. Domitian.
        ANSWER: c (p. 96)

21. Which of the statements <u>best</u> describes the Julio-Claudian emperors?
   a. were all completely competent rulers
   b. varied in ability and effectiveness
   c. were responsible for a tremendous amount of social legislation
   d. undid all the military reforms of Augustus
      ANSWER: b (p. 96)

22. Which of the following trends developed during the reigns of the Julio-Claudian emperors?
   a. Emperors took more and more responsibilities of rulership away from the old Senate.
   b. All efforts to achieve bureaucratic organization of imperial government eventually failed.
   c. Emperors turned over more and more of the daily affairs of government to the Senate.
   d. The power of imperial military forces stationed in Rome declined.
      ANSWER: a (p. 96)

23. The last of the Julio-Claudian emperors was
   a. Nero.
   b. Tiberius.
   c. Vespasian.
   d. Caligula.
      ANSWER: a (p. 96)

24. Among the five "good emperors" was
   a. Hadrian.
   b. Vespasian.
   c. Commodus.
   d. Tiberius.
      ANSWER: a (p. 97)

25. All of the following occurred during the reigns of the five "good emperors" <u>except</u> for
   a. a period of peace and prosperity for 100 years.
   b. the establishment of educational programs for the poor.
   c. the restoration of the powers of the Senate.
   d. extensive building programs.
      ANSWER: c (p. 97)

26. During the Early Empire (14-180 A.D.), the Empire reached its greatest extent under
   a. Hadrian.
   b. Marcus Aurelius.
   c. Trajan. .
   d. Titus.
      ANSWER: c (p. 97)

27. Trade and commerce in the Early Empire
   a. stimulated manufacturing.
   b. concentrated some industries in certain areas.
   c. was secondary in importance to agriculture.
   d. all of the above
      ANSWER: d (pp. 98-100)

28. The greatest historian of the "silver age" of Latin literature was
   a. Petronius.
   b. Tacitus.
   c. Seneca.
   d. Juvenal.
      ANSWER: b (p. 102)

29. The prolific "silver age" writer Seneca
   a. rejected the Stoic ideal of political service for a carefree life of opulence.
   b. satirized Rome's new rich class in his *Satyricon*.
   c. composed philosophical letters on the theme of Stoicism.
   d. died in a state of abject poverty despite remaining close friends with Nero.
      ANSWER: c (p. 102)

30. The most famous prose writer of Rome's golden age was
   a. Virgil.
   b. Livy.
   c. Ovid.
   d. Seneca.
      ANSWER: b (p. 101)

31. By the second century A.D., the *paterfamilias* had
   a. disappeared from Roman family life.
   b. become a complete dictator over his spouse and children.
   c. lost authority over his children.
   d. become the *Pontifex Maximus* of Rome.
      ANSWER: c (p. 102)

32. Which of the following is <u>not</u> true of the Colosseum:
   a. Its official name was the Flavian Amphitheater.
   b. It could seat 50,000 spectators.
   c. It was the scene of gladiatorial combats.
   d. It was destroyed by Caligula.
      ANSWER: d (pp. 103-104)

33. Imperial Rome's gladiatorial shows
   a. became increasingly associated with religious practices.
   b. were government-backed spectacles used to content the masses.
   c. were limited to fights between slaves and criminals trained at gladiatorial schools.
   d. paled in popularity to the Circus Maximus.
      ANSWER: b (p. 104)

34. The great epic poet of Rome's golden age was
   a. Ovid.
   b. Tacitus.
   c. Horace.
   d. Virgil.
      ANSWER: d (p. 149)

35. One of the most famous jurists of the Early Empire responsible for completing the basic natural rights principles vital to the Western world was

a. Galen.
b. Alcon.
c. Ulpian.
d. Acilius.

ANSWER: c (p. 102)

36. Among the greatest achievements of the classical age of Roman law was

a. the right to trial by jury.
b. the right of *habeus corpus*.
c. the concept of human natural rights implying that all are equal before the law.
d. the concept of no self-incrimination by defendants in criminal trials.

ANSWER: c (p. 102)

37. Among the upper classes of the Early Empire

a. birthrates increased.
b. the power of the *paterfamilias* increased.
c. women had considerable freedom and independence.
d. contraception and abortion fell into disfavor.

ANSWER: c (p. 102)

38. Which of the following statements was <u>not</u> true of Roman society in the early Empire:

a. The gladiators were usually condemned prisoners or slaves.
b. Slavery was abolished by Augustus Caesar.
c. The "classical age" of Roman law occurred in this era.
d. Upper-class women gained considerable freedom and independence.

ANSWER: b (pp. 102-103)

39. Which of the following statements does <u>not</u> apply to pre-Christian Roman religion:

a. Imperial officials were intolerant of foreign religions.
b. The official state religion did not provide emotional satisfaction.
c. Mithraism was the most important mystery cult.
d. The imperial cult of Roma and Augustus bolstered support for the emperors.

ANSWER: a (p. 107)

40. The mystery cult of Mithraism in the Early Empire

a. was widely practiced by women.
b. was completely opposed to the practices of Christianity.
c. centered around the worship of the gods Roma and Augustus.
d. was a religion especially favored by soldiers.

ANSWER: d (p. 107)

41. The early values of Christianity, as exemplified in Jesus' sermon on the mount,

a. emphasized total devotion to humility, charity, and true brotherly love.
b. were similar to those of Greco-Roman civilization.
c. emphasized the equality between the earthly and spiritual kingdoms.
d. all of the above

ANSWER: a (p. 108)

42. Early Christianity was
   a. molded into a broader religious movement by Paul of Tarsus.
   b. systematically persecuted by all of the Early Empire's rulers.
   c. spread throughout the Aegean and Asia Minor by Peter.
   d. never seen as a threat to the Roman state because of its private ceremonies.
      ANSWER: a (p. 108)

43. Paul of Tarsus
   a. founded the Christian church at Rome.
   b. preached Christianity only to the non-Jews.
   c. believed Christianity should be preached to Jews and non-Jews.
   d. was unable to put his beliefs into writing before his execution.
      ANSWER: c (p. 108)

44. The Roman Empire's persecution of Christians in the first two centuries after Christ's death
   a. began during the reign of Tiberius.
   b. was sporadic and local.
   c. forced most Christians into participating in Roman public, religious festivals.
   d. was known as the Agape.
      ANSWER: b (p. 109)

45. The "terrible third century" was made terrible by all of the following <u>except</u>
   a. ignorance of military affairs by the Severan emperors.
   b. civil wars and Germanic invasions.
   c. a series of natural disasters.
   d. serious inflation and devaluation of coinage.
      ANSWER: a (p. 104)

46. Constantine's most enduring reform came in the creation of
   a. a tetrarchy.
   b. a "New Rome."
   c. wage and price controls.
   d. the *coloni*.
      ANSWER: b (p. 106)

47. The political, economic, and social policies of the restored empire under Diocletian and Constantine
   a. meant the destruction of the civil and military bureaucracies.
   b. renewed the support of the Roman peasants and lower classes for the Empire.
   c. led to the economic rejuvenation of the Empire.
   d. were based on coercion and the loss of individual freedom.
      ANSWER: d (p. 106)

48. The successful growth of Christianity from the second through fourth centuries can be attributed to
   a. the centralized organization of its various church communities.
   b. its satisfying a human emotional need to belong.
   c. its universal appeal to all classes.
   d. all of the above
      ANSWER: d (pp. 109-110)

49. The Edict of Milan
   a. made Christianity the official state religion of the Empire under Julian.
   b. was Constantine's document officially tolerating the existence of Christianity.
   c. officially divided the Roman Empire into eastern and western halves.
   d. officially deposed the last Roman emperor, Romulus Augustulus, from his throne.
      ANSWER: b (p. 110)

50. Christianity was made the official religion of the Roman Empire by the emperor
   a. Valens
   b. Romulus Augustulus
   c. Odovacer
   d. Theodosius
      ANSWER: d (p. 110)

RELEVANT WORLD-WIDE WEB SITES/RESOURCES

1. Biblical Archaeology, BibArch:
http://www.bibarch.com
(Site maintained by High Top Media with extensive information on archaeological digs and analyses pertinent to the people and cultures of the Bible.)

2. J. Paul Getty Museum, Los Angeles, ArtsEdNet,
The Forum of Trajan in Rome:
http://www.artsednet.getty.edu/ArtsEdNet/Browsing/Trajan/index.html
(One of the finest online virtual reality tours of an ancient monument. Structures of the forum displayed magnificently as they appeared in 200 A.D.)

3. Roman Emperors–DIR–De Imperatoribus Romanis
An Online Encyclopedia of Roman Emperors
http://www.salve.edu/~dimaiom/deimprom.html
(Fine web site complete with images of statuary and coins displaying the imperial visage.)

4. Search the Great Buildings Online:
http://www.greatbuildings.com/gbc/search.html
(Fine site enabling users to view and gather information on structures central to the history of Western Civilization. Many Roman imperial sites available here.)

RELEVANT VIDEO RESOURCES

Ancient History: The Romans, 2-Disc Series on CD-ROM,Films for the Humanities and Sciences. (Virtual reality tour of Roman provincial town circa 250 A.D.)

Early Christianity and the Rise of the Church, 2 Programs, (30 minutes each program). Insight Media. (Visual history of early church focusing on works of Paul and theological debates of the era.)

Hail Caesar, PBS Home Video, 5 Programs on 6 cassettes, (55 minutes each program). (Excellent series focusing on key rulers of the late Republic and Empire--east and west: Julius Caesar, Augustus, Nero, Constantine, Hadrian, and Justinian. Excellent archaeological site visits and information.)

The Trial and Testimony of the Early Church: From Christ to Constantine, 6 Programs (30 minutes each program). Insight Media.
(Using narration and reenactments, series surveys rise of church and apostolic activity of Christian sectarians.)

The Western Tradition, Part I, Annenberg/CPB Collection/PBS Home Video, (30 minutes each program), Program 10, "The Roman Empire."

SUGGESTED STUDENT ACTIVITIES

1. There are those that have compared the late Roman Empire with the United States. Have students do a comparative study of Roman problems around 250 A.D. with the problems faced by the United States today.

2. Have students do outside reading on the various theories on the fall of Rome. They should choose one of these theories and develop an argument as to its validity.

3. Students are often fascinated by the Roman games. Have them do projects in which they report on such people and places as the Hippodrome, the Flavian Amphitheater, the Circus Maximus, or the most famous of all gladiators, Spartacus. Ample Web resources, text and images, for this project.

4. Students should do research on the "Good Emperors." Have them write a specific essay on why these emperors were "good" when compared to the Flavian or Julio-Claudian Emperor

CHAPTER 7
THE PASSING OF THE ROMAN WORLD AND THE EMERGENCE OF MEDIEVAL CIVILIZATION

CHAPTER OUTLINE

I. Transformation of the Roman World: The Role of the Germanic Peoples
- A. End of the Western Empire
- B. The New Kingdoms
  - 1. The Ostrogothic Kingdom of Italy
  - 2. The Visigothic Kingdom of Spain
  - 3. The Frankish Kingdom
  - 4. Anglo-Saxon England
- C. The Society of the Germanic Peoples
  - 1. The Frankish Family and Marriage

II. The Role and Development of the Christian Church
- A. Organization and Religious Disputes
- B. The Power of the Pope
- C. The Monks and Their Missions
  - 1. Benedictine Monasticism
  - 2. Monks as Missionaries
  - 3. Women and Monasticism
- D. Christianity and Intellectual Life

III. The Byzantine Empire
- A. The Reign of Justinian (527-565)
  - 1. Life in Constantinople: The Emperor's Building Program
- B. From Eastern Roman to Byzantine Empire
  - 1. The Byzantine Empire in the Eighth Century

IV. The Rise of Islam
- A. Muhammad and Islam
- B. The Expansion of Islam

V. Conclusion

CHAPTER SUMMARY

The migration of the Germanic peoples was a cause as well as a consequence of the fall of the Western Roman Empire. Germanic kingdoms were established in the West, including the Ostrogoths in Italy, the Visigoths in Spain, several Anglo-Saxon kingdoms in Britain, and a Frankish kingdom in old Gaul. Socially, there was often a fusion between old Roman elites and the new Germanic aristocracy, but Roman laws were replaced by the blood feud and the ordeal.

Christianity was the official religion of the Empire from the fourth century, with bishops heading the Church in major cities. The Bishop of Rome claimed supremacy over the Church, relying upon the prestige of Imperial Rome as well as the Petrine theory wherein Jesus gave Peter the keys to heaven. According to tradition Peter became the first Bishop of Rome (or pope), and his successors claimed his authority. One of the most significant was Gregory I the Great (590-604): the Church would build upon

Gregory's foundations, both religious and political.

Monasteries were crucial to the success of the Church. Early Christian monks were often hermits who practiced extreme forms of asceticism. Benedict of Nursia (d. c.543) established rules for communities of monks, who were required to take oaths of poverty, chastity, and obedience. There were also female monks, or nuns, who followed the Benedictine Rule.

The Church was the intellectual force in the Middle Ages. The early Church was greatly influenced by Greek philosophy in defining doctrine. Augustine (d. 430) was trained in classical culture, and his *Confessions* and *The City of God* have influenced Christian theology to the present. Jerome (d. 420) was also classically trained, and translated the Bible into Latin; his Vulgate edition remained the authoritative text in the Catholic Church for many centuries.

The Eastern Roman Empire suffered no decline and fall as had the West. Constantinople was the largest city in Europe and Justinian (r. 527-565) was among its greatest rulers. In an attempt to restore the old Empire, he invaded Italy, but although successful in battle, he ultimately failed to reunite West with East. A more lasting success was his codification of centuries of Roman law in the *Corpus Iuris Civilis*, which was adopted in the West toward the end of the Middle Ages.

But the Eastern Empire was overextended, and plagues and wars reduced its territory to Asia Minor and the Balkans. The use of Latin declined in favor of Greek, and the Eastern Empire became known as the Byzantine Empire. However, the differences between East and West were not just linguistic. The pope was the recognized head of Western Christendom, but in the East it was the emperor who not only ruled the state but also the church. Eventually the differences led to two different Christian churches, Catholic and Orthodox.

Muhammad, one of the most significant figures in world history, was born in the Arabian city of Mecca, traditionally important because of a shrine called the *Ka'ba*. Muhammed received numerous religious revelations from Allah (or God), which were written down in the Qur'an, the holy book of Islam, the religion of those who submit to Allah. Muhammed was Allah's Prophet, the successor of earlier prophets such as Moses and Jesus. Although differences emerged after his death in 632, in part over who should succeed him, Islam expanded rapidly, with Moslem Moors moving into Spain c.710 and into France until defeated at the battle of Tours in 732. Constantinople repelled Muslim armies, surviving until 1453, indirectly protecting Christian Europe. Not only did Muslims capture vast territories, they also created a great culture.

LECTURE AND DISCUSSION TOPICS

1. Explore the parameters of Medieval European civilization.

2. Examine the various Roman and Germanic elements which became the foundation of the various Germanic states which emerged after the decline of the Western Roman Empire.

3. Discuss the background to the rise and spread of Islam, including the tenets of that faith, and its impact upon the West.

4. Compare Islamic civilization with the Christian West in the two centuries after the death of Muhammad.

5. Discuss the impact and the influence of the early Church Fathers in the codification of the several doctrines of the Christian church, such as the contributions of Augustine and Jerome.

6. Explore the origins of western monasticism and its profound importance to the West in the Middle Ages.

7. Examine the question of whether or not the c. 500-800 era was a "dark age" in the West.

8. Discuss some of the factors that might explain why the Western Roman Empire "fell" but the Eastern Roman Empire survived.

9. Explore the history of the Eastern Roman Empire, its transition to the Byzantine Empire, examining its religious and cultural contributions to the peoples of Eastern Europe as well as its relationship to Islam.

MAP EXERCISES

1. Barbarian Migration and Invasion Routes. MAP 7.1. Note the places of origin of the various barbarian tribes, both Germanic and Hun. What factors, geographic and other, might explain their ultimate destinations. Why there and not elsewhere? (page 115)

2. The New Kingdoms of the Old Western Empire. MAP 7.2. How closely did the new Germanic kingdoms coincide with the borders of the Western Roman Empire? What areas or regions of Western Europe remained outside of the German kingdoms? Why? (page 116)

3. The Spread of Christianity. MAP 7.3. Note the extent of Christian areas at c.300. Where were the major areas of expansion between 300 and 600, and from 600 to 800? What might have been the causes of that expansion? (page 123)

4. The Eastern Roman Empire in the Time of Justinian. MAP 7.4. Note the parameters of Justinian's western campaign. Was it Justinian's single greatest mistake? Why and or why not? (page 126)

5. The Expansion of Islam. MAP 7.5. Where did Islam have its greatest territorial successes? Can it be claimed that the continued existence of the Byzantine Empire "saved" Western Civilization? Why and or why not? (page 130)

DISCUSSION QUESTIONS FOR THE PRIMARY SOURCES (BOXED DOCUMENTS)

1. "Germanic Customary Law: The Ordeal": What was the purpose of the ordeal of hot water? What does it reveal about the nature of the society that used it? What do you believe to be the conception of justice held by this society? (page 118)

2. "The Life of Saint Anthony": Based on the account by Athanasius, how would you characterize the ascetic ideals of early Christian monks? How important were those ideals to the growth of early Christianity? What do you believe to be the broader cultural effects of a Christian hatred of the human body? (page 120)

3. "Irish Monasticism and the Penitential": What does the Penitential of Cummean reveal about the nature of Irish monasticism? What do you think was the theory of human sexuality held by early Irish Christianity? How might the strong emphasis here on the identification and expiation of human sin work to empower the church at its agents over time? (page 122)

4. "The Qur'an and the Spread of the Muslim Faith": What are the basic ideas of Chapter 47 of the Qur'an? What are the theological beliefs illustrated in this excerpt? What might be the social and political impact of these ideals on the development of Islamic civilization. (page 129)

STUDENT RESEARCH AND PROJECT TOPICS

1. What is the doctrine of Petrine supremacy and what are its implications for the history of the early Christian church? How is the doctrine of Petrine supremacy related to the problem of the relationship between church and state?

2. What role did monks and nuns play in early medieval society? What does the author mean when he says that "monks became the heroes of Christian civilization"?

3. What contributions did the Germanic peoples make to the new political, economic, and social conditions of early European civilization?

4. "Western Europe experienced a Dark Age between the 400s and the 700s." Discuss, pro and con.

5. In what ways were the teaching of Islam similar to Christianity? How were they different?

6. What impact did Christianity have on the intellectual life of the emerging European civilization? How important was Saint Augustine to that intellectual life?

7. What were Justinian's major goals and how did he try to achieve them? How successful was he in actually achieving those goals?

8. Discuss the possible religious and non-religious reasons for the rapid spread of Islam from Arabia to Spain in the West and across the Persian Empire in the east.

9. What were the major contributions of Islam to Western Civilization? Be specific.

10. In what ways were the Byzantine and Islamic civilizations of the east different from the civilization developing in western Europe? In what ways were they the same?

IDENTIFICATIONS

1. Theodoric and the Ostrogoths
2. Vandals and Visigoths
3. Romulus Augustulus and Odoacer
4. Franks

5. Clovis
6. *wergeld*
7. compurgation and ordeal
8. heresy
9. Council of Nicaea
10. Arianism
11. Gregory I, the Great
12. St Anthony and St. Simeon the Stylite
13. St. Augustine's *The City of God*
14. Rule of Saint Benedict
15. monasticism
16. St. Boniface
17. Jerome
18. Cassiodorus
19. *trivium* and *quadrivium*
20. Justinian
21. *Corpus Iuris Civilis*
22. Hagia Sophia and Hippodrome
23. Byzantine Empire
24. Muhammad
25. Arabia
26. *Qur'an*
27. Allah
28. Five Pillars of Islam
29. *Hegira*
30. *Shari'a*
31. *jihad*
32. caliph
33. Umayads
34. Shi'ites and Sunnites
35. Battle of Tours

MULTIPLE CHOICE QUESTIONS

1. The Council of Nicaea in 325
    a. first organized a system of bishoprics.
    b. elected the first pope.
    c. defined Christ as being "of the same substance" as God.
    d. centered around the heresy of Donatism.
        ANSWER: c (page 119)

2. The problem of heresy was an important factor contributing to
    a. the decline of Rome.
    b. the church's formal organization.
    c. the construction of churches.
    d. the growing power of the Byzantines.
        ANSWER: b (p. 119)

3. The heresy of Arianism
   a. questioned the divinity of Jesus.
   b. denied the existence of God the Father.
   c. denied the existence of the Holy Spirit.
   d. reverted to Roman polytheistic religious beliefs.
      ANSWER: a (p. 110)

4. The Donatism heresy involved
   a. church taxes refused by the laity.
   b. church services performed by the laity.
   c. the efficacy of the Sacraments.
   d. proper punishments for killing priests.
      ANSWER: c (p. 170)

5. Inasmuch as Jesus gave the keys of heaven to Peter
   a. the bishops of Rome claimed the paramount position in the church.
   b. the Council of Nicaea gave its approval of Arianism.
   c. heresy became the main problem of the church.
   d. deacons should have the same spiritual powers as bishops.
      ANSWER: a (p. 119)

6. The title of *papa* has traditionally been given to
   a. the bishop of Rome.
   b. the patriarchs of Constantinople.
   c. Emperors after Constantine.
   d. the bishops of Milan.
      ANSWER: a (p. 119)

7. Augustine did all of the following <u>except</u>
   a. translate Scripture into the Latin Vulgate.
   b. write *The City of God*.
   c. use pagan culture in the service of Christianity.
   d. advocate marriage for the procreation of children as a good alternative for Christians incapable of upholding the ideal of celibacy as a means to holiness.
      ANSWER: a (p. 124)

8. Augustine's *The City of God*
   a. stated that its ultimate location was the kingdom of heaven.
   b. was a warning to unbelievers that the City of the Word was unnecessary.
   c. an epic poem to rival the works of the greatest pagan poets.
   d. an account of his own miraculous personal conversion.
      ANSWER: a (p. 124)

9. Augustine's work shows best
   a. how Christian theologians used pagan culture in the service of Christianity.
   b. his influence on the emperors.
   c. his skills as a linguist.
   d. his creation of new scripture in Latin.
      ANSWER: a (p. 124)

10. The Latin Father of the Church, Jerome, is known for all of the following except
   a. his mastery of Latin prose.
   b. his skills as a linguist.
   c. his translations of the Old and New Testaments from Hebrew and Greek into Latin.
   d. his final return to pagan heresy and rejection of key Christian doctrines.
      ANSWER: d (p. 124)

11. The father of hermit monasticism was
   a. Saint Pachomius.
   b. Saint Augustine.
   c. Saint Ambrose.
   d. Saint Anthony.
      ANSWER: d (p. 120)

12. The basic rule for western monastic living was developed by
   a. Basil.
   b. Pachomius.
   c. Benedict.
   d. Ambrose.
      ANSWER: c (p. 120)

13. Benedictine monasticism was not characterized by
   a. the communal life..
   b. an ideal of moderation.
   c. asceticism and extremism.
   d. isolated, self-sustaining communities.
      ANSWER: c (p. 120)

14. The first monastic rule for women in convents was produced in the fifth century A.D. by
   a. Pachomius.
   b. Caesarius of Arles.
   c. Empress Theodosia.
   d. Marcella.
      ANSWER: b (p. 121)

15. The last Roman Emperor in the West was
   a. Odoacer.
   b. Theodosius.
   c. Theodoric.
   d. Romulus Augustulus.
      ANSWER: d (p. 114)

16. The only German state on the continent which proved long-lasting was the kingdom of the
- a. Ostrogoths.
- b. Vandals.
- c. Franks.
- d. Bulgars.

ANSWER: c (p. 116)

17. The Germanic tribe to most maintain Roman tradition and synthesize their culture with that of the Romans was the
- a. Visigoths.
- b. Angles.
- c. Ostrogoths.
- d. Vandals.

ANSWER: c (p. 114)

18. In 410 A.D., Rome was sacked by the
- a. Burgundians.
- b. Visigoths.
- c. Huns.
- d. Persians.

ANSWER: b (p. 114)

19. Theodoric, the Ostrogothic king who took control of Italy, was determined to
- a. destroy Roman civilization and culture forever.
- b. destroy the Jews in Italy.
- c. sack the Byzantine Empire and depose the pope.
- d. maintain Roman customs and practices in Italy.

ANSWER: d (p. 114)

20. After the death of Theodoric, the Ostrogothic kingdom
- a. prospered under very able rulers.
- b. was attached by the Byzantines and devastated, destroying Rome as a center of Mediterranean culture.
- c. allied itself with the Vandals against the Visigoths.
- d. dominated Mediterranean trade for the next fifty years.

ANSWER: b (p. 115)

21. The essential similarity between the Ostrogoths of Italy and the Visigoths of Spain was in
- a. the Visigoths' rejection of beliefs heretical to Catholic Christians.
- b. Latin domination of military affairs.
- c. the maintenance of Roman structures of government.
- d. coexistence between the Germanic and Roman populations.

ANSWER: d (p. 115)

22. Which of the following was <u>not</u> true of the Frankish kingdom?
   a. Clovis established the kingdom under the Merovingians.
   b. It was dominated by a warrior class.
   c. It was a supporter of Arian Christianity.
   d. Its combination of Frankish, Gallo-Roman, and Christian cultures would produce a new European civilization.
      ANSWER: c (p. 116)

23. After the death of Clovis
   a. his son Charles Martel succeeded to the throne.
   b. the Frankish kingdom was absorbed by the Visigoths.
   c. the Frankish kingdom was divided into three major areas.
   d. nobles lost much of their power
      ANSWER: c (p. 116)

24. The successful Battle of Tours in 732
   a. destroyed the Visigoths.
   b. pushed the Burgundians back across the Rhone river.
   c. drove Muslim armies back to Spain.
   d. sacked Paris.
      ANSWER: c (p. 131)

25. Guilt under Germanic customary law was determined by
   a. trial by jury.
   b. the decisions of the *major domus*.
   c. the *wergeld.*
   d. compurgation and ordeal.
      ANSWER: d (p. 117)

26. The withdrawal of Roman armies from Britain enabled
   a. Celtic Britons to overrun the island.
   b. Angles and Saxons, Germanic tribes from Denmark and Germany, to invade and to establish new kingdoms on the isle.
   c. the rise of medieval Scottish culture.
   d. local Roman elites to rebuild English Latin culture.
      ANSWER: b (p. 117)

27. The Germans believed that the ordeal could
   a. reveal the truth by showing who God favored in a dispute.
   b. purify the spirit and bring one closer to God.
   c. cause eternal damnation because it was heresy.
   d. justify the acts of physically strong men.
      ANSWER: a (p. 117)

28. Frankish marriage customs
   a. prohibited sexual union until a year after marriage.
   b. placed women on an equal footing with their husbands.
   c. did not allow divorce.
   d. placed strong sanctions (sometimes death) on adulterous women.
      ANSWER: d (p. 118)

29. Pope Gregory the Great was responsible for all of the following <u>except</u>
   a. creating the Papal States.
   b. urging the Frankish rulers to reform the church in Gaul.
   c. supporting the work of Christian missionaries in England.
   d. writing *The Ecclesiastical History of the English People.*
      ANSWER: d (p. 119)

30. The primary instrument of Pope Gregory for converting the Germanic peoples of Europe was
   a. the imperial army.
   b. monasticism.
   c. bribery.
   d. his oratory.
      ANSWER: b (p. 119)

31. Irish monasticism from the sixth through eighth centuries tended to be highly
   a. ascetic.
   b. isolationist.
   c. scornful of pagan practices.
   d. scornful of classical education.
      ANSWER: a (p. 122)

32. Penitentials of Irish monasticism
   a. outlined the services monks were to perform freely in the lay community.
   b. were primarily concerned with punishing criminals.
   c. stressed atonement and provided strict guidelines for introspection and examination of one's life for signs of sinful behavior.
   d. established elaborate rules for accounting to inventory the great wealth and luxuries typical of Irish monks.
      ANSWER: c (p. 122)

33. For many Christian converts in the west, the major difference from Roman religion was the
   a. use of Greek instead of Latin in worship.
   b. promise of salvation.
   c. absence of any ritual in worship.
   d. abandonment of Rome as a "holy city."
      ANSWER: b (p. 124)

34. One of the greatest nuns of the seventh monastery, and founder of the Whitby monastery was
   a. St. Catherine.
   b. St. Joan.
   c. St. Hilda.
   d. St. Jesmine.
      ANSWER: c (p. 124)

35. Pope Gregory's conversion efforts in England
   a. advocated the use of force against heretics.
   b. relied more on learned persuasion than on brute force.
   c. caused new Christian British kings to murder their own subjects.
   d. resulted in the destruction of virtually all old English pagan temples.
      ANSWER: b (p. 122)

36. The great Christian scholar of late antiquity, Cassiodorus, divided the seven liberal arts into the *trivium* and *quadrivium*. According to Cassiodorus, the *trivium* includes

a. grammar, rhetoric, and music.
b. geometry, music, and astronomy.
c. grammar, rhetoric, and dialectic or logic.
d. arithmetic, logic, and astronomy.

ANSWER: c (p. 125)

37. Justinian's military conquests under general Belisarius

a. included Spain and Gaul in 552.
b. were the most damaging contributions to the eastern Empire's economic problems.
c. helped Italy economically.
d. were very short-lived.

ANSWER: d (p. 125)

38. Justinian's most important contribution to Western civilization was his

a. codification of law.
b. reconquest of western Europe.
c. preventing the migration of eastern peoples to the west.
d. spreading the use of Latin.

ANSWER: a (p. 125)

39. The *Corpus Iuris Civilis (Body of Civil Law)* compiled under Justinian

a. was not immediately adopted by the Byzantine Empire.
b. was the last Byzantine contribution to the west to be written in Latin.
c. marked a turning away from Roman law.
d. served to undermine economic prosperity in the empire.

ANSWER: b (p. 126)

40. The Germanic tribe which moved into Italy after Justinian's destruction of the Ostrogoths was the

a. Vandals.
b. Lombards.
c. Burgundians.
d. Bulgars.

ANSWER: b (p. 125)

41. Which of the following was not a great building in the city of Constantinople?

a. Hagia Sophia
b. Circus Maximus
c. Hippodrome
d. Royal Palace complex

ANSWER: b (pp. 126-127)

42. During the seventh century, the Byzantines fought all of the following except

a. Arabs.
b. Bulgars.
c. Visigoths.
d. Persians.

ANSWER: c (p. 127)

43. Which of the following is <u>not</u> true of the Byzantine emperors?
a. They were portrayed as chosen by God.
b. They maintained a permanent war economy.
c. Subjects had to prostrate themselves in front of them.
d. They rejected Greek and Roman classics and education.
ANSWER: d (p. 125)

44. During the period of the Roman Empire, the Arabian peninsula was dominated by the
a. Ostrogoths.
b. Vandals.
c. Bedouins.
d. Huns.
ANSWER: c (p. 128)

45. The cardinal principle of the Islamic faith is that there is only God and his prophet is
a. Gabriel.
b. Jesus.
c. Moses.
d. Muhammad.
ANSWER: d (p. 129)

46. Muhammad's flight from Mecca to Medina in 622 is known as the
a. *Ka'ba*.
b. *razzia*.
c. *jihad*.
d. *Hegira*.
ANSWER: d (p. 128)

47. Which of the following would <u>not</u> be a similarity between Christianity and Islam?
a. Each of the faiths had a holy book.
b. Both Muhammad and Jesus considered themselves to be divine.
c. Both religions were monotheistic.
d. Both religions had as part of their scriptures divine revelation.
ANSWER: b (p. 128)

48. The successors to Muhammad's leadership of the Muslims were known as
a. holy emperors.
b. caliphs.
c. sultans.
d. anti-popes.
ANSWER: b (p. 129)

49. Muslim societies abide by a strict code of law, much of it derived from the holy book *Qur'an*, and regulating all aspects of Muslim life. This law code is called
a. *Shari'a*.
b. *jihad*.
c. *hajj*.
d. Ramadan.
ANSWER: a (p. 129)

50. In Islam, "Striving in the way of the Lord" is the

a. *Hegira*.
b. *Jihad*.
c. *Jihad.*
d. *Sunnis*.

ANSWER: b (p. 131)

RELEVANT WORLD-WIDE WEB SITES/RESOURCES

1. Benedictine Order: Monasticism and the Writings of St. Benedict:
http://www.osb.org/osb/rb/text/toc.html
(Excellent text site with links on the life, works, and writing of Benedict and the Benedictines.)

2. Byzantine and Medieval Studies:
http://www.fordham.edu/halsall/medweb/
(A superb site with hundreds of links to major websites offering texts and images on these subjects.)

3. Byzantium: Byzantine Studies on the Internet:
http://www.byway.net/~halsall/byzantium.html
(A more specialized site with excellent links to text sources and museum collections on the Web.)

4. Orthodox Christianity:
http://www.orthodoxinfo.com
(A comprehensive website offering a survey and explanation of fundamental Orthodox Christian religious practices and rites accompanied by a reliable timeline on Orthodox Church history. Many additional links here to relevant sites regarding the faith and its history.)

5. The Topkapi Palace Museum, Istanbul
http://www.ee.bilkent.edu.tr/~history/topkapi.html
(A richly illustrated site with information on all aspects of Byzantine and Turkish cultural history.)

RELEVANT VIDEO RESOURCES

Cities of the World, PBS Home Video, 5 cassettes, (60 minutes each). (Tape 2 devoted to Istanbul, Jerusalem, and Marrakech.)

History and Holy Sacraments of Orthodox Christianity, 3 programs (30 minutes each program). Insight Media. (Comprehensive visual survey of the religious and cultural history of Christian Orthodox Church. A highly rated series illustrating the material and intellectual histories of the church.)

The Western Tradition: Part I, PBS Home Video, Annenberg/CPB Collection, (30 minutes each program), Programs 14 and 15 " The Fall of the Roman Empire" and "The Byzantine Empire." These are finely illustrated lectures conducted by Eugen Weber, professor of history, UCLA.)

Byzantium, PBS Home Video, 2 cassettes.

Quran (CD-ROM for Windows), Insight Media. (A comprehensive and multi-lingual edition of the Islamic Holy Book complete with commentaries and explanations of the important themes.)

The Story of Islam, 2 programs (60 minutes each program). Insight Media.
Comprehensive visual history of Islam covering entire development and variations within the faith.)

SUGGESTED STUDENT ACTIVITIES

1. Have students do a study of the law code of Justinian, being sure to point out the similarities between the code and modern day American law.

2. Arabic civilization has contributed greatly to the civilization of the west, especially in the field of science and mathematics. Have students investigate these contributions. Web sites on history of medicine and technology particularly helpful here.

3. Have students investigate the specific contributions of the Germanic kingdoms to Western civilization.

4. The monastic orders performed wonders in preserving civilization during the Middle Ages. Have students pick a monastic order and write a short essay on the group's specific contributions in the preservation of culture in the West.

CHAPTER 8
EUROPEAN CIVILIZATION IN THE EARLY MIDDLE AGES, 750-1000

CHAPTER OUTLINE

I. The World of the Carolingians
- A. Charlemagne and the Carolingian Empire (768-814)
  - 1. Governing the Empire
  - 2. Charlemagne as Emperor
- B. The Carolingian Intellectual Renewal
- C. Life in the Carolingian World
  - 1. The Family and Marriage
  - 2. Christianity and Sexuality
  - 3. Diet and Health

II. Disintegration of the Carolingian Empire
- A. Invasions of the Ninth and Tenth Centuries
  - 1. The Vikings

III. The Emerging World of Lords and Vassals
- A. The Manorial System

IV. The Zenith of Byzantine Civilization

V. The Slavic Peoples of Central and Eastern Europe

VI. The World of Islam
- A. Islamic Civilization

VII. Conclusion

CHAPTER SUMMARY

Early medieval Europe was a land of isolated villages. Famine was common and life expectancy low. In France, Charlemagne (r.768-814) gained a vast European kingdom through military conquest, but governing it was difficult; roads were largely nonexistent, and there was no bureaucracy but only the king's royal appointees, or counts, who had their own ambitions. Charlemagne made use of Church officials, and on Christmas Day, 800, Pope Leo III crowned him Roman emperor. There was also a Carolingian intellectual revival. Monasteries maintained *scriptoria* for the copying of manuscripts, and the Carolingian minuscule standardized the script. A palace school was established, where classical Latin taught what later became liberal arts.

The Church attempted to establish formal monogamous marriages. Sex outside of marriage was condemned, as was homosexuality. Clergy were to be celibate. Unwanted children were often taken into monasteries, which were also expected to provide hospitality for travelers. The fundamental food for all classes was bread, consumed in great quantities. Cows and oxen were used for dairy produce and plowing and sheep were raised for wool. Drunkenness was common, as was overeating (gluttony), though malnutrition also was widespread. Bleeding, herbs, magical charms, and appeals to God and the saints were resorted to in curing diseases.

Charlemagne's grandchildren divided his lands into a Latin-French west and a Germanic east, with the middle region to be fought over. Invasions by Scandinavian Vikings, Muslims, and Magyars occurred in the ninth and tenth centuries. Divided leadership and the invasions led to feudalism, or lordship, where government became localized and powerful nobles controlled vast lands. Other free men, vassals, served the lords, promising military service, and were granted lands, known as fiefs. Relations between lords and vassals were formalized by the oath of homage. Peasants, free and bound (serfs), worked.

The tenth century was the "Golden Age of Byzantine civilization." Under the Macedonian dynasty (867-1081), trade flourished, the Bulgars were defeated, Muslim armies were repelled, and Byzantine territory was increased. In Eastern Europe the Slavic kingdoms of Poland and Bohemia were established, whose peoples were converted to Christianity by Catholic missionaries. The eastern and southern Slavs, such as the Bulgars, the Serbs, and the Russ, adopted Orthodox Christianity, initially under the missionary leadership of Cyril and Methodius, who devised the Cyrillic or Slavonic alphabet, making the Bible available to Slavs.

Under the Umayyad dynasty, Damascus was the capital of Islam until the eighth century when the new Abbasid dynasty moved it east to Baghdad, where Persian influence was more pronounced. Greek, Syrian, and Persian scientific and philosophic writings were translated into Arabic, and an urban culture blossomed, not only in the Near East but also in Umayyad Spain's Cordoba, which later became a gateway of classical knowledge to the Christian west. Political unity, however, was lost, with separate caliphates established in Spain, Egypt, and elsewhere.

LECTURE AND DISCUSSION TOPICS

1. Assess Charlemagne and the Carolingian Empire, its rise and its fall.

2. Discuss the Carolingian Renaissance as a "renaissance."

3. Examine the Viking migrations and contrast those with the earlier Germanic barbarian invasions.

4. Explore relationships between Church and State from the eighth-century through the tenth-century.

5. Discuss the emergence of the church as one of the central institutions of the West.

6. Define feudalism, considering why it was a satisfactory solution to many of the challenges of the medieval society.

7. Compare and contrast European feudalism with feudalism in Japan.

8. Explore the central role the manor played in the world of the Middle Ages.

9. Discuss the impact that the Byzantine Empire had upon the peoples of Eastern Europe during the Middle Ages and after.

10. Compare and contrast the Abbasid civilization with Western society from the 700s through the 900s, and consider the impact of Islam on the West, in fact and in imagination.

MAP EXERCISES

1. The Carolingian Empire. MAP 8.1. Which areas of Western Europe became part of Charlemagne's empire during his reign? Could the expansion of the empire into Italy lead to friction with the Church? Why? Did it during Charlemagne's reign? (page 137)

2. Invasions of the Ninth and Tenth Centuries. MAP 8.2. Which invading group had the greatest impact upon Europe in the ninth and tenth centuries? Why? Geographically, what was the reason for the Vikings' success? (page 142)

3. A Typical Manor. MAP 8.3 Discuss the various geographical subsections of the manor from both an economic and a social perspective. (page 144)

4. The Migration of the Slavs. MAP 8.4. What might have been the causes of the migration of the Slavic peoples into Eastern Europe during the 500s and the 600s? (page 147

DISCUSSION QUESTIONS FOR THE PRIMARY SOURCES (BOXED DOCUMENTS)

1. "The Achievements of Charlemagne": Based on Einhard's account, discuss the strengths and weaknesses of Charlemagne. Which characteristics help to explain Charlemagne's success as a ruler? Does Einhard exaggerate Charlemagne's strengths? Why? What purposes do you believe this medieval historian intended his history writing to serve? (page 136)

2. "Advice from a Carolingian Mother": What advice does Dhouda, the wife of Bernard, marquis of Septimania, give her son on his duties to his new lord, King Charles the Bald? Why her and perhaps not her husband? What does this selection tell us about aristocratic women and their relationship with power? (page 140)

3. "A Western View of the Byzantine Empire": What impressions of the Byzantine court do we receive from Liudprand of Cremona's account? Do you find Liudprand's account to be fair and accurate? Why and/or why not? What is the modern meaning of the word "byzantine"? How does this account help to explain the modern meaning of the word? (page 146)

4. "A Muslim's Description of the Rus": What was Ibn Fadlan's impression of the Rus? What are the several possible reasons why he was so critical of their behavior? Was his criticism justified? Why or why not? What would the Rus have said about Ibn Fadlan? (page 148)

STUDENT RESEARCH AND PROJECT TITLES

1. Discuss the political organization of the empire created by Charlemagne. How did he rule? Why did it not survive after his death?

2. Of what significance was the Carolingian intellectual renaissance to western European civilization?

3. To what extent did the Catholic church alter Germanic practices in regard to family, sexuality, and children?

4. What positive and negative impacts did the Vikings make on the history and culture of medieval Europe?

5. Describe feudalism. It has been said that feudalism was the perfect political system for the Middle Ages. Explain.

6. Describe manorialism. What was its relationship to feudalism?

7. Why does the author use the title, the "zenith of Byzantine civilization," to describe the Byzantine civilization of the ninth and tenth centuries?

8. Describe the conversion to Christianity of the various peoples of Eastern Europe, including a discussion about the responsibilities of Rome and of Constantinople in that process.

9. Discuss the changing relations between Islam and the Byzantine Empire between 750 and 1000.

10. Compare Islamic civilization to the civilization of western Europe in the ninth and tenth centuries. Why was it superior? How did they mutually affect one another?

IDENTIFICATIONS

1. Pepin
2. Charlemagne
3. Einhard
4. *missi dominici*
5. Christmas Day, 800
6. *scriptoria*
7. clerical celibacy
8. Carolingian Renaissance
9. Carolingian minuscule
10. Louis the Pius
11 Treaty of Verdun
12. Magyars
13. battle of Lechfeld
14. Vikings
15. Danelaw and Normandy
16. feudalism
17. lords and vassals
18. stirrup
19. fief
20. subinfeudation
21. manorialism
22. serfs
23. the Photian Schism
24. Macedonian emperors
25. Slavs
26. Orthodox Christianity
27. Cyril and Methodius
28. Slavonic/Cyrillic alphabet
29. Varangians
30. Rurik

31. the Rus
32. Kiev
33. Vladimir
34. Umayyad
35. Abbasids
36. Baghdad
37. Harun al-Rashid
38. Cordoba
39. algebra and the astrolabe
40. Avicenna

MULTIPLE CHOICE QUESTIONS

1. In the ninth century, all of the following posed threats to European civilization except the
   a. Slavs.
   b. Magyars.
   c. Muslims.
   d. Vikings.
      ANSWER: a (page 135)

2. By the end of the seventh century, the ecclesiastical government of the Catholic church
   a. was on a par with that of the eastern Orthodox church.
   b. had improved its administrative and intellectual standards since the days of Constantine.
   c. was providing many administrators to assist Charlemagne in governing his empire.
   d. had disintegrated from earlier times and was in need of reform
      ANSWER: d (pp. 136-137)

3. The medieval church held that
   a. marriage is superior to celibacy.
   b. celibacy constituted a superior state to marriage.
   c. homosexuality was immoral but not a "sin".
   d. rulers should have only one official wife but could have concubines.
      ANSWER: b (p. 139)

4. The first Frankish king to be anointed in holy ceremony by an agent of the pope was
   a. Zacharias.
   b. Charlemagne.
   c. Charles Martel.
   d. Pepin.
      ANSWER: d (p. 135)

5. One of Charlemagne's most disappointing military campaign came against the
   a. Basques.
   b. Avars.
   c. Saxons.
   d. Lombards.
      ANSWER: a (p. 135)

6. The expansion of the Carolingian Empire under Charlemagne
    a. was carried out with the largest army up to its time.
    b. was most successful against the German tribes to the east.
    c. resulted in the quick destruction of the Saxons
    d. resulted in the capture of all of Europe except for Italy.
        ANSWER: b (p. 135)

7. Which of the following were not a Frankish official under Charlemagne?
    a. counts
    b. regents
    c. nobles
    d. *missi dominici*
        ANSWER: b (pp. 135-136)

8. The administration of Charlemagne's Carolingian Empire was carried out
    a. with the support of the Catholic church.
    b. with the resources of the nobles and his household staff.
    c. by Charlemagne's counts, who were watched over by the *missi dominici*.
    d. all of the above
        ANSWER: d (pp. 135-136)

9. The coronation of Charlemagne in 800 as emperor of the Romans
    a. was performed by Pope Zacharias I.
    b. was defended by the Donation of Constantine.
    c. symbolized the fusion of Roman, Germanic, and Christian cultures in the foundation of the new European civilization.
    d. greatly pleased the new emperor who had long coveted this office.
        ANSWER: c (pp. 134-155)

10. The Carolingian monks
    a. were known for the production of *scriptoria*, a type of paper.
    b. through their preservation of Latin manuscripts communicated classical Roman learning to western Europe.
    c. were best known for their hospitality to travelers.
    d. were known for their educational innovations.
        ANSWER: b (p. 138)

11. Charlemagne's Carolingian Renaissance was characterized by
    a. outstanding creativity and original thought.
    b. illuminated manuscripts done in Merovingian cursive script.
    c. the works of Alcuin, who rejected all classical educational ideals.
    d. new copies of classical literary works produced in Benedictine monastic *scriptoria*.
        ANSWER: d (p. 138)

12. An early biography of Charlemagne was written by
    a. Einhard.
    b. Alcuin.
    c. Cyril.
    d. Leo III.
        ANSWER: a (p. 136)

13. Initially, the greatest effect of the church on Frankish marriage
a. was to make it one of the sacraments.
b. was to limit sexual license.
c. emphasized the indissolubility of marriage.
d. prohibit the marriage of priests.
ANSWER: b (p. 139)

14. Regarding sexuality, the Catholic church in the Early Middle Ages
a. could not enforce clerical celibacy.
b. continued the Roman Empire's condemnation of homosexuality.
c. accepted sex for the purpose of pleasure within marriage only.
d. viewed coitus interruptus as the only legitimate birth control method.
ANSWER: a (p. 139)

15. Socially and culturally, the church's advocacy of indissoluble marriage resulted in
a. more bachelors who never married.
b. the development of the nuclear family at the expense of the extended family.
c. a great proportion of widows in communities.
d. the birth of fewer children in medieval times.
ANSWER: b (p. 139)

16. What percentage of ancient Roman works that survive today exist because they were copied by Carolingian monks?
a. ten percent
b. twenty-five percent
c. fifty percent .
d. ninety percent
ANSWER: d (p. 138)

17. The staple food in the Carolingian diet was
a. bread.
b. mutton.
c. beef.
d. pork.
ANSWER: a (p. 139)

18. Which of the following was a similarity between medicine in the Early Middle Ages and medicine in the ancient world?
a. Both relied heavily on primitive surgery.
b. In both periods, magical rites, charms, and amulets were used.
c. Anesthesia was unknown in both eras.
d. Medical training was unknown in both periods.
ANSWER: b (p. 40)

19. Carolingian society was marked by all of the following <u>except</u>
a. the use of bleeding to cure illness.
b. a total disinterest in bodily cleanliness.
c. different patterns of consumption of foodstuffs among rich and poor.
d. the vices of gluttony and drunkenness.
ANSWER: b (pp. 139-140)

20. What was the name of the treaty that divided the Carolingian Empire in 843?
   a. Treaty of Verdun
   b. Treaty of Aix-la-Chapelle
   c. Treaty of York
   d. Treaty of Leipzig
      ANSWER: a (p. 140)

21. The division of Europe into three kingdoms after the death of Louis the Pious led to
   a. the capture of the eastern German lands by Muslim forces.
   b. an incessant struggle between Louis the German, Charles the Bald, and their heirs over disputed territories.
   c. two centuries of relative calm.
   d. the eventual emergence of Lothair as the next ruler of a united Europe.
      ANSWER: b (pp. 140-141)

22. The most successful Muslim raids in the ninth century occurred in
   a. northern Italy.
   b. the western Frankish territories.
   c. Sicily.
   d. central Europe.
      ANSWER: c (p. 141)

23. The Magyars
   a. helped end Muslim expansion in northern Spain.
   b. were originally from western Asia.
   c. won their most successful victory at the battle of Lechfeld against German troops.
   d. were wiped out as a people in the tenth century for their rejection of Christianity.
      ANSWER: b (p. 141)

24. Which of the following statements was <u>not</u> true of the Vikings?
   a. Their iron weapons and superior ship were largely responsible for their successful raids.
   b. Their settlements tended to be limited to coastal areas in the Frankish kingdom.
   c. Their raids and settlements aided the growth of fief-holding.
   d. Christianity assimilated them into European civilization.
      ANSWER: b (p. 142)

25. One of the most famous Vikings, who discovered Greenland, was
   a. Leif Erikson.
   b. Erik the Red.
   c. Olaf the Bald.
   d. Wilbur the Swede.
      ANSWER: b (p. 142)

26. In western Europe, the chief political repercussion of frequent Viking raids was
   a. the strengthening of centralized royal authority.
   b. an increase in the power of the church.
   c. an increase in the power of local aristocrats to whom threatened populations turned for effective protection.
   d. a decline in the power of local aristocrats whose inability to stop the raids drove ordinary people into royal cities.
      ANSWER: c (p. 142)

27. Feudalism of medieval Europe was primarily
a. a complex system of vassalage by which the weak sought protection and sustenance from powerful local nobles.
b. a relationship between social equals.
c. limited to southern and western Europe.
d. a rigid hierarchical system that varied little from place to place.
ANSWER: a (pp. 142-143)

28. The "hierarchical" fief-holding system in which vassals in turn had vassals owing them services was known as
a. *comitatus*.
b. subinfeudation.
c. primogeniture.
d. the benefice.
ANSWER: b (p. 144)

29. The lord-vassal relationship in the Germanic practice of medieval Europe
a. marked a complete separation from the German traditions of lordship and loyalty.
b. meant fiefs could never become hereditary.
c. was a direct form of servitude.
d. was an honorable relationship between free men choosing to associate under physically threatening conditions.
ANSWER: d (p. 144)

30. The major obligation of the lord to the vassal was
a. economic support and protection either militarily or through grants of land.
b. scutage.
c. the tithe.
d. free use of the manorial mill.
ANSWER: a (p. 143)

31. Under feudalism of the Early Middle Ages
a. the major obligation of a vassal to his lord was to provide military service.
b. a vassal was not required to provide legal assistance at his lord's court.
c. a lord has no formal responsibilities toward his vassals.
d. there was no outlet for the breaking of the bond between lord and vassal.
ANSWER: a (pp. 143-144)

32. The military innovation clearly contributing to the rise of feudal vassalage was
a. the introduction of artillery in royal armies.
b. the growing importance of cavalry (mounted knights) in royal armies.
c. new weapons for foot soldiers.
d. the popularity of single combat among feuding nobles.
ANSWER: b (p. 143)

33. The Byzantine dynasty which effectively dealt with the many challenges facing the empire was the
a. Ottonian.
b. Bulgarian.
c. Macedonian.
d. Umayyad.
ANSWER: c (p. 145)

34. The Photian Schism
   a. divided Christianity and Islam over the role of Jesus as God.
   b. was a dispute which led to civil war between Charlemagne's grandsons at Lechfeld.
   c. was a dispute between Roman and Orthodox Christians over the Holy Spirit.
   d. was ended by the Treaty of Verdun.
      ANSWER: c (p. 145)

35. In manorialism, serfs
   a. paid their rent through military service.
   b. could marry only with their lord's permission. .
   c. were excommunicated if they married.
   d. were "free" but had nowhere to go as there were no alternatives to the manor.
      ANSWER: b (p. 145)

36. The economic structure of the Early Middle Ages
   a. saw feudalism replace manorialism.
   b. saw nearly the entire free peasant class become serfs.
   c. was underdeveloped and predominantly agricultural.
   d. witnessed the complete disintegration of trade.
      ANSWER: c (p. 145)

37. Manorialism
   a. marked an end to the fief-holding system of the Early Middle Ages.
   b. was an economic system based upon landed estates.
   c. brought about a rejuvenated increase in European slavery.
   d. devastated the social mobility of the lowest classes in European society.
      ANSWER: b (p. 144)

38. Which of the following statements were true of trade during the Middle Ages?
   a. During the early centuries of the Middle ages, trade drastically declined.
   b. During the sixth and seventh centuries, silk and perfumes were brought from China.
   c. By the ninth century, luxury goods were brought in from the Byzantine Empire.
   d. a and c
      ANSWER: a (p. 145)

39. The Byzantine Empire by the eleventh century
   a. reached its largest territorial boundaries since the seventh century.
   b. was looked upon as a land of barbarians by western Europeans.
   c. was beset by invasions and internal dissent, especially under Emperor Basil II.
   d. was devoid of any intellectual creativity.
      ANSWER: a (p. 147)

40. The Slavs
   a. were originally a single people from central Europe.
   b. adopted Roman Catholicism as their sole religion.
   c. were completely absorbed by the Bulgars in the ninth century.
   d. became bitter enemies of western European rulers for their rigid opposition to Christianity.
      ANSWER: a (p. 145)

41. The Poles, Czechs, and Hungarians
  a. ignored all efforts of German kings to Christianize them.
  b. were united by their cultural links to the Byzantine Empire.
  c. were greatly influenced by assimilation into the Catholic church and Latin culture.
  d. rejected western Christianity and became increasingly antagonistic toward Christianity.
    ANSWER: c (p. 147)

42. The Swedish Vikings–the Varangians–became known or assimilated with which of the following groups:
  a. Magyars
  b. Czechs
  c. Russians
  d. Bulgars
    ANSWER: c (p. 148)

43. The Slavic people of the Rus were best known for
  a. their defeat over Rurik, head of the Swedish Vikings, in 862.
  b. their preoccupation with cleanliness.
  c. their unflinching loyalty to the Roman Catholic church.
  d. founding the state that became known as Russia.
    ANSWER: d (p. 148)

44. The cruel and vicious Russian leader responsible for tying Russian political and religious ideals to the Byzantine Empire was
  a. Oleg.
  b. Vladimir.
  c. Prince Mieszko.
  d. Rurik.
    ANSWER: b (p. 148)

45. A comparison of Islam and Western Civilization in the eighth and ninth centuries shows
  a. the west's clear superiority in urban culture.
  b. Muslim creation of a brilliant and sophisticated urban culture while western society remained a world of petty and violent agricultural villages.
  c. a common fascination with decorative arts depicting living things.
  d. a greater respect for ancient civilizations and their cultures in the west.
    ANSWER: b (p. 149)

46. Muslim scholars were well known in the west for their original contributions in
  a. algebra.
  b. astronomy.
  c. medicine.
  d. all of the above
    ANSWER: d (p. 150)

47. The Islamic city in Spain that served as the Umayyad capital was
  a. Damascus.
  b. Cordoba.
  c. Baghdad.
  d. Ibn Sina.
    ANSWER: b (pp. 149-150)

48. The capital city of the Umayyad Caliphate and center of an Islamic empire was
  a. Jerusalem.
  b. Cairo.
  c. Damascus.
  d. Mecca.
    ANSWER: c (p. 149)

49. The major socio-political change associated with the Abbasid Caliphate is
  a. promotion of warrior captains to positions of supreme power.
  b. reduction in the power of judicial officials.
  c. promotion of judges, merchants, and government officials over warriors as ideal citizens.
  d. rejection of Persian influence in the structures of state rulership.
    ANSWER: c (p. 149)

50. The Abbasids
  a. chose all officials exclusively from the Arabic community.
  b. translated the Qur'an into Persian, making it the official language of Islam.
  c. ruled Spain from Cordoba.
  d. broke down the distinctions between Arab and non-Arab Muslims.
    ANSWER: d (p. 149)

RELEVANT WORLD-WIDE WEB SITES/RESOURCES

1. Internet Medieval Source Book:
http://www.fordham.edu/halsall/sbook.html
(Extensive online collection of key medieval texts.)

2. Monarchs in Medieval France:
http://lcweb.loc.gov/exhibits/bnf/bnf0003.html
(Richly illustrated site from U.S. Library of Congress exhibition including images of Carolingian fine and decorative arts.)

RELEVANT VIDEO RESOURCES

Europe in the Middle Ages, Films for the Humanities and Sciences, 7 cassettes, (30-45 minutes each). (Excellent video survey course covering early medieval Europe, Charlemagne, Feudalism, Medieval Spain, Byzantium, and Viking raids.)

Quran (CD-ROM for Windows), Insight Media. (A comprehensive and multi-lingual edition of the Islamic Holy Book complete with commentaries and explanations of central themes of Islam.)

The Story of Islam, 2 programs (60 minutes each program). Insight Media.
(Comprehensive visual history of Islam covering entire development and variations within the faith.)

The Western Tradition: Part I, Annenberg/CPB Collection/
PBS Home Video, (30 minutes each program), Programs 17 and 18, "The Dark Ages" and "The Age of Charlemagne."

SUGGESTED STUDENT ACTIVITIES

1. Have students do an essay on the importance of the Carolingian Renaissance. Have them answer the question: Why did Renaissance not spread to other eras?

2. The Byzantine civilization has been called eclectic. Have students do a study of the various sources that influenced the development of Byzantine civilization.

3. Have students do a project on the various types of feudalism and how the political system developed in the various European countries.

4. There are several good books on life on a medieval manor. Have students write a paper or do a presentation on an average day on a medieval manor.

CHAPTER 9
THE RECOVERY AND GROWTH OF EUROPEAN SOCIETY IN THE HIGH MIDDLE AGES

CHAPTER OUTLINE

I. Land and People in the High Middle Ages
- A. The New Agriculture
- B. Daily Life of the Peasantry
- C. The Aristocracy and the High Middle Ages
  - 1. The Way of the Warrior
  - 2. Aristocratic Women

II. The New World of Trade and Cities
- A. The Revival of Trade
- B. The Growth of Cities
  - 1. Life in the Medieval City
- C. Industry in Medieval Cities

III. The Intellectual and Artistic World of the High Middle Ages
- A. The Rise of the Universities
- B. A Revival of Classical Antiquity
- C. The Development of Scholasticism
- E. Literature in the High Middle Ages
- F. Romanesque Architecture: "A White Mantle of Churches"
- G. The Gothic Cathedral

IV. Conclusion

CHAPTER SUMMARY

The period from 1000 to 1300, known as the High Middle Ages, saw a doubling of the European population and the growth of cities and trade. The climate improved, contributing to increased food production, and forests were cleared and lands reclaimed from swamps. Iron plowshares brought heavy soils under cultivation, and horses, with the invention of horse collars, replaced the slower-moving oxen in the fields. Watermills and windmills came into wider use. A three-field system of crop rotation meant that one-third rather than one-half lay fallow each year, and the increased demand for agricultural products improved the lot of the peasants.

While peasants labored, the aristocratic ideal was to wage war. Tournaments allowed knights to train for battle, but it also provided a social outlet, contributing to the ideals of chivalry. The Church, with mixed success, attempted to limit warfare by forbidding fighting on Sundays and feast days, and by redirecting the ardor for battle into crusades. Castles served as fortresses and homes for the ruling class. Aristocratic women married young and were to be subservient, but they often had financial responsibilities, and some had considerable influence.

The revival of urban life occurred first in northern Italy and in Flanders, where the wool-cloth trade developed. Regional fairs, such as at Champagne in northern France, facilitated trade. In the cities, the largest with a population of 100,000, artisans, organized into monopolistic craft guilds, played a major role. New laws and customs evolved, and many towns gained charters of liberty from local lords, which guaranteed certain freedoms. The urban inhabitants lived and worked in close proximity, fire was a constant threat, and dirt and disease was rampant.

There was also an artistic and intellectual renaissance in the High Middle Ages. The earlier monastic and cathedral schools were dedicated to clerical rather than lay education. The first university was founded in Bologna, Italy, where the recently discovered *Body of Civil Law* was the focus of study. Students, mostly laymen, obtained a charter as a student guild, or *universitas*, in 1158. Paris, Oxford, and Cambridge soon followed. Teaching was in Latin, and the curriculum was the seven liberal arts of grammar, rhetoric, logic, arithmetic, geometry, astronomy, and music. Books were rare, thus instructors read the texts to students, adding their own interpretations. Many graduates took positions in the royal and church bureaucracies.

There was a renewed interest in classical writings, particularly those of Aristotle, which were translated into Latin in the twelfth century. Knowledge of Greek had largely disappeared in the west, but Muslims had made translations into Arabic, which in turn were translated into Latin. Christian theology was the "queen of the sciences," and scholars attempted to reconcile faith with reason, using logic to validate revelation in a system known as *scholasticism.* The most influential of the scholastics was Thomas Aquinas (d. 1274), who used Aristotelean logic and the dialectical method of posing and answering questions in his *Summa Theologica*.

In literature, Latin began to give way to the vernacular. Troubadour poetry was written in the vernacular, as were heroic epics such as the *Song of Roland.* In architecture, Romanesque, with its barrel vaults and massive pillars and walls with little space for windows gave way in the twelfth century to the Gothic. Ribbed vaults and pointed arches allowed for higher cathedrals, and flying buttresses, by redistributing the weight, made for thin walls and stained glass windows, whose natural light symbolized God's divine light. Cathedral construction would take decades: it was a community endeavor, an act of faith in this world and the next.

LECTURE AND DISCUSSION TOPICS

1. Outline the technological advances that increased European agricultural productivity, and their links to trade and urban development between 900 and the 1200s.

2. Explore the influence of climate and environment on medieval agricultural practices and development.

3. Compare and contrast the High Middle Ages with the earlier Carolingian era.

4. Assess the accomplishments of the High Middle Ages, including the growth of universities, scholasticism, and urban Gothic architecture.

5. Present through slides or a video/DVD an examination of the Gothic art and architecture, perhaps contrasting the Gothic era 's accomplishments with those of the earlier Romanesque period.

6. Examine the aristocratic code of chivalry, contrasting its noble values with its military realities. A comparison with the Bushido ethos of medieval Japan might be illuminating.

7. Discuss the growth of medieval towns and cities, both as opportunity and as challenge.

8. Compare and contrast the roles of aristocratic women, urban women, and peasant women during the High Middle Ages.

9. Explore the origin of the medieval university and its impact or role in the society of the Middle Ages. A comparison with modern universities could be fruitful.

10. Discuss: "The Gothic Cathedral as Material and Spiritual Machine."

MAP EXERCISES

1. Medieval Trade Routes. MAP 9.1. What geographical features might explain why northern Italy and Flanders were the earliest centers of the revival of cities and commerce? (page 159)

2. Main Intellectual Centers of Medieval Europe. MAP 9.2. What were the causes, historic and geographical, which might account for France being the intellectual capital of late medieval Europe? (page 163)

DISCUSSION QUESTIONS FOR THE PRIMARY SOURCES (BOXED DOCUMENTS)

1. "The Elimination of Medieval Forests": What does Abbot Suger's search for wooden beams reveal about the environmental challenges of the High Middle Ages? What factors defined the relationship of medieval people to the earth and to nature? (page 155)

2. "Women in Medieval Thought": What common assumptions about the nature of women underlie the arguments advanced in these two medieval documents? Are there any differences between the jurist and the merchant in their attitudes towards women? Why and/or why not? (page 158))

3. "The Value of Money": What are the advantages of money, according the Juan Ruiz? How do his attitudes compare with ideology and assumptions of the medieval Church? Do Ruiz' statements appear to be relevant to the twenty-first century? Why and or why not? (page 161)

4. "University Students and Violence at Oxford": What does this document reveal about the nature of town and gown conflicts in the Middle Ages? Do institutions of higher learning, over time, work to reduce social violence or simply create new opportunities for and ways to express human violence? Does this excerpt sound modern? If so, how? (page 165)

STUDENT RESEARCH AND PROJECT TOPICS

1. How important were new agricultural practices to the production of food in the High Middle Ages?

2. Discuss the structures and changes in daily life of the ordinary European medieval village. How did most Europeans live and what were the material factors shaping their behavior at the communal level?

3. Assume that you are a member of the European medieval nobility. Discuss the primary aspects of your lifestyle and explain how these characteristics positively and negatively affect your entire society.

4. What burdens did medieval female aristocrats have to confront and what freedoms did they enjoy?

5. Discuss the life of a medieval peasant family, including work and non-work experiences.

6. What were some of the reasons for the revival of trade and the growth of cities in the Middle Ages?

7. A German proverb of the medieval period states: "The city air will set you free." What reasons can you give to justify or to refute the accuracy of this proverb for ordinary medieval townspeople?

8. What were the advantages and what were the disadvantages of living in a medieval city?

9. What were the causes and what were the consequences of the development of the early medieval universities?

10. What were some of the reasons for the revival of classical antiquity in the High Middle Ages?

11. Discuss the fusion of Christian theology and classical logic in the High Middle Ages. Which thinkers and writers took active roles in achieving this synthesis and what did they contribute?

12. Compare and contrast Romanesque and Gothic architecture.

13. "The Gothic cathedral was the supreme accomplishment of the High Middle Ages world." Discuss.

14. In what ways does the artistic and literary culture of the High Middle Ages reflect the religious preoccupations and problems of medieval society?

IDENTIFICATIONS

1. the *carruca*
2. horse collar
3. three-field system
4. chivalry
5. tournaments and melees
6. a castle keep
7. knighthood
8. Eleanor of Aquitaine
9. Venice
10. Flanders
11. Champagne fairs
12. *borough/burgh*
13. charters of liberty
14. craft guilds
15. *universitas*
16. University of Bologna
17. Irnerius
18. the liberal arts
19. *artium baccalaureus*
20. town vs. gown
21. Aristotle

22. Averroes
23. “the queen of the sciences”
24. scholasticism
25. Thomas Aquinas’ *Summa Theologica*
26. troubadours
27. vernacular
28. *chanson de geste*
29. *The Song of Roland*
30. Romanesque
31. barrel vault
32. Gothic
33. pointed arch and flying buttress
34. Abbot Suger
35. church of Saint-Denis

MULTIPLE CHOICE QUESTIONS

1. The dramatic increases in European population between 1000 and 1300
   a. occurred despite detrimental climatic patterns.
   b. especially benefited women of child-bearing age.
   c. were primarily due to an increased birth rate outstripping relatively high medieval mortality rates.
   d. led to populations with many more women than men due to constant warfare.
   ANSWER: c (page 154)

2. Between 1000 and 1300, European population
   a. doubled.
   b. fell by half.
   c. increased very slowly.
   d. stagnated due to severe outbreaks of disease and war.
   ANSWER: a (p. 154)

3. One negative result of the new agriculture of the Early Middle Ages was
   a. the destruction of the forests.
   b. the contamination of the water supply.
   c. increased dependence of serfs on their lords.
   d. both b and c
   ANSWER: a (pp. 154-155)

4. The "agricultural revolution" of the High Middle Ages
   a. caused little change in the forested areas of Europe.
   b. was in part brought about by a change from the two-field to the three-field system.
   c. led to the demise of the cooperative agricultural villages.
   d. was in large part due to the development of the *aratum*, an iron ploughshare.
   ANSWER: b (p. 155)

5. New technological developments in agriculture improving productivity of foodstuffs included all of the following <u>except</u>

a. iron hoes.
b. the use of horse shoes.
c. the heavy-wheeled, iron-tipped plow (*carruca*).
d. harnesses for draft animals without collars.

ANSWER: d (p. 155)

6. Which of the following was <u>not</u> used as a source of power by medieval farmers?

a. horses
b. coal
c. water
d. windmills

ANSWER: b (p. 155)

7. The peasant's life during the Middle Ages was largely determined by

a. the whims of the lord.
b. religious holidays.
c. the natural rhythm of the seasons.
d. peace and warfare.

ANSWER: c (p. 156)

8. The basic staple of the peasant diet was

a. potatoes.
b. rice.
c. pork.
d. bread.

ANSWER: d (p. 156)

9. By the thirteenth century,

a. food prices fell because of decreased demand.
b. many free peasants were becoming serfs.
c. the growing demand for agricultural products in cities led to higher food prices.
d. the lords were increasing their political and legal powers at the expense of kings.

ANSWER: c (p. 155)

10. The most common drink of the medieval peasant was

a. ale.
b. beer.
c. wine.
d. cider.

ANSWER: a (p. 156)

11. The high number of fights and accidents described in medieval court records may plausibly be attributed to
a. the violence of lords.
b. the enormous quantities of alcohol consumed by all ranks of society.
c. generally poor diet and nutrition.
d. fears of witchcraft.
ANSWER: b (p. 157)

12. Male nobles of the High Middle Ages
a. were almost solely preoccupied with warfare as a distinguishing characteristic.
b. gradually became more involved in economic pursuits.
c. had previously been successful merchants.
d. were very effeminate and shunned the warlike ways of their predecessors.
ANSWER: a (p. 157)

13. In medieval thought, women were considered
a. equal to men in most things, but still inferior.
b. by nature subservient and lesser beings than men.
c. an equal partner of men in theory, but not in practice.
d. totally evil and in need of discipline.
ANSWER: b (p. 158)

14. The main part of the medieval castle was called the
a. motte.
b. bailey.
c. keep.
d. tower.
ANSWER: c (p. 157)

15. The knightly code of ethics known as chivalry included all of the following requirements except
a. knights were to fight to defend the church.
b. knights were to protect the weak and defenseless.
c. knights were to love the poor.
d. winning glory should be the knight's highest aim and motivating force.
ANSWER: c (p. 157)

16. Combative tournaments involving knights
a. were sanctioned by the church as a testing ground for faith.
b. consisted of the "melee" in which knights with a grudge fought to the death.
c. were considered excellent and necessary training for warfare.
d. were banned by 1100.
ANSWER: c (p. 158)

17. Marriages among the aristocracy of the High Middle Ages were
a. more frequently motivated by the love brides and grooms felt for one another.
b. still included violent blood rituals of betrothal dating back to pagan times.
c. usually occurred when both bride and groom were in their teens.
d. were generally between older men and younger women.
ANSWER: d (p. 166)

18. Eleanor of Aquitaine was noted for all of the following *except*
   a. she was an heiress.
   b. she was married to two kings.
   c. she became a saint in the church because of her pious celibacy.
   d. she took an active role in politics, rebelling against her second husband.
      ANSWER: c (pp. 158-59)

19. The area that assumed a leading role in the revival of trade in the Early Middle Ages was
   a. England.
   b. Spain.
   c. Germany.
   d. Italy.
      ANSWER: d (p. 159)

20. The revival of long-distance trade in the eleventh and twelfth centuries was due to all of the following <u>except</u>
   a. trade links with eastern Mediterranean cities forged by Italian port towns during the crusades.
   b. the emergence of Flanders as a great center of cloth production.
   c. the demise of local trade throughout Europe's rural world.
   d. the establishment of trading fairs by local northern European nobles.
      ANSWER: c (p. 159)

21. The growing independence of medieval urban areas was largely attributable to
   a. the refusal of lords and kings to grant liberties to the townspeople.
   b. the granting of self-government to the townspeople by bishops, especially in cathedral cities.
   c. their huge populations.
   d. the revival of commerce.
      ANSWER: d (p. 160)

22. The term "burg" or "borough" referred to
   a. a fortress.
   b. a trade association.
   c. a group of advisors to a city mayor.
   d. a private banking establishment.
      ANSWER: a (p. 160)

23. Cities in medieval Europe
   a. were usually ruled by a lord in a manner similar to the manorial system.
   b. rivaled those of the Arabs and Byzantines.
   c. often attained privileges purchased from neighboring territorial lords.
   d. were independent of the surrounding countryside for their food supplies.
      ANSWER: c (p. 160)

24. To protect their interests against nobles, townspeople often
   a. obtained charters of liberties. .
   b. formed trade unions.
   c. established chambers of commerce.
   d. created municipal police forces.
      ANSWER: a (p. 160)

25. A major motive contributing to the revolutionary political behavior of European townspeople was their
a. early embrace of religious heresy.
b. constant need to ally themselves with more heavily armed aristocrats.
c. great need for unfettered mobility to conduct trade efficiently.
d. unwillingness to pay lay and clerical lords for privileges of self-government.
ANSWER: c (p. 160)

26. On the whole, medieval cities tended to be
a. huge, rivaling modern cities in population.
b. relatively undemocratic; the wealthy usually ruled and voted in civic elections.
c. totally dominated by rural nobles.
d. devoid of sophisticated internal systems of government.
ANSWER: b (pp. 160-161)

27. Medieval cities
a. were generally clean and covered a large area.
b. had low population densities.
c. contained more men than women.
d. lacked public or private baths.
ANSWER: c (p. 162)

28. A major cause of pollution in medieval cities was
a. the smell and waste of animals and humans.
b. spills of oil, a common fuel of the era.
c. the production of iron in urban smelters.
d. the use of lead paint in private and public buildings.
ANSWER: a (p. 162)

29. The guild system of medieval European cities did all of the following <u>except</u>
a. enforced standards and methods of production for various articles.
b. fixed prices at which finished goods could be sold.
c. set the numbers of people who could enter key trades and the procedures by which they could do so.
d. discouraged the use of apprenticeships for training new workers.
ANSWER: d (p. 162)

30. Drinking water in the cities of the Middle Ages usually came from
a. mountain streams, piped in by aqueducts.
b. rivers.
c. wells.
d. rainwater.
ANSWER: c (p. 162)

31. The first university to be founded in Europe appeared in
a. Bologna.
b. Paris.
c. Oxford.
d. Frankfurt.
ANSWER: a (p. 163)

32. The first university in northern Europe was
   a. Oxford.
   b. Cambridge.
   c. Heidelberg.
   d. Paris.
   ANSWER: d (p. 163)

33. Due to its many cathedral schools, the intellectual center of Europe by the twelfth century was
   a. England.
   b. Holy Roman Empire.
   c. France.
   d. Spain.
   ANSWER: c (p. 163)

34. Students in medieval universities
   a. came strictly from the upper class.
   b. usually started their instruction while in their late twenties.
   c. often engaged in quarrels with one another and in confrontations with townspeople.
   d. were both male and female.
   ANSWER: c (p. 164)

35. The University of Bologna initially specialized in
   a. scholastic philosophy.
   b. Roman law.
   c. Greek medicine.
   d. Christian theology.
   ANSWER: b (163)

36. Concerning the curriculum of the medieval university
   a. students studied the liberal arts.
   b. it allowed for a wide degree of student choice.
   c. it was determined by the professors of the universities.
   d. it was based on the classics of Rome.
   ANSWER: a (p. 163)

37. The renaissance of the twelfth century was primarily caused by
   a. the university movement of the previous century.
   b. circulation in the west in Latin translation of many ancient philosophical and scientific works previously saved by Muslim scholars.
   c. the elaborate and dialectical writings of St. Thomas Aquinas.
   d. the generous financial support of scholars by new European monarchs.
   ANSWER: b (p. 164)

38. The renaissance of the twelfth century saw all of the following <u>except</u>
   a. Muslim scientific discoveries made available to the west.
   b. scholarly receptiveness to the works of Jewish thinkers.
   c. the end of the domination of Latin in scholarly works.
   d. a great influx of Aristotle's writings previously available only to brilliant Arab scholars.
   ANSWER: c (p. 164)

39. The primary preoccupation of scholasticism was
   a. the reconciliation of faith with reason.
   b. to prove the superiority of faith over rational thought.
   c. to disprove the writings of the church fathers through rational thought.
   d. to show the superiority of Greek thought over medieval theological thought.
      ANSWER: a (pp. 165-166)

40. The most significant figure from the ancient world to influence medieval theology and philosophy was
   a. Marcus Aurelius.
   b. Plato.
   c. Aristotle.
   d. St. Paul.
      ANSWER: c (p. 164)

41. The *Summa Theologica* of Thomas Aquinas
   a. raised questions concerning theology and solved them by the dialectical method.
   b. rejected the scholastic method of dialectical reasoning.
   c. suggested that truths derived by reason were far inferior to those derived by faith.
   d. preached for an acceptance of homosexuality when most members of the church condemned it.
      ANSWER: a (p. 165)

42. The first fully Gothic church was
   a. Westminster Abbey outside of London.
   b. Saint-Denis near Paris.
   c. Vienne in southern France.
   d. St. Peter's in Rome.
      ANSWER: b (p. 167)

43. The most popular form of vernacular literature in the twelfth century was
   a. troubadour poetry.
   b. the *fabliaux*.
   c. the *chanson de geste*.
   d. genealogical history.
      ANSWER: a (p. 166)

44. Troubadour poetry was chiefly concerned with
   a. religious imagery.
   b. the courtly love of nobles, knights, and ladies.
   c. the highly irreverent life of wine, women, and song.
   d. rhyme and a meter based on accent.
      ANSWER: b (p. 166)

45. *The Song of Roland* is one of the finest examples of
   a. the medieval *chanson de geste*.
   b. twelfth-century courtly romance.
   c. the Arthurian legend.
   d. Latin religious verse.
      ANSWER: a (p. 166)

46. Much of the surplus resources of medieval urban society went into

a. the salaries of more numerous royal officials.
b. the purchase of modern weaponry by kings for expanded royal armies.
c. the construction of castles and churches reflecting its basic preoccupations, warfare and God.
d. new church taxes going directly to the pope in Rome.

ANSWER: c (p. 166)

47. The dominant style of the church architecture in the eleventh and twelfth centuries was

a. Gothic.
b. Baroque.
c. Romanesque.
d. naturalistic.

ANSWER: c (p. 166)

48. Which of the following was <u>not</u> a characteristic of Romanesque architecture?

a. churches in this style were built in rectangular shape
b. massive pillars and walls were required for support, leaving no room for many windows
c. interiors were designed to be as bright as possible
d. heavy barrel vaults with rounded stone roofs replaced flat wooden roofs

ANSWER: c (pp. 166-167)

49. Gothic cathedrals seem to soar upward as light and airy constructions due to all of the following innovations <u>except</u>

a. ribbed vaults and pointed arches.
b. flying buttresses.
c. thin walls pierced by huge stained glass windows.
d. the wide use of classical columns on Greek models.

ANSWER: d (p. 167)

50. The Gothic style of architecture emerged and was perfected in

a. France.
b. the Netherlands.
c. Spain.
d. Sweden.

ANSWER: a (p. 167)

RELEVANT WORLD-WIDE WEB SITES/RESOURCES

1. Images of Medieval Art and Architecture
http://info.pitt.edu/~medart/
(A magnificent site offering detailed images of more than 40 great medieval buildings and monuments located across Europe.)

2. Metropolitan Museum of Art, New York, Arms and Armor Collection:
http://www.metmuseum.org/htmlfile/gallery/first/arms.html

3. Vatican Museums, Rome:
http://www.christusrex.org/www1/vaticano/0-Musei.html
(A superb and amply illustrated site ideal for research on cultural patronage of medieval and Renaissance papacy.)

RELEVANT VIDEO RESOURCES

Castle, PBS Home Video, (55 minutes). (From the David Macaulay Collection, focuses on 13th-century Welsh castle through site visit and computer animation.)

The Western Tradition, Part I, Annenberg/CPB Collection/PBS Home Video, (30 minutes each program), Programs 21 and 22, "Common Life in the Middle Ages" and "Cities and Cathedrals of the Middle Ages."

Medieval London, Films for the Humanities and Sciences, (20 minutes). (Examines medieval reconstruction and expansion of the city.)

A World Inscribed: The Illuminated Manuscript, Films for the Humanities and Sciences, (23 minutes). (Merited O'Connor Film Award from American Historical Assoc. Covers book illumination and noble bibliographic patronage from fifth to fourteenth centuries.)

RELEVANT MUSICAL PERFORMANCES

The Age of Cathedrals: Music from the Magnus Liber Organi, Harmonia Mundi France CD (No. 907157).

Guillaume de Machaut (1300-1377), Mass de Notre Dame, Harmonia Mundi France CD (No. 901590).

"Sumer is icumen in:" Medieval English Chants, Harmonia Mundi France CD (No. 901154). (Thirteenth-century popular and elite musical forms and performances.)

Troubadours, Harmonia Mundi France CD (No. 94396). (Twelfth-century music performed by itinerant musicians for royal and humble audiences.)

SUGGESTED STUDENT ACTIVITIES

1. Have students pick a famous castle in Europe, perhaps in England, and write an essay describing and telling the history of the structure. Suggest castles like Dover, Windsor, Leeds, etc.

2. Have students research medieval urban culture, pointing out how the material culture of these cities has influenced manners and behavior today.

3. For male and some female students, medieval warfare with its knights, armor, weapons, and tournaments, is fascinating. Have students research the armor and weapons of a medieval knight using online museum collections of arms and armor.

4. There are several good books on life during the Middle Ages. Have students do some outside reading on the subject and write an essay on the typical day in the life of a medieval peasant.

CHAPTER 10
THE RISE OF KINGDOMS AND THE GROWTH OF CHURCH POWER

CHAPTER OUTLINE

I. The Emergence and Growth of European Kingdoms, 1000-1300
- A. England in the High Middle Ages
- B. The Growth of the French Kingdom
- C. Christian Reconquest: The Spanish Kingdoms
- D. The Lands of the Holy Roman Empire: Germany and Italy
- E. New Kingdoms in Eastern Europe
- F. The Mongol Empire
- G. The Development of Russia

II. The Recovery and Reform of the Catholic Church
- A. The Problems of Decline
- B. The Cluniac Reform Movement
- C. The Reform of the Papacy

III. Christianity and Medieval Civilization
- A. Growth of the Papal Monarchy
- B. New Religious Orders and Spiritual Ideals
- C. Popular Religion in the High Middle Ages
- D. Voices of Protest and Intolerance
  - 1. Persecution of the Jews
  - 2. Intolerance of Homosexuality

IV. The Crusades
- A. Background to the Crusades
  - 1. Islam and the Seljuk Turks
  - 2. The Byzantine Empire
- B. The Early Crusades
- C. The Crusades of the Thirteenth Century
- D. Effects of the Crusades

V. Conclusion

CHAPTER SUMMARY

In the High Middle Ages monarchs consolidated their power, using the profits of trade and taxes on commerce to employ mercenary soldiers and professional bureaucrats instead of relying upon their nobles. When William, Duke of Normandy, conquered England in 1066, he created a centralized monarchy. Henry II (d.1189) established a system of royal courts and laws common to the entire kingdom, but Henry's youngest son, John (d.1216) was forced to accept the Magna Carta in 1215, which established the principle that the king was also bound by the laws. Edward I (d.1307) advanced representative government in the institution of Parliament when he summoned representatives from the cities and the non-titled knightly class to meet with the higher nobility, which eventually evolved into the House of Lords and the House of Commons.

The early Capetian kings of France had little authority over their nobility, but Philip II Augustus (d.1223) strengthened the monarchy by depriving the English kings of their French lands. By the reign of Philip IV the Fair (d.1314) a royal bureaucracy was firmly in place. In 1302, Philip summoned representatives of the nobility, clergy, and the cities, thus instituting the Estates-General, but which never gained the power of England's Parliament.

In the eleventh century several small Christian kingdoms in northern Spain began to wage war against the Muslims, a struggle which continued until 1492 when the Moors were expelled. The German monarchs, preoccupied with controlling northern Italy, lessened their authority in Germany; centralized royal power never materialized in Germany. Unified monarchies appeared in Scandinavia, and in eastern Europe German Teutonic Knights battled Slavs. Further east, the Mongols conquered Russia.

The Church remained powerful, but its spirituality was compromised by its secular involvements. From the abbey of Cluny a reform movement transformed monastic life and the papacy as well. In the Investiture Controversy, wherein the German kings had been appointing church officials, Pope Gregory VII forced Henry IV to beg his forgiveness, an event which symbolized of the pope's authority. The Church's power reached its apex under Pope Innocent III (r.1198-1216), who excommunicated kings and authorized crusades.

The High Middle Ages was an era of religious enthusiasm. Several new non-cloistered religious orders such as the Franciscans, the Dominicans, and the Beguines, worked in the secular world. Among the saints, Mary, the mother of Jesus, was particularly popular. Collecting holy relics and embarking on pilgrimages was widespread. Innocent III supported a crusade against the heresy of Cathar dualism, and instituted the holy inquisition. Homosexuals and Jews were also victims of popular passions, and the latter were driven out of France and England.

The crusades exemplified the power of the papacy and popular religious enthusiasm. The Moslem Seljuk Turks defeated a Byzantine army at the battle of Manzikert in 1071, and in 1095 Pope Urban II urged a holy war against Islam. The motives of the crusaders were mixed, including religion, adventure, and the quest for riches, and they captured Jerusalem in 1099 and established several small states in the region. The Turks struck back, leading to later crusades. The Fourth Crusade, at the urging of the Venetians who were providing transportation, sacked Constantinople; the Byzantine Empire never fully recovered. Other crusades followed, but in 1291 the last western outpost fell to Islam. The crusades contributed to the revival of trade, already underway, but they also encouraged the spread of religious bigotry and violence.

LECTURE AND DISCUSSION TOPICS

1. Discuss the development of the national states of England, France, and Germany, examining both their similarities and difference.

2. Assess the geopolitical implications of the lack of unified monarchies in medieval Germany and Italy, and the possible explanations for no political unification in those two regions.

3. As a test case, examine the particular circumstances of the Iberian Peninsula in the Middle Ages in comparison to the kingdoms of France and England and the Holy Roman Empire.

4. Assess the differences and the reasons for those differences between the new kingdoms of Eastern Europe and the established kingdoms of the west.

5. Discuss the role that the Mongols played in Christian Eastern Europe and the Moslem Near East.

6. Present a narrative and an analysis of the history of the church from the Dark Ages to the reign of Innocent III, including the reform of the church under Gregory VII and the often larger-than-life confrontations between church and state.

7. Explore the power and significance of the institutional church in the Age of Faith.

8. Examine "popular religion" in the High Middle Ages, including a discussion of the new religious orders of the Franciscans and Dominican, and the role each played in the more urban society of that era.

9. Explore the interrelationship between faith and intolerance in the High Middle Ages.

10. Discuss the religious and material motivations of the Crusades and assess their long-term effects upon the West and well as upon the Moslem world.

MAP EXERCISES

1. England and France in the High Middle Ages. MAP 10.1. Compare the losses and the gains of England and the French demesne in the twelfth and thirteenth centuries. Who gained the most, and why? What factor did geographical considerations play? (page 174)

2. Christian Reconquests in the Western Mediterranean. MAP 10.2. Trace the reconquest of Spain from Islam between 1000 and 1492. How might the north-to-south conquest be explained? (page 175)

3. The Holy Roman Empire in the Twelfth Century. MAP 10.3. From a geographical perspective, discuss its impact on the relations between the Holy Roman Empire and the Papacy. (page 176)

4. Eastern Europe. MAP 10.4. Locate the Germanic and the Slavic territories of northern and eastern Europe. What geographical features might explain the prevalence of wars and conquests in the region? (page 177)

5. The Early Crusades. MAP 10.5. What factors might explain why it was only the Third Crusade and not the earlier crusades which made use of sea travel to the Holy Land? (page 185)

DISCUSSION QUESTIONS FOR THE PRIMARY SOURCES (BOXED DOCUMENTS)

1. "Magna Carta": Summarize the major principles of the Magna Carta as seen in this excerpt. Why has the Magna Carta been considered such an important historical document? What groups were affected by the Magna Carta, and which were not? Is the Magna Carta a "modern" document? Why and/or why not? (page 173)

2. "A Miracle of Saint Bernard": What does this story illustrate about the nature of a medieval "holy man?" How might such documents drive and shape recruitment of new members to Catholic monastic orders? (page 181)

3. "Treatment of the Jews": What do these documents reveal about Christian attitudes toward the Jews? What fears or base motives in Christian communities may have aggravated the development of such virulently anti-Semitic attitudes? (page 183)

4. "The Siege of Jerusalem: Christian and Muslim Perspectives": What do these documents reveal about the crusading ideals of Europeans? Given the great murders, robberies, and other crimes committed by the Christian crusaders, what can you say about the probable affects of the Crusades on European society? On Muslim society–then and since? (page 186)

STUDENT RESEARCH AND PROJECT TOPICS

1. Compare the political developments in France and England with those in the Holy Roman Empire and Italy. What similarities do you find? What differences do you find? How do you explain the differences?

2. Discuss the attempts at reform of the Catholic church. What were the effects of reform on the relationship between popes and emperors? How was their conflict resolved?

3. Discuss the background to the crusades. What key events precipitated these forays of European knights toward the Holy Land? What were the underlying reasons for the crusades? What were the principal motivations of the crusaders?

4. The crusades have been called "successful failures." In your opinion, why is this statement true?

5. Discuss specifically the role of monastic orders, old and new, in shaping the politics and culture of medieval Europe.

6. The papacy underwent dramatic reforms and modifications in medieval times. How did this institution change at this time? What powers did it gain? What powers or influence did it lose?

7. What was the inquisition? Who founded the court and what was its purpose? What factors in medieval European society prompted the creation of this body? How effective was its operation in the great medieval proliferation of heresy?

8. Briefly explain intolerance in the thirteenth century. What groups were singled out for attack? Why were they attacked?

9. How does the behavior of Saint Francis of Assisi exemplify a return to early Christian ideals of church organization and operation? What does his great popularity and veneration among ordinary Europeans tell you about popular religion in medieval times?

10. What were the chief spiritual aims of the Catholic mendicant orders? How did the means they chose to reach these spiritual goals affect European society and politics especially in cities?

11. Discuss how the church administration of the seven sacraments shaped the lives of ordinary Europeans from cradle to grave.

IDENTIFICATIONS

1. Battle of Hastings
2. Plantagenets
3. common law
4. Thomas Becket
5. Magna Carta
6. Parliament
7. Capetian dynasty
8. Philip II Augustus
9. Philip IV the Fair
10. Estates-General
11. Aragon and Castile
12. Holy Roman Empire
13. Otto I
14. Frederick I Barbarossa and Frederick II
15. Florence and Milan
16. Teutonic Knights
17. the Mongols and Genghis Kahn
18. Alexander Nevsky
19. abbey of Cluny
20. Pope Gregory VII
21. lay investiture/Investiture Controversy
22. Concordat of Worms
23. papal monarchy.
24. Pope Innocent III
25. Cistercians
26. St. Bernard of Clairvaux
27. Hildegard of Bingen
28. St. Francis of Assisi
29. Dominicans

30 sacraments and holy relics
31 the Virgin Mary
32 Cathars/Albigensians
33 Holy Office/Inquisition
34 the Crusades
35 Seljuk Turks
36 Battle of Manzikert

37. Pope Urban at Clermont
38. crusader states
39. Saladin
40. Fourth Crusade

MULTIPLE CHOICE QUESTIONS

1. Feudalism in England under William I differed from feudalism in other countries in that
    a. he de-emphasize the role of knights.
    b. he required subvassals to swear allegiance to him.
    c. homage was eliminated.
    d. fiefs were drastically reduced in size.
        ANSWER: b (page 171)

2. Under William of Normandy and his son Henry I, medieval England
    a. saw its Anglo-Saxon institutions abolished and replaced by Norman ones.
    b. was isolated from continental affairs.
    c. developed a strong, centralized monarchy.
    d. saw all of its land become part of the Norman family's demesne.
        ANSWER: c (p. 171)

3. William of Normandy's conquest of England in 1066
    a. saw the Anglo-Saxon nobility retain their power and influence.
    b. resulted in the death of King Harold at the Battle of Hastings.
    c. was condemned by Pope Innocent III.
    d. led directly to the First Crusade.
        ANSWER: b (p. 171)

4. Henry II's conflict over legal jurisdictions with the church culminated in
    a. his assassination by a fanatic priest.
    b. his flight to France to escape excommunication.
    c. the murder of the Archbishop of Canterbury, Thomas Becket.
    d. the bankruptcy of his treasury.
        ANSWER: c (p. 171)

5. One of the great political developments in England in the thirteenth century was
    a. the Magna Carta, in which King John ended medieval rights and feudal obligations between king and nobles.
    b. the establishment of the English parliament.
    c. Edward I's successful unification of all the British Isles into a single feudal kingdom.
    d. Edward I's Great Estates Council.
        ANSWER: b (p. 172)

6. The Magna Carta was drawn up in
    a. France.
    b. England.
    c. Italy.
    d. Germany.
        ANSWER: b (p. 172)

7. The Magna Carta
   a. asserted royal rights over the church.
   b. gave the king the right to regulate all economic matters.
   c. limited the power of the English king.
   d. served to centralize government authority.
      ANSWER: c (p. 172)

8. Parliament in England originally arose from
   a. the popular demand of the people.
   b. the insistence of the nobles.
   c. the king's need to collect new taxes.
   d. the old Celtic tradition of Druidic councils.
      ANSWER: c (p. 172)

9. When the rule of the Capetians began at the end of the tenth century
   a. France was the most powerful country in Europe.
   b. the French king only controlled an area known as the Ile-de-France.
   c. the French had just defeated the English in the Hundred Year's War.
   d. Bordeaux was the French capital.
      ANSWER: b (p.172)

10. During the fourteenth-century development of the French monarchy
   a. Philip II suffered defeats at the hands of King John.
   b. Louis IX was known for his blatant denial of his subjects' rights.
   c. King Alfonso X encouraged the development of three religions.
   d. Philip IV inaugurated the Estates-General, France's first parliament.
      ANSWER: d (p. 173)

11. By the end of the twelfth century, Spain was
   a. free of Muslim control in the northern half of the country.
   b. a fully united Christian kingdom.
   c. once again completely under the control of the Muslims.
   d. the most powerful nation in Europe.
      ANSWER: a (p. 174)

12. The Christian reconquest of Spain in the thirteenth century
   a. brought an economic revival, especially for the Andalusian region.
   b. saw a politically united Spain.
   c. saw the king of Castile, Alfonso X, expel all Jews and Muslims.
   d. left Granada the last Muslim kingdom on the Iberian peninsula.
      ANSWER: d (p. 174)

13. During the eleventh and twelfth centuries, Holy Roman Emperors
   a. expanded the boundaries of the Empire.
   b. increased the size of their armies dramatically.
   c. attempted to exploit the resources of Italy.
   d. bankrupted their kingdom with their lavish spending.
      ANSWER: c (p. 175)

14. Frederick II of Hohenstaufen

a. was a dynamic man, but allowed his kingdom to fall into chaos by leading military ventures in Italy.
b. was considered incompetent by his contemporaries.
c. was a brilliant scholar who wrote treatises on political philosophy.
d. was perhaps the greatest military leader of the Middle Ages.

ANSWER: a (p. 176)

15. The Saxon king who was crowned emperor of the Romans in 962 was

a. Charlemagne.
b. Otto I.
c. Hugh Capet.
d. Henry II.

ANSWER: b (p. 174)

16. The Mongol invasions of eastern Europe and Russia eventually led to

a. the dominance of Alexander Nevsky's descendants over all of Russia.
b. a cultural legacy that had great influence on eastern Europe.
c. the Mongols' defeat at the hands of the Teutonic Knights in Silesia in 1241.
d. the temporary destruction of the Russian church.

ANSWER: a (p. 178)

17. Between the eighth and tenth centuries, serious challenges to the power of the papacy included all of the following except

a. Italy's political fragmentation.
b. recurrent outbreaks of plague in Constantinople.
c. military threats from Muslim powers.
d. attempts by German emperors to rule northern and central Italy.

ANSWER: b (p. 178)

18. The secularization of bishops and abbots in the Early Middle Ages led to

a. the collapse of Christian worship in many places.
b. greater popular respect for the church.
c. a serious decline in the execution of their spiritual duties weakening the moral authority of the church.
d. greater respect shown to the church and its officials by nobles.

ANSWER: c (p. 178)

19. The Cluniac reform movement

a. argued that the Holy Roman Emperor received his power from God.
b. sought to reform monasteries and then to uphold the highest spiritual ideals in the church.
c. began in Germany.
d. saw the papacy lose control over the church.

ANSWER: b (pp. 178-179)

20. The abbot of Cluny and the Cluniac reform movement

a. remained free of secular control.
b. frowned on communal worship and stressed individualism.
c. tied monasteries more closely to lay noble lords.
d. became most influential in England in the tenth century.

ANSWER: a (pp. 178-179)

21. "Lay investiture" refers to the process by which
   a. secular lords took a decisive role in choosing prelates for all types of church offices.
   b. worthy lay people were educated for high office by the church.
   c. clerics guilty of high crimes were imprisoned in noble castles.
   d. lords were selected by clerics to become chivalric defenders of the church.
      ANSWER: a (p. 179)

22. Pope Gregory VII
   a. claimed that popes had authority even over emperors.
   b. stated that popes should not be involved in the everyday activities of the church.
   c. increased the Church's missionary activities to China.
   d. collected new taxes to finance building programs.
      ANSWER: a (p. 179)

23. The investiture controversy refers to
   a. the right of imperial courts to pass judgment on clerics.
   b. the argument over who should get funds from church tithes.
   c. the designation of heirs to the imperial throne.
   d. the struggle between popes and lay rulers over who possesses the real power to appoint important clerics like bishops and abbots.
      ANSWER: d (p. 179)

24. All of the following is correct about the Mongols *except*
   a. they established a ruling dynasty in China.
   b. they defeated the Byzantines at the Battle of Manzikert.
   c. they were initially unified under Genghis Kahn.
   d. they were unsuccessful in permanently conquering western Europe.
      ANSWER: b (p. 177)

25. By the Concordat of Worms, in 1122,
   a. the pope excommunicated the German emperor.
   b. German lay rulers abandoned Catholicism.
   c. the papacy and German kings resolved the investiture controversy by giving royal and papal officers equal roles in the creation of new bishops.
   d. the papacy unilaterally declared its supreme authority over all appointments of clerics to church posts anywhere.
      ANSWER: c (p. 179)

26. The church during the twelfth century became very centralized, chiefly due to
   a. the work of very capable bishops.
   b. an efficient and well-organized Papal Curia.
   c. the influence of the monastic orders.
   d. a series of democratic and efficient popes.
      ANSWER: b (p. 179)

27. The papacy reached its zenith of power in the thirteenth century during the papacy of
   a. Urban II.
   b. Pius III.
   c. Innocent III.
   d. Boniface VIII.
      ANSWER: c (p. 179)

28. The interdict was
   a. used by emperors to remove popes from office.
   b. used by the church, forbidding priests from administering the sacraments.
   c. a new ritual used in the Cistercian monasteries.
   d. was employed by Moslems again the First Crusade.
      ANSWER: b (p. 181)

29. The Cistercians, a new reform-minded monastic order,
   a. grew very slowly in the eleventh century.
   b. decorated their churches with numerous religious and non-religious subjects.
   c. spent more time in private prayer and manual labor by curtailing religious services.
   d. endorsed serfdom and were supported by peasant labor services.
      ANSWER: c (p. 180)

30. Saint Bernard of Clairvaux was well known for his
   a. portrayal of Christ and the saints in personalized terms.
   b. founding of Cistercian scholasticism.
   c. support of Thomas Aquinas' writings.
   d. criticism of the militant, crusading attitude of medieval Christianity.
      ANSWER: a (pp. 180-181)

31. Hildegard of Bingen, one of the most accomplished nuns of the twelfth century, is noted for all of the following <u>except</u>
   a. her three books.
   b. her mystical visions of the divine.
   c. her fame as abbess of a convent.
   d. her abuse by kings and popes as a "false prophet."
      ANSWER: d (p. 180)

32. Female monasticism in the twelfth century
   a. was a new phenomenon.
   b. was a refuge for women of all classes.
   c. declined due to the changing, negative view of women.
   d. had its strongest intellectual tradition in Germany.
      ANSWER: d (p. 180)

33. Saint Dominic, founder of the new Dominican order of preachers,
   a. was chiefly concerned with limiting papal power.
   b. did not embrace the necessity of poverty for the members of new church orders.
   c. distinguished himself as an intellectual and sought to create a new order of learned prelates to fight heresy within the church.
   d. worked most closely with popes to reform the Papal Curia.
      ANSWER: c (p. 181)

34. The most important saint in the High Middle Ages was
   a. Paul.
   b. Mary.
   c. Nicholas.
   d. Augustine.
      ANSWER: b (pp. 181-182)

35. Francis of Assisi and his followers
  a. retreated from the secular world into isolated monasteries.
  b. sought the favor of popes in the papal campaign against heretics.
  c. led the First Crusade in capturing Jerusalem.
  d. preached repentance aided the poor.
    ANSWER: a (p. 181)

36. The sacramental system of the Catholic church
  a. would not be clearly defined until the fifteenth century.
  b. made the church an integral part of the people's lives from birth to death.
  c. was deemed unnecessary as part of salvation by the Fourth Lateran Council in 1215.
  d. made the weekly reception of the Eucharist mandatory for all Christians.
    ANSWER: b (p. 181)

37. The Dominican monastic order
  a. was officially recognized by the pope as an order.
  b. emphasized on elite education and protection of orthodox theology.
  c. rejected of a vow of poverty for members.
  d. accepted women for service in the order.
    ANSWER: b (p. 181)

38. The Third Crusade was all of the following *except*
  a. it was a consequence of the fall of Jerusalem.
  b. it was a reaction to the conquests of Saladin.
  c. it permanently recaptured Jerusalem for Christendom.
  d. three Christian monarchs participated.
    ANSWER: c (pp. 186-187)

39. The Albigensians believed
  a. in a dualism between good spiritual things and evil material ones.
  b. that the Waldensians and Cathars were the emissaries of Satan.
  c. that the Catholic church was the proper institution for all Christians.
  d. that procreation helped free the soul from earthly bondage.
    ANSWER: a (p. 182)

40. The Albigensian heresy was viciously attacked and brutally crushed by the church because
  a. the Cathars, or "pure ones," believed that the Catholic Church was a materialistic institution and thus evil.
  b. the movement antagonized local nobles, and clerics sought to gain favor with them by killing the heretics.
  c. many cardinals took up its beliefs.
  d. sympathizers with the movement lived throughout Christendom.
    ANSWER: a (p. 182)

41. The papal inquisition was
  a. also known as he Holy Office.
  b. often utilized Dominican monks as inquisitors.
  c. devised to deal with heretics.
  d. used against the Jews.
    ANSWER: d (p. 182)

42. The persecutions against European Jews in the High Middle Ages were
a. openly encouraged by Christian mendicants and preachers.
b. continually opposed by European Christian monarchs.
c. led by rural peasants.
d. only temporary and had no lasting impact.
ANSWER: e (pp. 182-183)

43. By the thirteenth century, a previous acceptance of homosexuality by church and society had been replaced by Christian persecution of homosexuals due to all of the following <u>except</u>
a. the writings of Thomas Aquinas.
b. a rising tide of intolerance in Europe.
c. the identification of homosexuals with other detested minority groups in society.
d. papal decrees which had condemned the lifestyle since the Early Middle Ages.
ANSWER: d (p. 183)

44. The Islamic world in the mid-eleventh century was unified and dominated by the
a. Fatimids.
b. Seljuks.
c. Berbers.
d. Abbasids.
ANSWER: b (p. 184)

45. In 1071, at Manzikert, the Seljuk Turks defeated the
a. Fatimids.
b. Normans.
c. Byzantines.
d. Germans
ANSWER: c (p. 184)

46. Pope Urban II at the Council of Clermont in 1095
a. promised remissions of sins for joining the crusades to recapture the Holy Land.
b. appointed Peter the Hermit as leader of the crusades.
c. urged the destruction of all Jewish settlements on the crusaders' way to the Holy Land.
d. urged religious toleration.
ANSWER: a (p. 185)

47. After taking the city of Jerusalem in 1099, the Christian soldiers of the First Crusade
a. massacred most of the men, women, and children in the captured city of Cairo.
b. created four Christian crusader states with feudal institutions.
c. sacked Constantinople on their way home.
d. traveled to Rome to receive the pope's blessing.
ANSWER: b (p. 186)

48. An important result of the First Crusade was
a. a cultural exchange between Christian soldiers and Muslims.
b. the establishment of four Latin kingdoms in Palestine, ruled by Emperor Alexius I.
c. rapid economic growth and wealth for Italian commercial cities with maritime ties to the crusader states.
d. the economic rejuvenation of the Byzantine Empire.
ANSWER: c (p. 188)

49. All of the following were aspects of the fourth crusade except the
a. Venetian use of Christian forces to attack their economic rivals.
b. sack of Constantinople by Christian crusaders.
c. restoration of the Byzantine Empire as a great Mediterranean power.
d. establishment of the Latin Empire of Constantinople.
ANSWER: c (p. 187)

50. Which of the following was not a result of the crusades?
a. some cultural exchanges between Christians and Muslims
b. new economic growth of Italian port cities
c. the growth in power of eastern crusader states
d. increasingly common and violent attacks on European Jews by Christians
ANSWER: c (pp. 187-188)

RELEVANT WORLD-WIDE WEB SITES/RESOURECES

1. The Bayeux Tapestry:
http://orb.rhodes.edu/schriber/bayeux_tapestry.html
(Beautiful illustrations and commentary on this visual chronicle of the Normans' invasion of England.)

2. Internet Islamic History Source Book:
http://www.fordham.edu/halsall/islam/islamsbook.html
(An excellent on-line source of major original documents in translation with extensive links to other relevant sites on the web. Excellent for both Islam and Byzantium.)

3. Vatican Museums, Rome:
http://www.christusrex.org/www1/vaticano/0-Musei.html
(A superb and amply illustrated site ideal for research on cultural patronage of medieval and Renaissance papacy.)

RELEVANT VIDEO RESOURCES

Crescent and Cross: Rise of Islam and the Age of the Crusades,
Films for the Humanities and Social Sciences, (52 minutes).
(Examines geopolitics of the crusades, role of Christian monastic orders in these conflicts, and rise of Christian religious intolerance.)

The Western Tradition, Part I, Annenberg/CPB Collection/PBS Home Video, (30 minutes each program), Programs 19 and 20, "The Middle Ages" and "The Feudal Order."

A World Inscribed: The Illuminated Manuscript, Films for the Humanities and Sciences, (23 minutes). (Merited the O'Connor Film Award from the American Historical Assoc. Covers book illumination and noble bibliographic patronage from fifth to fourteenth centuries.)

Great Kings of England, PBS Home Video, 5 cassettes, (45 minutes each). (Profiles here include William the Conqueror, Alfred the Great, and Richard the Lionheart.)

The Magna Carta, Films for the Humanities and Sciences,(22 minutes). (Prize-winning production on the content, meaning, and influence of the charter.)

Medieval Realms: Britain from 1066-1500, CD-ROM (Windows Format Only), Films for the Humanities and Sciences.
(Contents: illuminated manuscripts, historic documents, pictures of historic structures, modern English extracts from letters, charters, and court documents of the era, and musical/spoken word performances all drawn from collections of British Library.)

RELEVANT MUSICAL PERFORMANCES

Music and Poetry at Saint Gall, Harmonia Mundi France CD. (Ninth-century monastic music and prayer.)

Les premières polyphonies françaises (Earliest French Polyphony), Virgin Veritas CD (No. 7243 5 4513527). (Eleventh-century monastic chants and sung prayers.)

Monastic Song: 12th-Century Monophonic Chant, Harmonia Mundi France CD. (Hymns and laments composed by Peter Abelard, one of the finest academic minds of the era.)

Hildegard von Bingen, Ordo Virtutem (The Play of the Virtues), Deutsche Harmonia Mundi 2 CDs (No. 05472-77394-2). (Twelfth-century music drama for church celebration written by most noted early medieval nun and female composer of sacred music.)

SUGGESTED STUDENT ACTIVITIES

1. Culture in Spain has a definite Muslim influence. Have students write a synopsis of Muslim contributions to the culture of Spain.

2. Scholars consider the two most powerful popes of the Middle Ages to be Gregory VII and Innocent III. Have students do an essay comparing the lives of these two great pontiffs.

3. Have students do a comparative study of the lives of Saint Francis of Assisi and Saint Bernard of Clairvaux, being sure to bring out similarities and differences.

4. A few scholars have maintained that the Jews have not gone through one holocaust but several and that the first great persecution took place during the Middle Ages. Have students prove or disprove this idea in the form of a paper or debate.

CHAPTER 11
THE LATE MIDDLE AGES: CRISIS AND DISINTEGRATION IN THE FOURTEENTH CENTURY

CHAPTER OUTLINE

I. A Time of Troubles: Black Death and Social Crisis
- A. The Black Death
  - 1. Life and Death: Reactions to the Plague
- B. Economic Dislocation and Social Upheaval
  - 1. Peasant Revolts
  - 2. Revolts in the Cities

II. War and Political Instability
- A. The Hundred Years' War
- B. Political Instability
- C. Western Europe: England and France
- D. The German Monarchy
- E. The States of Italy

III. The Decline of the Church
- A. Boniface VIII and the Conflict with the State
- B. The Papacy at Avignon (1305-1378)
- C. The Great Schism

IV. Culture and Society in an Age of Diversity
- A. The Development of Vernacular Literature
- B. Art and the Black Death
- C. Changes in Urban Life
- D. Inventions and New Patterns

V. Conclusion

CHAPTER SUMMARY

The fourteenth century was an era of crisis. A "little ice" age led to famine, but a greater disaster followed: the Black Death. The bubonic plague was spread by black rats' fleas, carrying the bacterium *Yersina pestis*, while the pneumonic variety was transmitted through the air from person to person. It reached Europe in 1347. In a few years, up to 50 percent of the population died, with higher mortality rates in urban areas. It returned every few years for centuries.

Reactions differed. Some escaped into alcohol, sex, and crime. Others, believing the Black Death to be a punishment from God, attempted to atone for their sins through self-inflicted pain. The Jews became scapegoats. People fled, carrying the plague with them. The resulting labor shortage could benefit peasants, although the demand for products was also reduced. When the ruling classes reduced wage rates there were peasant revolts. The ruling classes quelled the revolts, but social upheaval continued to plague the post-plague world.

Wars were also part of the crisis, notably the Hundred Years War between England and France. In 1328 the French Capetian line ended. England's Edward III (d.1377) claimed the French throne, but a cousin to the Capets, Philip of Valois, became king (d.1350). War soon began. Armored knights on horseback was the backbone of medieval armies, but English peasants using the longbow had begun to change the face of war. When the French king was captured, a treaty was signed in 1360: France agreed to pay ransom, the English received land in France, and Edward renounced his claim to the throne. Using guerilla tactics, the French regained their lands, but in 1415 England's Henry V (d.1422) invaded. The French cause was saved by Joan of Arc (d.1431), a young peasant woman who claimed to have been told by an angel and saints that she should offer her support to the dauphin-the heir to the throne. Her leadership inspired the French, who also began to rely on cannon, and by 1453 France had won.

During Edward III's reign, Parliament gained control over taxes, increasing its power. In France, however, the Estates-General failed to achieve the same influence. Both kingdoms were also driven by aristocratic factions. In Germany, dukedoms and city-states went their own way, independent of the Holy Roman Emperor, itself an elective office. Italy was divided into small kingdoms in the south, the Papal States in central Italy, and several city-states in the north, notably Milan and the oligarchic republics of Florence and Venice. Warfare was endemic.

The papacy declined. Confrontation between France's Philip IV (d.1314) and Pope Boniface VIII led to the removal of the papacy to Avignon on France's border in 1305. From 1377 there were two competing popes. Some argued that a general council, not the pope, should rule the church, and Conciliarism did end the Great Schism. There was a preoccupation with salvation. Some turned to good works, others to mysticism and devotional movements. The scholastics' confidence in reason was attacked: God's existence could only be "proved" by faith.

Vernacular literature was exemplified in Italy by Dante in Italy, Chaucer in England, and Christine de Pizan in France. In art, Giotto explored three-dimensional realism. After the Black Death, artists frequently portrayed subjects of death and decay. The impact of the plague led to urban public health regulations, to younger marriages, and to a greater division of gender roles under the assumption that women were the weaker sex. Technological developments included the perfection of the clock and eyeglasses, and paper began to replace parchment. Finally, the development of gunpowder blew the Middle Ages into history.

LECTURE AND DISCUSSION TOPICS

1. Discuss the interrelationship of disease and history, using the Black Death as a case study.

2. Assess both the causes and the consequences of the Black Death.

3. Examine the Hundred Years' War as a transition event between the Middle Ages and the modern world.

4. Explore the phenomena of uprisings and revolts from the underside of society, using the post-plague Peasant Revolts as a historical model.

5. Compare and contrasts the lives of Henry V of England and France's Joan of Arc, both as historical events and as national symbols.

6. Discuss the breakdown of the feudal system, the wars and conflicts which resulted, and the eventual emergence of stronger monarchies, using France and England as examples.

7. Examine the "German problem" and the "Italian problem" in the fifteenth century.

8. Assess the causes and the consequences of the decline of papal authority and its impact on church-state relations in the fourteenth and fifteenth centuries.

9. Discuss the similarities and differences between western society after the decline of the Western Roman Empire and Europe in the aftermath of the Black Death.

10. Explore the impact of late medieval technology and inventions upon European society, including their beliefs and values.

MAP EXERCISES

1. The Spread of the Black Death. MAP 11.1. What areas were largely spared from the impact of the plague, and was geography, including distance from the eastern Mediterranean, the primary explanation? (page 194)

2. The Hundred Years' War. MAP 11.2. Compare the lands in France controlled in England in 1360 with those held in 1429. How do they differ? What part did geographical proximity to England as well as the regions in France historically and traditionally under English control play in England's successes d during the war? (page 197)

DISCUSSION QUESTIONS FOR THE PRIMARY SOURCES (BOXED DOCUMENTS)

1. "The Black Death" from Giovanni Boccaccio, *Decameron*": What evidence does this excerpt provide on the total collapse of Italian urban civilization as it was structured before the advent of the plague? What might have been the political, economic, religious, and social consequences of such an event? (page 193)

2. "The Trial of Joan of Arc": What does the career of Joan as a royal advisor and soldier tell you about the culture of late medieval France? How do kings and courtiers respond to Joan and what forces may conspire to explain her extraordinary accomplishments and horrific end? (page 199)

3. "Boniface VIII's Defense of Papal Supremacy": What claims does Boniface VIII make in *Unam Sanctam*? To what extent are these claims a logical continuation of the development of the papacy in the Middle Ages? If you were a monarch, would you object to this papal bull? Why and/or why not? (page 203)

4. "Dante's Vision of Hell": What realism does Dante convey with this scene? How would this piece of literature compare with earlier medieval works? Why would the church oppose this work? What lessons do you think this work was intended to teach its readers? (page 204)

STUDENT RESEARCH AND PROJECT TOPICS

1. To what extent were climate and disease key factors in producing economic and social changes?

2. Discuss the factors that led to the urban and rural revolts in the fourteenth century. Was desperate poverty a chief cause? Why or why not?

3. "When Adam delved and Eve span, who was then a gentleman?" Discuss the key characteristics and implications of this revolutionary slogan as it contributed to the formation of English peasant political culture.

4. Discuss the Hundred Years' War: What were its causes? Why did the war continue for so long a period in the fourteenth century? What advantages did each side possess? What were the results of the war in the fourteenth century for France and England?

5. What major problems did European states face in the fourteenth century? How are these problems evident in the history of England, France, and the Holy Roman Empire?

6. What changes occurred in the political life of Italy during the fourteenth century?

7. Trace the events of the papacy's decline during the fourteenth century.

8. What was the main causes of the Great Schism? What were the major results of this great political and religious conflict?

9. What do we mean by vernacular literature? Give some examples of fourteenth-century vernacular literature and compare them to the vernacular literature of the twelfth and thirteenth centuries. Was there a significant change in subject matter? Why or why not? What common themes remained?

10. How did the adversities of the fourteenth century affect urban life and medical practices at the time?

IDENTIFICATIONS

1. "little ice age"
2. Black Death
3. bubonic plague
4. *Yersinia pestis*
5. pneumonic plague
6. flagellants
7. pogroms
8. the *Jacquerie*
9. Wat Tyler and John Ball
10. the *ciompi*
11. the longbow
12. Battle of Crecy
13. Henry V
14. Battle of Agincourt

15. Joan of Arc
16. Orleans
17. Charles VII
18. gunpowder
19. dukes of Burgundy and Orleans
20. Golden Bull of Charles IV
21. Italian communes
22. the Visconti and the d'Este
23. Pope Boniface VIII's *Unam Sanctam*
24. Avignon
25. Catherine of Siena
26. Great Schism
27. the "Antichrist"
28. Council of Constance
29. the vernacular
30. Dante's *Divine Comedy*
31. Chaucer's *Canterbury Tales*
32. Christine de Pizan's *Book of the Ladies*
33. *ars moriendi*
34. Giotto
35. clocks

MULTIPLE CHOICE QUESTIONS

1. Among the adverse economic and population changes in fourteenth-century Europe were
    a. global warming.
    b. disastrous weather conditions.
    c. a rapidly increasing population.
    d. a transition to incompetent urban commune governments which led to violent riots.
        ANSWER: d (p. 192)

2. What was the main cause of the fourteenth century famines?
    a. a blight that struck the wheat crop
    b. a lack of knowledge of scientific agriculture
    c. droughts throughout most of Europe
    d. a little ice age inducing bad weather with heavy rains
        ANSWER: d (p. 192)

3. The Black Death was most devastating in
    a. Italy.
    b. Germany.
    c. Eastern Europe.
    d. Scandinavia.
        ANSWER: a (p. 192)

4. The Black Death
   a. was one of many European plagues from the eighth century.
   b. started in northern Europe and moved southward to Italy.
   c. recurred in severe outbreaks for centuries.
   d. never reached England.
      ANSWER: c (p. 193)

5. The percentage of the European population believed to have been wiped out by the Black Death was
   a. ten to twenty.
   b. twenty-five to fifty.
   c. fifty to sixty.
   d. over seventy-five.
      ANSWER: b (p. 193)

6. All of the following were psychological reactions to the great plague <u>except</u>
   a. an increase in violence and murder due to a sense of life's cheapness.
   b. the formation of groups like the flagellants, who physically maimed themselves to save the world.
   c. a reduction in the persecution of religious minorities because of the displeasure it caused God.
   d. morbidity and preoccupation with death in everyday life.
      ANSWER: c (p. 194)

7. The flagellants
   a. were praised by the Catholic church for their miraculous deeds.
   b. were groups that physically punished themselves to win the forgiveness of God.
   c. were a new phenomenon that arose in response to the Hundred Years' War.
   d. would remain a popular religious movement throughout the fourteenth century.
      ANSWER: b (p. 193)

8. The persecutions against Jews during the Black Death
   a. were instigated at the calling of the Catholic church.
   b. led to the execution of nearly all of the Jews in eastern Europe.
   c. reached their worst excesses in German cities.
   d. had little to do with financial motives.
      ANSWER: c (p. 194)

9. The devastation of the great plague in the fourteenth century led to
   a. the perception of life as something cheap and passing.
   b. a decrease in crime due to an increase in religious piety.
   c. an increase in the number of clergy.
   d. all of the above
      ANSWER: a (p. 194)

10. Economically, the great plague and the crises of the fourteenth century
   a. devastated peasants but not nobles.
   b. brought an economic boom to landlords.
   c. caused only minor changes in agricultural practices.
   d. raised wages because of a scarcity of labor.
      ANSWER: d (p. 195)

11. Overall, due to the socioeconomic dislocations caused by the plague, the incomes of European aristocrats after 1347

a. increased as they developed crushing monopolies on food supply.

b. f ell dramatically as the wages they paid to laborers went up while prices for their agricultural products fell due to lower aggregate demand.

c. remained largely unchanged especially in England.

d. rose slowly as disruptions in urban trade cut into their profit margins for food supply.

ANSWER: b (p. 195)

12. The European aristocracy responded to the adversity of the great plague by

a. seeking to lower wages especially for farm laborers.

b. producing only the most basic foodstuffs, such as grain.

c. petitioning kings to order the relocation of laborers.

d. forming agricultural cooperatives linking landowners, laborers, and city consumers.

ANSWER: a (p. 195)

13. Post-plague socioeconomic relations between rich and poor in Europe

a. got much worse as materially threatened nobles began to regard wealthier peasants as base animals.

b. improved noticeably as Christians sought to make peace with one another to please an angry God.

c. quickly resumed their pre-plague character.

d. suffered as richer nobles rebuffed the sincere efforts of peasants to maintain the manorial system.

ANSWER: a (p. 195)

14. A key economic consequence of the plague was

a. the rapid expansion of European civic banking to rebuild industry.

b. a decline in manorialism and weakening of feudalism as noble landlords desperate for cash converted peasant labor service to market rents freeing their serfs.

c. the more frequent bankruptcy of monarchs as they emptied their treasuries trying to provide poor relief.

d. the very slow enrichment of middling peasant laborers who began to dominate rural communities.

ANSWER: b (p. 195)

15. The *Jacquerie* refers to

a. a revolt of the peasants in England in 1381.

b. elite French troops.

c. a peasant's revolt in France in 1358.

d. a group of French advisors to the king.

ANSWER: c (p. 195)

16. The English Peasants' Revolt of 1381 differed from some other revolts in that it

a. was caused by rising economic expectations of ordinary people.

b. was brutally crushed by the nobles.

c. succeeded in getting the government to agree to the peasants' demands.

d. gained long-term results for the peasants.

ANSWER: a (p. 195)

17. Among the leaders of the English Peasants' Revolt of 1381 was/were
   a. Wat Tyler and John Ball.
   b. John Froissart.
   c. the archbishop of Canterbury.
   d. Etienne Marcel.
      ANSWER: a (p. 195)

18. Merchants and manufacturers responded to the economic tribulations of the fourteenth century by
   a. increasing their prices.
   b. restricting competition and resisting the demands of the lower classes.
   c. blaming the Jews and persecuting them.
   d. pressuring the government to raise the prices of their products.
      ANSWER: b (p. 196)

19. The Hundred Years' War between France and England grew out of
   a. the strong personalities of Philip IV and Edward III.
   b. the dispute over the duchy of Gascony.
   c. economic problems and revolts in Portugal.
   d. a and b
      ANSWER: d (p. 196)

20. The progress of the Hundred Years' War was characterized by
   a. early French successes.
   b. a steady return to feudal-style armies.
   c. English use of peasant soldiers and the longbow.
   d. the English political subjugation of much of France.
      ANSWER: c (pp. 196-197)

21. An important element in the ultimate French victory in the Hundred Years' War was
   a. the use of peasants and longbows.
   b. armored warriors on horseback.
   c. the French capture and execution of England's King Edward III.
   d. the use of cannon and gunpowder.
      ANSWER: d (p. 198)

22. In the conduct of the Hundred Years' War, a sure sign of feudalism's decline was
   a. the inability of feuding kings to raise armies of knights.
   b. the reliance of kings on artillery as the main component of royal armies.
   c. the decisive role of peasant foot soldiers rather than mounted knights.
   d. the clear intention of kings to destroy the estates of their own vassals.
      ANSWER: c (pp. 197-198)

23. Joan of Arc
   a. helped defeat the British at the Battle of Agincourt.
   b. liberated Orleans and the Loire Valley from English control.
   c. saw her task accomplished when Henry V was crowned king of France in 1429.
   d. permanently confessed to the charges of heresy but recanted and was hanged by the neck.
      ANSWER: b (p. 198)

24. In 1415, the Hundred Years' War was restarted by the English King
a. Henry III.
b. Charles V.
c. Henry V.
d. Edward VIII.
ANSWER: c (p. 197)

25. During the reign of Edward III of England, the Great Council
a. became the chief advisory body of the king.
b. relinquished most of its main powers.
c. became the House of Lords forming a hereditary body of peers in Parliament.
d. became subservient to the House of Commons.
ANSWER: c (p. 199)

26. England under the reign of Edward III witnessed
a. the temporary demise of Parliament.
b. the House of Commons dominating the House of Lords in Parliament.
c. the defeat of Richard II in the War of the Roses.
d. the crown's acceptance of Parliament's right to approve royal taxation and to inspect government accounts.
ANSWER: d (p. 199)

27. Politically, France by the end of the fourteenth century saw
a. the dominance of the Estates-General in determining government policy and administering taxes.
b. no new forms of government revenue due to royal opposition.
c. chaos and civil war as rival noble factions fought for control of the realm.
d. new rights of political participation in the Parlement of Paris for poor townspeople.
ANSWER: c (pp. 199-200)

28. The Golden Bull of 1356 in Germany
a. made Emperor Charles IV the first in a line of hereditary rulers.
b. ensured the independence of the ecclesiastical states.
c. gave seven electors the power to choose the "King of the Romans."
d. ensured strong central authority for Germany in the next century.
ANSWER: c (p. 200)

29. Prior to the Golden Bull of 1356, Germany was a land composed of
a. free imperial city-states.
b. independent princely states.
c. ecclesiastical states.
d. all of the above
ANSWER: d (p. 200)

30. Politically, Italy and Germany were similar in the fourteenth century because
a. the plague had equally devastated both regions.
b. both regions failed to develop a centralized monarchical state.
c. local nobles and town governments lost much influence over reigning kings.
d. mercenary captains usurped royal authority and ruled violently.
ANSWER: b (pp. 200-201)

31. In the fifteenth century, Italy was
   a. united under the papacy.
   b. ruled by the Bourbons.
   c. divided up into numerous independent states.
   d. conquered by the Tudors.
      ANSWER: c (p. 201)

32. In the fifteenth century, Florence was ruled by
   a. the Hohenstaufen emperors.
   b. Venetian aristocrats.
   c. a merchant oligarchy.
   d. the papacy.
      ANSWER: c (p. 201)

33. The power of the Venetian city-state in the fourteenth century was based upon
   a. political control of the Mediterranean Sea region.
   b. being the bankers to the papacy.
   c. its maritime commercial empire.
   d. its mainland agricultural estates which produced wool for the eastern markets.
      ANSWER: c (p. 201)

34. Pope Boniface VIII
   a. reasserted papal supremacy with great success in the fourteenth century.
   b. renounced his claims to full temporal authority in *Unam Sanctam*.
   c. came into conflict with Edward I of England over the issue of taxing the clergy.
   d. died in 1305 after his captivity at the hands of Philip IV of France.
      ANSWER: d (p. 202)

35. The first of the French popes to reside at Avignon was
   a. Clement V.
   b. Boniface VIII.
   c. Gregory XI.
   d. John Paul II.
      ANSWER: a (p. 202)

36. The papacy at Avignon
   a. saw a decline in its prestige.
   b. gained the church much prestige.
   c. suffered due to a lack of incoming revenue.
   d. remained there until the seventeenth century.
      ANSWER: a (p. 202)

37. The Great Schism
   a. occurred when French forces executed the Italian pope on charges of heresy.
   b. further damaged the prestige and authority of the church.
   c. ended with the victory of Pope Clement VII.
   d. ended with the victory of Pope Urban VI.
      ANSWER: b (p. 203)

38. One overall result of the Great Schism was to
  a. put an end to the church's previous financial abuses.
  b. introduce institutional uncertainty into the lives of Christians.
  c. rejuvenate Christianity as it had been on the decline throughout Europe.
  d. end the abuse of pluralism.
    ANSWER: b (p. 203)

39. The Great Schism is known as that period in the history of the Catholic Church marked by
  a. the creation and feuding of multiple popes.
  b. the rise of new and powerful heretical movements.
  c. the division of Christendom over the question of toleration for Jews.
  d. disagreements among Christian theologians over the justice of killing those condemned for witchcraft.
    ANSWER: a (p. 203)

40. The chief accomplishment of the Council of Constance (1414-1418) was
  a. to set the earliest conditions for ending the Great Schism.
  b. to order the sack of Rome by French forces.
  c. to end once and for all the Great Schism by forcing the resignation or deposing all existing popes and paving the way for election of only one new pope, Martin V.
  d. to support biblical scholarship revealing clear support in scripture for multiple popes.
    ANSWER: c (pp. 203-204)

41. The fifteenth century artist who attempted to imitate nature was
  a. William of Occam.
  b. Gerhard Groote.
  c. Giotto.
  d. Boccaccio.
    ANSWER: c (p. 205)

42. The basic unit of the late medieval urban environment was the
  a. extended family.
  b. nuclear family.
  c. commune.
  d. Church council.
    ANSWER: b (p. 206)

43. All are correct about the *Divine Comedy except*
  a. it was written in Latin.
  b. it was the story of a soul's quest for salvation.
  c. its author was Dante Alighieri.
  d. it was written in the vernacular.
    ANSWER: b (p. 204)

44. What was Christine de Pizan's most famous work?
  a. *The Divine Comedy*.
  b. *Book of the City of Ladies*.
  c. *The Prince*.
  d. *Spiritual Exercises*.
    ANSWER: b (p. 205)

45. Dante's *Divine Comedy*
a. is considered a synthesis of medieval Christian thought.
b. was one of the last fourteenth-century works to be written in Latin.
c. lashed out at the "barbarity" of the classical tradition.
d. attacked the science of Aristotle, the Holy Roman Emperor, and the Catholic church.
ANSWER: a (p. 204)

46. Among the great and influential female religious mystics of the fourteenth century was
a. St. Ingrid of Bohemia.
b. Catherine of Siena.
c. Judith of Vienna.
d. Isabella of Ravenna.
ANSWER: b (p. 202)

47. A leading vernacular author in medieval England was
a. William Shakespeare.
b. Geoffrey Chaucer.
c. The Venerable Bede.
d. John Donne.
ANSWER: b (pp. 204-205)

48. Changed urban attitudes in the fourteenth century included
a. the promotion of equality between men and women in the workplace.
b. later marriages and increases in the number of extended families.
c. children being seen as valuable only in their capacity to work and earn money for the family.
d. strengthen the development of gender roles and limit employment opportunities for women.
ANSWER: d (p. 206)

49. A Chinese invention that made its appearance in the west in the fourteenth century was
a. paper.
b. gunpowder.
c. rice.
d. porcelain.
ANSWER: b (p. 206)

50. The most effective and revolutionary of fourteenth-century inventions occurred in the area of
a. the printing press.
b. paper.
c. eyeglasses.
d. clocks.
ANSWER: d (p. 206)

RELEVANT WORLD-WIDE WEB SITES/RESOURCES

1. Medieval France Documents:
http://history.hanover.edu/medieval/france.htm
(An excellent site in the Hanover College history series offering an array of primary documents and links on the history of France in the Middle Ages.)

RELEVANT VIDEO RESOURCES

The Circles of Light: The Divine Comedy, Films for the Humanities and Sciences, from the series "The Medieval Mind," (50 minutes).

Civilisation, PBS Media Video/BBC Television, Program 3, "Romance and Reality: The Middle Ages in France and Italy," (50 minutes).

The Western Tradition, Part I, Annenberg/CPB Collection/PBS Home Video, (30 minutes each program), Programs 23 and 24, "The Late Middle Ages" and "The National Monarchies."

SUGGESTED STUDENT ACTIVITIES

1. Have students do a short paper or a panel presentation on the different ways people in the Middle Ages reacted to the Black Plague.

2. Students could trace the development of the English Parliament from the time of the Great Council through the end of the 13th century.

3. Venice became a rich Italian city-state during the late Middle Ages. Have students write a short history of the great Italian city-state.

4. Joan of Arc was a fascinating woman, and there are several good books on her. Have students do a report, written or oral, on Joan.

5. Have students find evidence of medieval popular religion and mysticism in modern religious movements, perhaps both Christian and non-Christian.

CHAPTER 12
RECOVERY AND REBIRTH: THE RENAISSANCE

CHAPTER OUTLINE

I. Meaning and Characteristics of the Italian Renaissance
II. The Making of Renaissance Society
- A. Economic Recovery
- B. Social Changes in the Renaissance
  - 1. The Nobility
  - 2. Peasants and Townspeople
- C. Family and Marriage in Renaissance Italy

III. The Italian States in the Renaissance
- A. Machiavelli and the New Statecraft

IV. The Intellectual Renaissance in Italy
- A. Italian Renaissance Humanism
  - 1. Humanism and Philosophy
- B. Education in the Renaissance
- C. The Impact of Printing

V. The Artistic Renaissance
- A. The Northern Artistic Renaissance

VI. The European State in the Renaissance
- A. The Renaissance State in Western Europe
- B. Central Europe: The Holy Roman Empire
- C. The Struggle for Strong Monarchy in Eastern Europe
- D. The Ottoman Turks and the End of the Byzantine Empire

VII. The Church in the Renaissance
- A. The Problems of Heresy and Reform
- B. The Renaissance Papacy

VIII. Conclusion

CHAPTER SUMMARY

Beginning in Italy, the Renaissance (or "rebirth") was an era which rediscovered the culture of ancient Greece and Rome. It was also a time of recovery from the fourteenth century. In comparison with medieval society, the Renaissance had a more secular and individualistic ethos, but might best been seen as evolutionary in its urban and commercial continuity from the High Middle Ages. In the North Sea, the Hanseatic League competed with merchants from the Mediterranean, where the Venetians had a commercial empire. In Florence, profits from the woolen industry were invested in banking.

The aristocracy remained the ruling class, its ideals explicated in Castiglione's *The Book of the Courtier*. Peasants were still the vast majority, but serfdom and manorialism were dying out. An important minority were the inhabitants of towns and cities, with merchants and bankers at the apex and the unskilled workers at the bottom. The extended family was dominated by the father or husband as a dictator, and marriages were arranged for social and economic advantage. Wives were much younger than their husbands, with their primary function being to bear children; the mortality rate in childbirth and for infants and young children remained high.

Italy was dominated by five major states: the duchy of Milan, Florence, Venice, the Papal States, and the kingdom of Naples. There were also other city-states which were centers of culture and where women played vital roles. At the end of the fifteenth century, Spain and France invaded the divided peninsula. The exemplar of the new statecraft was Niccolo Machiavelli (d.527), whose *The Prince* described the methods of gaining and holding political power: moral concerns are irrelevant, for the ends justify the means.

There was an increased emphasis upon the human. Among the influential humanists was Petrarch (d.1374) in his advocacy of classical Latin writers. Civic humanism posited that the ideal citizen was not only an intellectual but also a patriot, actively serving the state, and. humanist education was to produce individuals of virtue and wisdom. The printing press was perfected, multiplying the availability of books. In art, the aim was to imitate nature by the use of realistic perspective. Masaccio (d.1428), Donatello (d.1466) and Michelangelo (d.1564) made Florence a locus of the arts. The High Renaissance of Michelangelo, Leonardo da Vinci (d.1519) and Raphael (d.1520) combined natural realism with Platonic idealism. The artisan might become a great artist, and thus transform his social and economic status.

It was the era of the "new monarchies." In France, Louis XI (d.1483), the Spider, established a centralized state. England's Henry VII (d.1509) limited the private armies of the aristocracy, raised taxes, and left a more powerful monarchy. In Spain, Isabella (d.1504) and Ferdinand (d.1516) created a professional army and enforced religious uniformity by the conversion and expulsion of Jews and Moslems. The Holy Roman Empire remained weak, but the Habsburg emperors created a strong state of their own through numerous marriages. The were no "new monarchies" in eastern Europe, but Russia's Ivan III (d.1505) ended Mongol control. Lastly, in 1453 the Ottoman Turks captured Constantinople.

The church was besieged by problems. John Hus (d.1415) condemned the papacy for corruption, its temporal concerns, and demanded the Bible in the vernacular. The popes reflected their era, and their secular involvements overshadowed their spiritual responsibilities. Some preferred war and politics to prayer and piety, and others ignored their vows of celibacy, ambitiously advancing their families over the needs of the faithful. Most were great patrons of the arts, but religious concerns ranked behind the pleasures of this life.

LECTURE AND DISCUSSION TOPICS

1. Explore the concept of the word "Renaissance," both as a satisfactory and also as an unsatisfactory designation for the West in the fifteenth and sixteenth centuries.

2. Discuss the essential characteristics and accomplishments of the Italian Renaissance and compare and contrast those with the Northern Renaissance.

3. Assess the development of printing and its impact on the development of western civilization, possibly with a comparison to the impact of the Internet today.

4. Explore the concept of "humanism" in the context of Renaissance society.

5. Discuss the role of women in the Renaissance: was rebirth and humanism only for men?

6. Present a slide lecture on the art of the Renaissance.

7. Examine urban society in the Renaissance with an emphasis upon who benefited and who did not in the Renaissance world.

8. Assess Machiavelli as historian and as prophet.

9. Explore the question of whether the "New Monarchies" were really new?

10. Discuss the church and the Renaissance, and the church's relationships to demands for church and spiritual reform.

MAP EXERCISES

1. Renaissance Italy. MAP 12.1. Because of historical proximity, what likely role did ancient Rome play in explaining why the Renaissance began in Italy? If so, why not Greece? Would the Renaissance have evolved in the same manner if Italy had been politically united, say under the Holy Roman Empire or the Papacy, rather than made up of several different and competitive states? (page 215)

2. Europe in the Renaissance. MAP 12.2. What are the geographical and historical reasons why state building was most successful in England, France, and Spain, and less successful in Italy and the Holy Roman Empire? Are geographical factors a possible explanation? (page 225)

DISCUSSION QUESTIONS FOR THE PRIMARY SOURCES (BOXED DOCUMENTS)

1. "A Renaissance Banquet": Describe the kinds of people who would be present at a banquet where the foods listed on this menu would be served. What does this excerpt tell you about the material culture of the Renaissance and the associations of food with social status? (page 211)

2. "Marriage Negotiations": What were the most important considerations in marriage negotiations? Why were they so important? Did personal choice play any role? If not, why not? (page 214)

3. "Machiavelli: 'Is It Better to be Loved than Feared?'": What does Machiavelli have to say about being loved rather than feared? How do his theories in this regard make his politics modern and distinguish his advice from Greco-Roman notions of good rulership? Is Machiavelli a cynic or a realist? Why? (page 217)

4. "A Woman's Defense of Learning" What were the reasons Laura Cereta complained about her status in Renaissance society? Does she see herself as unique? What were the expected interests and accomplishments of Renaissance women? Why were Renaissance women rarely taken seriously in their quest for educational opportunities and recognition for their intellectual talents? Were any of those factors unique to the Renaissance era? (page 219)

STUDENT RESEARCH AND PROJECT TOPICS

1. What were the characteristics of the Italian Renaissance? How did it differ from the Renaissance of the Twelfth Century?

2. In what ways did the European world experience an economic recovery in the fifteenth century? Did the revived economy differ greatly from what it had been?

3. Discuss the major social changes of the Renaissance era. Were these changes actually a rejection of medieval trends? Why or why not?

4. Discuss the political development of Italy during the Renaissance. What new political practices (statecraft) did the Italians contribute to Europe? How are these new political practices reflected in the work of Machiavelli?

5. Compare warfare in the Middle Ages with that of the Renaissance. Consider the differences and the continuities, as regards to causes, aims, financing, technology, as well as who fought and for what motives.

6. Discuss Italian Renaissance humanism. What does the word humanism mean? Who were the humanists? What were their goals? Did they achieve them?

7. Assume that you are a pupil in a Renaissance school. How would the curriculum differ from a medieval church school? Explain what kind of education you plan to receive. For what occupations will you be prepared?

8. What were the distinctive characteristics of the Renaissance artists? How does their art reflect the political and social events of the period?

9. "The major characteristic in the development of the 'new monarchies' was the expansion of central government authority in the areas of economic, political, judicial, military, and religious policy." Is this a valid statement in regard to England, Spain, and France? Was the pattern of political development the same in eastern Europe?

10. Discuss the major characteristics of the Renaissance papacy. What impact did the policies of the Renaissance popes have on the Catholic church?

IDENTIFICATIONS

1. *renaissance*
2. Jacob Burckhardt
3. Leon Battista Alberti
4. Hanseatic League
5. house of Medici
6. Castiglione's *Book of the Courtier*
7. Francisco Sforza
8. Cosimo d'Medici
9. Lorenzo the Magnificent
10. the Papal States
11. Isabella d'Este
12. 1527 sack of Rome
13. Machiavelli's *The Prince*
14. civic humanism

15. Petrarch
16. Bruni's *The New Cicero*
17. Marcilio Ficino and neoplatonism
18. Renaissance hermeticism
19. Pico della Mirandola's *Oration on the Dignity of Man*
20. "liberal studies"
21. Johannes Gutenberg
22. Masaccio
23. Donatello's *David*
24. Brunelleschi
25. High Renaissance
26. Leonardo da Vinci's *Last Supper*
27. Raphael's *School of Athens*
28. Michelangelo's ceiling of the Sistine Chapel
29. Northern Renaissance
30. Jan van Eyck and Albrecht Durer
31. "new monarchies"
32. Louis XI the Spider and Henry VII
33. Ferdinand and Isabella
34. Spanish Inquisition
35. the Habsburgs
36. Poland's *Sejim*
37. Ivan III
38. Constantinople and 1453
39. John Hus
40. Renaissance popes

MULTIPLE CHOICE QUESTIONS

1. The Italian Renaissance was primarily
    a. a mass movement of the peasants.
    b. characterized by a preoccupation with religion.
    c. a product of rural Italy.
    d. a recovery or rebirth of antiquity and Greco-Roman culture.
        ANSWER: d (page 210)

2. The word "Renaissance" means
    a. rebirth.
    b. new world.
    c. maturation.
    d. escape.
        ANSWER: a (p. 210)

3. Economic developments in the Renaissance included
   a. a revival in trade.
   b. increased employment due to the change from wool to luxury manufacturing.
   c. a boom rivaling that of the High Middle Ages.
   d. new trade routes made possible by the Ottoman Turks.
   ANSWER: a (p. 211)

4. According to Jacob Burckhardt, the Renaissance in Italy represented
   a. a distinct break from the Middle Ages and the true birth of the modern world.
   b. the greatest period of economic recovery in the history of civilization.
   c. a period of moral decline.
   d. an era of tremendous graft and corruption in Italian government.
   ANSWER: a (p. 210)

5. The Medici controlled the finances of the Italian city state of
   a. Venice.
   b. Rome.
   c. Milan.
   d. Florence.
   ANSWER: d (p. 212)

6. What was the commercial and military league set up off the north coast of Germany?
   a. Delian League
   b. Prussian Confederation
   c. Hanseatic League
   d. League of German Cities
   ANSWER: c (p. 211)

7. Two key areas of Renaissance technological innovation were
   a. fireworks and glass making.
   b. mill construction and hydraulics.
   c. mining and metalworking, including manufacture of firearms.
   d. optical instruments and lens grinding.
   ANSWER: c (p. 212)

8. The cultural center of the European Renaissance was
   a. London.
   b. Florence.
   c. Paris.
   d. Rome.
   ANSWER: b (p. 215)

9. Castiglione's *The Courtier* was
   a. a primer on military training for nobles.
   b. a very popular handbook laying out the new skills in politics, the arts, and personal comportment expected of Renaissance aristocrats.
   c. a sharp denunciation of the wasteful noble life.
   d. a treatise against active participation in public life.
   ANSWER: b (p. 212)

10. The achievements of the Italian Renaissance were the products of
a. an elite movement, involving small numbers of wealthy patrons, artists, and intellectuals.
b. a mass movement in which all sections of society participated and contributed.
c. a narrow religious movement directed almost entirely by clerics.
d. a political movement in essence controlled mainly by kings.
ANSWER: a (p. 210)

11. The aristocracy of the sixteenth century was
a. to dominate society as it had done in the Middle Ages.
b. largely surpassed by the upcoming merchant class.
c. still powerful, but with little new blood to keep it vital.
d. extremely uneducated compared to the nobility of the Middle Ages.
ANSWER: a (p. 212)

12. In most European countries of the Renaissance, nobles made up what percentage of the total population?
a. 10-12 percent
b. 15-20 percent
c. 2-3 percent
d. 7-8 percent
ANSWER: c (p. 212)

13. Banquets during the Renaissance
a. expressed the simplicity of the life idealized in courtly society.
b. were not held on Holy Days and on such celebrations as weddings.
c. were used to express wealth and power of an aristocratic family.
d. were banned by the papacy.
ANSWER: c (p. 213)

14. The Third Estate of the fifteenth century was
a. predominantly urban.
b. essentially free from the manorial system, especially in eastern Europe.
c. relatively free from violence and disease in urban areas.
d. made up of peasants, merchants, and artisans.
ANSWER: d (p. 212)

15. Western Europe in the Renaissance saw
a. a decline in serfdom.
b. a decline in centralized royal government.
c. a reduction in urban trade networks.
d. a rise in famine.
ANSWER: a (p. 212)

16. Outside of the urban areas of northern Italy and Flanders, peasants made up approximately what percentage of the total population?
a. 50 percent.
b. 70 percent.
c. 90 percent.
d. 98 percent.
ANSWER: c (p. 212)

17. Within urban society, the workers without property and the unemployed made up what percentage of the population?

a. 20 percent.
b. 40 percent.
c. 60 percent.
d. 80 percent.

ANSWER: b (p. 213)

18. Which of the following statements best describes marriage in Renaissance Italy?

a. Young men asked women for their hand in marriage, after a lengthy courtship.
b. Husbands were generally the same age as their spouses.
c. Marriages were usually arranged, to strengthen familial alliances.
d. Men and women waited longer to get married than in the Middle Ages.

ANSWER: c (p. 213)

19. Marriages in Renaissance Italy were

a. based on love and mutual affection.
b. easy to dissolve or annul.
c. an economic necessity of life involving complicated family negotiations.
d. often worked out hastily with little thought.

ANSWER: c (p. 213)

20. By the fifteenth century, Italy was

a. a centralized state.
b. dominated by the Papal States exclusively.
c. dominated by five major regional independent powers.
d. the foremost European power.

ANSWER: c (p. 215)

21. Perhaps the most famous of Italian ruling woman was

a. Battista Sforza.
b. Isabella d'Este.
c. Christina of Milan.
d. Catherine de Medeci.

ANSWER: b (p. 214)

22. Federigo da Montefeltro of Urbino was

a. a fine example of a skilled, intelligent, independent Italian warrior prince.
b. an outspoken advocate of Italian unification.
c. a callous, disloyal prince, loathed by the papacy.
d. strictly opposed to the proliferation of *condottieri* in Italy.

ANSWER: a (p. 215)

23. The Roman statesman and intellectual who became a model for many Renaissance humanists was

a. Marcus Aurelius.
b. Virgil.
c. Horace.
d. Cicero.

ANSWER: d (p. 218)

24. Machiavelli's ideas as expressed in *The Prince* achieve a model for
    a. a republican state in Italy.
    b. a new attitude of moral responsibility among politicians.
    c. a modern secular concept of power politics.
    d. a deeply religious conception of the sanctity of the state.
        ANSWER: c (pp. 216-217)

25. Italian Renaissance humanism in the early fifteenth century, above all else
    a. increasingly became alienated from political life.
    b. was based on the study of the Greco-Roman classics.
    c. rejected the church and Christianity in general.
    d. helped revive Greek as a "living" language.
        ANSWER: b (p. 217)

26. In the late fifteenth century, Italy became a battleground for the competing interests of
    a. France and England.
    b. England and Spain.
    c. France and Spain.
    d. Spain and Germany.
        ANSWER: c (p. 216)

27. Neoplatonism in mid-fifteenth century Italy
    a. rejected a hierarchy of substances.
    b. was revived when Marsilio Ficino translated many of Plato's works.
    c. postulated that humanity's highest duty was obedience to God.
    d. logically denied the previously held belief in the idea of Platonic love.
        ANSWER: b (p. 218)

28. Neoplatonism was based on two primary ideas
    a. a hierarchy of substances and a theory of spiritual love.
    b. dualism of nature and stress on the feminine side.
    c. love of God and order of the universe.
    d. knowledge of the mind and knowledge of the spirit.
        ANSWER: a (p. 218)

29. The *Corpus Hermeticum*
    a. contained histories written by papal secretaries.
    b. radically conflicted with the ideas of Pico della Mirandola's *Oration on the Dignity of Man*.
    c. contained writings on the occult as well as theological and philosophical speculations of great interest to humanists.
    d. advocated the final rejection of neoplatonic thought.
        ANSWER: c (p. 218)

30. Pico della Mirandola's *Oration on the Dignity of Man* stated that
    a. humans were fallen creatures, but regain their place by following God's will.
    b. human beings were nothing more than undifferentiated animals.
    c. humans were divine and destined to spiritual life.
    d. humans could be whatever they chose or willed.
        ANSWER: d (p. 218)

31. A subject of particular interest to fifteenth-century humanists was
   a. botany.
   b. the Greek language.
   c. accounting.
   d. engineering.
      ANSWER: b (218)

32. The liberal education of the Renaissance
   a. envisioned as its primary goal the creation of well-rounded, virtuous and ethical citizens.
   b. was for all segments of society, rich and poor.
   c. advocated concentration on science and research, not rhetoric and verbal skills.
   d. entirely excluded Christian teachings.
      ANSWER: a (p. 218)

33. Liberal education in the Renaissance included all of the following <u>except</u>
   a. the mastery of Greek and Latin.
   b. a stress on physical education.
   c. the study of martial arts such as mastering the use of gunpowder.
   d. the study of music.
      ANSWER: c (p. 218)

34. A Humanist education in the Renaissance was
   a. a possibility for all men regardless of class.
   b. was exclusively reserved for upper class men.
   c. was occasionally available for some upper class women.
   d. a monopoly of the church.
      ANSWER: c (p. 219)

35. Who played a leading role in perfecting movable type for printing?
   a. Johannes Gutenberg
   b. Francois Rabelais
   c. Francesco Guicciardini
   d. Lorenzo Valla
      ANSWER: a (p. 219)

36. The development of printing in the fifteenth century
   a. pertained predominantly to secular works, as theological works were still done by hand.
   b. saw the invention of movable type by Nicholas Fabian.
   c. ensured that literacy and new knowledge would spread rapidly in European society.
   d. actually made communication and collaborative work between scholars more difficult due to competition.
      ANSWER: c (pp. 219-220)

37. Italian artists in the fifteenth century began to
   a. ignore nature and paint for expression.
   b. experiment in areas of perspective.
   c. copy the works of previous artists.
   d. move away from the study of anatomical structure.
      ANSWER: b (p. 220)

38. Which of the following groups of Italian artists dominated the High Renaissance?
- a. Donatello, da Vinci, Mirandola
- b. Raphael, Donatello, da Vinci
- c. da Vinci, Botticelli, Raphael
- d. de Vinci, Raphael, Michelangelo

ANSWER: d (pp. 221-222)

39. What was the name of the Renaissance painter who achieved fame earlier in his career for his beautiful madonnas?
- a. Titian
- b. Raphael
- d. Leonardo
- d. Donatello

ANSWER: b (p. 223)

40. Which of the following is <u>not</u> true of Northern Renaissance artists?
- a. They had less mastery of the laws of perspective than many Italian painters.
- b. The most influential artist was Jan van Eyck.
- c. There was an emphasis on illuminated manuscripts and wooden panel painting.
- d. They valued the secular human form as the primary vehicle of expression.

ANSWER: d (p. 233)

41. The most influential northern school of art in the fifteenth century was centered in
- a. Paris.
- b. Flanders.
- c. Canterbury.
- d. Burgundy.

ANSWER: b (p. 223)

42. The "new monarchs" of the late fifteenth century in Europe
- a. continued the trend toward decentralization.
- b. were often obsessed with the acquisition and expansion of power.
- c. attempted to build up the nobility for support.
- d. accepted the domination of the church as a matter of course.

ANSWER: b (p. 224)

43. The results of the Hundred Years' War
- a. reinvigorated and strengthened the French monarchy.
- b. caused economic turmoil in England.
- c. temporarily strengthened the nobility in England.
- d. all of the above

ANSWER: d (pp. 224-225)

44. Under Ferdinand and Isabella, Spain
- a. became increasingly corrupt and inefficient.
- b. saw society become more secular.
- c. saw Muslim power vanish from the peninsula.
- d. had little remaining dissension and was thoroughly unified.

ANSWER: c (p. 226)

45. All of the following monarchs were successful in continuing the centralization of their "new monarchies" except

a. Maximilian I of the Holy Roman Empire.
b. Henry VII of England.
c. Ferdinand of Aragon in Spain.
d. Louis XI the Spider of France.
ANSWER: a (p. 226)

46. The Habsburg dynasty ruled in

a. Poland.
b. Italy.
c. Holy Roman Empire.
d. Russia.
ANSWER: c (p. 226)

47. The Byzantine Empire was finally destroyed in 1453 by

a. the crusaders.
b. the Persians.
c. the Russians.
d. the Turks.
ANSWER: d (p. 227)

48. John Huss did all *except*

a. he condemned the Church for all of the following except that the
b. he said that popes should be given greater power to eliminate heresy.
c. he said popes should be stripped of their authority and their property.
d. he condemned the clergy for being too corrupt and worldly.
ANSWER: b (p. 227)

49. The Renaissance popes did all of the following except

a. patronize Renaissance culture.
b. participate in temporal authority at the expense of their spiritual responsibilities.
c. attempt to return to the papacy to more humble times.
d. combat church councils.
ANSWER: c (pp. 227-228)

50. The Renaissance papacy

a. was exemplified by the spartan existence of Leo X.
b. saw popes build dynasties over several generations to maintain power.
c. was little concerned with war and politics, as shown by Julius II.
d. was often seen as debauched, especially under Pope Alexander VI.
ANSWER: d (p. 228)

RELEVANT WORLD-WIDE WEB SITES/RESOURCES

1. The Columbus Letter:
http://www.usm.maine.edu/~maps/columbus/toc.html
(Excellent site maintained by Osher Map Library at the University of Southern Maine showing 1494 printed Basel Edition of Columbus' first letter detailing his discoveries in the New world. Fine online images of this Renaissance printer's masterwork with translations of all passages into English. Excellent online source for the material history and culture of printing in the northern European Renaissance.)

2. Galleria degli Uffizi (Uffizi Museum, Florence, Italy):
General Uffizi entrance site (in Italian):
http://musa.uffizi.fi.it/
Uffizi Museum guide (room by room) in English:
http://musa.uffizi.firenze.it/discrezioneE.html
(One of the absolutely finest museum web sites in the world with superb room by room tours enabling you to see and enlarge representative works from every major Italian painter and school of painting present in this exceptionally fine collection. This site is highly recommended to illustrate and illuminate themes in this chapter and in subsequent chapters.)

3. The Last Supper:
http://hpux.dsi.unimi.it/imaging/LAST_SUPPER/lastsupper.html
(A magnificent site blending architectural illustration and art to show the emplacement and cultural significance of da Vinci's Last Supper.)

4. Plague and Public Health in Renaissance Europe:
http://jefferson.village.virginia.edu/osheim/intro.html
(Excellent site for development of public health and novel medical practices in Florence, Lucca, and Pisa after 1348.)

5. WebMuseum, Paris:
http://metalab.unc.edu/louvre/paint/auth/
(A superb arts site on the Web with hundreds of screens showing masterworks by a long, long list of painters. Bulk of online collection is comprised of works from late medieval times, the Renaissance, Baroque eras and Ancien Regime. Site is thus an appropriate complement to this and later chapters.)

RELEVANT VIDEO RESOURCES

Civilisation, Public Media Video/BBC Television, multiple programs (50 minutes each program). Program 4, "Man as the Measure of All Things." (Central focus here on the city of Florence and the Italian Renaissance.)

Life of Leonardo Da Vinci, PBS Home Video, 4 programs on 3 cassettes, (approx. 60 minutes each).

Power of the Past: Florence, PBS Home Video, (90 minutes).
(Excellent video documentary on the Arno city and its magnificent cultural history.)

Scientific Imagination in the Renaissance, Insight Media, (53 minutes).
(Excellent study of how new scientific inquiries and theories of the era, especially in applied mathematics, shaped the culture of the Renaissance.)

The Western Tradition, Part I, Annenberg/CPB Collection/PBS Home Video, multiple programs, (30 minutes each program). Program 25, "The Renaissance and the Age of Discovery."

RELEVANT MUSICAL PERFORMANCES

Antoine Brumel, Mass "Et ecce terrae motus", Sony Vivarte CD (No. SK 46348).

Josquin Desprez, Stabat Mater and Motets, Harmonia Mundi France CD (No. 901243).

Josquin Desprez, Masses, Gimell CD (No. 454 919-2).

Jacob Obrecht, Missa Maria Zart, Gimell CD, (No. 454 932-2).

SUGGESTED STUDENT ACTIVITIES

1. Assign students parts of Castiglione's *The Book of the Courtier*. Have them determine what Renaissance courtly manners are still evident in society today.

2. Assign students parts of Machiavelli's *The Prince*. Have them find evidence of Machiavelli's prince in world rulers today.

3. Have students do an essay on a Renaissance painter of their choice. The student should write about the artist's life, most famous paintings, and the characteristics of the painter's art.

4. Have students pick a Renaissance Pope and do a short essay on the life of that pope, showing the contributions of the pontiff to the decline of the Catholic church.

CHAPTER 13
REFORMATION AND RELIGIOUS WARFARE IN THE SIXTEENTH CENTURY

CHAPTER OUTLINE

I. Prelude to Reformation
- A. Christian or Northern Renaissance Humanism
- B. Church and Religion on the Eve of the Reformation

II. Martin Luther and the Reformation in Germany
- A. The Early Luther
- B. The Development of Lutheranism
- C. Germany and the Reformation: Religion and Politics

III. The Spread of the Protestant Reformation
- A. The Zwinglian Reformation
- B. The Radical Reformation: The Anabaptists
- C. The Reformation in England
- D. John Calvin and the Development of Calvinism

IV. The Social Impact of the Protestant Reformation
- A. The Family
- B. Religious Practices and Popular Culture

V. The Catholic Reformation
- A. The Society of Jesus
- B. A Revived Papacy
- C. The Council of Trent

VI. Politics and the Wars of Religion in the Sixteenth Century
- A. The French Wars of Religion (1562-1598)
- B. Philip II and the Cause of Militant Catholicism
- C. The Revolt of the Netherlands
- D. The England of Elizabeth

VIII. Conclusion

CHAPTER SUMMARY

The roots of the religious reformations of the sixteenth century were several, including Christian humanism, where the focus was on the Bible and the writings of the church fathers. Among the humanists was Desiderius Erasmus (d.1536), who stressed inner piety and Christ as a guide for daily life rather than dogma and ritual. The Church was criticized for corruption, materialism, and for abuses such as pluralism and absenteeism. For many the quest for salvation was often merely mechanical: collecting relics, going on pilgrimages, purchasing indulgences to reduce time in purgatory. To the medieval church, the sacraments administered by the clergy ensured salvation, but Martin Luther (d.1546) argued that faith alone was the answer, and that the Bible, not the Church, was the sole authority. In 1517 Luther went public in his criticisms. Outlawed after being condemned by pope and emperor, he translated the Bible into German.

Erasmus agreed with Luther's ideas, but feared that they would destroy Christian unity. When peasants rose in rebellion, Luther condemned them: equality before God did not mean equality on earth, and pragmatically, Luther needed the support of the German princes against Emperor Charles V (r.1519-1556). In 1555, Charles and the princes agreed to the Peace of Augsburg, by which each prince would determine the religion of his subjects. Lutheranism became the state religion Scandinavia. In Switzerland, Ulrich Zwingli (d.1531) removed stained glass windows and eliminated music from worship. When Pope Clement VII was unable to annul the marriage of England's Henry VIII (d.1547), Parliament established a separate church with the monarch as its head. John Calvin (d.1564) agreed with Luther's theology, but went further in emphasizing God's sovereignty and the concept of predestination: some were predestined for heaven, others for hell. His leadership made Geneva, Switzerland, the locus of Protestantism.

For Protestants the family was the center of human society, but theological equality did not lead to equality in marriage: the wife's role was to obey her husband and bear children. Education was encouraged because of the necessity to read God's word. Catholic holy days and religious carnivals were abolished; some went further, closing theaters and abolishing dancing.

Within the Catholic church, the most important religious order was the Society of Jesus, or the Jesuits, founded by Ignatius Loyola (d.1556), whose *The Spiritual Exercise* was a primer on how to find God. Pope Paul III (r.1534-1549) called the council of Trent, which met from 1545 to 1563; its final report reaffirmed traditional Catholic doctrine.

It was a violent century. In France, 3,000 Protestants, or Huguenots, were massacred on Saint Bartholomew's Day, 1572. The Catholic king, Henry III, was assassinated by a monk in 1589, and the Huguenot head of the Bourbon family became Henry IV (d.1610). He converted to Catholicism, reconciling the majority, and he issued the Edict of Nantes, granting religious toleration to the Huguenots: both actions were take for political reasons. Spain's Philip II's authoritarian rule and persecution of Protestants led to rebellion in the Netherlands. It was crushed in the south, but not the north: the Dutch became independent in 1648.

Elizabeth (d.1603) was a moderate Protestant, whose policies satisfied most, but not the radical Puritans who wanted to rid the Church of England of its Catholic-like rituals nor her exiled Catholic cousin, Mary Queen of Scots, who plotted against her and was beheaded. English seamen attacked Spanish forces in the Americas and Elizabeth supported the Dutch. In retaliation, Philip II sent a naval Armada against England in 1588. It ended in defeat for Spain.

LECTURE AND DISCUSSION TOPICS

1. Discuss the motives and accomplishments of such diverse religious reformers as Erasmus, Luther, Calvin, and Henry VIII.

2. Assess the religious and non-religious causes of the sixteenth century Reformations.

3. Discuss the careers, including motives, accomplishments, and consequences of Luther and Calvin, both as products of the Age of Faith and as founders of the modern world.

4. Examine the politics of the Reformation and particularly the role of Charles V.

5. Analyze social implications of the Reformation: Was Europe transformed by religious divisions?

6. Assess the relationships between the Renaissance and the Reformation.

7. Discuss several of the radical Reformation movements such as the Anabaptists.

8. Compare and contrast the Protestant Reformation with the Catholic Reformation or Counter-Reformation.

9. Assess the careers of Ignatius Loyola, Teresa of Avila, and other Catholics as Catholic reformers and as Counter-reformers.

10. Discuss the religious and non-religious causes and consequences of the Wars of Religion.

MAP EXERCISES

1. The Empire of Charles V. MAP 13.1. What were the key regions of conflict between the Holy Roman Empire and France and between the Holy Roman Empire and the Ottoman Empire, and why? What particular difficulties, religious and otherwise, did the Holy Roman Emperor, Charles V, face? (page 238)

2. Catholics and Protestants in Europe by 1560. MAP 13.2. Can it be claimed that the Protestant Reformation was largely a northern European phenomenon? If so, why, or if not, why not? What were the factors, political and otherwise, which might have guaranteed the success of Catholicism in the European south? (page 242)

DISCUSSION QUESTIONS FOR THE PRIMARY SOURCES (BOXED DOCUMENTS)

1. "Luther and the Ninety-Five Theses": Summarize the major points of Luther's Ninety-Five Theses. Why did they have such a strong appeal in Germany? What might have been the religious and non-religious elements of his support? (page 235)

2. "A Reformation Debate: The Marburg Colloquy": Based on this example, why do you think Reformation debates led to further hostility rather than the compromise and unity between religious and sectarian opponents? What were the specific issues which divided Luther from Zwingli at Marburg? (page 239)

3. "Loyola and Obedience to 'Our Holy Mother, the Hierarchical Church'": What are the fundamental assumptions that underlie Loyola's rules for "thinking with the church"? What do these assumptions tell you about the nature of the Catholic reform movement? Why would Protestants such as Luther and Zwingli object to Loyola's rules? (page 243)

4. “Queen Elizabeth Addresses Parliament (1601)”: What qualities are evident in Elizabeth’s speech which would endear her to her listeners? How was her popularity connected to the events of the late sixteenth century? Would the members of Parliament have responded differently to a king? Why and or why not? (page 247)

STUDENT RESEARCH AND PROJECT TOPICS

1. What was Christian humanism and how did it help prepare the way for the Protestant Reformation? Did Erasmus' works pave the way for Luther's break with Rome and Catholicism? How?

2. What were the sources of discontent among the Catholic clergy on the eve of the Reformation? What were the manifestations of popular religious piety on the eve of the Reformation?

3. What was Luther's fundamental religious problem? Trace the development of this problem and how Luther solved it. How did Luther's religious ideas differ from those of Catholicism?

4. What role did politics play in the establishment of Lutheranism? Use examples from Germany and perhaps Scandinavia.

5. Compare and contrast the chief ideas of Zwinglianism, Anabaptism, and Lutheranism. What did they have in common? How were they different?

6. How did the English Reformation differ from the reformation in other countries? Be sure to mention specific monarchs and acts of Parliament.

7. Discuss the chief ideas of Calvinism and show how they were similar to the ideas of Lutheranism. How did they vary from the ideas of Lutheranism? Why did Calvinism become the major international form of Protestantism?

8. What impact did Reformation doctrines have on the family, education, and popular religious practices?

9. What were the contributions of the papacy, Council of Trent, and the Jesuits to the revival of Catholicism?

10. How might the entire Reformation be seen as both an elite and a popular simultaneous attack on the Catholic sacraments and sacrementalism?

IDENTIFICATIONS

1. Christian humanism
2. Desiderius Erasmus's *The Praise of Folly*
3. pluralism and absenteeism
4. Thomas a Kempis' *Imitation of Christ*
5. Martin Luther
6. salvation by faith
7. Johann Tetzel and indulgences
8. Ninety-Five Theses
9. Edict of Worms
10. Peasants' War, 1524
11. the Protestant minister
12. Charles V
13. Pope Clement VII
14. Suleiman the Magnificent

15. Peace of Augsburg
16. Ulrich Zwingli
17. Marburg Colloquy
18. Anabaptists
19. Menno Simons
20. Henry VIII's wives
21. Act of Supremacy
22. Book of Common Prayer
23. Edward VI and "bloody Mary"
24. John Calvin
25. predestination
26. Geneva
27. the Protestant family
28. Puritans
29. Catholic Reformation
30. Ignatius Loyola
31. Jesuits
32. Pope Paul III
33. Council of Trent
34. Huguenots
35. *politiques*
36. Henry IV and the Edict of Nantes
37. Philip II
38. Battle of Lepanto
39. United Provinces of the Netherlands
40. Elizabeth and the Spanish Armada

MULTIPLE CHOICE QUESTIONS

1. The northern Christian humanists
    a. felt pessimistic about the future of humanity.
    b. were sophisticated and realistic in their expectations.
    c. championed study of classical and early Christian antiquity to reform the Church.
    d. doubted that education could solve the world's problems.
        ANSWER: c (p. 232)

2. Northern European humanists studiously learned Greek expressly to
    a. comprehend ancient Greek pagan culture more deeply.
    b. read the New Testament in its original Greek version and comprehend better the early writings of Greek church fathers.
    c. avoid use of lowly vernacular languages.
    d. outshine southern civic humanist competitors in public debate.
        ANSWER: b (p. 232)

3. Erasmus wanted to reform the church by
   a. returning to the simplicity of the early church and understanding the teachings of Christ via new translations of the Bible.
   b. stressing the sacraments and ritual of the church.
   c. accepting all the ideas of Luther.
   d. eliminating the Pope and increasing the power of archbishops.
   ANSWER: a (p. 232)

4. Just prior to Luther's reform movement, in Europe's clergy
   a. the practice of pluralism ended.
   b. the nobility and wealthy middle class dominated the highest church offices.
   c. the practice of collecting relics disappeared.
   d. declining revenue hit all clerical ranks.
   ANSWER: b (p. 233)

5. Popular religion in the Late Middle Ages and Renaissance was marked by
   a. greater popular belief in the spiritual utility of relics and indulgences.
   b. outbursts of church burnings to chase away "devil priests."
   c. efforts to do away with traditional beliefs and practices of the Catholic Church.
   d. the rise of several new neo-pagan, polytheistic cults.
   ANSWER: a (p. 233)

6. Martin Luther's early life was characterized by
   a. failure to follow the daily routine of monastic life.
   b. an obsession with his own sins and questions over the efficacy of the sacraments.
   c. his love for the study of law.
   d. his rejection of the Bible as a 'contradictory' work.
   ANSWER: b (p. 234)

7. To Martin Luther, the question of "How can I be saved" was answered through
   a. the doctrine of justification by grace through faith alone.
   b. doing good works for one's universal brotherhood.
   c. a strict devotion to monastic order, as with his own Augustinian order.
   d. the sacramental system.
   ANSWER: a (p. 234)

8. The event that eventually led to Luther's break with the church was
   a. the Council of Pisa's declaration that maintained the necessity of Purgatory for salvation.
   b. the increase of Papal taxes on the German peasantry.
   c. widespread sale of indulgences by preaching monks.
   d. the declaration that the German clergy must pay taxes.
   ANSWER: c (p. 234)

9. According to Luther, "justification" is
   a. how we explain our acts to god through prayer.
   b. how the faithful must demand proofs of their pastors' intelligence and educational qualifications.
   c. the act by which a person is made deserving of salvation.
   d. how Christians must demand that politicians live up to the rules of moral behavior set down in the Bible.
   ANSWER: c (p. 234)

10. "As soon as the coin in the coffer rings, the soul from purgatory springs" was a German advertising slogan used by the Catholic Church to sell

a. church offices.
b. special pilgrimage trips to Rome.
c. indulgences.
d. cookies baked by nuns for donation to poor children.
ANSWER: c (p. 234)

11. Luther's pamphlet, *The Babylonian Captivity of the Church*,

a. attacked the sacramental system of the church.
b. outlined the doctrine of Luther in German.
c. explained the Lutheran liturgy.
d. attacked abuses of the Catholic clergy in the Middle East.
ANSWER: a (p. 234)

12. The Edict of Worms

a. contained Luther's refutation of Johann Eck's accusations.
b. expressed Luther's rejection of Pope Leo I's spiritual authority.
c. called Luther to appear before Emperor Charles V to recant his "heresies."
d. made Luther an outlaw within the Holy Roman Empire.
ANSWER: d (p. 234)

13. The German university city that served as a center for the diffusion of Luther's ideas was

a. Wittenberg.
b. Frankenhausen.
c. Nurenberg.
d. Berlin.
ANSWER: a (p. 235)

14. The Peasants' War of 1524-1525

a. was led by a radical ax-follower of Luther, Philip Melanchthon.
b. furthered the spread of Lutheranism throughout all of Europe.
c. as praised by Luther as it destroyed the great Catholic princes of Germany.
d. was primarily a revolt by peasants against local lords but was strongly opposed by Luther who saw it as a social revolution from below against God's order.
ANSWER: d (p. 235)

15. All of the following were part of Luther's new religious services *except*

a. liturgy in German.
b. prayers in Latin.
c. Bible reading and preaching.
d. song.
ANSWER: b (p. 235)

16. At its outset, the Reformation in Germany was

a. a rural phenomenon.
b. largely an urban phenomenon.
c. a movement with strong urban and rural backing.
d. only a minor quarrel among monks.
ANSWER: b (p. 235)

17. To popularize his message of essential religious reform Luther used
    a. pamphlets illustrated with vivid woodcuts.
    b. daily newspapers edited and published by his followers.
    c. music, especially the Gregorian chant.
    d. speaking tours throughout Italy.
        ANSWER: a (p. 235)

18. The Catholic doctrine of transubstantiation opposed by Luther holds that
    a. clerics could move freely from one church office to another anywhere in Europe.
    b. Angels freely visit the earth.
    c. the devil could take any form or shape he or she pleased.
    d. at communion the bread and wine are miraculously turned into the body and blood of Jesus.
        ANSWER: d (p. 245)

19. Among the other religious innovations championed by Luther were all of the following except
    a. a new worship service conducted in German.
    b. denunciations of clerical celibacy and encouragement that all clerics should marry.
    c. assertions that the authority of scripture must be supplemented by church decrees.
    d. dissolution of all single-sex monastic orders.
        ANSWER: c (p. 235)

20. Although Charles V had many adversaries, his chief concern during his reign was
    a. Henry VIII of England.
    b. Ludwig II of Bavaria.
    c. Charles XII of Sweden.
    d. Francis I of France.
        ANSWER: d (p. 236)

21. The Habsburg-Valois Wars led to
    a. the defeat of Francis I of France in 1544.
    b. the development of the Lutheranism in Germany.
    c. Charles V's sacking of Wittenberg in 1527.
    d. the final defeat of the Turks in Austria at the Battle of Mohács in 1526.
        ANSWER: b (pp. 236-237)

22. Religious warfare in Germany ended in 1555 with
    a. the Battle of Mühlberg.
    b. the Battle of Mohács.
    c. the Peace of Augsburg.
    d. the Diet of Augsburg.
        ANSWER: c (p. 237)

23. Who said "I speak Spanish to God, Italian to women, French to men, and German to my horse"?
    a. Philip II of Spain.
    b. Emperor Charles V.
    c. Ignatius Loyola.
    d. Martin Luther.
        ANSWER: b (p. 236)

24. Outside of Germany, Luther's ideas were most readily accepted in
  a. England.
  b. France.
  c. Scandinavia.
  d. Spain.
    ANSWER: c (p. 235)

25. Prior to the Zwinglian Reformation, Switzerland
  a. was unified under the rule of Maximilian in 1499.
  b. was composed of thirteen self-governing cantons.
  c. became Europe's greatest economic power under the Swiss confederation.
  d. was the principal source of religious books in all of Europe.
    ANSWER: b (p. 237)

26. Zwingli's interpretation of the Lord's Supper differed from Luther's in that
  a. Luther held to the Catholic belief in transubstantiation.
  b. Luther said that the ceremony was totally symbolic.
  c. Zwingli said the ceremony was only symbolic and that no real transformation in the bread and wine occurred.
  d. Zwingli held to the belief called consubstantiation.
    ANSWER: c (p. 239)

27. The Marburg Colloquy of 1529
  a. produced no agreement or alliance between the Lutheran and Zwinglian movements.
  b. was fought over the fundamental issue of baptism.
  c. pitted Martin Bucer against Landgrave Philip of Hesse over the issue of the Lord's Supper.
  d. swayed Ulrich Zwingli to accept Lutheran doctrine.
    ANSWER: a (p. 239)

28. The Anabaptists
  a. were most radical and militant under Menno Simons in Zürich.
  b. were not regarded as a political threat as they preached separation between church and state.
  c. were founded by Conrad Grebel, beginning as an elitist movement.
  d. considered all believers to be equal as priests spreading the spirit of early Christianity.
    ANSWER: d (p. 240)

29. Anabaptism in the Netherlands was rejuvenated by
  a. the radical Johann Sebastian.
  b. the elderly Michael Sattler.
  c. the dissenter John of Leiden.
  d. the pacifist Menno Simons.
    ANSWER: d (p. 241)

30. The Reformation in England under Henry VIII
  a. was triggered by Henry's desire to annul his marriage.
  b. witnessed the complete transformation of Catholic doctrine.
  c. nearly ended with Thomas Cromwell's mishandling of the treasury.
  d. led to Parliament's leadership over the Church of England.
    ANSWER: a (p. 240)

31. The most important religious work which came out of the English Reformation was
a. Tyndale's *New Testament.*
b. *In Praise of Folly*.
c. *The Book of Common Prayer*.
d. *The Institutes of the Christian Religion*.
ANSWER: c (p. 240)

32. England's break with the Roman church became official with the passage of the
a. Act of Supremacy.
b. Six Articles.
c. Act of Toleration.
d. Act of Succession.
ANSWER: a (p. 240)

33. The Edwardian Reformation
a. began with the brilliant regency of the Duke of Somerset.
b. saw King Edward strip away the powers granted to Parliament by Henry VIII.
c. witnessed rapid changes to a more Protestant doctrine and liturgy.
d. ended with the military coup of the duke of Northumberland.
ANSWER: c (p. 240)

34. The reign of Queen Mary of England was most noted for
a. a failed Catholic restoration.
b. constant war with Spanish territories.
c. permanently ending the Protestant Reformation in England.
d. the issuing of the Act of Supremacy and the Treason Act in 1534.
ANSWER: a (p. 240)

35. Which of the following are among the chief characteristics of John Calvin's reform movement?
a. Calvin's acceptance of "justification by faith alone"
b. predestination and the absolute sovereignty of God
c. the belief that humans must obey secular authorities
d. a belief in congregational church covenant
ANSWER: b (p. 240)

36. John Calvin's *Institutes of the Christian Religion*
a. had little popular impact as it was only written in Latin.
b. was a new and masterly synthesis of Protestant thought.
c. systematically explained the fundamental difference between Calvinist and Lutheran doctrines.
d. led to his eviction from France by Francis I.
ANSWER: b (p. 240)

37. In Geneva, the Calvinists
a. imposed strict penalties for blasphemy and immoral behavior.
b. reformed the city with little opposition from an enthusiastic populace.
c. saw their reforms jeopardized by the execution of Michael Servetus.
d. withdrew the Ecclesiastical Ordinances in 1541.
ANSWER: a (p. 241)

38. The Reformation changed conceptions of the family by
a. substantially transforming women's subordinate place in society.
b. creating new career avenues for women outside the home.
c. extolling the superior state of marriage over celibacy.
d. encouraging women to take more active roles in religious life, as exemplified by Catherine Zell of Germany.
ANSWER: c (p. 241)

39. By the mid-sixteenth century, the city which was the fortress of the Reformation was
a. Wittenberg.
b. London.
c. Zurich.
d. Geneva.
ANSWER: d (p. 241)

40. The Reformation successfully abolished all of the following from the lives of Europe's Protestant community <u>except</u> for
a. indulgences.
b. the celebrations of religious holy days.
c. taverns.
d. clerical celibacy.
ANSWER: c (p. 242)

41. The most important religious order in the Catholic Reformation was the
a. Theatines.
b. Jesuits.
c. Dominicans.
d. Oratory of Divine Love.
ANSWER: b (p. 243)

42. The Catholic Reformation's ultimate refusal to compromise with Protestantism was exemplified by
a. Pope Paul III, who proved to be an ultra-conservative in refusing changes within the church.
b. the Roman Inquisition and the creation of the Index.
c. the Council of Trent, at which moderate Catholics and Jesuits heard the Protestants proclaim their doctrines.
d. Pope Paul IV, a moderate pope who proposed compromise in Catholic-Protestant disputes.
ANSWER: b (p. 244)

43. The Council of Trent
a. compromised with the Protestants on the doctrine of Justification by Faith.
b. agreed with most Protestants that there were only two sacraments.
c. reaffirmed traditional Catholic beliefs against the Reformation.
d. asserted the importance of doctrine over ritual.
ANSWER: c (pp. 244-245)

44. In France, the Protestant minority were known as
a. Anabaptists.
b. Huguenots.
c. Calvinists.
d. Bourbonites.
ANSWER: b (p. 245)

45. In France, the *politiques* were
a. heads of various religious and political factions during the civil wars.
b. administrators in provincial towns, appointed by the king.
c. those who placed politics ahead of religion in an attempt to end the wars of religion.
d. advisors to Catherine de'Medici.
ANSWER: c (p. 245)

46. The Edict of Nantes was all of the following except it
a. was an acknowledgment that Catholicism was the official religion in France.
b. expelled the Huguenots from France.
c. recognized the rights of the Protestant minority.
d. was a political decision.
ANSWER: b (p. 245)

47. The greatest advocate of militant Catholicism was
a. Philip II of Spain.
b. Henry VII of England.
c. Charles V of the Holy Roman Empire.
d. Henry IV of France.
ANSWER: a (p. 245)

48. By 1648, Spain admitted ultimate defeat at the hands of
a. France.
b. the Dutch Republic.
c. the Holy Roman Empire
d. the Ottoman Empire.
ANSWER: b (p. 246)

49. Elizabeth of England's religious policy could best be described as
a. radical Protestantism.
b. moderate agnosticism.
c. moderate Protestantism.
d. indifferent Catholicism.
ANSWER: c (p. 247)

50. The event that guaranteed that England would remain a Protestant country was
a. its defeat of the Spanish Armada.
b. Henry VIII's divorce from Catherine of Aragon. .
c. the Edict of Nantes.
d. the execution of Bloody Mary.
ANSWER: d (p. 248)

RELEVANT WORLD-WIDE WEB SITES/RESOURCES

1. Horus' History Links (at Univ. of Calif. Riverside):
http://www.ucr.edu/h-gig/horuslinkswork.html
(Vast online history site with links to hundreds of web pages on all aspects of European and world history including links to sites on the history of specific countries, eras, and regions. Very good for western Europe, the Reformation, and the Counter-Reformation.)

2. Project Wittenberg:
http://www.iclnet.org/pub/resources/text/wittenberg/wittenberg-home.html
(Excellent documents online and complete suite of links to other relevant Reformation pages on the Web.)

3. Reformation Ink: Reformation Classics:
http://www.remembrancer.com/ink/classic.htm
(Excellent site with a great number of original and rare documents central to the Reformation online for student use. Wide selection of original sermons, pamphlets, and tracts on religious reform in the era.)

4. The Reformation: Modern European History Advanced Placement:
http://pw2.netcom.com/~giardina/protestant.html
(A fine web site with a good selection of relevant Reformation documents online including such items as Luther's 95 Theses and works by other major church reformers.)

5. Treasures of the Saxon State Library: The Reformation in Germany:
http://rs7.loc.gov/exhibits/dres/dres3.html
(A wonderful site with original Reformation documents from the Saxon State Archives online—excellent for the history of printing, material culture, and the book trade in the era. Highly recommended.)

6. University of Toronto: Centre for Reformation and Renaissance Studies:
http://citd.scar.utoronto.ca/crrs/databases/www/bookmarks.html
(Excellent assortment of online primary and secondary sources for the study of Europe in the ages of Renaissance and Reformation. Excellent and extensive links to other sites.)

7. Brown University: Renaissance Women Online Collection:
http://wwp.stg.brown.edu/texts/RWOentry.html
(A fine site with documents written by the Queen Elizabeth I of England as well as a variety of original works written by English and European women during early modern times. Highly recommended.)

8. Tudor England:
http://tudor.simplenet.com/
(Excellent site with many sections devoted to art, architecture, cartography, history, and politics of England in Tudor times.)

RELEVANT VIDEO RESOURCES

Civilization, Public Media Video/BBC Television, multiple programs (50 minutes each program). Programs 5 and 6, "The Hero as Artist" (on Rome in the sixteenth century)"Protest and Communication," (on Germany in the fifteenth and sixteenth centuries with special reference to printing and the spread of printing to other European kingdoms. References here also to France and to the England of Shakespeare).

King Henry VIII, Films for the Humanities and Sciences, (55 minutes).

Reformation Overview, Insight Media, 2 programs (60 minutes each program). (Excellent video profiles of major reformers coupled with strong emphasis on the material history of printing as an agency of religious change. Highly recommended.)

Where Luther Walked, Insight Media, 1 program (30 minutes). (Video excursion through the German regions and townscapes home to Luther and his followers. Excellent on the environments of the Reformation.)

Civilization, Public Media Video/BBC Television, multiple Programs, (50 minutes each program). Program 7, "Grandeur and Obedience: Rome and Europe in the Counter-Reformation."

RELEVANT MUSICAL PERFORMANCES

William Byrd, Masses for 3, 4 and 5 Voices, EMI CD (No. D 102333)

Carlo Gesualdo, Madrigals.

Orlandus Lassus, Mass "Osculetur Me," Gimell CD (No. CDGIM 018).

Giovanni Palestrina, Missa pro defunctis (Requiem), Teldec CD (No. D 106302).

Heinrich Schutz, Musikalische Exequien, Harmonia Mundi France CD, (No. 901261).

Thomas Tallis, Motets or Lamentations of Jeremiah.

Tomas Luis de Victoira, Officium defuntorum (Requiem), Archiv CD (No. D 112440).

SUGGESTED STUDENT ACTIVITIES

1. Have students do a study of the modern Lutheran, Presbyterian, Baptist, and Catholic churches, determining how these churches' beliefs have changed since the Reformation.

2. Henry VIII and his six wives seem to interest students. Have students do a study of his marriages. Was Henry really the great "womanizer" of history? Was he a good king?

3. Give students a library assignment and have them answer the question: What evidence of religious practices of the Reformation period can be found in the modern day church and family?

4. Have students do research to answer the hypothetical question: Could the Reformation have been stopped? Why or why not? Make sure students are specific in their answers.

5. England during the reign of Elizabeth was a fascinating period. Have students pick out one aspect of Elizabethan England and do an essay, perhaps on Elizabethan society or culture, or the politics of the age.

CHAPTER 14
EUROPE AND THE NEW WORLD: NEW ENCOUNTERS, 1500-1800

CHAPTER OUTLINE

I. On the Brink of a New World
- A. The Motives and Means

II. New Horizons: The Portuguese and Spanish Empires
- A. The Development of a Portuguese Maritime Empire
- B. Voyages to the New World
- C. The Spanish Empire in the New World
  - 1. Early Civilizations in Mesoamerica
  - 2. The Spanish Conquest of the Aztec Empire
  - 3. The Inca and the Spanish
  - 4. Administration of the Spanish Empire

III. New Rivals On the World Stage
- A. Africa: The Slave Trade
  - 1. Growth in the Slave Trade
- B. The West in Southeast Asia
- C. The French and British in India
  - 1. The Impact of Western Powers
- D. China
  - 1. Western Inroads
- E. Japan
  - 1. Opening to the West
- F. The Americas
  - 1. The West Indies
  - 2. North America

IV. Toward a World Economy
- A. Economic Conditions in the Sixteenth Century
- B. The Growth of Commercial Capitalism
- C. Mercantilism
- D. Overseas Trade and Colonies: Movement Toward Globalization

V. The Impact of European Expansion
- A. The Conquered
  - 1. Catholic Missionaries
- B. The Conquerors

VI. Conclusion

CHAPTER SUMMARY

The fifteenth and sixteenth centuries were times of Western global expansion. Among the motives, economics ranked first, followed by religion, and adventure or fame, or, as the text quotes, "God, glory, and gold." It occurred when it did because of the emergence of centralized monarchies, sufficient wealth to finance such endeavors, and new technologies such better maps and charts, more seaworthy ships, the compass and astrolabe, and knowledge of Atlantic winds.

The first to venture forth were Portugal and Spain. Portuguese ships were exploring and trading along Africa's west coast by the mid-fifteenth century, bringing back slaves and gold. Southern Africa was rounded in 1488, and India was reached in 1498, followed by the Malay peninsula and the Spice Islands (Indonesia). The Portuguese empire was one of trade; its population was too small to establish large colonies, but Spain had greater resources. Seeking the same Asian goal as Portugal, the Italian Christopher Columbus (d.1506), sailing for Spain, reached the Caribbean West Indies in 1492, believing it was part of Asia. It was not, and the new found land became known as the New World or America, after Amerigo Vespucci, an early geographer. Spanish conquistadors arrived on the mainland of Mesoamerica in 1519. Aztec resistance was quickly overcome thanks to assistance from other native states, gunpowder and horses, and European diseases such as smallpox, for which the native population had no immunity. In South America, the Incas were conquered by the 1530s. The natives became Spanish subjects, but were often exploited by Spanish settlers. Two viceroys (vice kings) ruled in Mexico City and Lima, Peru; Catholic missionaries, under the control of the Spanish crown, brought Christianity, including cathedrals, schools, and the inquisition, to the native population.

Although originally less prized than gold and spices, slaves became a major object of trade, and by the nineteenth century ten million African slaves had been shipped to America. Slavery was common in Africa, and the African terminus of the trade was in the hands of the Africans, but the insatiable demand for slaves led to increased warfare on that unfortunate continent. It was not until the late 1700s that slavery came under criticism in Europe.

The Dutch expelled Portugal from the Spice Islands by 1600, and in India, the British East India Company controlled the Mughal Empire by the mid-1700s. Trade with China was limited, its rulers believing the West offered nothing that China needed, and Japan gave only the Dutch even minimal trading rights. In the New World, the Dutch, French, and the British also established colonies. Eventually British North America consisted of thirteen colonies. France established an empire in Canada, but its French population remained small.

In Europe, a commercial revolution led to integrated markets, joint-stock trading companies, and banking and stock exchange facilities. Mercantilist theory posited that a nation should acquire as much gold and silver as possible, there must be a favorable balance of trade, or more exports than imports, and the state would provide subsidies to manufactures, grant monopolies to traders, build roads and canals, and impose high tariffs to limit imports.

The impact of European expansion was mixed. In the Americas, the native culture was largely destroyed and a new multiracial society evolved. That was less true in British America, which became mainly European in population and culture. The Columbian exchange saw Europeans bringing horses, cattle, sugarcane, wheat as well as disease and gunpowder to the New World and adopting the potato, maize (corn), and chocolate in turn. Native cultures were least affected in Asia, particularly in Japan and China. Missionaries, mostly Catholic, were mainly successful in the New World, and within Europe, imperial rivalries could lead to war.

LECTURE AND DISCUSSION TOPICS

1. Explore the various possible explanations why it was the West rather than elsewhere (e.g. China, Islam) which "encountered" the rest of the world.

2. Analyze the role geography played in understanding the Age of Discovery.

3. Assess the possible explanations why it was the states of the Iberian peninsula who led the West in encountering the world

4. Discuss the Columbian Exchange and its consequences for both the Old World and the New World.

5. Discuss the geopolitics of mercantilism and the economic imperatives for the development of European colonialism.

6. Analyze the long-term socioeconomic consequences of European encounter with the New World.

7. Examine the African slave trade, both before and after the Europeans arrived.

8. Explore the causes and motives as well as the consequences of Europe's involvement in the African slave trade.

9. Assess the impact of the European encounters with the peoples and societies of Asia: Where did the West have the greatest impact and where the least?

10. Explore the Chinese responses to the arrival of the West.

MAP EXERCISES

1.European discoveries and Possessions in the Fifteenth and Sixteenth Centuries. MAP 14.1. What were the major the geopolitical reasons why the Spanish succeeded mainly in the Western Hemisphere and the Portuguese in Southeast Asia in establishing colonial possessions? Were the reasons historical or geographical? Other explanations? (page 253)

2. Global Trade Patterns of the European States in the Eighteenth Century. MAP 14.2. It was later said that "the sun never set on the British Empire." Was that true in the eighteenth century. Which European nations were Britain's major rivals in the Western Hemisphere, in Africa, in South Asia, and in Southeast Asia? (page 262)

DISCUSSION QUESTIONS FOR THE PRIMARY SOURCES (BOXED DOCUMENTS)

1. "The Spanish Conquistador: Cortés and the Conquest of Mexico": What does Cortés focus on in his description of the Aztec city of Tenochtitlan? What were the justifications, religious and non-religious, for his overthrow of Moctezuma's empire? (page 255)

2. "The Atlantic Slave Trade": Given the horrific realities of the slave trade, why were European governments and public opinion so slow to respond its inhuman practices? What role did religion, economics, race, and sheer ignorance play in ignoring the plight of the African slaves? (page 258)

3. "West Meets East: An Exchange of Royal Letters": What were France's Louis XIV motives for wanting to increase contact with Vietnam's King of Tonkin? What other motives should be taken into account? (page 260)

4. “The Mission”: What changes did the Jesuit missionaries impose upon the Guarani Indians of Paraguay? Could the Jesuit rule be described as a “socialist dictatorship”? Why and or why not? (page 267)

STUDENT RESEARCH AND PR0JECT TOPICS

1. What factors contributed to the successes of the West in the age of discovery or encounter?

2. Compare and contrast Portuguese and Spanish reasons and methods of exploration and expansion.

3. Who were the “winners” and who were the “losers” in the slave trade–in Europe, in Africa, and in the New World?

4. What correlation is there between overseas expansion and economic, social, and political development in Europe?

5. Given its relatively small population and lack of obvious resources, why was the Dutch Republic so successful in establishing a profitable overseas empire?

6. What role did private investment and initiative play in the development of European imperialism. Give specific examples.

7. Was it sheer chance or luck which allowed Britain to gain control of much of India, or were there other political, social, and economic factors which gave Britain an advantage over the French, Dutch, Portuguese, and other potential European rivals?

8. Why and how did Japan succeed in keeping Europeans largely away from its nation from 1600 to the 1850s?

9. What role did religion play as a motivation in the age of discovery? Was it as important a motive as economics? Give examples.

10. Discuss the Columbian exchange. What was “exchanged” and who gained the most?

11. What is the doctrine of mercantilism? How did European countries practice it? How is it related to European colonial expansion?

12. Assume that you are a nobleman and also a merchant. Of the following countries, England, France, Prussia, or Poland, which country would you prefer to live in? Why?

IDENTIFICATIONS

1. Prester John
2. *The Travels of John Mandeville*
3. Marco Polo

4. "God, glory, and gold"
5. *portolani*
6. Ptolemy's *Geography*
7. Prince Henry the Navigator
8. Bartholomeu Dias
9. Vasco da Gama and Calicut
10. Alfonso de Albuquerque
11. Spice Islands
12. Christopher Columbus
13. John Cabot
14. Amerigo Vespucci
15. Ferdinand Magellan
16. Treaty of Tordesillas
17. Hernan Cortés and Moctezuma
18. the Aztecs and Tenochtitlan
19. the Inca and Pachakuti
20. Francisco Pizarro
21. *encomienda*
22. slave trade
23. "sugar factories"
24. Dutch East India Company
25. Batavia
26. Mughal Empire
27. British East India Company
28. Robert Clive and the "Black Hole of Calcutta"
29. Ming and Qing dynasties
30. Lord Macartney and Emperor Qianlong
31. Tokugawa shoguns
32. Nagasaki
33. the New Netherlands
34. Massachusetts Bay Company
35. joint stock trading companies
36. Bank of Amsterdam and the Amsterdam Exchange
37. mercantilism
38. mestizos and mulattoes
39. the Columbian exchange
40. Gerardus Mercator

MULTIPLE CHOICE QUESTIONS

1. The primary motive for European exploration during the Renaissance was
    a. social, to relieve the population pressure on Europe.
    b. religious, to spread the Gospel.
    c. economic, the desire for precious metals and new areas for trade.
    d. military, to provide new bases for the army.
        ANSWER: c (page 251)

2. When he began to envision his voyage across the Atlantic, Columbus had a copy of
a. *The Travels of John Mandeville.*
b. Machiavelli's *The Prince.*
c. Ptolemy's *Portolani.*
d. Marco Polo's *Travels.*
ANSWER: d (p. 251)

3. The religious crusading motive for exploration was strongest in
a. Spain and Portugal.
b. Florence and Venice.
c. the Byzantine Empire.
d. England and France.
ANSWER: a (pp.251-252)

4. All of the following facilitated the European discoveries *except*
a. the compass and astrolabe.
b. seaworthy ships.
c. representative government.
d. adequate maps.
ANSWER: c (p. 252)

5. The astronomer of the second century A.D. whose map had a significant influence upon the European voyages in the fifteenth and sixteenth centuries was
a. Cicero.
b. Augustine.
c. Ptolemy.
d. Pompey.
ANSWER: c (p. 252)

6. Prince Henry the Navigator
a. sponsored the exploration the west African coast.
b. was the first to round the Cape of Good Hope.
c. discovered the Spice Islands.
d. discovered the island of Madagascar.
ANSWER: a (p. 252)

7. Portugal became the early leader in European expansion largely through
a. direct trade policies with China.
b. defeating Muslim opposition in establishing trade opportunities with India.
c. spending its wealth on ships and manpower.
d. winning the race of exploration to the New World.
ANSWER: b (p. 252)

8. When Vasco da Gama reached India, he announced he was searching for
a. "gold and slaves."
b. "Christians and spices."
c. "tea and coffee."
d. "gunpowder and paper."
ANSWER: b (p. 252)

9. In the 1440s, among the first profits the Portuguese derived from their maritime exploration and returning ships came from the sale of

a. silver.
b. copper.
c. African slaves.
d. precious stones.

ANSWER: c (p. 257)

10. The development of a Portuguese maritime empire encompassing Malacca and the Malay peninsula was achieved, in part, through

a. ruthless attacks on all prior Arab settlers in the region including the murder and mutilation of male and female Islamic prisoners.
b. the negotiation of four commercial treaties with Arab traders.
c. scrupulous business practices with local residents.
d. massive bribery to local Arab overlords.

ANSWER: a (p. 253)

11. Spanish expansion and exploration of the New World was best characterized by

a. the first circumnavigation of the globe by Amerigo Vespucci.
b. the conquest of the Aztec Empire by Cortés.
c. the conquest of the Incas by Magellan.
d. Pizarro's rounding of South America in 1519.

ANSWER: b (p. 255)

12. The European who first referred to the Native Americans as "Indians" was

a. Hernan Cortez.
b. Amerigo Vespucci.
c. Christopher Columbus.
d. Ferdinand Magellan.

ANSWER: b (p. 254)

13. The first known circumnavigation of the earth was by

a. Amerigo Vespucci.
b. Ferdinand Magellan.
c. John Cabot.
d. Christopher Columbus.

ANSWER: d (pp.251, 254)

14. The Treaty of Tordesillas divided

a. the Spice Islands between Portugal and the Dutch Republic.
b. South Africa between the English and the Dutch.
c. the New World between Spain and Portugal.
d. the North Atlantic between England and France.

ANSWER: c (p. 254)

15. The Mesoamerica civilization which existed at the time of European exploration was the

a. Maya.
b. Inca.
c. Toltec.
d. Aztec.

ANSWER: d (p.255)

16. The major European disease that resulted in high rates of mortality among the natives of the New World was

a. syphilis.
b. AIDS.
c. smallpox.
d. scurvy.

ANSWER: c (pp. 256-257)

17. The capital of the Aztec empire was

a. Batavia.
b. Cuzco.
c. Quito.
d. Tenochtitlan.

ANSWER: d (p. 256)

18. In reality, the *encomienda* made the natives of the new world

a. equal to the Spanish.
b. slaves of the Spanish.
c. masters of the Spanish.
d. local rulers for the Spanish.

ANSWER: b (pp. 256-257)

19. The Spanish conquistador who conquered the Incas was

a. Bartholome de Las Casas.
b. Hernan Cortez.
c. Alfonso de Albuquerque.
d. Francisco Pizarro.

ANSWER: a (p. 256)

20. Because of the impact of European diseases such as smallpox, the 100,000 population of Hispaniola when Columbus arrived in 1493 had, by 1570, been reduced to

a. 30,000.
b. 10,000.
c. 3,000.
d. 300.

ANSWER: d (p. 257)

21. Between the sixteenth and the nineteenth centuries, the number of African slaves shipped to the New World is estimated at

a. one million.
b. two million.
c. ten million.
d. twenty-five million.

ANSWER: c (p. 257)

22. The African slave trade
a. had little impact upon the number of wars in Africa.
b. reduced the number of wars in Africa because all the African states united against the European slavers.
c. increased the number of wars in Africa because of the increasing demand for prisoners who could be sold as slaves.
d. died out with the discovery of the South Asian Spice Islands.
ANSWER: c (p. 258)

23. The first religious group in Europe to criticize slavery and the slave trade were the
a. Catholics.
b. Lutherans.
c. Quakers.
d. Anabaptists.
ANSWER: c (p. 258)

24. Portugal's handicap in its attempt to dominate Southeast Asian trade was that
a. Portugal was too far away.
b. the kingdom was too small, lacking a sufficient population to govern an empire.
c. it was too religious.
d. the Portuguese were satisfied by their control of Brazil, which brought more wealth.
ANSWER: b (pp. 258-259)

25. The European nation which took over the spice trade from Portugal was
a. the Dutch Republic.
b. England.
c. Spain.
d. France.
ANSWER: a (p. 259)

26. The mainland states of Southeast Asia had better success in resisting European encroachment than did the Spice Islands and Malay states because
a. they had greater natural resources desired by the Europeans.
b. they were more cohesive politically.
c. the Europeans were not aware of their existence.
d. they were Christians, and the Europeans never bothered their fellow Christians.
ANSWER: b (p. 259)

27. India's Mughal dynasty was
a. Hindu in religion.
b. Mongol in origin.
c. successful in expelling the British East India Company.
d. long native to the Indian subcontinent.
ANSWER: b (p. 260)

28. Which of the following was <u>not</u> a British enclave in India:
a. Batavia.
b. Madras.
c. Calcutta.
d. Surat.
ANSWER: a (p. 261)

29. The British East India Company official who fought off the French threat in India was
a. Lord Macartney.
b. Robert Clive.
c. Robert Walpole.
d. Lord Byron.
ANSWER: b (pp. 260-261)

30. The local British population in India's Fort William was imprisoned in
a. "the bilious swamp of Madras."
b. "the icy Ajanta caves."
c. "the black hole of Calcutta."
d. "the Red Fort of the Mughals."
ANSWER: c (p. 261)

31. The European nation which had the first direct contact with China since Marco Polo was
a. Portugal.
b. Spain.
c. the Dutch Republic.
d. Russia.
ANSWER: a (p. 261)

32. The first European nation to establish diplomatic relations with China was
a. England.
b. Russia.
c. the Dutch.
d. Venice.
ANSWER: b (p. 262)

33. Which empire at the end of the eighteenth century was dismissive of trading with Great Britain?
a. the Mughal Empire
b. the Spanish Empire
c. the Chinese Empire
d. the Russian Empire
ANSWER: c (p. 263)

34. Japan was closed to all European trade except for _____ at the port of ______.
a. the Spanish/Tokyo.
b. the English/Edo
c. the Dutch/Nagasaki
d. the Portuguese/Osaka
ANSWER: c (p. 263)

35. The most valuable product from the West Indies was
a. cotton.
b. sugar.
c. coffee.
d. hemp.
ANSWER: b (p. 264)

36. The major difference between England's North American colonies and those of France was that

a. French Canada had a larger European population than did England's colonies.
b. the English colonial population was considerable less than the population of New France.
c. the English colonial population was much greater than the European population of New France.
d. there were no natural resources in New France to export to Europe.
ANSWER: c (p. 264)

37. Spain's importance as a commercial power declined in the seventeenth century because

a. of the drop in output of the New World silver mines.
b. the destruction of the tobacco crop because of a virulent new virus.
c. the take-over of the West Indies sugar islands by the French.
d. the Treaty of Tordesillas.
ANSWER: a (pp. 263-264)

38. One of the major economic problems of the sixteenth century in Europe was

a. deflation.
b. inflation.
c. depression.
d. a population decline which led to massive unemployment.
ANSWER: b (p. 264)

39. The inflation of the sixteenth and early seventeenth centuries

a. severely hampered commercial expansion.
b. caused a shift in industry to urban locales.
c. caused a decline in the standard of living for wage earners.
d. was caused largely by a declining labor force.
ANSWER: c (p. 265)

40. Which of the following statements best applies to the economy of sixteenth-and-seventeenth-century Europe?

a. The joint stock company enabled the raising of spectacular sums of capital for world trading ventures.
b. The early seventeenth century saw a general stagnation in the areas of mining and metallurgy.
c. Technological innovations made the lives of peasants improve dramatically.
d. The population explosion made for urban growth and more social equality in cities.
ANSWER: a (p. 266)

41. The Spice Islands were opened up for European trade by the

a. Amsterdam Exchange Bank.
b. British East India Company.
c. Dutch East India Company.
d. House of Fugger.
ANSWER: c (p. 265)

42. By the early seventeenth century the greatest commercial and banking center of Europe was

a. London.
b. Amsterdam.
c. Florence.
d. Vienna.
ANSWER: b (p. 265)

43. Mercantilism includes all of the following ideas <u>except</u>:
a. Economic activity was war carried on by peaceful means.
b. The prosperity of a nation depended upon its gold and silver reserves.
c. Colonies were not desirable because they consumed too many natural resources.
d. Government should stimulate trade through high tariffs and subsidizing industry.
ANSWER: c (p. 265)

44. Which of the following was <u>not</u> a result of European expansion and exploration?
a. the influx of tremendous amounts of precious metals into Europe
b. the introduction of new foods into Europe
c. the establishing of the Catholic faith in many areas of the New World
d. the introduction of smallpox into Europe
ANSWER: d (p. 257)

45. By the end of the seventeenth century,
a. international trade was much greater than intra-European trade.
b. wealth was being transferred back to the New World from Europe in the form of raw materials.
c. local, regional, and intra-European trade was considerably greater than international trade.
d. slavery was in decline in both Africa and the New World.
ANSWER: c (p. 265)

46. Which nation(s) or continent was least affected by European power and influence, including religious influence?
a. China and Japan
b. Africa
c. the America
d. India
ANSWER: a (p. 267)

47. A multiracial society appeared first in
a. British North America.
b. Latin America.
c. Northern Europe.
d. Southern Europe.
ANSWER: b (p. 266)

48. Christianity failed to take root in China in part because of
a. papal condemnation of ancestor worship.
b. lack of interest on the part of Catholic religious orders.
c. opposition by Muslims.
d. the inability of westerners to learn Chinese.
ANSWER: a (p. 267)

49. What was <u>not</u> part of the Columbian exchange?
a. Potatoes from Europe and chocolate from the New World.
b. Horses and cattle from Europe and corn from the New World.
c. Gunpowder from Europe and tobacco from the New World.
d. Smallpox from Europe and gold and silver from the New World.
ANSWER: a (p. 268)

50. The most famous map projection in history is

a. the *portolani*.

b. Ptolemy's *Geography*.

c. that of Gerardus Mercator.

d. Galileo's *The Starry Messenger*.

ANSWER: d (p. 269)

RELEVANT WORLD-WIDE WEB SITES/RESOURCES

1. Hanover History Texts Project (at Hanover College):
http://history.hanover.edu/project.html
(Fine site referenced earlier containing good original source documents arranged by era. Excellent material early modern Europe and the Ancient Regime.)

RELEVANT VIDEO RESOURCES

Conquistadors with Michael Wood. PBS Home Videos, 2 cassettes.

SUGGESTED STUDENT ACTIVITIES

1. Have students do oral reports from their research on one of the Spanish or Portuguese explorers. Be sure to have them determine the reason(s) or motives for the explorer's venture.

2. Have students debate the issue of whether the New World could have become economically profitable for the West without the resources of the Africa slave trade.

3. Suggest that selected students research the reasons for the Chinese and Japanese responses to Western incursions into their territories and present their findings to the class.

4. Have students debate the advantages and disadvantages which the Europeans and the non-Europeans gained from the Columbian exchange.

CHAPTER 15
STATE BUILDING AND THE SEARCH FOR ORDER IN THE SEVENTEENTH CENTURY

CHAPTER OUTLINE

I. Social Crises, War, and Rebellions
  A. The Witchcraft Craze
  B. The Thirty Years' War (1618-1648)
  C. Rebellions
II. The Practice of Absolutism: Western Europe
  A. France and Absolute Monarchy
    1. The Reign of Louis XIV (1643-1715)
  B. The Decline of Spain
III. Absolutism in Central and Eastern Europe
  A. The German States
    1. The Rise of Brandenburg-Prussia
  B. The Emergence of Austria
  C. Russia: From Fledgling Principality to Major Power
    1. The Reign of Peter the Great (1689-1725)
  D. The Ottoman Empire
  E. The Limits of Absolutism
IV. Limited Monarchy: The Dutch Republic and England
  A. The Golden Age of the Dutch Republic
  B. England and the Emergence of Constitutional Monarchy
    1. Revolution and Civil War
    2. Restoration and a Glorious Revolution
    3. Responses to Revolution
V. The Flourishing of European Culture
  A. The Changing Faces of Art
    1. Mannerism and the Baroque
    2. French Classicism and Dutch Realism
  B. A Wondrous Age of Theater
VI. Conclusion

CHAPTER SUMMARY

The seventeenth century experienced economic recession and population decline as well as continued religious conflict between Catholics and Protestants. The breakdown of community and the growth of a more individualistic ethic resulted in a world of greater uncertainty. One reflection of anxieties was an epidemic of witchcraft accusations, usually against women.

Protestant and Catholic animosities remained a prime cause for war, notably the Thirty Years War (1618-1648). There were also national and dynastic rivalries such as those between the Bourbon kings of France and the Habsburgs of Spain and the Holy Roman Empire. By the end, religious convictions had become secondary to secular political ambitions in public affairs. The Peace of

Westphalia gave the German princes the right to determine the religion of their domains, France gained territory, Spanish power declined, and the Habsburg authority as German emperors was diminished. Conscript standing infantry armies became the norm.

The century is known as the age of absolutism or the age of Louis XIV, although no seventeenth century ruler had the power of modern totalitarian dictators. Monarchs justified their absolutist claims by divine right–God had chosen kings to rule. Louis XIV (r.1643-1715), the Sun King, was the model for other rulers. His palace of Versailles symbolized his authority, where the aristocracy was entertained and controlled by ceremony and etiquette. Louis revoked his grandfather's Edict of Nantes, and he fought four costly wars, mainly to acquire lands on France's eastern borders. The Hohenzollern rulers of Brandenburg-Prussia became kings. Austrian power waned in the empire but it gained lands in the east and in Italy. Russia's Peter the Great (r.1689-1725) attempted to westernize Russia, especially militarily, and built a new capital, St. Petersburg, to be his window on the west. The last major invasion by the Ottoman Empire into central of Europe resulted in its defeat in 1683.

The oligarchic Dutch republic was a success during its so-called Golden Age of the seventeenth century. The States General was controlled by wealthy merchants, many from Amsterdam with its population of 200,000. During wars, the military leader, or stadholder, gained power, with William of Orange becoming the monarch during the crisis resulting from the wars against Louis XIV and France.

The Stuart kings of Scotland, advocates of divine right absolution, became the rulers of England in 1603. Religious disputes occurred within Protestantism, between the Church of England and Puritan reformers. Civil war between Charles I (r.1625-1649) and Parliament led to the creation of a republic, the Commonwealth. The monarchy was restored under Charles II (r.1660-1685). Parliament's Test Act required worship in the Church of England to hold office. James II (r.1685-1688), a Catholic, suspended the law, and his Protestant daughter, Mary, and her husband, William of Orange, the Dutch stadholder, invaded. Before ascending the throne they accepted the Bill of Rights, limiting royal power. John Locke (d.1704) justified the Glorious Revolution, claiming that government is created by a social contract to protect the natural rights of life, liberty, and property, and if it fails to do so, there is a right of revolution.

In art, Mannerism, with its emotional and religious content, was followed by the Baroque, which used dramatic effects to convey religious and royal power, which in turn gave way to French Classicism. Rembrandt (d.1669) made it the golden age of Dutch painting. It was also a golden age of theater with England's Shakespeare (d.1616), Spain's Lope de Vega (d.1635), and France's Moliere (d.1673).

LECTURE AND DISCUSSION TOPICS

1. Discuss: "Europe, 1550-1650: Why Was It an Age of Crisis?"

2. Analyze the several possible causes of the witchcraft craze of the sixteenth and seventeenth centuries.

3. Explore the nature of Absolutism, noting to the degree to which it was less than "absolute," possibly comparing with twentieth century Totalitarianism.

4. Examine the Thirty Years' War as to its causes and its consequences: Was it the last of the wars of religion or the first of Europe's modern wars?

5. Analyze the significance of Louis XIV in the "Age of Louis XIV."

6. Examine life and society at the Palace of Versailles and its environment of noble etiquette.

7. Assess the impact of the Ottoman Empire upon the European mind of the sixteenth and seventeenth centuries.

8. Compare and contrast absolutism in Western Europe with that of Eastern Europe.

9. Compare and contrast French absolutism with England's constitutional monarchy as paradigms of seventeenth century state building.

10. Present a slide lecture of late sixteenth and seventeenth century art, from Mannerism and the Baroque to French classicism and Dutch realism.

MAP EXERCISES

1. The Thirty Years' War. MAP 15.1. What role did dynastic struggles play in the Thirty Years' War? Which were the key regions of conflict, and were they national-dynastic or religious in their importance to the participants? Identify the Protestant-core areas and the Catholic-core regions. Were the core-areas of crucial significance to the outcomes of the war? Why and/or why not? (page 275)

2. The Growth of Brandenburg-Prussia. MAP 15.2. Compare the territories of Brandenburg-Prussia in 1415 and 1792. What particularly valuable lands were obtained? What might have been the geographical justifications or explanations for Prussian expansion? (page 279)

4. The Growth of the Austrian Empire. MAP 15.3. Trace the growth of the Austrian Empire from its Holy Roman Empire beginnings to its eventual multi-ethnic empire. In the east, at whose expense did Austria benefit, and why? What role, if any, might religion have played in lessening Austria's role in the Germanies? (page 280)

5. Russia: From Principality to Nation-State. MAP 15.4. Which nations lost territory as a result of Russian expansion? Which of Russia's new territorial acquisitions most significantly upset the status quo and why? What geographical history does the United States share with Russia? (page 282)

DISCUSSION QUESTIONS FOR THE PRIMARY SOURCES (BOXED DOCUMENTS)

1. "A Witchcraft Trial in France": What does this document tell us about the spread of witchcraft persecutions in the seventeenth century? What does this document tell you about the legal procedures involved in the trial of witches and how might these procedures have worked to condemn the innocent? What do these passages tell you about early modern European conceptions of justice? (page 273)

2. "Peter the Great Deals with a Rebellion": How did Peter deal with the revolt of the Streltsy? What does his approach to this problem tell us about the tsar? Is it possible that this account is exaggerated? Why or why not? (page 281)

3. "The Bill of Rights": The author states that the "Bill of Rights" laid the foundation for a constitutional monarchy? How? What key aspects of this document testify to the exceptional nature of English state politics in the seventeenth century? How was the Bill of Rights a radical departure from sovereignty in France? (page 285)

4. "William Shakespeare: In Praise of England": Beside patriotism, what other motives may Shakespeare have had in writing this tribute to England? How does this passage reflect Shakespeare's, and England's, attitude toward foreigners? (page 289)

STUDENT RESEARCH AND PROJECT TOPICS

1. What were the economic and social problems that troubled Europe from 1560 to 1650? Do these problems constitute a "crisis"?

2. Why have some historians labeled the Thirty Years' War as the "last of the religious wars," while others have called it the "first modern war"? Which do you believe is the more accurate assessment? Why?

3. What was the "military revolution" and what effect did it have on warfare in the sixteenth and seventeenth centuries?

4. What does the witchcraft craze tell us about European society and the place of women in that society in the sixteenth and seventeenth centuries?

5. Define absolutism and determine to what extent France's government in the seventeenth century can be labeled an absolute monarchy.

6. What did Louis XIV hope to accomplish in his domestic and foreign policies? To what extent did he succeed? Be specific in giving examples of his successes and failures.

7. Compare the reigns of Frederick William of Brandenburg-Prussia and Peter the Great of Russia. How are their policies similar? How are they different?

8. What role did the nobility play in politics and government in Poland and England?

9. England in the seventeenth century witnessed a general revolutionary upheaval that involved a struggle between king and Parliament. What were the issues (causes) of this struggle? What role did the Puritans play in its course? In what ways was England changed by it?

10. Compare and contrast developments in the United Netherlands and England. Can it be said that both states were moving in the direction of constitutional monarchy by the end of the seventeenth century? Why or why not?

11. How did the art and literature of the second half of the seventeenth century reflect the political and social life of that period? Give examples.

IDENTIFICATIONS

1. witches
2. Thirty Years War
3. Peace of Westphalia
4. absolutism
5. Jean Bodin
6. "divine right"
7. Cardinals Richelieu and Mazarin
8. the Fronde
9. Louis XIV
10. Edict of Fontainebleau
11. Versailles
12. Jean-Baptiste Colbert
13. Louis XIV's wars
14. Brandenburg-Prussia
15. the Great Elector
16. the Hohenzollerns
17. the Habsburgs
18. the Romanovs
19. Peter the Great
20. Saint Petersburg
21. Great Northern War
22. Vienna and the Ottoman Empire
23. house of Orange
24. the Stuarts
25. Puritans
26. English Civil War
27. Oliver Cromwell
28. the Restoration
29. Test Act
30. James II and the Glorious Revolution
31. Thomas Hobbes
32. John Locke
33. Bill of Rights
34. Mannerism
35. Baroque
36. French Classicism
37. Rembrandt van Rijn
38. William Shakespeare
39. Lope de Vega
40. Jean-Baptiste Moliere

MULTIPLE CHOICE QUESTIONS

1. Seventeenth-century European population
    a. increased dramatically due to greater food production.
    b. decreased dramatically due to disease and war.
    c. experienced great fluctuations as European nations established colonies.
    d. fluctuated narrowly, constrained by famines and diseases.
        ANSWER: d (page 272)

2. The witch hunts of the sixteenth and seventeenth centuries
    a. came out of the social unrest deriving from the shift from individualism to communalism.
    b. were generally directed at the wealthy by jealous neighbors.
    c. resulted in accusations against mainly lower-class women.
    d. were primarily restricted to rural areas.
        ANSWER: c (p. 274)

3. Recent scholarship cites which of the following reasons for the witchcraft craze of the sixteenth and seventeenth centuries?
    a. the outbreak of religious fervor of the same period
    b. social conditions that threatened old communal values
    c. local politicians used "witches" as scapegoats for their own political problems
    d. an indirect result of the Protestant-Catholic struggle
        ANSWER: b (pp. 273-274)

4. The Thirty Years' War
    a. eventually involved every country in Europe and Asia.
    b. is considered by most to be the first "modern" war.
    c. is considered by most to be part of the larger Bourbon-Habsburg struggle.
    d. was primarily fought in Spain.
        ANSWER: c (p. 274)

5. The event that sparked the Thirty Years' War was
    a. a Protestant noble rebellion against the Catholic ruler Ferdinand in Bohemia.
    b. the invasion of France by Frederick IV.
    c. the Spanish conquest of the Netherlands and subsequent local enforcement of the bloody Inquisition.
    d. the overthrow of Spanish rule in the new world by roving bands of Dutch pirates.
        ANSWER: a (p. 274)

6. As a result of the Peace of Westphalia of 1648
    a. the German population was to be converted to Catholicism.
    b. all German states could choose their own religions, except for Calvinism.
    c. German states were allowed to determine their religion.
    d. the institution of the Holy Roman Empire was to be the ruling force in Germany for the next 100 years.
        ANSWER: c (p. 274)

7. Following the Thirty Years' War, what country became dominant in Europe?
   a. Sweden
   b. France
   c. Germany
   d. Spain
      ANSWER: b (p. 274)

8. The Thirty Years' War
   a. was largely confined to agreed upon battlefields.
   b. witnessed the devastation of much of the German countryside.
   c. was fought according to chivalric codes.
   d. was fought mainly in Italy.
      ANSWER: b (p. 274)

9. According to Jean Bodin, sovereign power included all of the following except
   a. determining foreign policy.
   b. establishing political democracy.
   c. control the state's administrative system.
   d. make laws, tax, and administer justice.
      ANSWER: b (p. 275)

10. A similarity between Louis XIII and Louis XIV was that they both were
   a. Protestant Huguenots, descended from Henry of Navarre.
   b. intimately involved with the day-to-day governing of France.
   c. came to the throne as young boys.
   d. remained under the control of strong advisors during their entire reigns.
      ANSWER: c (p. 276)

11. Absolutism means
   a. the real power in any state must be religious and exercised by churchmen.
   b. ultimate authority rests solely in the hands of a king who rules by divine right.
   c. subordinate powers have an absolute right to advise the king on conducting the affairs of state.
   d. no matter how humble, male citizens have an absolute right to participate in politics.
      ANSWER: b (p. 275)

12. As Louis XIII's chief minister, Cardinal Richelieu was most successful in
   a. evicting the Huguenot presence from France after the La Rochelle rebellion.
   b. strengthening the central role of the monarchy in domestic and foreign policy.
   c. creating a reservoir of funds for the treasury.
   d. emerging victorious in the Fronde revolts of the nobility.
      ANSWER: b (p. 276)

13. The series of noble revolts known as the Fronde resulted in
   a. the assassination of Cardinal Mazarin in 1661.
   b. renewed power for the Parliament of Paris.
   c. a unified noble army securing and increasing its own power.
   d. French citizens looking to the monarchy for stability.
      ANSWER: d (p. 276)

14. Louis XIV's first step in transforming the French state into an absolute monarchy was
a. gaining control of the military.
b. decreasing the power of the French merchants.
c. restructuring and centralizing governmental administration.
d. dismissing Mazarin's advisors.
ANSWER: c (pp. 276-277)

15. Louis XIV restructured the policy-making machinery of the French government by
a. delegating considerable authority to his ministers and secretaries.
b. stacking the royal council with loyal followers from relatively new aristocratic families.
c. selecting his ministers from established aristocratic families.
d. all of the above
ANSWER: b (p. 277)

16. The economic policies of Jean-Baptiste Colbert, Louis XIV's controller general of finances
a. were noted for their innovation and originality.
b. used new accounting practices to take the tax burden off the peasants.
c. were based on the economic theory of mercantilism that stressed government regulation of economic affairs to benefit the state.
d. gave Louis the large surplus in the treasury needed to carry out his wars.
ANSWER: c (p. 277)

17. The costly palace built by Louis XIV, that became the envy of all European monarchs, was
a. Fountainebleau.
b. Versailles.
c. Aix-la-Chapelle.
d. Avignon.
ANSWER: b (p. 277)

18. The chief reason for the wars of Louis XIV was
a. to reduce the power of the Habsburgs.
b. his desire to insure the dominance of France and his Bourbon dynasty in all Europe..
c. to destroy the commercial superiority of the Dutch.
d. to gain ports on the Adriatic Sea.
ANSWER: b (p. 277)

19. All of the following resulted from the wars of Louis XIV <u>except</u>
a. new territories were added to France's northwestern frontier.
b. France was left impoverished and surrounded by enemies.
c. the Habsburgs were permanently driven from the Germanies by French armies.
d. a member of Louis' Bourbon dynasty became the monarch of Spain.
ANSWER: c (p. 278)

20. The overall practical political purpose of the court of Versailles was
a. to exclude the high nobility and royal princes from real power.
b. to serve as Louis XIV's residence from which to survey Paris.
c. to act as a reception hall for state affairs.
d. to give Louis XIV a life of privacy away from spies.
ANSWER: a (p. 277)

21. Louis XIV's Edict of Fontainebleau
a. created new ranks of intendants to govern various regions of France.
b. revoked the earlier Edict of Nantes, curtailed the rights of French Protestants, and caused thousands of highly skilled Huguenot to flee the country.
c. established new standards of court etiquette and was intended to diminish the power of great nobles.
d. removed most French bishops from their sees and replaced them with nobles to strengthen Louis' control of the French Catholic Church.
ANSWER: b (p. 277)

22. During the reign of Philip IV, Spain
a. suffered under the misrule of the Duke of Lerma.
b. won back its European possessions in the Thirty Years' War.
c. received a respite from the civil wars and internal revolts of Philip's predecessors.
d. failed to make any real progress, despite reforms under the count of Olivares.
ANSWER: d (p. 278)

23. After 1648, the "Holy Roman Empire"
a. became one of the most powerful and centralized monarchies in Europe under the domination of Spanish grandees.
b. was not really and empire at all but rather a loose association of 300 German states.
c. became divided into three great warring states: Prussia, Poland, and Silesia.
d. continued to acknowledge the temporal power of the pope.
ANSWER: b (p. 278)

24. Frederick William the Great Elector built Brandenburg-Prussia into a significant European power by
a. establishing religious uniformity in his kingdom, as evidenced in his eviction of the Huguenots.
b freeing the peasants from the dominion of the nobles.
c. using his army whenever possible to gain his ends.
d. making the General War Commissariat the bureaucratic machine of his state.
ANSWER: d (p. 278)

25. The Austrian Empire in the seventeenth century
a. was unified by linguistic and ethnic ties.
b. was defeated at Vienna by a Turkish army in 1687.
c. was a highly centralized, absolutist state under Leopold I.
d. lost a German empire, but gained one in eastern Europe.
ANSWER: d (p. 279)

26. The first Russian ruler to take the title of "tsar" (Caesar) was
a. Rurik.
b. Ivan the Terrible.
c. Michael Romanov.
d. Peter the Great.
ANSWER: b (p. 279)

27. Russian society in the seventeenth century
    a. witnessed the reign of Ivan the Terrible.
    b. witnessed profound religious reforms in the Russian Orthodox church.
    c. was characterized by a highly oppressive system of serfdom, where peasants were bound to the land..
    d. saw the rise of the merchant class to power.
        ANSWER: c (p, 279)

28. The most significant Romanov ruler of the eighteenth century was
    a. Ivan the Terrible.
    b. Nicholas III.
    c. Olaf the Great.
    d. Peter the Great.
        ANSWER: d (pp. 279-280)

29. Which of the following statements best applies to Peter the Great of Russia?
    a. His program of Europeanization was predominantly technical and aimed at modernizing the military.
    b. His respect for western governments led to increased powers for the Duma.
    c. His traditional, conservative attitude stripped away all previous social gains for women.
    d. His desire to teach Russians western customs could not be enforced among the old-fashioned nobles.
        ANSWER: a (p. 280)

30. Peter the Great's foreign policy had as its primary goal
    a. the opening of a warm-water port accessible to Europe.
    b. the destruction of the Ottoman Empire.
    c. the capture of the Scandinavian countries.
    d. the control of Constantinople and the Dardanelles.
        ANSWER: a (p. 281)

31. Scandinavia in the seventeenth and eighteenth centuries witnessed
    a. Denmark expand so as to dominate the Baltic.
    b. Sweden become a second-rate power after the Great Northern War.
    c. Sweden and Denmark join forces to defeat and occupy Poland in 1660.
    d. the economic dominance of Sweden over the rest of northern Europe.
        ANSWER: b (p. 281)

32. The Ottoman Empire suffered a major defeat in 1683 at
    a. Vienna.
    b. Budapest.
    c. Istanbul.
    d. Venice.
        ANSWER: a (p. 282)

33. The "Golden Age" of the Dutch Republic in the seventeenth century witnessed
a. William of Orange become the monarch.
b. the economic prosperity of the United Provinces burdened by a series of wars late in the century.
c. the temporary weakening of the States General.
d. all of the above.
ANSWER: d (p. 283)

34. James I of England alienated most of the members of Parliament by
a. encouraging an alliance with Spain.
b. insisting on his right to govern through Divine Right.
c. persecuting Puritans.
d. lavishly spending money on the English army.
ANSWER: b (p. 283)

35. The Petition of Right (1628), among other things,
a. stated that the King of England was elected.
b. maintained that the King could pass no new tax without the consent of Parliament.
c. restored order in the English military.
d. made the English monarch purely ceremonial.
ANSWER: b (p. 283)

36. The Parliamentarians were successful in the English Civil War because
a. they received aid from the French.
b. their weaponry was superior to that of the King's forces.
c. of the effectiveness of Oliver Cromwell's New Model Army.
d. their army was much larger than the Royalist army.
ANSWER: c (p. 284)

37. The Restoration in England was the
a. restoration of Catholicism.
b. reestablishment of the Stuart monarchy..
c. coronation of Oliver Cromwell.
d. creation of an oligarchic republic under William and Mary..
ANSWER: b (p. 284)

38. The devout Catholic English monarch who instigated a constitutional crisis for England in 1687-1688 was
a. Charles II.
b. James II.
c. William I.
d. Charles IV.
ANSWER: b (p. 284)

39. The "Glorious Revolution" in 1688 in England was significant for
a. restoring Charles II and the Stuart dynasty to power.
b. bloodlessly deposing James II in favor of William of Orange.
c. returning England to a Catholic commonwealth.
d. Parliament's establishment of a new monarch through a series of bloody wars.
ANSWER: b (p. 285)

40. The incident that prompted the nobles to depose James II was:
   a. his marriage to the Duchess of Orange.
   b. the death of his first wife.
   c. the birth of a Catholic son.
   d. a religious alliance with France.
      ANSWER: c (p. 285)

41. The English Bill of Rights
   a. laid the foundation for a future constitutional monarchy.
   b. resolved England's seventeenth-century religious questions.
   c. reaffirmed the divine-right theory of kingship while limiting the king's power.
   d. confirmed the king's right to raise standing armies without parliamentary consent.
      ANSWER: a (p. 285)

42. Thomas Hobbes
   a. felt that man was suited best to be in a pristine state of nature, without government interference.
   b. stated that mankind was animalistic, and needed a strong government to maintain social order.
   c. was a firm believer in democracy.
   d. said that the best form of government was a theocracy.
      ANSWER: b (p. 286)

43. John Locke was responsible for
   a. synthesizing previous doctrines on international law.
   b. the idea of society as being in a constant state of war.
   c. advocating political democracy for the entire populace.
   d. *Two Treatises of Government*, which emphasized the social contract between the people and government.
      ANSWER: d (p. 286)

44. The artistic movement of Mannerism
   a. was similar to that of the High Renaissance.
   b. followed the Baroque. .
   c. was exemplified by the paintings of Peter Paul Rubens.
   d. broke down the High Renaissance principles of balance, harmony, and moderation.
      ANSWER: d (p. 287)

45. Baroque art
   a. was a revolt against the ideals of the Italian Renaissance.
   b. attempted to blend the feelings of the religious reformations with Renaissance art.
   c. was very similar to the French Impressionists of a later period.
   d. was eclectic, featuring elements of Renaissance, medieval, and Mannerist art.
      ANSWER: b (p. 287)

46. The greatest figure of Baroque art was
   a. Rembrandt van Rijn.
   b. Gian Lorenzo Bernini.
   c. El Greco.
   d. Nicholas Poussin.
      ANSWER: b (p. 287)

47. The patriotic enthusiasm and pride of the English during the Elizabeth era is best characterized by

a. the philosophy of John Cabot.
b. the plays of William Shakespeare.
c. the New Model Army.
d. all of the above

ANSWER: b (p. 289)

48. Baroque art was superseded by which of the following artistic styles?

a. Impressionism
b. English landscape art
c. French Classicism
d. Dutch portraiture

ANSWER: c (p. 288)

49. The Dutch painter Rembrandt van Rijn was most noted for

a. his formation of the French Academy of Painting and Sculptors.
b. reflecting the values of the Dutch aristocracy in his works.
c. being the great Protestant painter of the seventeenth century.
d. rejecting the Dutch preoccupation with realism for the Baroque style of French classicism.

ANSWER: c (p. 288)

50. The French playwright Moliére is noted for all of the following except

a. *Tartuffe*.
b. benefited from the patronage of Louis XIV.
c. satirizing French religious and social customs.
d. perfecting neoclassical tragedy.

ANSWER: d (p. 289)

RELEVANT WORLD-WIDE WEB SITES/RESOURCES

1. French Royal Absolutism: The Path to Absolutism (at the Library of Congress):
http://lcweb.loc.gov/exhibits/bnf/bnf0004.html
(A site offering beautiful images and documents in translation on the origins and development of the French monarchy over the period 1448-1661. Highly recommended.)

2. Johnson Museum of Art, Cornell University, Dutch Collection:
http://www.museum.cornell.edu/hfj/permcoll/euro/euro_du.html
(Beautiful online images of Dutch seventeenth-century art.)

3. North Carolina Museum of Art, Dutch Collection:
http://www2.ncsu.edu/NCMA/collections/european/dutch/indexlow.html
(A fine site with several beautiful Dutch masterworks online.)

4. Jan Steen Gallery (at Rice University):
http://spacsun.rice.edu/~rss/jsteen.html
(A superb art site with many of Jan Steen's finest genre scenes online, showing popular culture and urban folkways in the early modern Dutch Republic. Highly recommended.)

RELEVANT VIDEO RESOURCES

Daily Life at the Court of Versailles, Films for the Humanities and Sciences, (60 minutes). (Available through Wadsworth Publishing.)

The West and the Wider World 1500-1800, Landmark Films, (60 minutes). (Available through Wadsworth Publishing.)

RELEVANT MUSICAL PERFORMANCES

Giovanni Fontana, Giovanni Cima, Francesco Turini, Sonatas for Violins, Virgin Veritas 2 CD's (No. 7243 5 45199 2 5).

Giovanni Gabrieli, Music for San Rocco, Archiv CD (No. 449 180-2).

Biagio Marini, Curiose & Moderne Inventioni (Sonatas for Strings), Harmonia Mundi France CD (No. 907175).

Music of Versailles (Various Composers), Deutsche Harmonia Mundi CD (No. 77145-2R6)

SUGGESTED STUDENT ACTIVITIES

1. Have students do an essay on witchcraft during the 15th and 16th century; have them choose a particular aspect of such phenomena as demonology, Catharism, the Inquisition, or Antinomianism.

2. Versailles is/was a remarkable palace; have students do an essay on an aspect of this royal residence. For example, what was life at the palace like when the King was there? Or perhaps on the famous Hall of Mirrors.

3. Peter the Great is one of the most colorful figures in Russian history; have students prepare a report on a part of Peter's "westernization" program.

4. Have students determine the specific reasons for the New Model Army's superiority over the Royalist army during the English Civil Wars.

5. Have students compare and contrast the characteristics of French Classicism and Dutch Realism with Renaissance and Baroque art.

CHAPTER 16
TOWARD A NEW HEAVEN AND A NEW EARTH: THE SCIENTIFIC REVOLUTION AND THE EMERGENCE OF MODERN SCIENCE

CHAPTER OUTLINE

I. Background to the Scientific Revolution
II. Toward a New Heaven: A Revolution in Astronomy
- A. Copernicus
- B. Kepler
- C. Galileo
- D. Newton

III. Advances in Medicine
IV. Women in the Origins of Modern Science
V. Toward a New Earth: Descartes, Rationalism, and a New View of Humankind
VI. Science and Religion in the Seventeenth Century
VII. The Spread of Scientific Knowledge
- A. The Scientific Method
- B. The Scientific Societies

VIII. Conclusion

CHAPTER SUMMARY

There was an interest in nature, "God's handiwork," in the Middle Ages" but the world was seen through a theological prism, relying on a few ancient authorities, particularly Aristotle. Other ancient authors were rediscovered in the Renaissance, and its artists made use of science, mathematics, and nature in portraying the real world. New technologies also contributed. The quest for scientific truths was often combined with a belief in magic and alchemy.

From the Scientific Revolution of the sixteenth and seventeenth centuries came a new cosmology. Aristotle and Claudius Ptolemy had posited a geocentric universe, with the fixed earth in the center and crystal spheres moving around it in perfect circular orbits. The inner crystal spheres were the heavenly bodies (the moon, planets, and fixed stars), and the outer was the God's Empyrean Heaven. But it was difficult to reconcile the Ptolemaic system with actual astronomical observations until Nicolaus Copernicus (d.1543) theorized a heliocentric or sun-centered universe. Johannes Kepler (d.1630) discovered that planetary orbits were elliptical and that a planet's speed is variable, thus destroying the idea of perfect circular orbits.

Galileo Galilei (d.1642), using the new telescope, discovered the moon's craters, moons of Jupiter, and sunspots; the universe was not perfect and unchanging as the Aristotelian system had claimed. Galileo was condemned by the Catholic Church, which feared a cosmology where humanity was no longer at the center of the universe and where God's heavens were material. In his *Principia*, Isaac Newton (d.1722) put forth mathematical proofs to support his universal law of gravitation: the entire universe is a mechanistic entity, operating though mathematical laws.

There were advances in medicine. Galen, the ancient Greek physician, claimed that there were two separate blood systems and that the body was made up of four humors, imbalances between them leading to disease. Andreas Vesalius (d.1564) used anatomical dissection, discovering that Galen was often incorrect. The discovery a single system of blood which circulates through veins and arteries was made by William Harvey (d.1657). In spite of gender discrimination, the lack of formal educational opportunities, and the assumption that females were inferior, many women made contributions to the Scientific Revolution, including Margaret Cavendish (d.1673) and the astronomer Maria Winkelmann (d.1720).

The Scientific Revolution led to doubt. Rene Descartes (d.1650) questioned all that he had learned and began again. What he could not doubt was his own existence–*I think therefore I am*–truth relies upon reason. Mind and matter differed; the mind could only achieve knowledge of the material world through reason and mathematics. Francis Bacon (d.1626) contributed the scientific method or the inductive method, where a study of the particular would lead to correct generalizations. To "conquer nature in action" was Bacon's goal.

Traditional religious beliefs were challenged. Blaise Pascal (d.1662) claimed that Christianity was not contrary to reason, that reason and emotions were inseparable. Ultimately, his faith was in the human heart, not the rational mind.

Knowledge of the new science was spread through universities, royal patronage, scientific societies, and scientific journals. The Scientific Revolution was more than merely intellectual theories. Its appeal was also to non-scientific elites because of its practical implications in economic progress and profits and in maintaining the social order, including the waging of war.

LECTURE AND DISCUSSION TOPICS

1. Discuss the revolutionary nature of the Scientific Revolution.

2. Assess the significance of the Scientific Revolution for the development of Western Civilization.

3. Explore the impact that the Hermetic tradition had on the emergence of the Scientific Revolution.

4. Discuss the central role that the revolution in astronomy played in the Scientific Revolution.

5. Explore the advances that took place in medicine during the sixteenth and seventeenth centuries, using additional examples other than those found in the text.

6. Examine the role of women in the Scientific Revolution, including personages, motivations, and accomplishments, as well as their reception by their male colleagues, and why.

7. Elaborate on the role of Isaac Newton in the Scientific Revolution, and his profound centrality in the intellectual world of the West until the theories of Einstein and Planck.

8. Examine the possible explanations why organized religion so vehemently supported Ptolemy's and Galen's systems.

9. Discuss the possibility that "science" became a new or alternative religion in the seventeenth century.

10. Examine the central role that Descartes played in the intellectual community of the seventeenth century.

DISCUSSION QUESTIONS FOR THE PRIMARY SOURCES (BOXED DOCUMENTS)

1. "On the Revolutions of the Heavenly Spheres": What major new ideas did Copernicus discuss in this selection? What was the source of these ideas? Why might one say that European astronomers finally destroyed the Middle Ages? (page 296)

2. "The Starry Messenger": What was the significance of Galileo's use of the telescope? What impressions did he receive of the moon? Why were his visual discoveries so stunning and how did he go about publicizing them? Why would these irrefutable discoveries have been so threatening to clergymen of all faiths? (page 297))

3. "The 'Natural Inferiority' of Women": What arguments did Spinoza use to support the idea of female inferiority? How would you refute these arguments? What was the effect of his line of reasoning upon the roles women could play? (page 301)

4. "Pascal: What is a Man in the Infinite?'": Why did Pascal question whether human beings could achieve scientific certainty? What does the sheer scale of Pascal's thought (and disquiet) tell you about the impact of the Scientific Revolution on the consciousness and conscience of Europeans? (page 303)

STUDENT RESEARCH AND PROJECT TOPICS

1. What were the roots of the Scientific Revolution? How do you explain its emergence?

2. How did seventeenth-century science differ from medieval science? Renaissance science? What was the old Ptolemaic conception of the universe and what did Copernicus, Kepler, and Galileo contribute to the development of the heliocentric theory of the cosmos? What was the reaction of the church to their findings?

3. What do we mean by the Newtonian world-machine? How did Newton arrive at this conception? What are the broader social, political, and cultural implications of viewing the entire universe as a machine?

4. What did Vesalius and Harvey contribute to a scientific view of medicine? Be specific and give examples.

5. How did women contribute to the beginnings of modern science? How did male scientists view women and female scientists?

6. What was rationalism? Why was Descartes considered the founder of "modern rationalism?"

7. Compare the methods used by Bacon and Descartes. Would Pascal agree with the methods and interests of these men? Why or why not?

8. How was the new scientific knowledge spread in the seventeenth century?

9. Why were seventeenth-century European intellectuals so intent on developing methods of study for entire bodies and specific fields of human knowledge? What did it mean then to become a methodical (or systematic) thinker or researcher?

10. What was "new" and what was not new about the seventeenth century's "New Heaven and a New Earth"? Be specific and give examples.

IDENTIFICATIONS

1. "God's handiwork"
2. "natural philosophers"
3. hermetic magic
4. Ptolemaic universe
5. Aristotle
6. geocentric universe
7. the Empyrean Heaven
8. Nicolaus Copernicus
9. *On the Revolutions of the Heavenly Spheres*
10. heliocentric universe
11. Johannes Kepler's elliptical orbits
12. Galileo Galilei's *The Starry Messenger*
13. the Inquisition
14. Isaac Newton's *Principia*
15. universal law of gravitation
16. Galen
17. Andreas Vesalius
18. *On the Fabric of the Human Body*
19. William Harvey
20. *On the Motion of the Heart and Blood*
21. Margaret Cavendish
22. Maria Winkelmann
23. Rene Descartes' *Discourse on Method*
24. "I think therefore I am"
25. Descartes' deductive method
26. Scientific Method
27. Francis Bacon's inductive method
28. "to conquer nature in action"
29. Blaise Pascal's *Pensees*
30. English Royal Society and French Royal Academy of Sciences

MULTIPLE CHOICE QUESTIONS

1. The Scientific Revolution of the seventeenth century
   a. was stimulated by a revived interest in Galen and Aristotle.
   b. directly resulted from reaction and revolt against the social and historical conditions of the Middle Ages.
   c. was largely due to a monastic revolution.
   d. although an innovative phase in western thinking, was based upon the intellectual and scientific accomplishments of previous centuries.
   ANSWER: d (page 293)

2. The origins of the Scientific Revolution can be traced to
   a. the work of thousands of ordinary artisans and mechanics making daily discoveries.
   b. the concentrated efforts of Protestant and Catholic clerics.
   c. the work of a very small number of great European intellectuals.
   d. a secretive group of alchemists and magicians.
   ANSWER: c (p. 294)

3. All of the following are considered possible influences and causes of the Scientific Revolution <u>except</u>
   a. the practical knowledge and technical skills emphasized by sixteenth-century universities.
   b. mathematical and naturalistic skills of Renaissance artists.
   c. the Hermetic belief in magic and alchemy.
   d. the humanists' rediscovery of Greek mathematicians and thinkers.
   ANSWER: a (pp. 293-294)

4. Which of these ancient authorities was not relied on by medieval scholars?
   a. Aristotle
   b. Galen
   c. Ptolemy
   d. Galileo
   ANSWER: d (p. 293)

5. According to Leonardo da Vinci, what subject was the key to understanding the nature of things?
   a. astronomy
   b. art
   c. mathematics
   d. the Bible
   ANSWER: c (p. 293)

6. Scholars devoted to Hermeticism believed
   a. that the world was a very recent creation still imperfect.
   b. credited the devil with control over the dark secrets of nature.
   c. saw the world as a living embodiment of divinity where humans could use mathematics and magic to dominate nature.
   d. retreated from study of the natural world to concentrate on mastery of theories of magic.
   ANSWER: c (p. 294)

7. The general conception of the universe before Copernicus was that

a. it was orderly with heaven at the center and the earth circling around it.
b. the earth was the stationary center and heavenly spheres orbited it.
c. the earth rested on the shell of a giant tortoise.
d. it could not be revealed according to God's will.

ANSWER: b (p. 294)

8. The greatest achievements in science during the sixteenth and seventeenth centuries came in what three areas?

a. astronomy, mechanics, and medicine
b. astronomy, biology, and chemistry
c. biology, mechanics, and ballistics
d. engineering, physics, and dentistry

ANSWER: a (p. 298)

9. The Ptolemaic conception of the universe was also known as

a. God's master plan.
b. the geocentric conception.
c. the lunacentric conception.
d. the expanding universe.

ANSWER: b (p. 294)

10. Copernicus's heliocentric theory was

a. based on the observations of several earlier astronomers and his own computations.
b. published without fear of scorn or reprisal.
c. derived from a vision he had.
d. a hoax he thought up to win an award in science.

ANSWER: a (p. 295)

11. Copernicus was a native of

a. Lithuania.
b. Poland.
c. Prussia.
d. Italy.

ANSWER: b (p. 295)

12. The immediate reaction to the theories of Copernicus

a. was immediate condemnation by clerics.
b. was broad acceptance by the majority of educated persons.
c. had little immediate impact.
d. the calling of the Council of Dort by Protestants and Catholics to question the astronomer closely prior to trial for blasphemy.

ANSWER: c (p. 295)

13. The ideas of Copernicus were

a. radically different from Aristotle's principle of the existence of heavenly spheres.
b. nearly as complicated as those of Ptolemy.
c. not too different from the ideas of today.
d. quite consistent with Biblical ideas.

ANSWER: b (p. 295)

14. Following upon Copernicus's heliocentric theories
   a. Johannes Kepler used data to derive laws of planetary motion that confirmed Copernicus's heliocentric theory but that showed the orbits were elliptical.
   b. Kepler observed the heavens and proved that planetary motion was circular around the sun.
   c. Kepler used magic to prove that the earth moved in a manner based on geometric figures, trying to bring harmony of the human soul into alignment with the universe.
   d. Galileo and Kepler demonstrated that the motion of the planets is steady and unchanging.
   ANSWER: a (p. 295)

15. Copernicus claimed that
   a. space was infinite and that the stars were billions of miles away.
   b. God resided in the center of the universe.
   c. the universe consisted of eight spheres with the sun motionless at the center.
   d. the church would always be correct in spite of contradictory appearances.
   ANSWER: c (p. 295)

16. Kepler's laws of planetary motion
   a. proposed a solution to the riddle about what substances made up planets.
   b. reverted to the Ptolemaic system with the earth at the center.
   c. gained acceptance despite disproving the great Aristotle's conviction that the motion of planets was steady and unchanging.
   d. showed that planets are constantly gaining speed.
   ANSWER: c (p. 296)

17. One of the dramatic findings of Galileo's observations was
   a. that orbits of planets were elliptical rather than circular.
   b. that planets were not made of some perfect substance but had natural properties similar to the earth.
   c. that the solar system was much larger than previously thought .
   d. that the stars were smaller than previously thought.
   ANSWER: b (p. 296)

18. The first European to make systematic observations of the heavens by telescope was
   a. Galileo.
   b. Copernicus.
   c. Brahe.
   d. Kepler.
   ANSWER: a (p. 296)

19. The Catholic Roman Inquisition attacked Galileo for his scientific ideas with the encouragement of
   a. European monarchs fearful of losing their authority.
   b. even Protestant theologians who hated Galileo, an Italian Catholic scholar.
   c. elements within the church pledged to defend ancient Aristotelian ideas and Catholic orthodoxy.
   d. the pope who refused to believe that the earth and planets really move.
   ANSWER: c (p. 296)

20. Galileo published his observations of the heaven in
    a. *The Starry Messenger.*
    b. *The Principia.*
    c. *On the Revolution of the Heavenly Spheres.*
    d. *Discourse on Method.*
        ANSWER: a (p. 296)

21. What actions did the Catholic church pursue concerning Galileo and his ideas?
    a. authorities reluctantly agreed to his theories
    b. turned him over to the Papal Curia.
    c. allowed Galileo six months to change his mind concerning his theories
    d. ordered him to recant in a public trial.
        ANSWER: d (p. 297)

22. After Galileo's condemnation by the Inquisition, leadership in science passed to
    a. Italy and Greece.
    b. Spain and Portugal.
    c. Poland and Russia.
    d. England, France and the Dutch Republic.
        ANSWER: d (p. 297)

23. Isaac Newton's scientific discoveries
    a. were resisted more in his own country, England, than in the rest of Europe.
    b. although readily accepted in his own country, were resisted on the continent.
    c. were modern in their removal of God from universal laws.
    d. were among the first to be printed in a language other than Latin.
        ANSWER: b (p. 298)

24. In Newton's *Principia*, he demonstrated through his rules of reasoning that the universe was
    a. a chaotic, unpredictable place.
    b. in fact, a mathematical impossibility.
    c. a regulated machine operating according to universal laws.
    d. finite and its boundaries are clearly defined.
        ANSWER: c (p. 298)

25. Newton's universal law of gravitation proved that
    a. through its mathematical proof it could explain all motion in the universe.
    b. motion in the universe operated on a series of distinct universal laws.
    c. people could never comprehend why the planets moved the way they did.
    d. the universe began with the "big bang".
        ANSWER: a (p. 298)

26. The Greco-Roman doctor who had the most influence on medieval medical thought was
    a. Hippocrates.
    b. Rhazes.
    c. Galen.
    d. Aristotle.
        ANSWER: c (p. 298)

27. The most famous of the female astronomers in Germany was
   a. Margaret Cavendish.
   b. Maria Winkelmann.
   c. Aphra Benn.
   d. Gillian Larson.
      ANSWER: b (p. 300)

28. Among the following, who is <u>not</u> associated with major changes in sixteenth and seventeenth-century medical research?
   a. Andreas Vesalius.
   b. William Harvey.
   c. Paracelsus.
   d. Galen.
      ANSWER: d (p. 298)

29. *On the Fabric of the Human Body*
   a. was Andreas Vesalius' masterpiece on anatomical structure.
   b. contained William Harvey's theories on blood circulation.
   c. contained Paracelsus' theories on a macrocosm-microcosm universe.
   d. was Galen's masterpiece that influenced so many doctors in the Middle Ages.
      ANSWER: a (p. 299)

30. William Harvey's *On the Motion of the Heart and Blood* refuted the ideas of
   a. the immune system being associated with the pancreas.
   b. the liver as the beginning point of circulation of blood.
   c. the independent functioning of the lymph system.
   d. herbal healing.
      ANSWER: b (p. 299)

31. The role of women in the Scientific Revolution is illustrated by
   a. the scientific community's growing acceptance of female members.
   b. Maria Merian's breakthrough in astronomy.
   c. Margaret Cavendish, who participated in her day's scientific debates.
   d Maria Winkelmann, an entomologist accepted into the Berlin Academy of Sciences.
      ANSWER: c (p. 299)

32. The overall effect of the Scientific Revolution on the argument about women was to
   a. dispel traditional myths of female inferiority.
   b. increase the role of women in the child-bearing process.
   c. generate facts about differences between men and women that were used to prove male dominance.
   d. demonstrate that there was no inherent skeletal differences between the sexes.
      ANSWER: c (p. 300)

33. Margaret Cavendish attacked the belief
   a. that humans through science were masters of nature.
   b. that science was for the benefit of all humanity.
   c. in women being equal to men, despite her position.
   d. of a Newtonian world-machine.
      ANSWER: a (p. 300)

34. Benedict Spinoza believed that women
   a. were equal to men.
   b. were little more than animals without a soul.
   c. were "naturally" inferior to men.
   d. could stand on their own, but society functioned far better when men alone ruled.
      ANSWER: c (p. 301)

35. The philosophy of René Descartes
   a. stressed a separation of mind and matter.
   b. stressed a holistic universe of mind and matter devoid of a creator-God.
   c. saw the material world as a living thing containing the human essence.
   d. would not have a wide influence upon Western thought until the nineteenth century.
      ANSWER: a (p. 301)

36. What was the name of Descartes' book that expounded his theories about the universe?
   a. *On the Revolution of Heavenly Bodies.*
   b. *On the Fabric of the Human Body.*
   c. *Discourse on Method.*
   d. *Mind Over Matter.*
      ANSWER: c (p. 301)

37. Descartes believed that the world could be understood by
   a. the same principles inherent in mathematical thinking.
   b. quiet contemplation and following of the Scriptures.
   c. mystical experiences.
   d. interpreting dreams and applying that knowledge to our everyday lives.
      ANSWER: a (p. 301)

38. Francis Bacon was important to the Scientific Revolution for his emphasis on
   a. empirical, experimental observation.
   b. pure theoretical science.
   c. reaching deductive conclusions by moving from general to particular principles.
   d. science's urgent need to catalogue all of nature's diversity.
      ANSWER: a (p. 304)

39. Showing the disputatious nature of European scientific thinkers, Francis Bacon rejected
   a. the ideas of Copernicus and Kepler and misunderstood Galileo.
   b. the theories of Vesalius.
   c. the publications of the Royal Society.
   d. the political views of John Locke.
      ANSWER: a (p. 304)

40. Organized religions in the seventeenth century generally
   a. conceded the accomplishments of science and separated theology from science proper.
   b. rejected scientific discoveries that conflicted with the Christian view of the world.
   c. contributed greatly to scientific research.
   d. largely ignored science as merely a "toy for the minds of God's children."
      ANSWER: b (pp. 297, 302)

41. The eighteenth century used anatomy and physiology to establish the
a. equality of men and women.
b. superiority of men over women.
c. superiority of women over men.
d. the theory of natural selection.
ANSWER: b (p. 300)

42. Descartes
a. used the inductive method.
b. denied the existence of God.
c. claimed that "I think, therefore I am."
d. agreed in all matters with Francis Bacon.
ANSWER: c (p. 301)

43. In his work *Pensees*, Pascal
a. showed that science and religion were incompatible.
b. popularized the scientific method.
c. offered his thoughts on the heliocentric theory.
d. attempted to convince rationalists that Christianity was valid by appealing to their reason and emotions.
ANSWER: d (p. 302)

44. For Blaise Pascal, humans
a. could know infinity through reason.
b. were the summation of all things.
c. could only understand that which is revealed to them by the Bible.
d. could not understand infinity, only God could.
ANSWER: d (p. 303)

45. Concerning the first important scientific societies, the French Academy differed from the English Royal Society in the former's
a. government support and control.
b. publication of scientific journals.
c. focus on theoretical work in mechanics and astronomy.
d. belief that science should proceed along the lines of a cooperative venture.
ANSWER: a (p. 304)

46. During the seventeenth century, royal and princely patronage of science
a. declined greatly.
b. was common only in Italy.
c. became an international phenomenon.
d. replaced funding by the church.
ANSWER: c (p. 305)

47. The first of the scientific societies appeared in what country?
a. Italy
b. Russia
c. Poland
d. Scotland
ANSWER: a (p. 304)

48. The scientific societies of early modern Europe
a. were always s under government control.
b. submitted their discoveries and observations to the churches for approval.
c. stressed only the theoretical findings of the their investigations.
d. initially stressed the practical benefits of science.
ANSWER: d (p. 305)

49. Science became an integral part of Western culture in the eighteenth century because
a. people perceived it to be rationally superior to other belief systems.
b. its mechanistic nature was popular with the lower classes.
c. the victory of radical political groups, such as the Levellers, following the Puritan Revolution encouraged freedom of expression.
d. it offered a new means to make profit and maintain social order.
ANSWER: d (p. 305)

50. The key figure of the Scientific Revolution who would inspire the search for natural laws in other fields, including society and economics, was
a. Galileo.
b. Newton.
c. Descartes.
d. Pascal.
ANSWER: b (p. 305)

RELEVANT WORLD-WIDE WEB SITES/RESOURCES

1. The Galileo Project:
http://es.rice.edu/ES/humsoc/Galileo
(A massive site devoted to all aspects of Galileo's life and work equipped with numerous links to documents and other relevant source readings. Highly recommended.)

2. The Scientific Revolution, Modern European History Advanced Placement:
http://pw2.netcom.com/~giardina/newton.html
(A fine site with good biographical material on all the major scientists and philosophers active in the period.)

3. Internet History of Science Sourcebook:
http://www.fordham.edu/halsall/science/sciencesbook.html
(Superb site on the history of science within the context of western civilization. See in particular the subsections on Classical Science and the Scientific Revolution.)

RELEVANT VIDEO RESOURCES

Ascent of Man: The Starry Messenger, Time-Life Video, (52 minutes).

Ascent of Man: The Majestic Clock-Work, Time-Life Video, (52 minutes).

(Both programs above, from the superb Ascent of Man series with Jacob Bronowski, are among the finest documentary productions ever made on the history of science and technology in early modern Europe. Other segments of the series can be highly recommended to accompany the study of western civilization and the history of science from 1600 to 1970.)

SUGGESTED STUDENT ACTIVITIES

1. Have students answer the following question: What medical practices and knowledge of the sixteenth century are still used today? This project could possibly include an interview with the students' family physician.

2. Have students determine what religious/theological assumptions if any have been proven or discovered by science.

3. Suggest that students recreate in class the trial of Galileo.

CHAPTER 17
THE EIGHTEENTH CENTURY: AN AGE OF ENLIGHTENMENT

CHAPTER OUTLINE

I. The Enlightenment
- A. The Paths to Enlightenment
  1. New Skepticism
  2. The Impact of Travel Literature
  3. The Legacy of Locke and Newton
- B. The Philosophes and Their Ideas
  1. Montesquieu and Political Thought
  2. Voltaire and the Enlightenment
  3. Diderot and the Encyclopedia
  4. Toward a New "Science of Man"
  5. The Later Enlightenment
  6. The "Woman's Question" in the Enlightenment
- C. The Social Environment of the Philosophes

II. Culture and Society in the Enlightenment
- A. Innovations in Art, Music, and Literature
- B. The High Culture of the Eighteenth Century
- C. Popular Culture
- D. Crime and Punishment

III. Religion and the Churches
- A. Toleration and Religious Minorities
- B. Popular Religion in the Eighteenth Century

IV. Conclusion

CHAPTER SUMMARY

The eighteenth century was the age of the Enlightenment, an era when intellectuals, known as *philosophes*, wished to apply the scientific method with its reason and rationality to the challenges of society. The result would be progress and improvement in the human condition. The findings of the scientific revolution reached a wider audience through the works of numerous popularizers. Travel books increased the awareness of different cultures: some glorified the so-called "natural man" as superior to the civilized European, others admired Chinese civilization. Newton's scientific laws became a paradigm for discovering natural laws, and John Locke's *tabula rasa*, or blank sheet, indicated that reason and sense experience could create a better world.

A cosmopolitan group, the philosophes used reason to improve society. State censorship was overcome by having works published in Holland or writing about the Persians when they really meant French society, as did the baron de Montesquieu (d.1755). His *The Spirit of the Laws* praised the system of checks and balances and separation of powers which he believed were the essence of the British political system, an important concept of the United States Constitution. Voltaire (d.1778) attacked the intolerance of organized religion, and many philosophes adopted Deism with its mechanistic god and a universe operating according to natural laws.

Denis Diderot (d.1784) compiled a multi-volume *Encyclopedia*, a compendium of Enlightenment ideas. In economics, the Physiocrats rejected mercantilism in favor of the laws of supply and demand and *laissez-faire*, as did Adam Smith's *Wealth of Nations*. Jean-Jacques Rousseau (d.1778), like Locke, believed in the social contract theory, arguing that society must be governed by the general will. In claiming that in education children should follow their instincts--reason was not enough--he was a precursor of Romanticism. Many of the philosophes had traditional attitudes towards women, but Mary Anstell (d.1731) and Mary Wollstonecraft (d.1797) argued for the equality of the sexes and the right of women to be educated. The Enlightenment appealed mostly to the urban middle classes; it passed the peasants by. Its ideas were discussed in Parisian salons, coffeehouses, reading clubs, lending libraries, and societies like the Freemasons.

In art, the lightness and curves of the Rococo replaced the Baroque. In classical music there were major development in the opera, oratorio, sonata, concerto, and the symphony by Johann Sebastian Bach (d.1750), George Frederick Handel (d.1759), Franz Joseph Haydn (d.1809), and Wolfgang Amadeus Mozart (d.1791). In England, the novel became a new literary form. There was an increase in the reading public with books, magazines, and newspapers. Elite private schools emphasized the Greek and Latin classics, but new middle class education stressed modern languages and other relevant subjects. The theories of Cesare Beccaria (d.1794) and others contributed to a decline in the use of torture and capital punishment.

There was a separation between popular culture and the culture of the elites, although the rate of literacy was rising among the majority, in part because of an increase in primary education. State churches, traditional and conservative, were the norm. There was some gain in religious toleration for minorities including the Jews, although anti-Semitic attitudes continued. Popular religious movements appealed to the non-elites. In England, John Wesley (d.1791) led a religious revival movement among the common people. It was a century of both change and tradition.

LECTURE AND DISCUSSION TOPICS

1. Discuss the significance of the philosophes to the Enlightenment, and examine their ideas and beliefs, using specific examples.

2. Examine the Enlightenment as an elite movement.

3. Explore the Scientific Revolution roots of the Enlightenment.

4. Assess the significance of Newton and Locke upon the later philosophes.

5. Discuss the Enlightenment as an urban and middle class phenomenon.

6. Compare and contrast the political and social ideas of Voltaire, Montesquieu, and Rousseau.

7. Discuss the impact that the Enlightenment had, or did not have, upon religion in the eighteenth century.

8. Explore the Enlightenment as the beginning of modernity.

9. Discuss the historic and symbolic importance of the Parisian salon and the London coffeehouse.

10. Compare and contrast the high culture and the popular culture of the eighteenth century.

MAP EXERCISES

1. The Enlightenment in Europe. MAP 17.1. Where were the centers of the Enlightenment and why were they located where they were? What role did geography play in explaining the centers of the Enlightenment? What role did history play? (page 310)

DISCUSSION QUESTIONS FOR THE PRIMARY SOURCES (BOXED DOCUMENTS)

1. "The Attack on Religious Intolerance": Compare the two approaches of Voltaire to the problem of religious intolerance. Do you think one is more effective than the other? Why? Is Voltaire merely a product of his own era, that of the Enlightenment, or did he help make or construct that era? (page 312)

2. "A Social Contract": What is Rousseau's concept of the social contract? What implications did it contain for political thought, especially in regard to the development of democratic ideas? What does Rousseau mean by "the general will"? Might that concept lead as much to dictatorship and totalitarianism as to democracy? Why and/or why not? (page 313)

3. "The Rights of Women": What arguments does Mary Wollstonecraft make on behalf of the rights of women? What contemporary trends in other aspects of eighteenth-century life would have brought the condition of women into sharper focus as an essential topic of enlightened investigation and improvement? What might explain Wollstonecraft's relative failure to achieve her objectives in her own era? (page 315)

4. "The Conversion Experience in Wesley's Methodism": How does the emotionalism of this passage relate to enlightened thinkers' fascination with the passions and the workings of human reason? Did eighteenth-century religious thinkers and religious practices accept or reject new enlightened ideas about human nature and behavior? How would Voltaire have responded to Wesley and his revivalism? (page 320)

STUDENT RESEARCH AND PROJECT TOPICS

1. Discuss the major intellectual changes that led to the Enlightenment.

2. What specific contributions did Montesquieu, Voltaire, and Diderot make to the age of the Enlightenment? Compare and contrast their political ideas with Thomas Hobbes and Machiavelli.

3. Discuss the significance and the influence of John Locke and Isaac Newton on the Enlightenment.

4. What new ideas did the philosophes contribute on the following subjects: politics, the "new science of man," economics, education, and religion?

5. What were the major ideas of Jean-Jacques Rousseau? In what ways were Rousseau's ideas unique, differing from those of his predecessors

6. What role did women play in the development of the Enlightenment?

7. How do the art and literature of the eighteenth century reflect the political and social life of the period?

8. Define "high culture." In what ways was high culture expressed in the eighteenth century?

9. What is "popular culture" and how was it expressed in the eighteenth century? How do you explain the differences between high and popular culture at the time?

10. What kinds of experiences would you associate with the popular religion of the eighteenth century? How did the intellectual and emotional debates of the Enlightenment play themselves out in the realm of human spirituality and the churches?

IDENTIFICATIONS

1. Immanuel Kant
2. *reason, natural law, progress*
3. Fontenelle's *Plurality of Worlds*
4. James Cook
5. John Locke's *tabula rasa*
6. *Essay Concerning Human Understanding*
7. *philosophes*
8. Montesquieu's *The Spirit of the Laws*
9. Voltaire's *Treatise on Toleration*
10. Denis Diderot's *Encyclopedia*
11. A science of man
12. Physiocrats
13. Francois Quesnay
14. Adam Smith's *Wealth of Nations*
15. *laissez-faire*
16. Jean-Jacques Rousseau
17. *The Social Contract* and the general will
18. Mary Astell
19. Mary Wollstonecraft>s *Vindication of the Rights of Woman*
20. the salon and the coffeehouse
21. Marie-Therese de Geoffrin
22. Rococo
23. Antoine Watteau
24. Balthasar Neumann
25. Johann Sebastian Bach
26. George Frederick Handel
27. Franz Joseph Haydn
28. Wolfgang Amadeus Mozart
29. daily newspapers
30. Cesare Beccaria=s *On Crimes and Punishments*
31. Carnival
32. gin
33. Ashkenazic and Sephardic Jews
34. Joseph II
35. John Wesley and Methodism.

MULTIPLE CHOICE QUESTIONS

1. The scientist-philosopher who provides a link between the scientists of the 17th century and the philosophes of the next was
   a. Voltaire.
   b. Diderot.
   c. Fontenelle.
   d. Beccaria.
      ANSWER: c (page 308)

2. Enlightened thinkers can be understood as secularists because they strongly recommended
   a. the application of the scientific method to the analysis and understanding of all aspects of human life.
   b. the rational dismantling of all churches and their competing but empty ideologies.
   c. a complete stop to all efforts at the reform of justice.
   d. rigorous state control of all forms of education.
      ANSWER: a (p. 308)

3. The German philosopher Immanuel Kant proclaimed the motto of the Enlightenment to be
   a. "Death to Priests!"
   b. "Convert the Kings to Peace!"
   c. "Dare to Know!"
   d. "Free Women from the Tyranny of Males!"
      ANSWER: c (p. 308)

4. European intellectual life in the eighteenth century was marked by the emergence of
   a. anti-Semitism and sharper persecution of minorities.
   b. secularization and a search to find the natural laws governing human life.
   c. sophism and the mockery of past traditions.
   d. monastic schools and medieval modes of training religious thinkers.
      ANSWER: b (p. 308)

5. The works of Fontenelle announce the Enlightenment because they
   a. popularize a growing skepticism toward the claims of religion.
   b. portray churches as allies of scientific progress.
   c. discourage amateur conversations about scientific matters.
   d. question the capacity of women to comprehend scientific discourse.
      ANSWER: a (p. 308)

6. A major inspiration for travel literature in the eighteenth century were the Pacific adventures of
   a. James Cook.
   b. Ferdinand de Lesseps.
   c. Zheng He.
   d. David Hume.
      ANSWER: a (p. 308)

7. John Locke's philosophy contributed to the development of Enlightenment ideas by arguing that a person's character was shaped by
  a. that person's environment, not by innate ideas implanted in the brain by God.
  b. that person's genetic heritage.
  c. the person's elementary education.
  d. that person's personal relationships.
    ANSWER: a (p. 309)

8. The French philosophes
  a. were literate intellectuals who meant to change the world by advancing reason and rationality.
  b. flourished in an atmosphere of government support.
  c. sought no extension of Enlightenment to other states.
  d. supported state censorship of ideas contrary to their own.
    ANSWER: a (p. 310)

9. Isaac Newton and John Locke
  a. created two antagonistic religious systems of thought.
  b. provided deep inspiration for the Enlightenment by arguing that through rational reasoning and the human acquisition of knowledge one could discover natural laws governing all aspects of human society.
  c. claimed that mathematics and science would bring about the cure for the evils of society but only very slowly.
  d. said the philosophes were the prophets of the future and that their rejection of the scientific revolution was justified.
    ANSWER: b (p. 309)

10. The French philosophes mostly included people from
  a. the nobility and the middle class.
  b. the lower class and the lower middle class.
  c. aristocracy and nobility.
  d. urban artisans.
    ANSWER: a (p. 309)

11. Above all, Montesquieu's *The Spirit of the Laws* was concerned with
  a. the superior position of executive leadership.
  b. the importance of the legislature.
  c. the judiciary being the most important element of government.
  d. maintaining balances among the various branches of government.
    ANSWER: d (p. 311)

12. The recognized capital of the Enlightenment was
  a. Geneva.
  b. Berlin.
  c. London.
  d. Paris.
    ANSWER: d (p. 310)

13. A key new type of enlightened writing fueling skepticism about the "truths" of Christianity and European society was
a. psychological autobiography.
b. travel reports and comparative studies of old and new world cultures.
c. ribald stories of peasant ignorance.
d. aristocratic joke books showing the bad humor of supposed social elites.
ANSWER: b (pp. 308-309)

14. The leader of the Physiocrats and their advocacy of natural economic laws was
a. Denis Diderot.
b. Adam Smith.
c. Francois Quesnay.
d. Cesare Beccaria.
ANSWER: c (p. 312)

15. Voltaire was best known for his criticism of
a. the German monarchical system.
b. the separation of church and state.
c. religious intolerance.
d. Plato and the Greeks.
ANSWER: c (p. 311)

16. Deism was based on
a. the Newtonian world-machine with God as its benevolent mechanic, designing the universe in accord with rational laws.
b. God answering prayers directed to him in song.
c. the divinity of Jesus as prime mover of the rational universe.
d. the denial of the existence of a Supreme Being.
ANSWER: a (p. 311)

17. Which of the following statements best applies to Denis Diderot?
a. His materialistic, atheistic beliefs became tempered by his adoption of deism.
b. His *Encyclopedia* had considerable impact, particularly after its price was greatly reduced.
c. His *Encyclopedia* had little impact due to its limited elitist appeal.
d. The core of his educational beliefs expressed his devotion to sexual monogamy and chastity.
ANSWER: b (p. 312)

18. The belief in natural laws underlying all areas of human life led to
a. the social sciences.
b. an abandonment of the scientific method.
c. intellectual stagnation.
d. the formation of the Church of Latter-Day Saints.
ANSWER: a (p. 312)

19. Diderot's most famous contribution to the Enlightenment's battle against religious fanaticism, intolerance, and prudery was his

a. great play "Is Rome Burning?"
b. his 28-volume *Encyclopedia* compiling articles by many influential philosophes.
c. his autobiography published in French.
d. his biography of Newton, "the greatest Europe has ever known."
ANSWER: b (p. 312)

20. The best statement of laissez-faire was made in 1776 by

a. Thomas Jefferson.
b. John Locke.
c. John Adams.
d. Adam Smith.
ANSWER: d (p. 313)

21. Which the following works expressed Rousseau's political ideas on the "general will"?

a. *The Progress of the Human Mind*
b. *Emile*
c. *The Social Contract*
d. *Discourse on the Origins of the Inequality of Mankind*
ANSWER: c (p. 313)

22. Who said that individuals "will be forced to be free"?

a. Baron Paul d'Holbach.
b. Jean Jacques Rousseau.
c. Denis Diderot.
d. Francois Quesnay.
ANSWER: b (p. 313)

23. Montesquieu's *Persian Letters*

a. expressed his admiration of Islam and the East.
b. was a translation of a great literary work from ancient Persia.
c. allowed him to criticize the Catholic church and the French monarchy.
d. was first written in Latin and later translated into French..
ANSWER: c (p. 311)

24. In Rousseau's *The Social Contract*, he expressed his belief that

a. government was an evil that should be eliminated.
b. the individual's will is the most important.
c. freedom is achieved by being forced to follow what is best for all or the "general will.@
d. a child was a small adult with all the same abilities and obligations.
ANSWER: c (p. 313)

25. For Rousseau, what was the source of inequality and the chief cause of crimes?

a. private property
b. marriage
c. religion
d. ignoring the "general will"
ANSWER: a (p. 313)

26. Rousseau's influential novel, *Emile*, deals with these key Enlightenment themes:
   a. proper child rearing and human education
   b. the best roles for women in making modern society
   c. the necessity of church marriage and reform of church teaching on this sacrament
   d. the abolition of the pope's restrictions on religious practices and the content of sermons
      ANSWER: a (p. 314)

27. Of great importance to the Enlightenment were the salons, which
   a. gave social mobility to both men and women.
   b. were usually run by women but for male guests.
   c. provided a forum for the serious discussion of the ideas of the philosophes.
   d. all of the above
      ANSWER: d (pp. 314-315)

28. The strongest statement and vindication of women's rights during the Enlightenment was made by
   a. Mary Wollstonecraft.
   b. Beatrice Williams.
   c. Mary Astell.
   d. Princess Amelia of Austria.
      ANSWER: a (p. 314)

29. The Rococo architectural style of the eighteenth century was
   a. confined to France.
   b. best expressed in the architectural works of Baron d'Holbach.
   c. evident in the masterpieces of Balthasar Neumann.
   d. characterized by strict geometric patterns and an emphasis on power.
      ANSWER: c (p. 316)

30. Choose the correct relationship between the Rococo artist and his work.
   a. Antoine Watteau--Bishop's Palace at Würzburg
   b. Giovanni Battista Tiepolo' *Plurality of Worlds*
   c. Balthasar Neumann--pilgrimage church of the Vierzehnheiligen
   d. Domenikus Zimmermann--the salon
      ANSWER: c (p. 316)

31. Johann Sebastian Bach
   a. was best known for his operas.
   b. became a close German confidant of Voltaire.
   c. produced religious music as a way to worship God.
   d. all the above
      ANSWER: a (p. 317)

32. European music in the later eighteenth century was well characterized by
   a. Haydn and Mozart, who caused a shift from the Baroque to the classical.
   b. Handel, the most religiously inspired of the period's composers.
   c. the strictly elitist, aristocratic works of Haydn.
   d. the innovative, secular compositions of Bach.
      ANSWER: a (p. 317)

33. Which eighteenth-century composer was considered most innovative and wrote the opera, *The Marriage of Figaro*?

a. Bach
b. Handel
c. Haydn
d. Mozart

ANSWER: d (p. 317)

34. Eighteenth-century writers, especially in England, used this new form of literary expression to attack the hypocrisies of the era and provide sentimental entertainment to growing numbers of readers:

a. epic poetry
b. autobiography
c. novels
d. short stories

ANSWER: c (p. 317)

35. The establishment of the modern fictional novel is generally attributed to

a. the French.
b. the English.
c. the Germans.
d. the Italians.

ANSWER: b (p. 317)

36. The English writer who argued in *A Serious Proposal to the Ladies* that women should become better educated was

a. Anne Stuart.
b. Mary Astell
c. Jane Austin.
d. Mary Wollstonecraft.

ANSWER: b (p. 314)

37. The French Rococo painter who portrayed the aristocratic life as refined, sensual, and civilized was

a. Antoine Watteau.
b. Balthasar Neumann.
c. Madame Geoffrin.
d. Rembrandt.

ANSWER: a (p. 316)

38. Great Britain led the way in the eighteenth century in producing

a. magazines.
b. newspapers.
c. coffee houses.
d. all of the above

ANSWER: d (p. 318)

39. High culture in eighteenth-century Europe was characterized by

a. the enormous impact of the book publishing industry.
b. the decline of French as an international language.
c. the decline of the magazine with the rise of the novel.
d. the increased dependency of authors on wealthy patrons.

ANSWER: a (p. 317)

40. The musical composition which has been called Aone of those rare works that appeal immediately to everyone, and yet is indisputably a masterpiece of the highest order is

a. Bach's *St. Matthew's Passion.*
b. Haydn's *The Seasons.*
c. Handel's *Messiah.*
d. Mozart's *The Marriage of Figaro.*
ANSWER: c (p. 317)

41. A less brutal approach to justice in the eighteenth century is associated with

a. Voltaire.
b. Beccaria.
c. Montesquieu.
d. Hume.
ANSWER: b (p. 319)

42. Concerning the European legal system, by the end of the eighteenth century

a. a trend away from imprisonment and toward capital punishment began.
b. corporal and capital punishment were on the decline.
c. criminal punishments became more cruel as violent crimes increased.
d. all of the above
ANSWER: b (p. 319)

43. By the beginning of the eighteenth century, most European states

a. had a hierarchy of courts to deal with civil and criminal cases.
b. had abandoned the use of judicial torture to obtain evidence.
c. still had no separate judicial system.
d. lacked barristers and attorneys.
ANSWER: a (p. 319)

44. The punishment of crime in the eighteenth century was often

a. public and very gruesome.
b. carried out by mobs after the criminals were charged in court.
c. less severe than the crime would merit.
d. the responsibility of the army.
ANSWER: a (p. 319)

45. The Carnival of the Mediterranean world was

a. a period of intense sexual activity and gross excesses.
b. strictly a secular event with no spiritual function.
c. a popular, lower-class event seldom characterized by acts of violence or aggression.
d. none of the above
ANSWER: a (p. 318)

46. A cheap and popular alcoholic drink in eighteenth century England was

a. beer.
b. gin.
c. wine.
d. porter.
ANSWER: b (pp. 318-319)

47. In eighteenth-century Europe, churches, both Catholic and Protestant,
  a. declined in numbers and influence.
  b. still played a major role in social and spiritual areas.
  c. was responsible for the dramatic role in literary.
  d. had not changed much in two centuries.
    ANSWER: b (p. 319)

48. The Jews of eighteenth-century Europe
  a. were assimilated into French society through the unanimous calls of the philosophes for integration.
  b. were most persecuted in Poland and Lithuania.
  c. were most free in participating in banking and commercial activities in tolerant cities.
  d. won the right to publicly practice of their religion in Austria with Joseph II's Toleration
    ANSWER: c (p. 320)

49. John Wesley
  a. was responsible for the resurgence of Catholic piety.
  b. supported a rationalistic approach to Protestantism.
  c. spread the teachings of pietism through his Moravian Brethren.
  d. created and controlled his evangelical Methodist church using revivalist techniques.
    ANSWER: d (pp. 320-321)

50. Significant elements of rationalism and deism in what two countries led some ordinary Protestant churchgoers in reaction to new and dynamic religious movements?
  a. England and Germany.
  b. France and Austria.
  c. Italy and Spain.
  d. Sweden and Poland.
    ANSWER: a (p. 321)

RELEVANT WORLD-WIDE WEB SITES/RESOURCES

Numerous excellent sites exist covering various aspects of the European Enlightenments. Among the best of these are:

1. Eighteenth-Century Resources:
http://andromeda.rutgers.edu/~jlynch/18th
(A superb site maintained by a specialist in the era with numerous fine links to other online resources. Highly recommended.)

2. Eighteenth-Century Studies (at Carnegie Mellon University):
http://english-www.hss.cmu.edu/18th/
(Fine site with online excerpts from novels, plays, and memoirs of the era in English.)

3. The Enlightenment: From Age of Faith to Age of Reason:
http://www.stedwards.edu/cfpages/stoll/iw/enlightn.htm
(Excellent site with good links to other relevant resources.)

4. Internet Modern History Sourcebook (at Fordham University):
http://www.fordham.edu/halsall/mod/modsbook.html

(Site includes information, documents, and links arranged by era with extensive materials and links on the Ancien Regime, Scientific Revolution, and Enlightenments. Superb selection of online original documents from all eras for student use.)

RELEVANT VIDEO RESOURCES

Civilisation, Public Media Video/BBC Television, Programs 9 and 10, "The Pursuit of Happiness" and "The Smile of Reason," (50 minutes each). (Topics covered include Rococo Art, south German architecture, European palace building at Versailles and Blenheim, and the cultural history of Parisian salons.)

The Famous Composers Series, PBS Home Video, (multiple programs, 30 minutes each). (Programs available with profiles of J.S. Bach, J. Haydn, and W.A. Mozart.)

RELEVANT MUSICAL PERFORMANCES

Johann Sebastian Bach, The Well-Tempered Clavier; Four Orchestral Suites; or Mass in B Minor.

George Frederick Handel, Messiah or Water Music.

Franz Joseph Haydn, The Creation or Symphony No. 104, "The London."

Wolfgang Amadeus Mozart, The Magic Flute; Don Giovanni; Requiem; or Symphony No. 41.

SUGGESTED STUDENT ACTIVITIES

1. Have students choose a philosophe such as Montesquieu or Locke and have them trace the development of their political thought and how their ideas have influenced modern political thinking.

2. Students could do the same with one of the great eighteenth-century composers, tracing his musical development and influence. The published letters of Haydn or Mozart in English would be excellent sources here.

3. Have students do a comparative study of the Rococo, Baroque, and Renaissance styles of architecture.

CHAPTER 18
THE EIGHTEENTH CENTURY: EUROPEAN STATES, INTERNATIONAL WARS, AND SOCIAL CHANGE

CHAPTER OUTLINE

I. The European States
- A. Enlightened Absolutism?
- B. The Atlantic Seaboard States
  - 1. France: The Long Rule of Louis XV and Louis XVI
  - 2. Great Britain: King and Parliament
- C. Absolutism in Central and Eastern Europe
  - 1. Prussia: The Army and the Bureaucracy
  - 2. The Austrian Empire of the Habsburgs
  - 3. Russia under Catherine the Great
- D. Enlightened Absolutism Revisited

II. Wars and Diplomacy
- A. The Seven Years War (1756-1763)

III. Economic Expansion and Social Change
- A. Population and Food
- B. Family, Marriage, and Birthrate Patterns
- C. New Methods of Finance and Industry

IV. The Social Order of the Eighteenth Century
- A. The Peasants
- B. The Nobility
- C. The Inhabitants of Towns and Cities

V. Conclusion

CHAPTER SUMMARY

During the eighteenth century, royal authority was often justified by the service the monarch could render to the state and its people rather than by divine right. Some believed that the monarchs should have a monopoly of power in what is called "enlightened despotism" or "enlightened absolutism." Britain's constitutional monarchy was an alternative.

For much of the century, France was ruled by Louis XV (r.1715-1774). Only five when he ascended the throne, in his maturity he proved to be weak and lazy, controlled by his mistresses and advisors. His successor was little better. Louis XVI (r.1774-1793) was unprepared, and his wife, Marie Antoinette, an Austrian princess, became a focus of anti-royal attitudes. In Britain, power was shared between kings and parliament, with the latter gaining influence. The new ruling dynasty, from Hanover in Germany, was ignorant of British traditions and incompetent, which led to a new position in government, that of the Prime Minister. Trade and manufacturing were beginning to supercede the economic power of land and agriculture.

Prussia rose to major power status under Frederick William I (r.1713-1740) and Frederick II the Great (r.1740-1786), strengthening the kingdom through an efficient bureaucracy and a larger army. Frederick the Great was in the model of an enlightened despot: he reformed the laws, allowed religious toleration and considerable freedom of speech and the press, but he also increased the army to 200,000. In the Austrian Empire, Empress Maria Theresa (r.1740-1780) centralized the government and Joseph II (r.1780-1790) abolished serfdom, reformed the laws, and granted religious toleration, but his reforms did not outlast his reign. Russia's Catherine II the Great (r.1762-1796) also instituted reforms, but they favored the landed nobility rather than the peasants and serfs. Russia gained territory at the expense of the Ottoman Empire and Poland, and the latter disappeared from the maps, partitioned among Prussia, Russia, and Austria. In Italy, Austria replaced declining Spain as the paramount power.

War was endemic, with national interests and dynastic concerns prevailing in a system guided by the balance of power. The mid-century War of the Austrian Succession (1740-1748) and the Seven Years War (1756-1763) were fought not only in Europe but also in North America and India. Frederick the Great was the instigator, desiring Austrian Silesia, but Britain was the true victor, driving France from Canada and India, and creating a world-wide empire. Standing armies were the norm, and with religious passions more muted, wars were less ideological.

The population grew, mainly as the result of a declining death rate and improvements in agriculture thanks to a warmer climate, better livestock, improved soil fertility, and new crops such as the potato. Paper money or banknotes compensated for the dearth of gold and silver, and institutions such as the Bank of England mobilized the wealth of the kingdom through credit and loans. The seeds of the industrial revolution were planted, notably in the textile industry where new technologies transformed the manufacture of cotton cloth.

The patriarchal family remained the core of society. Late marriages limited the birthrate, but there was considerable illegitimacy. 85 percent of the population were peasants, freer in the west than the east, but still facing many legal obligations. The nobility were 2 or 3 percent. Their large country estates defined their life style, but anyone with sufficient wealth could generally enter their ranks. The Grand Tour also defined aristocratic life: sons of the elite traveled widely in search of culture and education. Townspeople were a small minority except in Britain and the Dutch Republic; London had a population of 1 million, Paris half that. Urban mortality rates were high and poverty widespread, with prostitution and begging the means of survival for many.

LECTURE AND DISCUSSION TOPICS

1.Discuss the concept of the eighteenth-century enlightened despots and enlightened absolutism as both myth and reality.

2. Survey the European states and their governments, comparing and contrasting Great Britain, France, Prussia, Austria, and Russia.

3. Assess just how "enlightened" were Frederick the great, Catherine the great, and Joseph II by considering their governing philosophies, their accomplishments, and their lasting influence.

4. Examine the nature of eighteenth-century warfare, focusing upon the War of the Austrian Succession and the Seven Years' War.

5. In an examination of the careers of Catherine the Great and Frederick the Great, what constitutes "greatness"?

6. Compare and contrast the family, marriage, birthrate, and population trends and practices of the eighteenth century with earlier periods in western civilization, noting what had changed and what had not.

7. Discuss the social, political, and cultural role of the nobility in the eighteenth-century.

8. Explore the increasing urbanization of European society in the eighteenth-century, or, was an urban revolution taking place?

9. Discuss eighteenth-century European imperialism and colonization in the contexts of the geopolitics of global warfare.

10. Assess the claim that the modern world began in the eighteenth century.

MAP EXERCISES

1. Europe in 1763. MAP 18.1. What were the geographical factors which encouraged conflict between Prussia and Austria rather than between Spain and France or France and Britain? What were the possible geographical reasons that other became involved in the Austro-Prussian quarrel? What role did geography play in the great wars of the eighteenth century? (page 326)

2. The Battlefields of the Seven Years' War, MAP 18.2. Why was the Seven Years' War called the "first world war"? Outside of Europe, where did the major conflicts take place, and who was/were the victor(s)? Why did the overseas battles take place where they did? (page 331)

DISCUSSION QUESTIONS FOR THE PRIMARY SOURCES (BOXED DOCUMENTS)

1. "Frederick the Great and His Father": Based on these documents, why was the relationship between Frederick the Great and his father such a difficult one? What does this troubled relationship tell you about the affects of rulership on the great kings of Europe and their families. What new duties and concerns of monarchs (like Frederick William) may have reshaped relations between kings and sons? (page 327)

2. "British Victory in India": What differences, if any, would Robert Clive had likely mentioned if the battle of Plassy had occurred in Europe? According to the letter, what part did native Indians seemingly play in the battle? Why such little mention? Does Clive's account seem reasonable and accurate? Why and/or why not? (page 332)

3. "Marital Arrangements": What does Richard Sheridan suggest about marriage among the upper classes in eighteenth-century Britain? Could the same comments be made about upper-class marriages elsewhere in Europe at the time? What were the social, political, and economic considerations which were significant in eighteenth-century marriages? Could he be over-stating the issue? Why or why not? (page 334)

4. "Poverty in France": What does this document reveal about the nature of poverty in France in the eighteenth-century? How would growing ranks of the poor in Europe further destabilize this society? Would traditional European modes of poor relief be in any way up to the challenge posed by more and more poor? Why or why not? (page 337)

STUDENT RESEARCH AND PROJECT TOPICS

1. Imagine that you are a philosophe serving Joseph II or Catherine the Great. What advice would you give him or her on the best way to rule Austria or Russia?

2. Compare the development of the two Atlantic seaboard states, France and Great Britain? How were they alike? How were they different?

3. Compare the development of absolutism in Prussia, the Austrian Empire, and Russia. What are the similarities and differences? What did the rulers achieve? How did they fail? How important was the character of the ruler in each case? How did Poland fit in the system and what was its impact on the three?

4. What do we mean by the phrase "enlightened politics" and to what extent was politics "enlightened" in the European states of the eighteenth-century?

5. What was the nature of war and diplomacy in the eighteenth century? How would you compare the nature of war and diplomacy in the eighteenth century with that of the seventeenth century? How can Balance of Power be seen as Balance of Terror?

6. How did the European social order change in the eighteenth century? Were the changes greater or lesser than in previous centuries?

7. How and why did the nobility play a dominating role in the European society of the eighteenth century?

8. How did life change, if it did, for the lower classes during the nineteenth century?

9. "The Seven Years War was the first world war." Discuss.

10. Given the numerous social and economic changes of the eighteenth century, those at the bottom of society often found themselves much worse off than in earlier centuries. Why?

IDENTIFICATONS

1. enlightened absolutism
2. Louis XV
3. Louis XVI
4. Marie Antoinette
5. the United Kingdom
6. "pocket boroughs"
7. the Hanovarians/the Georges
8. Robert Walpole
9. George III
10. William Pitt the Elder
11. Frederick William I
12. Junkers
13. Frederick II, the Great

14. Maria Theresa
15. Joseph II
16. Catherine the Great
17. serfs
18. Emelyn Pugachev
19. Treaty of Kuchuk-Kainarji
20. partitions of Poland
21. War of the Austrian Succession
22. Silesia
23. Robert Clive
24. Seven Years War
25. Great War for Empire
26. French-Indian War
27. Montcalm and Wolfe
28. Treaty of Paris, 1763
29. coitus interruptus
30. Bank of England
31. "banknotes"
32. the "putting-out" or "domestic system"
33. the country house
34. Thomas Gainsborough
35. London's one million

MULTIPLE CHOICE QUESTIONS

1. Politically, the period from 1715 to 1789 witnessed
   a. the rise of the masses in politics as advocated by the philosophes.
   b. the waning of monarchical power.
   c. the continuing process of centralization in the development of nation-state for efficient taxation and building armies.
   d. "enlightened absolutism" take its deepest roots in France.
   ANSWER: c (page 324)

2. During the eighteenth century, the idea of Divine Right
   a. remained a strong basis for government.
   b. was gradually replaced by more republican ideas concerning government.
   c. was gradually replaced by the idea of "enlightened absolutism" justified by utilitarian arguments.
   d. was best exemplified by the reign of Joseph II of Austria.
   ANSWER: c (p. 324)

3. France in the eighteenth century
   a. thrived under the strong leadership of Louis XV and Louis XVI.
   b. suffered from severe economic depression throughout the century.
   c. was torn apart by a series of civil wars.
   d. lost an empire while acquiring a huge pubic debt.
   ANSWER: d (p. 325)

4. The reign of Louis XVI was predominantly concerned with
   a. a ludicrous attention to court intrigues.
   b. solving the government's debt.
   c. establishing a strict code of moral behavior throughout France.
   d. regaining the empire lost in the Seven Years' War.
      ANSWER: a (p. 325)

5. Political developments in eighteenth-century Great Britain included
   a. the monarchy losing its few remaining powers to Parliament.
   b. the redistribution of boroughs to make the electoral system for the House of Commons more fair.
   c. William Pitt the Younger's corrupt power leading to calls for popular reform.
   d. the increasing influence of the king's ministers.
      ANSWER: d (p. 325)

6. As prime minister of Great Britain, Robert Walpole
   a. used the military to further Britain's world empire.
   b. was forced to follow closely the policies of George I and George II.
   c. pursued a peaceful foreign policy to avoid new land taxes.
   d. was a great advocate of Empire.
      ANSWER: c (p. 326)

7. Enlightenment political thought advanced the concept of human natural rights including all of the following except
   a. equality before the law.
   b. the right to assemble.
   c. freedom from taxation.
   d. freedom of worship.
      ANSWER: c (p. 324)

8. A continuing trend throughout eighteenth-century Prussia was
   a. the uncontrollable growth of the royal state bureaucracy.
   b. the social and military dominance of the Junker nobility.
   c. an avoidance of military entanglements, especially under Frederick the Great.
   d. social mobility for the peasants through the civil service.
      ANSWER: b (p. 327)

9. Under the reign of Frederick William I, Prussia
   a. saw the size of its army diminish.
   b. became a highly centralized European state.
   c. witnessed nobles dominate important administrative posts.
   d. failed to establish an efficient civil bureaucracy.
      ANSWER: b (p. 327)

10. Frederick the Great of Prussia
   a. was one of the most cultured monarchs of the eighteenth century.
   b. increased Prussian territory.
   c. increased the size of the Prussian military.
   d. all of the above
      ANSWER: d (pp. 327-328)

11. The Austrian Empire under Joseph II
    a. reversed the enlightened reforms of Joseph's mother, Maria Theresa.
    b. rescinded all of Hungary's privileges.
    c. saw the nobility's power permanently stripped away.
    d. witnessed the general discontent of the people due to Joseph's drastic reforms.
        ANSWER: d (p. 329)

12. In a sincere effort to reform his domains typical of enlightened rulers, the Austrian emperor Joseph II issued
    a. three new court circulars on improved operations for the imperial bureaucracy.
    b. 6,000 decrees and 11,000 new laws, most antagonistic to the majority of his subjects.
    c. 150 new ranks of imperial bureaucrats.
    d. at least 350 imperial decrees for the reform of judicial practice in Hungary.
        ANSWER: b (p. 329)

13. The enlightened legal reforms expressed by Catherine the Great in her *Instruction*
    a. succeeded in abolishing serfdom in all of Russia.
    b. succeeded in establishing an equal system of law for all Russian citizens.
    c. instigated changes in Russian government that sapped the power of the old nobility.
    d. accomplished nothing due to heavy opposition and were soon forgotten.
        ANSWER: d (p. 329)

14. Catherine the Great of Russia
    a. followed a successful policy of expansion against the Turks.
    b. instigated enlightened reforms for the peasantry after the revolt of Emelyn Pugachev.
    c. alienated the nobility with her extensive enlightened reforms.
    d. successfully eliminated the power of the Duma.
        ANSWER: a (p. 329)

15. Emelyn Pugachev is noted in Russian history for
    a. leading a successful rebellion among the peasantry.
    b. causing greater repression of the peasantry due to his unsuccessful rebellion.
    c. leading the Russian army in its capture of Turkish lands.
    d. the assassination of Catherine the Great.
        ANSWER: b (p. 329)

16. Which of the following countries did not participate in the partition of Poland:
    a. Austria
    b. Prussia
    c. Bavaria
    d. Russia
        ANSWER: c (p. 329)

17. In the Treaty of Kuchuk-Kainarji, Russia
    a. lost territory to the Ottoman Empire in the Caucuses.
    b. gained control over Istanbul.
    c. granted Emelym Pugachev his own independent state in the Ukraine.
    d. achieved the right to protect Greek Orthodox Christians in the Ottoman realm.
        ANSWER: d (p. 329)

18. Of the major rulers associated with enlightened absolutism, the only one who sought radical change based upon enlightenment ideas was

a. Frederick the Great.
b. Joseph II.
c. Catherine the Great.
d. Louis XVI.

ANSWER: b (p. 330)

19. The class which was most resistant to enlightenment reforms was the

a. monarchy.
b. aristocracy.
c. peasantry.
d. urban middle classes.

ANSWER: c, page 503

20. Enlightened absolutism in the eighteenth-century

a. could never overcome the political and social realities of the time.
b. was most successful in the strengthening of administrative systems.
c. was limited to policies that did not undermine the interests of the European nobility.
d. was successful in implementing legal reforms in many European states.

ANSWER: a (p. 330)

21. European diplomacy during the eighteenth century was predicated on the idea that

a. sea power was the basis of real power.
b. in a balance of power, one state should not achieve dominance over another.
c. a country's empire determined its greatness.
d. the charisma of a ruler determined a country's success in foreign policy.

ANSWER: b (p. 330)

22. The War of the Austrian Succession

a. was limited only to Habsburg territory.
b. made the Prussian king ruler or Austria.
c. was fought between Austria and France, with France gaining Silesia.
d. saw Prussia in control of Silesia when the war ended.

ANSWER: d (p. 330)

23. Speaking of politics in a supposedly enlightened age, King Frederick the Great of Prussia said, "the fundamental rule of governments is the principle of

a. respecting new human rights."
b. extending their territories."
c. combating church fanaticism."
d. raising taxes to meet all military needs of state spending."

ANSWER: b (p. 330)

24. The Diplomatic Revolution resulted when Maria Theresa of Austria refused to recognize the loss of

a. Hungary and fought the Spanish.
b. Galicia and took on the Bohemians.
c. Silesia and gained a French alliance.
d. Bosnia and allied herself defensively with England.

ANSWER: c p. 330)

25. Which of the following statements concerning the Seven Years' War is correct?
   a. Its immediate origins can be traced to the failure of Frederick II's Pragmatic Sanction.
   b. The French defeated the British in India due to their superior forces.
   c. Britain became the world's greatest colonial power.
   d. The continuation of rivalries from the War of the Austrian Succession led to Prussia's victory in the European theater.
      ANSWER: c (p. 332)

26. The Treaty of Paris, which concluded the Seven Years' War
   a. forced France to withdraw from India, leaving it to Great Britain.
   b. left France with the strongest navy in the world.
   c. forced William Pitt the Elder to remove British troops from North America.
   d. left France in control of Canada.
      ANSWER: a (p. 332)

27. The Austrian ruler at the time of the War of the Austrian Succession was
   a. Joseph II.
   b. Marie Antoinette.
   c. Maria Theresa.
   d. Charles VI.
      ANSWER: c (p. 330)

28. Of the great European powers, the only one <u>not</u> to possess a standing army and to rely on mercenaries by the eighteenth century was
   a. Prussia.
   b. Great Britain.
   c. Russia.
   d. France.
      ANSWER: b (p. 332)

29. European population growth in the second half of the eighteenth century
   a. saw all of the great powers grow in population except Russia.
   b. occurred despite increased death and infant mortality rates.
   c. was due to the absence of famines and elimination of most major diseases.
   d. was nearly double the rate of the first half of the century.
      ANSWER: d (p. 332)

30. A key financial advantage the British government enjoyed over French rulers in the eighteenth century was
   a. Britain's capacity to borrow large sums of money at low rates of interest.
   b. a lower total amount of British government debt.
   c. a strong policy against state borrowing of any kind in Britain.
   d. no real curbs on state borrowing in France.
      ANSWER: a (p. 334)

31. All of the following were persistent trends in the upper-class eighteenth-century European family except

a. an emphasis upon the family rather than upon the individual.
b. marriages were arranged on the basis of family interest rather than individual choice.
c. aristocrats married at a younger age than the general population.
d. children were often placed out to foundling homes for state or municipal care.
ANSWER: d (pp. 333-334)

32. European society in the eighteenth century witnessed

a. a pattern developing of marriage at earlier ages for brides and grooms.
b. the continued dominance of the nuclear family.
c. the declining importance of the woman in the "family economy.
d. rapidly declining rates of illegitimate births and a consequent decline in infanticide due to stringent laws prohibiting either.
ANSWER: b (p. 333)

33. The population of Europe by 1790 was

a. 90 million.
b. 120 million.
c. 150 million.
d. 190 million.
ANSWER: d (p. 332)

34. Europe's falling death rate in the eighteenth-century was due to all of the following except

a. more plentiful food due to an agricultural revolution.
b. the decline of the bubonic plague.
c. the ending of a little ice age.
d. significantly improved sanitary conditions in the cities.
ANSWER: d (pp. 332-333, 337)

35. The improvements in agricultural practices and methods in eighteenth-century Europe occurred primarily in

a. France.
b. the Netherlands.
c. Britain.
d. Russia.
ANSWER: c (p. 333)

36. The domestic system of industrial production in Flanders and England became known as the

a. household system.
b. cottage system.
c. mercantile system.
d. laissez-faire.
ANSWER: b (p. 335)

37. A key financial innovation of the eighteenth century was

a. the creation of insurance policies.
b. the circulation of paper bank notes compensating for a lack of coinage.
c. international currency markets and arbitrage speculation.
d. deficit spending by enlightened monarchs to pay for vital government reforms.
ANSWER: b (p. 334)

38. The New World food crop which became central to the died of many Europeans in the eighteenth-century was

a. wheat.
b. the potato.
c. rye.
d. the tomato.

ANSWER: b (p. 333)

39. By the eighteenth century, the largest European social class comprised

a. peasants.
b. the middle class.
c. the nobility.
d. serfs.

ANSWER: a (p. 335)

40. Europe's unequal social organization in the eighteenth century

a. was determined by the division of society into traditional orders.
b. was contrary to Christian teaching.
c. was least apparent in Prussia.
d. all of the above

ANSWER: a (p. 335)

41. The European peasantry in the eighteenth century

a. comprised nearly half of Europe's population.
b. was free from serfdom in all countries by 1789.
c. often owed extensive compulsory services to aristocratic landowners.
d. benefited the most in southern Italy and eastern Germany.

ANSWER: c (p. 335)

42. The nation which took the lead in the eighteenth-century agricultural revolution was

a. France.
b. England.
c. Prussia.
d. Spain.

ANSWER: b (p. 333)

43. The European nobility in the eighteenth century

a. played a significant role in the administrative machinery of European states.
b. lost its former dominance in military affairs.
c. composed twenty percent of Europe's population.
d. differed little in wealth and political power from state to state.

ANSWER: a (p. 336)

44. The special legal privileges of the European nobility included all of the following <u>except</u>:

a. judgment by peers.
b. immunity from severe punishment.
c. exemptions from most forms of taxation.
d guarantees against becoming poor.

ANSWER: d (p. 336)

45. The most important product of European industry in the eighteenth-century was
   a. manufacturing of weapons.
   b. textiles.
   c. ironmongery.
   d. pottery and glassware.
      ANSWER: b, page 515

46. Different social groups remained easily distinguishable everywhere in Europe by
   a. which church they worshipped in.
   b. their skin complexion.
   c. the clothes they wore.
   d. their birth certificates.
      ANSWER: c (p. 335)

47. Which of the following statements best described the eighteenth-century European city?
   a. They were remarkably cleaner than the medieval city.
   b. They were decreasing dramatically in population.
   c. They were still filthy and lacked proper sanitation.
   d. They were becoming more democratic in government.
      ANSWER: c (p. 337)

48. By the eighteenth century, the largest European city in terms of population was
   a. London.
   b. Paris.
   c. St. Petersburg.
   d. Amsterdam.
      ANSWER: a (p. 336)

49. Most cities in western and even central Europe were socially dominated by
   a. craft guilds.
   b. patrician oligarchies.
   c. urban communes.
   d. titled aristocrats.
      ANSWER: b (p. 337)

50. At the beginning of the eighteenth-century,
   a. the old order was under severe attack.
   b. the old order still remained strong.
   c. republicanism was in ascendant.
   d. enlightened absolutism had proved to be a failure.
      ANSWER: b (p. 338)

RELEVANT WORLD-WIDE WEB SITES/RESOURCES

1. Documents in Military History:
http://www.hillsdale.edu/dept/History/Documents/war/WarDocs.htm
(An excellent online collection of pertinent documents on the dynastic struggles and military conflicts of the era.)

2. The Homepage for Eighteenth-Century France:
http://www.geocities.com/Paris/Metro/2549
(An excellent site documenting the most important and powerful kingdom of the era. Highly recommended for excellent links to other sites.)

3. Internet Library of Early Journals: A Digital Library of 18th- and 19th-century Journals:
http://www.bodley.ox.ac.uk/ilej
(A fine site containing online copies in English of early journals tracking the major and minor issues of these eras. Highly recommended for student access to primary print sources of the times.)

RELEVANT VIDEO RESOURCES

Jean-Jacques Rousseau: Retreat to Romanticism, Films for the Humanities and Sciences, (55 minutes). (Available through Wadsworth Publishing.)

The Battle of Quebec: 1759, Films for the Humanities and Sciences, (55 minutes). (Available through Wadsworth Publishing.)

The English House and the English Country Garden. PBS Home Videos, 4 cassettes.

SUGGESTED STUDENT ACTIVITIES

1. Have students write a fictitious essay about an enlightened monarch who possesses all the attributes of the perfect enlightened king.

2. Have students debate the advantages and disadvantages of enlightened absolutism, both in the eighteenth century and even to many societies today.

3. Have students investigate the possible reasons why it was Great Britain rather than France or another European nation which established the first world-wide empire.

4. Suggest students organize a modern Grand Tour for the twenty-first century, comparable in aim/intent and experience with the Grand Tour of the eighteenth century.

CHAPTER 19
REVOLUTIONARY POLITICS: THE ERA OF THE FRENCH REVOLUTION AND NAPOLEON

CHAPTER OUTLINE

I. Start of a Revolutionary Era: The American Revolution
- A. Forming a New Nation

II. The French Revolution
- A. Background to the French Revolution
  1. The Three Estates
  2. Other Problems Facing the French Monarchy
  3. From Estates-General to a National Assembly
- B. The Destruction of the Old Regime
  1. A New Constitution
- C. The Radical Revolution
  1. A Nation in Arms
  2. The Committee of Public Safety and the Reign of Terror
  3. Equality and Slavery
  4. The Decline of the Committee of Public Safety
- D. Reaction and the Directory

III. The Age of Napoleon
- A. The Rise of Napoleon
- B. The Domestic Policies of Emperor Napoleon
- C. Napoleon's Empire and the European Response

IV. Conclusion

CHAPTER SUMMARY

An era of revolutions began with the American Revolution, justified ideologically by Locke's social contract and natural rights philosophy. The Constitution of 1787, with its Bill of Rights, provided a strong central government with a separation of power between the three branches. Its affect in Europe was immense: Enlightenment ideals could become reality.

But there were other causes for the French Revolution, such as the legal inequality of the three Estates of the clergy, the aristocracy, and commoners, who were the vast majority. In 1788, the government, facing financial collapse, summoned the Estates-General for the first time since 1614. Assembling at Versailles in May 1789, it deadlocked whether to vote as estates or by head. The Third Estate proclaimed itself the National Assembly, an illegal act which Louis XVI failed to repress, in part because of rural and urban uprisings, notably the capture of the Bastille prison in Paris on July 14. In August, the National Assembly adopted the Declaration of the Rights of Man and Citizen with its natural rights philosophy, and in October, the women of Paris walked to Versailles and forced the king to accompany them back to the city.

The constitution of 1791 subordinated the monarch to the Legislative Assembly. All were citizens, but only citizens who paid taxes had the vote. The lands of the Catholic Church were nationalized and the church placed under civil control. The regime faced opposition from the church, some aristocrats, and conservatives in general, but also from those who demanded even more revolution, such as the Jacobins. Louis' fellow European monarchs were also opposed, and the result was war in April 1792. In reaction to early military defeats the revolution entered into a more radical stage, abetted by the Paris Commune of artisans and merchants. A republic was proclaimed and the ex-king, Louis XVI, was executed in January 1793.

To meet the domestic and foreign threats, the Committee of Public Safety was given dictatorial power. Under the leadership of Maximilien Robespierre, it raised an army motivated by national patriotism rather than dynastic loyalties. Revolutionary courts were created to ferret out those not sufficiently supportive of the revolution, and 50,000 were executed during "the Terror." Price controls were placed upon food and other necessary items and slavery was abolished. Notre Dame Cathedral was designated the Temple of Reason and a new revolutionary calendar was adopted eliminating Sundays and church holidays. But in July 1794, the National Convention turned against Robespierre, who was quickly executed. A new government headed by a five-member Directory was established which satisfied neither the radicals nor the royalists, and in 1799, the Directory was overthrown and the Consulate established.

An outsider from Corsica, revolution and war gave Napoleon Bonaparte his opportunity. A controversial figure, he was more the enlightened despot than the democratic revolutionary. He made peace with the papacy on his terms, and his Civil Code guaranteed equality, though less so for women. In 1804 he crowned himself Emperor. His armies conquered much of the continent but his empire did not last. In June 1812, he invaded Russia with 600,000 troops, but ultimately the French were forced to retreat. National revolts, a reaction to French occupation armies, broke out, and Napoleon abdicated in 1814. He briefly returned to power but was defeated at the battle of Waterloo in 1815, and sentenced to exile on the island of Saint Helena in the South Atlantic, where he died in 1821. His shadow hung over Europe for decades.

At the end, order had triumphed over liberty, and the victors were the propertied classes. The ideals of liberty, equality, and fraternity inspired future generations, and the citizen nationalism created in France led to the development of modern nationalism elsewhere.

LECTURE AND DISCUSSION TOPICS

1. Discuss the possible causes of the French Revolution.

2. Explore some of the several major historical interpretations as to the meaning of the French Revolution.

3. Do individuals make history? Consider specific persons and their respective roles in the events of the French Revolution.

4. What was revolutionary about the French Revolution?

5. Consider the question: Was the Ancien Regime truly "old"?

6. Discuss the conservative reaction and response to the events of the French Revolution and the ideology of the revolutionaries.

7. Examine the popular opposition to state intervention and innovation in the revolutionary efforts to change French society.

8. Explore the origins of total war in the era of the French Revolution and Napoleon.

9. Assess the many faces of Napoleon, or who was the real Napoleon?

10. Was the French Revolution a success or a failure?

MAP EXERCISES

1. French Conquests During the Revolutionary Wars, 1792-1799. MAP 19.1. Which regions or areas of French conquest could be considered as areas long desired by royalist France and which conquered territories were not part of earlier French ambitions? Why were Austria and Prussia necessary allies against revolutionary France? (page 349)

2. Napoleon's Grand Empire. MAP 19.2. Compare MAPS 19.2 with 19.1. Were Napoleon's territorial ambitions significantly different from pre-1799 conquests? If so, where? Geographically, which territories would France find it most difficult to control and why? (page 356)

DISCUSSION QUESTIONS FOR THE PRIMARY SOURCES (BOXED DOCUMENTS)

1."The Fall of the Bastille": Discuss the fall of the Bastille and indicate why its fall came to mark the triumph of French "liberty" over despotism? Does the newspaper account seem objective or not? Why? Is the fall of the Bastille more important as fact or as symbol? Why? (page 345)

2. "The Declaration of the Rights of Man and the Citizen": What "natural rights" does this document proclaim for the French? To what extent do you believe that this document was influenced by the ideas or ideals of the philosophes? How does the Declaration of the Rights of Man and Citizen compare with America's Declaration of Independence? (page 346)

3. "Justice in the Reign of Terror": Was there anything "just" about the revolutionary courts? What explanations or reasons could be given to justify such a system? Compare the Bastille and the guillotine as revolutionary symbols. Could the guillotine be considered an "enlightened" method of execution? Why or why not? (page 350)

4. "Napoleon and Psychological Warfare": What themes did Napoleon use to play upon the emotions of his troops and inspire them to greater efforts? Do you think Napoleon believed any of these words? Why or why not? Would Napoleon's style of oratory be effective in the twenty-first century? Why or why not? (page 353)

STUDENT RESEARCH AND PROJECT TOPICS

1. What impact did the American Revolution have on Europe?

2. Discuss the causes of the French Revolution. Do you think there is one cause that is more important than the others? Why or why not?

3. How was France changed by the revolutionary events of 1789-1792? Who benefited the most from these changes?

4. Why did the French Revolution enter a radical phase? What did the radical phase accomplish? What role did the Reign of Terror play in the Revolution?

5. How did the French Revolution affect the roles of women in society? Did the Revolution and its consequences ultimately benefit or hurt female citizens? Did men win more out of this event than women? Why?

6. Compare and contrast the French Revolution with previous revolutions in England and America.

7. In what ways did Napoleon's policies repudiate the accomplishments of the French Revolution? In what ways did his policies strengthen the accomplishments of the French Revolution?

8. Napoleon has been considered the greatest general of all time. Using examples from the text, defend or refute this statement.

9. What innovations from the French Revolution in military organization and army motivation and morale did Napoleon capitalize on to build and employ the armed forces of his empire?

10. Which revolution–American or French–has had the greatest influence during the last two centuries, and why?

IDENTIFICATIONS

1. July 14, 1789
2. the Bastille
3. July 4, 1776
4. natural rights
5. Yorktown
6. First and Second Estates
7. the *taille*
8. Third Estate
9. the bourgeoisie
10. vote by order or by head?
11. the National Assembly
12. the Tennis Court Oath
13. *Declaration of the Rights of Man and Citizen*
14. Olympe de Gouges
15. "We are bringing back the baker...."
16. Civil Constitution of the Clergy
17. the Jacobins
18. Paris Commune
19. *sans-culottes*
20. Georges Danton
21. National Convention
22. Committee of Public Safety

23. Maximilien Robespierre
24. Reign of Terror
25. the guillotine
26. Law of General Maximum
27. "temple of reason"
28. Toussaint L'Ouverture
29. Thermidorean Reaction
30. Directory
31. Napoleon Bonaparte
32. Italian and Egyptian campaigns
33. First Consul and Emperor
34. the Concordat with the Papacy
35. the Civil Code
36. battle of Trafalgar
37. *fraternitie*
38. the Grand Army and the "Great Retreat"
39. Waterloo
40. Elba and Saint Helena

MULTIPLE CHOICE QUESTIONS

1. A key result of the Seven Years' War in North America was
   a. growing tensions between American colonists and the English government demanding more revenue from the colonies to pay for the victorious British army.
   b. the colonists' growing sympathy for the defeated French.
   c. greater acceptance of British policies by American colonists, especially in fiscal matters.
   d. weakening of the American colonial economy and the collapse of American maritime commerce.
   ANSWER: a (page 341)

2. After 1763, the British authorities and colonists came into conflict over
   a. British efforts to raise new revenues through increased taxes.
   b. freedom of trade on the high seas.
   c. freedom of religion.
   d. the expansion of rival French colonies in North America.
   ANSWER: a (p. 341)

3. The colonists would only win their war for independence due to
   a. generous military and financial aid from various European states, especially France.
   b. the collapse of the English colonial system.
   c. apathy of the English military.
   d. flaws in the English mercantile system.
   ANSWER: a (p. 341)

4. The defeat of General Cornwallis and his army at Yorktown in 1781, leading to British abandonment of the Revolutionary War, was achieved by
a. American colonial army and naval forces alone.
b. a combined American and French army.
c. a combined force of American, French, Spanish, and Dutch forces.
d. a combined American and French army supported by a French fleet.
ANSWER: d (p. 341)

5. The Constitution of the United States of 1789
a. was a revision of the Articles of Confederation.
b. was seen by European liberals as a utopian document that would never last.
c. created a republic in which the branches of government provided checks on one another.
d. had no real impact on the French Revolution.
ANSWER: c (p. 342)

6. The American Revolution affected Europeans by
a. proving that military force was the final diplomatic authority.
b. ending colonial expansion around the world.
c. proving that the new United States was the most powerful nation.
d. proving that the ideas of the Enlightenment could be realized politically.
ANSWER: d (p. 342)

7. A key conduit of "enlightened" American political and moral ideas back to Europe was formed by
a. returning British prisoners of war.
b. the hundreds of influential French army and navy officers who had fought on the American side during the Revolutionary War.
c. European nobles returning from expeditions to the new American frontier.
d. missionary priests returning from evangelical campaigns deep in the U.S. back country.
ANSWER: b (p. 342)

8. French society on the eve of their revolution
a. was dominated by the military.
b. saw a sharp decline in sexual morality.
c. was still largely dominated by the nobility and clergy.
d. was rapidly changing, with the middle class becoming vastly more influential.
ANSWER: c (p. 342)

9. The immediate cause of the French Revolution was
a. the government's failure to resolve its debts and other economic problems.
b. the blocking of attempted reforms by the French Parliaments.
c. the radical calls of the philosophes for reform.
d. Louis XVI's rejection of the cahiers de doléances.
ANSWER: a (p. 343)

10. The French economy of the eighteenth century was
a. growing due to an expansion of foreign trade and industrial production.
b. stagnant due to foreign competition in industry and trade.
c. declining rapidly due to overuse of arable land.
d. based largely on the silk industry.
ANSWER: a (p. 342)

11. The third estate was composed of all of the following <u>except</u>
a. shopkeepers.
b. peasants.
c. clergy.
d. skilled craftsmen.
ANSWER: c (p. 342)

12. Compared to the American Revolution, the French Revolution was
a. more violent.
b. more radical.
c. more influential in Europe as a model of rebellion.
d. all the above
ANSWER: d (p. 357)

13. By the eighteenth century, the French bourgeoisie and nobility were
a. growing further apart in social status.
b. increasingly less distinguishable from each other.
c. rapidly losing social status to the third estate.
d. openly hostile and frequently involved in street battles.
ANSWER: b (p. 343)

14. The Estates-General consisted of representatives of the three orders: the First Estate (clergy), the Third Estate (people), and the Second Estate, representing the
a. towns.
b. pope.
c. nobility.
d. army.
ANSWER: c (p. 342)

15. In 1789, the Estates-General was
a. Louis XVI's parliamentary body often consulted by the king.
b. in unanimous agreement that only radical changes could solve France's problems.
c. dominated by the first estate composed mostly of urban lawyers.
d. divided over the issue of voting by orders or by head.
ANSWER: d (p. 343)

16. Vital fiscal reform of the French state just prior to the French Revolution led the government to
a. declare war on England.
b. tax the clergy and the nobility.
c. call a meeting of the Estates General.
d. end serfdom..
ANSWER: c (p. 343)

17. When the Estates General met in 1789, two-thirds of the Third Estate were
a. nobles.
b. lawyers.
c. merchants and artisans.
d. wealthy peasants.
ANSWER: d (p. 343)

18. Just prior to the Revolution in France, the number of the poor in France
   a. actually declined.
   b. went up greatly.
   c. increased very slowly.
   d. remained fairly constant.
      ANSWER: b (p. 343)

19. In the summer of 1789, when the "revolution of the lawyers" appeared doomed by imminent royal use of armed force, the Revolution as a whole was saved by the
   a. betrayal of the monarchy by high clergymen.
   b. defection of key nobles of the sword to the rebels.
   c. intervention of armed commoners, especially in urban uprisings against royal forces and armories.
   d. the outside influence of mercenary troops paid by the rebels.
      ANSWER: c (p. 344)

20. In April 1792,
   a. Emperor Leopold II of Austria declared war on France.
   b. Napoleon invaded England.
   c. Louis XVI successfully escaped from France.
   d. the French Legislative Assembly declared war on Austria.
      ANSWER: d (p. 347)

21. The French revolutionary slogan neatly evoking the ideals of the rebellion was
   a. "Down with the aristocracy!"
   b. "Liberty, Equality, Fraternity!"
   c. "Death to the king and queen!"
   d. "Kill all priests and burn all churches!"
      ANSWER: b (pp. 355, 357)

22. The controversy over voting by order versus voting by head in the Estates-General saw
   a. the nobles of the robe advocate voting by head.
   b. the "lovers of liberty" effectively block voting by head.
   c. Abbé Sieyès's call for the expulsion of the Third Estate from the Estates-General.
   d. the Third Estate respond by forming a "National Assembly."
      ANSWER: d (p. 344)

23. All of the following were accomplished by the Constituent Assembly <u>except</u>
   a. the Declaration of the Rights of Man and the Citizen.
   b. the Civil Constitution of the Clergy.
   c. defense of seigneurial rights throughout the country.
   d. the reform of French voting procedures.
      ANSWER: c (pp. 344-345)

24. The Bastille was
   a. a royal castle.
   b. an arsenal and prison.
   c. the place where most state executions took place.
   d. a monastery.
      ANSWER: b (pp. 344-345)

25. The Declaration of the Rights of Man and the Citizen
   a. was drawn up by the monarchy to limit freedoms.
   b. was rejected by those influenced by the Enlightenment.
   c. owed much to the American Declaration of Independence and John Locke.
   d. allowed for aristocratic privileges to endure in France.
      ANSWER: c (pp. 344, 346)

26. The Declaration of the Rights of Woman and the Female Citizen
   a. became law by popular vote of the National Assembly.
   b. was ignored entirely by the males in the National Assembly who did little to improve the lot of women in French society.
   c. caused massive riots in its defense by ordinary men and women, especially in cities.
   d. was fully accepted by the crown and its ministers and then became enforceable law.
      ANSWER: b (p. 345)

27. In regard to the Catholic Church, the National Assembly
   a. left the institution alone.
   b. increased its power dramatically in France.
   c. passed legislation that secularized church offices and clergymen.
   d. abolished the faith in France.
      ANSWER: c (p. 345)

28. What type of government was set up by the Legislative Assembly?
   a. dictatorship.
   b. republic.
   c. democracy.
   d. limited constitutional monarchy.
      ANSWER: d (p. 346)

29. What group emerged as the most important radical element in French politics, at the beginning of the French Revolution?
   a. Jacobins
   b. Papists
   c. Communists
   d. Loyalists
      ANSWER: a (p. 346)

30. During the early stages of the "Radical Revolution," power passed from the Legislative Assembly to the
   a. Girondins.
   b. Paris Commune and the *sans-culottes*.
   c. Directory.
   d. Consulate.
      ANSWER: b (p. 347)

31. In September of 1792, the National Convention
   a. established a constitutional monarchy.
   b. abolished the monarchy and established a republic.
   c. voted to preserve the life of Louis XVI.
   d. was dismantled by Louis XVI.
      ANSWER: b (p. 348)

32. The Committee of Public Safety during the Reign of Terror
a. was headed by Maximilien Robespierre.
b. implemented a successful series of economic and price controls through France.
c. attempted to restore the church's influence over politics.
d. all of the above
ANSWER: a (p. 349)

33. The French Republic's army in the 1790s
a. received little backing from the home front.
b. was small, but effective in battle.
c. fueled modern nationalism and was raised through total mobilization of the population.
d. was totally defeated by foreign aristocratic forces.
ANSWER: c (p. 349)

34. In the Reign of Terror's "preservation" of the revolution from its internal enemies
a. the nobility was singled out as the most dangerous social group.
b. rebellious cities and districts were brutally defeated by the Revolutionary Armies.
c. no more than 5,000 people were killed by the guillotine.
d. the Committee of Public Safety played an insignificant role.
ANSWER: b (p. 350)

35. During the Reign of Terror, the majority of the victims were
a. nobles.
b. clergy.
c. middle class.
d. peasant and laboring classes.
ANSWER: d (p. 350)

36. In regard to religion, the National Convention
a. took measures to strengthen the Roman Catholic Church.
b. issued an edict allowing for total religious freedom.
c. took measures to de-Christianize the republic.
d. made the republic completely atheistic.
ANSWER: c (p. 351)

37. Which of the following is not true of the French revolutionary republican calendar?
a. Year 1 was 1792.
b. Most Christian holidays were kept.
c. *Sain*t was removed from street names.
d. It was meant to signal a new beginning for the nation.
ANSWER: b (p. 351)

38. A slave rebellion, inspired by the revolution, occurred in Saint-Domingue, and was led by
a. Maximilien Robespierre.
b. Georges Danton.
c. Toussaint L'Ouverture.
d. Olympe de Gouges.
ANSWER: b (p. 351)

39. The chief accomplishment of the National Convention was the
    a. creation of the revolutionary calendar.
    b. preservation of the revolution from being destroyed by foreign enemies.
    c. creation of the Directory.
    d. National French school system.
        ANSWER: b (p. 352)

40. The Thermidorean Reaction occurred after
    a. the death of Louis XVI.
    b. the invasion of Paris by the Prussians.
    c. Napoleon came to power.
    d. the death of Robespierre.
        ANSWER: d (p. 352)

41. The government of the Directory in the period of the Thermidorean Reaction
    a. primarily relied on the support of the royalists.
    b. was unicameral and directly elected by active citizens.
    c. was characterized by honest leadership and wise economic plans.
    d. increasingly had to rely on military support for its survival.
        ANSWER: d (p. 352)

42. The chief reason for Napoleon's rapid rise to power was his
    a. series of stunning defeats over the enemies of France.
    b. social programs that appealed to the masses.
    c. promises to make France great again.
    d. work of an inner clique of revolutionaries dedicated to the general.
        ANSWER: a (p. 353)

43. Which of the following statements best applies to Napoleon?
    a. He was a child of the Enlightenment and the French Revolution.
    b. He had a sense of moral responsibility to the people of France.
    c. He advocated an invasion of Britain in the 1790s.
    d. He was born the son of a Parisian merchant.
        ANSWER: a (pp. 352-354)

44. Which of the following statements best applies to Napoleon's domestic policies?
    a. Much autonomy was given to the provincial departments as the previous system of prefects was overhauled.
    b. His "new aristocracy" was actually little different from the old, as it was based on privilege and wealth.
    c. His Civil Code reaffirmed the ideals of the Revolution while creating a uniform legal system.
    d. As a devout Catholic, he reestablished Catholicism as the official state religion.
        ANSWER: c (p. 354)

45. The Concordat
    a. allowed for reforms in the French military.
    b. reestablished the Catholic Church and the pope's authority in France.
    c. was part of Napoleon's Civil Code.
    d. reformed the French civil service.
        ANSWER: b (pp. 353-354)

46. Napoleon's Grand Empire
   a. was composed of three different parts but united under the rule of Napoleon.
   b. revived the power of the nobility and clergy in all its states.
   c. included all of Europe with the defeat of Britain in 1805.
   d. had no long-standing impact on the conquered countries.
      ANSWER: a (p. 355)

47. Napoleon's Grand Empire included all of the following states except
   a. Italy.
   b. Spain.
   c. Holland.
   d. Great Britain.
      ANSWER: d (p. 355)

48. Not among the factors in the defeat of Napoleon was
   a. the failure of the Continental System.
   b. the defeat of the French navy at the Battle of Trafalgar.
   c. mass reactions to his brutal suppression of local customs in the conquered countries.
   d. the spread of nationalism in the conquered countries.
      ANSWER: c (p. 355)

49. The Continental System tried to defeat the British by
   a. massive invasion of Britain.
   b. preventing British trade.
   c. causing political unrest in Britain.
   d. none of the above
      ANSWER: b (p. 355)

50. Napoleon met his final defeat at the Battle of
   a. Leipzig.
   b. Borodino.
   c. Trafalgar.
   d. Waterloo.
      ANSWER: d (p. 357)

RELEVANT WORLD-WIDE WEB SITES/RESOURCES

1. Hanover College Historical Texts Project:
http://history.hanover.edu/project.html
(A comprehensive history site with excellent documents arranged by era. Numerous online original documents and other materials on the French Revolution. A good site to visit throughout a course on Western Civilization.)

2. Internet Modern History Sourcebook:
http://www.fordham.edu/halsall/mod/modsbook.html
(An excellent site covering in great depth and with extensive documentation all of the major eras of western history. Very useful for the American, French, and Industrial revolutions.)

3. Le Calendrier Républican:
http://ourworld.compuserve.com/homepages/pchapelin/calend.htm
(Site in French on the development and daily details of the French Revolutionary Calendar.)

RELEVANT VIDEO RESOURCES

The Campaigns of Napoleon, PBS Home Video, 3 programs on 3 cassettes, (50 minutes each). (Comprehensive history of all Napoleonic campaigns and battles with scholarly commentary by Dr. David Chandler, one of the finest historians for the period.)

Civilisation, Public Media Video/BBC Television, (50 minutes each program). Program 12, "Fallacies of Hope." (Covers the French Revolution, rise of Napoleon, and Romanticism in arts and letters.)

The Age of Revolutions, 1776-1848, Landmark Films, (60 minutes). (Available through Wadsworth Publishing.)

Napoleon Bonaparte, Films for the Humanities and Sciences, (55 minutes). (Available through Wadsworth Publishing).

RELEVANT MUSICAL PERFORMANCES

La Prise de la Bastille: Music of the French Revolution, Capriccio CD, (No. 10 280).

Ludwig van Beethoven, Symphony No. 3, "The Eroica."

SUGGESTED STUDENT ACTIVITIES

1. Have students write an essay comparing and contrasting the American Revolution with the French Revolution.

2. Have students research the ideas and principles that were birthed by the French Revolution. Which of these ideas do we hold dear to us today (i.e., egalitarian democracy, women's rights, etc.)?

3. Have students investigate the role of women in the French Revolution, especially mass female public protests and "the march to Versailles."

4. Have students analyze the defeats of Napoleon. Could he have succeeded? How? What would Europe be like had he been victorious?

CHAPTER 20
THE INDUSTRIAL REVOLUTION AND ITS IMPACT ON EUROPEAN SOCIETY

CHAPTER OUTLINE

I. The Industrial Revolution in Great Britain
   - A. Origins
   - B. Technological Changes and New Forms of Industrial Organization
     1. The Cotton Industry
     2. The Steam Engine
     3. The Iron Industry
     4. A Revolution in Transportation
     5. The Industrial Factory
   - C. Britain's Great Exhibition of 1851

II. The Spread of Industrialization
   - A. Limitations to Industrialization
   - B. Centers of Continental Industrialization
   - C. The Industrial Revolution in the United States
   - D. Limiting the Spread of Industrialization to the Non-industrialized World

III. The Social Impact of the Industrial Revolution
   - A. Population Growth
     1. The Great Hunger
   - B. The Growth of Cities
     1. Urban Living Conditions in the Early Industrial Revolution
     2. Urban Reformers
   - C. New Social Classes: The Industrial Middle Class
   - D. New Social Classes: Workers in the Industrial Age
     1. Working Conditions for the Industrial Working Class
   - E. Standards of Living
   - F. Efforts at Change: The Workers
   - G. Efforts at Change: Reformers and Government

IV. Conclusion

CHAPTER SUMMARY

The Industrial Revolution was one the transforming events in world history. Britain was in the forefront because of several advantageous circumstances. An agricultural revolution had increased the quantity of foodstuffs thus lowering the costs and a population increase supplied a surplus of labor for the new industrial technologies. Britain was a wealthy nation with capital for investment, and unlike in some continental countries, profit was a legitimate goal. Coal and iron were abundant, and a transportation revolution created a system of canals, roads, bridges, and later, steam-powered railroads. Parliament had established a stable government where property, one of Locke's natural rights, was protected. Finally, Britain was the world's major colonial power with access to overseas markets. The cotton industry led the way because of new technologies such as the spinning jenny and power loom. Most significant was the steam engine, perfected by James Watt (d.1819). London's Great Exhibition of 1851 showcased to the world Britain's industrial might.

Continental industrialization was delayed because of a lack of transport, the existence of internal tolls, less sympathetic governments, and the upheavals of the French Revolution and Napoleonic wars. Continental nations made use of British technology and artisans until they established schools to train their own engineers and mechanics. Unlike Britain's laissez-faire approach, continental industrialization was subsidized by governments through the building of railroads, establishing technical schools, and excluding cheaper British goods through tariffs. By 1860, the United States was also well along the road of industrialization.

In the non-western world industrial development was much slower, in part because it lacked the social-economic-political structures of the West, but also because Britain and other colonial powers prevented the growth of local industries in order to maintain a market for their manufactured goods: colonies were to produce raw materials and purchase industrial products.

The birthrate declined but the population increased because of a reduction in epidemics and wars and an increase in the food supply. Overpopulation, particularly in rural areas, led to disaster, such as in the potato famine in Ireland which led to the death of a million persons between 1845 and 1851. Cities grew dramatically: London grew from one million in 1800 to 2.35 million in 1850. Urbanization was slower on the continent, and until the twentieth century most workers were still engaged in agriculture. Urban living conditions were often horrendous and most cities lacked any semblance of sanitary facilities.

The new middle-class consisted of manufacturers and bankers. Even members of the traditional aristocracy became industrial entrepreneurs. Another new class was the working class. The work environment, especially in the factories, was dreadful: long hours, unsafe conditions, and child labor was the norm. Laws were passed, in Britain known as the Factory Acts, in the attempt to improve factory conditions, initially for women and children. Whether there were improvements in general living standards is difficult to determine. Statistics suggest that there was an increase in real wages, but miserable living and working conditions balanced off the gains. Labor unions were formed to improve wages and conditions but with limited success. Workers sometimes protested by destroying the factories and machines, as did the Luddites in England. England's Chartist movement petitioned Parliament, demanding reforms, but the politicians rejected their demands. In summary, the Industrial Revolution radically transformed western civilization and then the rest of the world–politically, economically, socially–for good and for ill.

LECTURE AND DISCUSSION TOPICS

1. Discuss and describe the emergence of the modern industrial system.

2. What was revolutionary about the Industrial Revolution?

3. Examine some of the reasons why Great Britain was the first nation in the world to industrialize.

4. Compare and contrast, both as to similarities and differences, the plight of factory workers in the early decades of the Industrial Revolution and the condition of workers today.

5. Discuss the emergence of the "working class" and "the middle class" in the context of the Industrial Revolution.

6. Consider how continental industrialization differed from the process of industrialization in Great Britain.

7. Examine the historical controversy about the impact of the Industrial Revolution on the standards of living of the majority of the population, or the masses.

8. Explore how the advent of factory time and attendant changes affected rhythms of life, work, and leisure in western society.

9. Discuss the responses to the negative impacts of the Industrial Revolution. What were they, who were they, what motivated them, and were they successful?

10. Examine the concept of Luddism, both in the early nineteenth century and today.

MAP EXERCISES

1. The Industrial Revolution in Britain. MAP 20.1. What is the relationship between areas of industrialization and major population centers? How important was the railroad to Britain's industrial development and why? (page 363)

2. The Industrialization of Europe by 1850. MAP 20.2. What are the possible geographic and non-geographic reasons why continental industrialization was centered in north and northwestern Europe rather than in the eastern and southeastern regions of the continent? What is the relationship, if any, between peasant emancipation and industrialization? Between urbanization and industrialization? (page 366)

DISCUSSION QUESTIONS FOR THE PRIMARY SOURCES (BOXED DOCUMENTS)

1."The Traits of the British Industrial Entrepreneur": As seen in the life of Richard Arkwright, what traits did Edward Baines think were crucial to be a successful entrepreneur? To what extent are these still considered the necessary traits for a successful entrepreneur in the twenty-first century age of the computer? (page 361)

2. "Discipline in the New Factories": As seen in this document, what impact did factories have on the lives of workers? To what extent have such "rules" determined much of modern industrial life? How is your life marked by the historical development of such rules? Are today's workers still only "hands" in the opinion of many employers? (page 364)

3. "S-t-e-a-m-boat A-comin'!": How does this document illustrate the impact of the transportation revolution on daily life in the United States? Is Mark Twain romanticizing his account of life on the Mississippi from his remembered past? If so, where in his account and why? (page 367)

4. "Child Labor: Discipline in the Textile Mills": What kind of working conditions did children face in the mills during the early Industrial Revolution? What were the benefits of child labor to the employers? Why not employ just adults? Why did entrepreneurs permit such conditions and such treatment of children? Is the problem of child labor still with the world today? Why or why not? If so, where? (page 372)

STUDENT RESEARCH AND PROJECT TOPICS

1. Why did the Industrial Revolution begin in Great Britain?

2. Discuss and trace the role of the factory in the early Industrial Revolution. What made the factory system possible? What impact did it have on the lives of workers, especially on women and children?

3. Compare and contrast the patterns of industrialization in continental Europe and the United States with those of Great Britain.

4. Discuss the role of government in the industrial development of the Western world. What were ways that government encouraged industrialization and how did it attempt to check its excesses? Are modern day efforts to curb industrial excesses the same or different from what they were in the early nineteenth century?

5. How are changes in population growth and the development of urbanization related to the Industrial Revolution?

6. Discus the impact of the early Industrial Revolution upon the family, the role of women, and the living and working conditions of the industrial workers?

7. What efforts did workers make to ameliorate the harsh working conditions of the early Industrial Revolution? How successful were they?

8. Assume that you are a small landowner who lost his land due to economic changes in the British countryside. In a brief essay, explain your changed position and lifestyle as you and your family move to Manchester to gain employment in one of the new factories.

9. Discuss the concept of the 'middle-class' and its relation to the Industrial Revolution.

10. "The 'working-class' is a product of the Industrial Revolution." Discuss.

IDENTIFICATIONS

1. Industrial Revolution
2. cotton industry
3. canals
4. Richard Arkwright and James Hargreaves
5. hand-loom weavers
6. coal and coke
7. James Watt and the rotary engine
8. Henry Cort and puddling
9. George Stephenson's *Rocket*
10. railroads
11. the factory
12. Great Exhibition of 1851

13. the Crystal Palace
14. the American system
15. steamboats
16. Ireland and the potato
17. suburbs
18. Poor Law Commissioners
19. Edwin Chadwick
20. bourgeois
21. "new elites"
22. working class
23. child labor
24. domestic servants
25. trades unions
26. Robert Owen
27. Luddites
28. Chartism
29. factory acts
30. Ten Hours Act

MULTIPLE CHOICE QUESTIONS

1. The Industrial Revolution had its beginnings in
    a. France.
    b. Belgium.
    c. Great Britain.
    d. the United States.
        ANSWER: c (page 360)

2. Britain's emergence as the first industrial power was aided by all of the following <u>except</u>
    a. a rapid population growth and a surplus pool of labor.
    b. the agricultural revolution of the eighteenth century.
    c. a ready supply of domestic and colonial markets.
    d. Parliament's heavy and controlling involvement in private enterprise.
        ANSWER: d (p. 360)

3. The Industrial Revolution in Britain was largely inspired by
    a. the urgent need to solve the great poverty in the eighteenth century.
    b. the failure of the cottage industry.
    c. entrepreneurs who sought and accepted the new manufacturing methods of inventions.
    d. the industrialization of the Dutch and French.
        ANSWER: c (p. 360)

4. The infrastructure advantages in Britain promoting rapid industrialization included all of the following <u>except</u>

a. canals.
b. roads.
c. bridges.
d. internal customs posts.
ANSWER: d (p. 360)

5. The British industrial entrepreneur Richard Arkwright

a. typified the highly educated and mannered entrepreneur of the Industrial Revolution.
b. invented the water frame spinning machine.
c. perfected the Compton's mule.
d. created the Spinning Jenny.
ANSWER: b (p. 361)

6. The first step toward the Industrial Revolution in Britain occurred within its

a. cotton textile industry.
b. mining industry.
c. iron industry.
d. railroad industry.
ANSWER: a (p. 361)

7. Britain's cotton industry in the late eighteenth century

a. could not keep up with French textile production.
b. was responsible for the creation of the first modern factories.
c. declined due to the lack of technical innovation.
d. immediately fell apart with the success of the Industrial Revolution.
ANSWER: b (p. 361)

8. The invention of the steam engine in Britain was initially triggered by

a. the textile industry's demand for new sources of power.
b. problems in the mining industry.
c. the railroad industry's call for a more efficient source of power.
d. the need for a more efficient mode of power for English ships.
ANSWER: b (p. 361)

9. Which of the following inventions proved vital to the industrialization of the British cotton manufacture?

a. Arkwright's spinning frame.
b. Hargreaves' spinning jenny.
c. Cartwright's power loom.
d. all the above
ANSWER: d (p. 361)

10. James Watt was vital to the Industrial Revolution for his invention of

a. the spinning jenny.
b. the mule-powered Newcomen engine.
c. a rotary engine that could spin and weave cotton.
d. the first steam-powered locomotive.
ANSWER: c (p. 361)

11. The development of the steam engine during the Industrial Revolution
a. was the work of Edmund Cartwright.
b. proved disastrous to Britain's mining industry.
c. made factories dependent upon the location of rivers.
d. made Britain's cotton goods the cheapest and most popular in the world.
ANSWER: d (p. 362)

12. The success of the steam engine in the Industrial Revolution made Britain dependent upon
a. timber.
b. coal.
c. water power.
d. electricity.
ANSWER: b (p. 362)

13. The Englishman Henry Cort was responsible for the process in iron smelting known as
a. puddling.
b. cottling.
c. the open hearth.
d. "skimming."
ANSWER: a (p. 362)

14. The development of such superior locomotives as the *Rocket*, used on the first public railway lines, is attributed to
a. Timothy Faulkner.
b. George Stephenson.
c. Richard Trevithick.
d. Walter Zofrin.
ANSWER: b (p. 362)

15. The development of the railroads in the Industrial Revolution was important in
a. increasing British supremacy in civil and mechanical engineering.
b. increasing the size of markets and the price of goods.
c. bringing about the demise of joint-stock companies.
d. all of the above
ANSWER: a (pp. 362-363)

16. The new set of values established by factory owners during the Industrial Revolution
a. was rejected by evangelical religions as being "unchristian."
b. was basically a continuation from the cottage industry system.
c. was never adopted by the working class.
d. relegated the worker to a life of harsh discipline subject to the clock and the rigors of highly competitive wage labor.
ANSWER: d (p. 363)

17. The most frequent method employed to make the many very young boys and girls working in new British industries obey the owner's factory discipline was
a. repeated beatings.
b. bribes of candy.
c. heavy fines for lost time.
d. lectures and schooling in the rules to parents.
ANSWER: a (p. 363)

18. The rise of the industrial factory system deeply affected the lives and status of workers who now
   a. were often paid in kind.
   b. no longer owned the means of economic production and could only sell their labor for a wage.
   c. were less vulnerable to more rapid cycles of economic boom and bust.
   d. got both good wages and many fringe benefits unknown before.
      ANSWER: b (p. 363)

19. The Great Exhibition of 1851
   a. showed how the Industrial Revolution had produced wealth from the coal mines of England.
   b. displayed Great Britain's industrial wealth to the world.
   c. was housed in the Royal Palace, a tribute to French engineering skills.
   d. showed British agricultural technology to the world.
      ANSWER: b (p. 364)

20. One of the chief reasons why Europe initially lagged behind England in industrialization was a lack of
   a. banking facilities.
   b. roads and means of transportation.
   c. manpower.
   d. capital for investment.
      ANSWER: b (p. 366)

21. To keep their industrial monopoly, Britain attempted to
   a. export fewer goods to continental countries.
   b. prohibit industrial artisans from going abroad.
   c. limit financial investment overseas.
   d. increase tariffs to keep out foreign manufactured goods.
      ANSWER: b (p. 365)

22. Industrialization began on the continent first in
   a. Spain and Italy.
   b. Belgium, France and Germany.
   c. Russia and Sweden.
   d. Norway and Denmark.
      ANSWER: b (p. 366)

23. One of the differences between British and Continental industrialization was that
   a. government played a larger role in British industrialization. .
   b. Britain relied upon railroads while Continental nations primarily made use of rivers and canals.
   c. government played a larger role in Continental industrialization.
   d. Continental industrialization relied more upon textile manufacturing that Britain.
      ANSWER: c (pp. 365-366)

24. The Industrial Revolution spread from Western Europe and the United States only after
   a. 1800.
   b. 1825.
   c. 1850.
   d. 1900.
      ANSWER: c (p. 364)

25. The initial application of machinery to production in the United States was
    a. entirely the result of American inventors and inventions.
    b. by borrowing from Great Britain.
    c. by learning from the mistakes made in France and doing the opposite.
    d. to use only adult males as factory workers.
        ANSWER: b (p. 367)

26. By 1850, all of the following countries were close to Britain in industrial output <u>except</u>
    a. Russia.
    b. Belgium.
    c. the United States.
    d. France.
        ANSWER: a (p. 368)

27. The Industrial Revolution on the continent
    a. was a generation behind Britain in cotton manufacture.
    b. neglected coal and iron technology in favor of the progress in the textile industry.
    c. benefited from the discovery of vast coal deposits in Germany in the 1820's.
    d. would remain far behind the British until the twentieth century.
        ANSWER: a (p. 366)

28. The first Continental nations to complete establish a comprehensive railroad system were
    a. France and Italy.
    b. Belgium and Germany.
    c. Prussia and Poland.
    d. Russia and Austria.
        ANSWER: b (p. 366)

29. The Industrial Revolution in the United States
    a. never matched Great Britain's due to a lack of internal transportation.
    b. employed large numbers of women in factories, especially the textile mills.
    c. utilized a labor-intensive economy with many skilled workers.
    d. occurred predominantly in the southern states.
        ANSWER: b (p. 368)

30. Due to the size of the country, industrialization in the United States was dependent upon
    a. a substantial labor source.
    b. improved technology.
    c. better industrial methodology.
    d. a good system of transportation.
        ANSWER: d (p. 367)

31. By 1860 what percent of the population in cities held 70 to 80 percent of the wealth in America?
    a. 10 percent
    b. 30 percent
    c. 60 percent
    d. 75 percent
        ANSWER: a (p. 368)

32. Compared to Britain, American industrialization was a capital-intensive endeavor because
   a. Britain had more unskilled laborers.
   b. there was a labor shortage in the U.S.
   c. there was a skilled labor surplus in Britain.
   d. there was a far larger pool of unskilled laborers in the U.S.
      ANSWER: d (p. 367)

33. The so-called American System was
   a. high tariffs to protect new industries.
   b. the use of interchangeable parts in manufacturing.
   c. a common market for the western hemisphere.
   d. none of the above.
      ANSWER: b (p. 367)

34. By 1850, the European population
   a. could not be closely approximated as government statistics were not yet kept.
   b. was close to figures from 1800.
   c. was over 150 million.
   d. was over 250 million.
      ANSWER: d (p. 368)

35. The European population explosion of the nineteenth century
   a. is mainly explained by the increased birthrates across Europe.
   b. was largely attributable to the disappearance of famine from western Europe.
   c. was due to the lack of emigration.
   d. occurred despite the preponderance of major epidemic diseases.
      ANSWER: b (p. 368)

36. The only European country with a declining population in the nineteenth century was
   a. Ireland.
   b. Italy.
   c. Austria.
   d. France.
      ANSWER: a (p. 369)

37. Urbanization in the first half of the nineteenth century
   a. was more dramatic for the Continent than Great Britain.
   b. caused over fifty percent of the Russian population to live in cities by 1850.
   c. was a phenomenon directly tied to industrialization.
   d. accounted for widespread poverty in rural areas of Europe.
      ANSWER: c (p. 369)

38. Which of the following statements best applies to urban life in the early nineteenth century?
   a. Government intervention prevented consumer fraud and food adulteration.
   b. A tremendous decline in death rates accounted for the increased population of most large cities.
   c. Lower-class family dwellings were on the whole much better than in the countryside.
   d. Filthy sanitary conditions were exacerbated by the city authorities' reluctance to take responsibility for public health.
      ANSWER: d (p. 370)

39. Demographic changes that resulted from industrialization saw
   a. the wealthy move from cities to escape the ill effects of factory development.
   b. the new middle class move to the suburbs of cities to escape the urban poor.
   c. laboring classes become more affluent and varied in their places of residence.
   d. rich and poor more commonly living together in new suburban housing developments.
      ANSWER: b (p. 369)

40. Edwin Chadwick
   a. was a leader in expressing the dislike of the middle class for the working poor.
   b. wrote the *Treatise on the Iron Law of Wages*.
   c. advocated modern sanitary reforms that resulted in Britain's first Public Health Act.
   d. was representative of the new entrepreneurial, industrial class.
      ANSWER: c (p. 370)

41. Members of the new industrial entrepreneurial class in the early nineteenth century
   a. particularly excluded aristocrats.
   b. were responsible for the predominance of giant corporate firms by 1850.
   c. were usually resourceful individuals with diverse social backgrounds.
   d. were more often from the lower classes than the bourgeoisie.
      ANSWER: c (p. 370)

42. The new social class of industrial workers in the early Industrial Revolution
   a. did not include women at all.
   b. worked under appallingly dangerous conditions for incredibly long hours at the mercy of profit-maximizing bosses.
   c. excluded large numbers of children from factory work.
   d. unionized and achieved a good amount of political power.
      ANSWER: b (p. 371)

43. Working conditions in the early decades of the Industrial Revolution were
   a. poor in all areas except for pottery and craft workshops.
   b. poor despite close government regulation of factories.
   c. satisfactory in the coal mines following the invention of steam power.
   d. probably worse in the cotton mills with their high temperatures and hazardous air.
      ANSWER: d (p. 371)

44. One of the primary reasons for the use of children as a source of labor in the Industrial Revolution was
   a. a lack of compulsory education laws.
   b. low-paid children could more easily move around large industrial equipment.
   c. there was an overabundance of children in society.
   d. poor parental supervision.
      ANSWER: b (p. 371)

45. Women who worked in the early factories of the Industrial Revolution
   a. were given the same pay as men.
   b. instigated dramatic change in pre-industrial kinship patterns.
   c. never represented a large percentage of the workers in textile factories.
   d. did not result in a significant transformation in female working patterns.
      ANSWER: d (p. 372)

46. The Industrial Revolution's effect on the standard of living
a. especially benefited the middle classes.
b. led to much increased disparity between the richest and poorest classes in society.
c. eventually led to an overall increase in purchasing power for the working classes.
d. all the above
ANSWER: d (p. 368)

47. The Chartist movement in Britain
a. was the skilled craftsmen's attempt to destroy industrial machinery.
b. gave millions of men and women a sense of working-class consciousness generated by terrible common working conditions in the factories.
c. coerced Parliament into instituting universal male suffrage.
d. none of the above
ANSWER: b (p. 373)

48. One of the major demands of the Chartists was
a. the abolition of women labor.
b. to achieve political democracy and a voice for working people in government.
c. paid vacations for all factory hands.
d. to have representatives elected to Parliament from the boroughs of London.
ANSWER: b (p. 373)

49. The Luddites
a. received little support in their areas of activity.
b. destroyed industrial machines that destroyed their livelihood.
c. were composed of the lowest unskilled workers in Great Britain.
d. was the first movement of working-class consciousness of the Continent.
ANSWER: b (p. 373)

50. Efforts at industrial reform in the 1830's and 1840's in Great Britain achieved all of the following <u>except</u> the
a. establishment of a national system of trade unions by 1847.
b. reduction of working hours for children to no more than 12 hours a day.
c. outlawing of women and children in coal mines.
d. requirement of daily education for working children.
ANSWER: a (p. 373)

RELEVANT WORLD-WIDE WEB SITES/RESOURCES

1. The Industrial Revolution:
http://www.stedwards.edu/cfpages/stoll/iw/industrl.htm
(One of the best sites regarding the subject. Multiple documents, images, and links online.)

2. Internet History of Science Sourcebook (at Fordham University):
http://www.fordham.edu/halsall/science/sciencesbook.html
(Excellent site for all aspects of scientific development over time arranged by regions/cultures and eras. Very fine material on Scientific Revolution, classical science, Enlightenment experimentation, and the Industrial Revolution.)

RELEVANT VIDEO RESOURCES

Civilisation, Public Media Video/BBC Television, (50 minutes each program), Program 13, "Heroic Materialism." (Covers nineteenth-century industrialization, rise of materialism and materialist values, and the growth of European cities.)

SUGGESTED STUDENT ACTIVITIES

1. Have students do research on one of the key figures in the Industrial Revolution, such as Robert Stephenson, Henry Bessemer, or James Watt. Have the students report to the class.

2. Students could do a detailed report on the Great Exhibition of 1851 in England.

3. If you have a small class, divide them into two groups to debate the pros and cons that have resulted from industrialization.

4. Have students do a comparative study on union movements in Europe with their American counterparts.

CHAPTER 21
REACTION, REVOLUTION, AND ROMANTICISM, 1815-1850

CHAPTER OUTLINE

I. The Conservative Order (1815-1830)
  A. The Peace Settlement
  B. The Ideology of Conservatism
  C. Conservative Domination: The Concert of Europe
    1. The Revolt of Latin America
    2. The Greek Revolt (1821-1832)
  D. Conservative Domination: The European States
    1. Great Britain: Rule of the Tories
    2. Restoration in France
    3. Intervention in the Italian States and Spain
    4. Repression in Central Europe
    5. Russia: Autocracy of the Tsars
II. Ideologies of Change
  A. Liberalism
  B. Nationalism
  C. Early Socialism
III. Revolution and Reform (1830-1850)
  A. Another French Revolution
  B. Revolutionary Outbursts in Belgium, Poland, and Italy
  C. Reform in Great Britain
  D. The Revolutions of 1848
    1. Yet Another French Revolution
    2. Revolution in Central Europe
    3. Revolts in the Italian States
    4. The Failures of 1848
  E. The Growth of the United States
IV. The Emergence of an Ordered Society
  A. New Police Forces
  B. Prison Reform
V. Culture in an Age of Reaction and Revolution: The Mood of Romanticism
  A. The Characteristics of Romanticism
  B. Romantic Poets and the Love of Nature
  C. Romanticism in Art and Music
  D. The Revival of Religion in the Age of Romanticism
VI. Conclusion

CHAPTER SUMMARY

One of the many "isms" of nineteenth century was conservatism. For conservatives, society and the state, not the individual, was paramount, in a world to be guided by tradition. The victors over Napoleon met at the Congress of Vienna, forming the Quadruple Alliance of Britain, Austria, Russia, and Prussia. Its guiding principle was "legitimacy," or monarchical government, to be maintained by a balance of power. A new German Confederation replaced the Holy Roman Empire. The Quadruple Alliance became the Quintuple Alliance with the admittance of France.

Acting as the Concert of Europe, the major powers intervened to uphold conservative governments. However, Britain, seeking new markets, opposed intervention when Spain's Latin American colonies declared their independence. Britain was under conservative Tory rule until 1830 despite economic protests and demands for electoral reform. The Bourbons returned to France with Louis XVIII (1814-1824) and Charles X (1824-1830). Bourbon Spain and Italy remained under conservative rule. Reform hopes of German students and professors was negated by the repressive measures of the Carlsbad Decrees. Order was maintained in multi-ethnic Austria, and in Russia a reform movement was crushed in 1825.

Liberalism grew out of the Enlightenment and the era of Revolutions. Freedom was the aim, both in politics and in economics; the state should have no responsibilities except in defense, policing, and public works construction. Natural rights and representative government were essential but most liberals limited voting to male property owners. Nationalism, with its belief in a community with common traditions, language, and customs, also emerged from the French Revolution, threatening the status quo in divided Germany and Italy and the multi-ethnic Austrian Empire. Utopian socialists envisioned cooperation rather than competitive capitalism, and voluntary communities were established and government workshops suggested.

In 1830, an uprising in France led to a constitutional monarchy headed by Louis-Philippe (1830-1848), supported by the upper middle-class. Belgium split off from the Netherlands, but national uprisings in Poland and Italy failed. In Britain, the franchise was widened to include the upper middle-classes, and free trade became the norm. The great revolutionary year was 1848. France's Louis-Philippe fled into exile and the Second Republic was established with universal manhood suffrage, but conflict developed between socialist demands and the republican political agenda. A unified Germany was the aim of the Frankfurt Assembly, but it failed. In Austria, liberal demands of Hungarians and others were put down. In Italy, there were uprisings against Austrian rule and a republic was proclaimed in Rome, but conservatives regained control.

To attain an ordered society, civilian police forces were created, such as London's "bobbies." Urban poverty was addressed through workhouses and technical institutes to teach productive trades. Sunday schools were established and churches campaigned against gambling and prostitution. In prisons, the incarcerated would be reformed through work or by isolation.

Romanticism, a reaction against Enlightenment reason, favored intuition, feeling, and emotion. Johann Wolfgang von Goethe wrote a popular novel about a youth who committed suicide for love. Folk tales were collected by the brothers Grimm, and the Middle Ages inspired Sir Walter Scott. Mary Shelley and Edgar Allan Poe wrote about the bizarre and Percy Bysshe Shelley and Lord George Byron were notable poets. Nature was often the subject in William Wordsworth's poetry and the paintings of Caspar David Friedrich and J.M.W. Turner. In music, Ludwig von Beethoven and Hector Berlioz were major figures. Religious Romanticism was to be found in Catholicism's medieval heritage and in Protestant revival movements.

LECTURE AND DISCUSSION TOPICS

1. Examine the forces of conservatism in theory and practice in the early nineteenth century and compare those to today's conservatism.

2. Discuss nineteenth century conservatism as a reaction to the eighteenth century Enlightenment and the events of the French Revolution.

3. Assess the impact of the Congress of Vienna on the history of the nineteenth century.

4. Define and describe nineteenth century liberalism in theory and practice, using Great Britain as a model.

5. Compare and contrast nineteenth century liberalism with today's liberalism.

6. Discuss the concept that "nationalism" became the new religion of the nineteenth century.

7. What is Romanticism?--The Romantic Movement in Art [a slide lecture]

8. Assess the several causes of the revolutions of 1848 and also the results: what were the successes and what were the failures in that revolutionary year?

9. Compare and contrast the year 1789 with the year 1848.

10. Discuss Romanticism as one possible reaction to the Enlightenment and the Industrial Revolution.

MAP EXERCISES

1. Europe after the Congress of Vienna, MAP 21.1. In comparison to 1789, what changes had occurred in the map of Europe by 1815? From the vantage point of 1815, what might be several predictions for the future of the German Confederation and the states of Italy? From the map, what nation might prove to be a potential threat to European security and stability in the later nineteenth and twentieth centuries? (page 379)

2. Latin America in the First Half of the Nineteenth century, MAP 21.2. What might be some of the factors, historical and geographic, which led to the breakup of South America into so many separate nation states? Geographically, which nation(s) might be best located and which nation(s) less satisfactorily situated to benefit from future nineteenth century western civilization developments, and why? (page 380)

3. The Distribution of Languages in Nineteenth Century Europe, MAP 21.3. Comparing this map with 21.1, what obvious challenges might face the Ottoman and Austrian empires in the decades after 1815? How did the linguistic distribution in those two empires compare with the linguistic circumstances in the German Confederation, France, Italy, and Great Britain? (page 384)

DISCUSSION QUESTIONS FOR THE PRIMARY SOURCES (BOXED DOCUMENTS)

1."The Voice of Conservatism: Metternich of Austria": Based on Metternich's discussion, how would you define conservatism? What experience obviously conditioned Metternich's ideas? Based on this selection, discuss the actual policies Metternich would have wanted his government to pursue. Does Metternich have any accurate insights regarding the future of Europe? If so, what are they? (page 378)

2. "The Voice of Liberalism: John Stuart Mill on Liberty": How do Mill's ideas fit into the concept of democracy, safety and national security? What is more important in his thought: the individual or society? What do you believe to be the historic sources or inspirations of Mill's ideas? Did Mill's ideas have any apparent impact on the future? Is so, how? (page 383)

3. "Revolutionary Excitement: Carl Schurz and the Revolution of 1848 in Germany": Why was Schurz so excited when he heard the news about the revolution in France? Do you think being a university student would help explain his reaction? Why or why not? Why might the United States have satisfied his hopes as expressed in the document? (page 387)

4. "Gothic Literature: Edgar Allan Poe": What characteristics of Romanticism are revealed in Poe's tale? How does Romanticism offer alternatives to the reigning influences of rationalism and industrialism? Does Poe's work reflect his own era and environment? If so, how? (page 390)

STUDENT RESEARCH AND PROJECT TOPICS

1. Discuss the Congress of Vienna. What did it try to accomplish in Europe? How well did it succeed in achieving its goals?

2. What were the chief ideas associated with the ideology of conservatism in the first half of the nineteenth century? How were these ideas put into practice between 1815 and 1830? How has conservative ideology changed over the last century?

3. What were the chief ideas associated with the ideologies of liberalism, nationalism, and early or utopian socialism? Why were liberalism, nationalism, and early socialism considered revolutionary by many people? How were these ideologies similar? How were they different?

4. How was Great Britain able to avoid revolution in the 1830's and 1840's?

5. Discuss the revolutions of 1848 in France, central Europe, and Italy. What caused them? What did they achieve initially? Why did the revolutionary forces fail? What did the revolutions actually achieve?

6. Compare and contrast the revolution of 1848 in France with the revolutions in the German and Italian states. How were they similar and how were they different?

7. In what specific ways did Europe respond to the need for order in society in the first half of the nineteenth century?

8. Discuss the major ideas of Romanticism and show why they were related to the social, artistic, and literary forces of the age.

9. What might be political romanticism? Define it and give examples from the first half of the nineteenth century.

10. Compare and contrast the concepts of romanticism as exhibited in Caspar David Friedrich's *Man and Woman Gazing at the Moon* with Eugene Delacroix's *The Death of Sardanapalus*.

IDENTIFICATIONS

1. Congress of Vienna
2. Klemens von Metternich
3. "legitimacy"
4. balance of power
5. Edmund Burke and conservatism
6. Concert of Europe
7. the congress system
8. Latin America revolts
9. Greek Revolt
10. Tories and Whigs
11. Louis XVIII and Charles X
12. German Confederation
13. the Decembrist Revolt
14. Tsar Nicholas I
15. classical economics
16. John Stuart Mill
17. *On the Subjection of Women*
18. utopian socialism
19. Robert Owen's New Lanark
20. July Revolution of 1830
21. Reform Act of 1832
22. France's Second Republic
23. Frankfurt Assembly
24. Giuseppe Mazzini and Young Italy
25. Jacksonian Democracy
26. Romanticism
27. *The Sorrows of Young Werther*
28. Percy Bysshe Shelley, Lord Byron, and William Wordsworth
29. Caspar David Friedrich and Eugene Delacroix
30. Ludwig von Beethoven

MULTIPLE CHOICE QUESTIONS

1. At the Congress of Vienna, the Austrian representative Prince Metternich pursued the policy of legitimacy, meaning
   a. he wished to legitimate the French defeat.
   b. he sought legitimate control over central Europe to benefit Austria.
   c. he endeavored to restore legitimate monarchs on the thrones of every major European power to preserve traditional institutions and values.
   d. he sought legitimate proof of England's economic and industrial support of Austria.
   ANSWER: c (page 377)

2. After Napoleon's defeat, the Quadruple Alliance
   a. sent troops to sack Paris.
   b. restored the old Bourbon monarchy to France in the person of Louis XVIII.
   c. returned Corsica to Italian control.
   d. delivered an ultimatum to the pope demanding full control over all of Italy.
   ANSWER: b (p. 377)

3. The Congress of Vienna
   a. gave Prussia complete control over Polish lands.
   b. created policies that would maintain the balance of power among the members of the Quadruple Alliance.
   c. failed to achieve long-lasting peace among European nations.
   d. treated France leniently following Napoleon's One Hundred Days.
   ANSWER: b (p. 377)

4. The foreign minister and diplomat who dominated the Congress of Vienna was
   a. Klemens von Metternich.
   b. Prince Talleyrand.
   c. Tsar Alexander I.
   d. Napoleon.
   ANSWER: a (p. 377)

5. Klemens von Metternich
   a. supported much of the revolutionary ideology after Napoleon's defeat.
   b. thought that a free press was necessary to maintain the status quo.
   c. believed European monarchs shared the common interest of stability.
   d. was anti-religious and supported atheistic causes.
   ANSWER: c (p. 377)

6. Conservatism, the dominant political philosophy following the fall of Napoleon
   a. was rejected by the Congress of Vienna as inappropriate in the new liberal age.
   b. expressed that individual rights remained the best guide for human order.
   c. was best expressed in Edmund Burke's *Reflections on the Revolution in France*, emphasizing the dangers of radical and "rational" political change.
   d. was too radical for Joseph de Maistre, the French spokesman for a cautious, evolutionary conservatism.
   ANSWER: c (p. 377)

7. At its most elementary level, conservatism
   a. sought to preserve the achievements of previous generations by subordinating individual rights to communal welfare.
   b. became the most popular political philosophy in Russia.
   c. sought above all else the achievement of individual rights.
   d. was never popular among the political elite of Europe.
   ANSWER: a (p. 378)

8. The Congress of Vienna was least successful in
   a. restoring monarchy to France.
   b. permanently maintaining the status quo through military interventions.
   c. establishing the Concern of Europe.
   d. instituting an era of conservatism.
   ANSWER: b (p. 378)

9. The most important factor in preventing the European overthrow of the newly independent nations of Latin America was
   a. British intervention.
   b. the Monroe Doctrine guiding American foreign policy.
   c. the sheer size of South America.
   d. growing support for pacifism in Europe.
   ANSWER: a (p. 379)

10. The Greek revolt was successful largely due to
   a. a well-trained guerrilla army.
   b. the Turks' lack of fortitude.
   c. European intervention.
   d. superior Greek military tactics.
   ANSWER: c (p. 379)

11. Which of the following areas was most directly controlled by the Austrians after 1815
   a. Britain.
   b. France.
   c. Spain.
   d. Italy.
   ANSWER: d (p. 381)

12. Intervention, designed to prevent revolution, was used to support revolution in the case of
   a. Spain.
   b. Italy.
   c. Greece.
   d. Poland.
   ANSWER: c (p. 379)

13. By 1815, following the Congress of Vienna, the Italian peninsula
   a. was entirely unified as a single country.
   b. remained divided into several states subject to the domination of northern European powers.
   c. had been devastated by the last campaigns of Napoleon.
   d. had been completely annexed by Austria, a move confirmed by the Congress.
   ANSWER: b (p. 381)

14. The Germanic Confederation, created in the Vienna settlement of 1815,
   a. created a united Germany.
   b. was dominated by Prussia and Bavaria.
   c. had little real power.
   d. was crushed by Imperial Austria.
      ANSWER: c (p. 381)

15. Of the two political factions in Great Britain in the early nineteenth century, the one supported by the new industrial middle class was
   a. Tories.
   b. Liberals.
   c. Radicals.
   d. Whigs.
      ANSWER: d (p. 381)

16. Tsar Alexander I of Russia did all of the following except
   a. become more reactionary after the defeat of Napoleon.
   b. grant a constitution, freeing the serfs.
   c. reform the Russian education system.
   d. revert to a program of arbitrary censorship as a tool of rulership.
      ANSWER: b (p. 381)

17. Following the death of Alexander I in 1825, Russian society under Nicholas I became
   a. a police state due to Nicholas's fear of internal and external revolution.
   b. the most liberal of the European powers.
   c. an industrial power after the abolition of serfdom.
   d. increasingly influenced by ultra-conservative societies, such as the Northern Union.
      ANSWER: a (p. 381)

18. Economic liberalism can also be described as
   a. mercantilism.
   b. socialism.
   c. *laissez-faire* economics.
   d. corporatism.
      ANSWER: c (p. 382)

19. All of the following are correct about nineteenth century liberals except they
   a. were democrats.
   b. demanded the protection of civil liberties.
   c. advocated religious toleration and the separation of church and state.
   d. desired ministerial responsibility, where the ministers of government were responsible to the legislatures rather than the monarchs.
      ANSWER: a (p. 382)

20. The foremost social group embracing liberalism was made up by
   a. factory workers.
   b. the industrial middle class.
   c. radical aristocrats.
   d. army officers.
      ANSWER: b (p. 382)

21. Among J.S. Mill's most provocative writings was his *On the Subjection of Women* in which he argued that

a. women should be kept in the home to improve men's chances of finding work.
b. the legal subordination of females to males is wrong since men and women did not possess different natures.
c. Parliament should admit women members immediately.
d. female convicts be shipped out to colonize Australia.
ANSWER: b (p. 382)

22. Central to the liberal ideology in the nineteenth century was

a. child labor laws.
b. the preservation of law and order.
c. an emphasis on individual freedom.
d. the buildup of a nation's military.
ANSWER: c (p. 382)

23. The growing movement of nationalism in nineteenth-century Europe

a. was resisted by liberal thinkers, who felt that all ethnic groups should live together harmoniously.
b. advocated the formation of one European nation to end economic and military conflicts.
c. was fundamentally radical since it encouraged people to shift their political loyalty away from present states and rulers.
d. found its best expression in the writings of John Stuart Mill.
ANSWER: c (p. 382)

24. The utopian socialists of the first half of the nineteenth century were best characterized by

a. a commitment to economic competition.
b. a desire to introduce equality and cooperation into social conditions.
c. distrustful of government, believing that societal solutions could result through *laissez-faire.*
d. believed that the class struggle could bring about a socialist utopia.
ANSWER: b (p. 383)

25. The socialist communities associated with Robert Owen included all of the following <u>except</u>

a. New Lanark in Scotland.
b. Old Priory in England.
c. Nashoba in Tennessee.
d. New Harmony in Indiana.
ANSWER: b (pp. 383-384)

26. King Louis-Philippe in France

a. did all he could to help the impoverished industrial workers.
b. cooperated with upper middle class.
c. allowed for great reforms in the electoral system.
d. was the son of the former reactionary King Charles X.
ANSWER: b (p. 385)

27. The most successful nationalistic European revolution in 1830 was in
a. Poland.
b. Belgium.
c. Italy.
d. Scandinavia.
ANSWER: b (p. 385)

28. The primary driving force in the revolutions of Belgium, Poland, and Italy in 1830 was
a. nationalism.
b. religion.
c. racism.
d. socialism.
ANSWER: a (p. 385)

29. As a consequence of the British Reform Bill of 1832,
a. the industrial middle classes triumphed over the landed classes.
b. the Charter of the working class was adopted by Parliament.
c. the manufacturing elite joined the landed interest in ruling Britain.
d. Victoria became Queen of the United Kingdom of Britain and Ireland.
ANSWER: c (p. 385)

30. The Reform Bill of 1832 in Britain primarily benefited the
a. landed aristocracy.
b. upper-middle class.
c. working class.
d. clergy.
ANSWER: b (p. 385)

31. The July Revolution of 1830 in Paris
a. brought the Bourbon dynasty under Louis XVIII back to power.
b. restored the Bonapartes to power with Louis Napoleon as president of France
c. established a constitutional monarchy under Louis-Philippe.
d. created the democratic Second Republic.
ANSWER: c (p. 385)

32. The revolution of 1848 in France ultimately resulted in
a. the continued rule of Louis-Philippe but with radical reforms.
b. new elections to the national Assembly, resulting in the dominance of the radical republicans.
c. Europe's first socialist state under the guidance of the workshops.
d. the Second Republic under Louis Napoleon as its first president.
ANSWER: d (p. 386)

33. The 1848 "national workshops" in France
a. became a vital part of the French economy.
b. were extremely important to the French radical aristocracy.
c. became little more than unemployment compensation units through public works projects.
d. built many national parks in France.
ANSWER: c (p. 386)

34. In 1848, the Frankfurt Assembly
   a. unanimously adopted a *Grossdeutsch* solution for the Germanies.
   b. succeeded in making Prussia's Frederick William IV president of a united Germany.
   c. failed in its attempt to create a united Germany.
   d. gained the support of Austria.
      ANSWER: c (p. 386)

35. Giuseppe Mazzini's nationalist organization Young Italy
   a. liberated Italy's northern provinces from Austrian control.
   b. failed to achieve his goal of republican unity by 1849.
   c. helped inspire successful liberal constitutions throughout Italy.
   d. used the liberals in governments to extend suffrage to Italy's working classes.
      ANSWER: b (p. 388)

36. Mazzini's republican goal
   a. was largely successful in political terms.
   b. failed due to opposition of the French, the Austrians, and the pope.
   c. became the basic ideology of contemporary German liberals.
   d. was most popular among the Italian middle classes.
      ANSWER: b (p. 388)

37. Which of the following best explains the failures of the revolutions of 1848?
   a. Liberalism triumphed over nationalism.
   b. Nascent imperialism seduced the middle classes away from revolutionary goals.
   c. There was a crucial absence of national passion in the major revolutionary locales.
   d. The many nationalities were often divided among themselves.
      ANSWER: d (p. 388)

38. In the United States, the Supreme Court became a strong national institution under
   a. Andrew Jackson.
   b. John Marshall.
   c. Thomas Jefferson.
   d. Alexander Hamilton.
      ANSWER: b (p. 388)

39. Mass democratic politics was introduced into the United States during the presidency of
   a. George Washington.
   b. Thomas Jefferson.
   c. Andrew Jackson.
   d. Abraham Lincoln.
      ANSWER: c (p. 389)

40. All of the following were characteristics of Romanticism except
   a. a strong, pantheistic worship of nature.
   b. the rejection of the supernatural and unfamiliar.
   c. a preoccupation with sentiment, suffering, and self-sacrifice.
   d. a romantic reverence for history that inspired nationalism.
      ANSWER: b (p. 389)

41. The romantic movement had many of its roots in
   a. Turkey.
   b. Britain.
   c. Germany.
   d. France.
      ANSWER: c (p. 389)

42. The literary model for early Romantics was
   a. *The Last Days of Socrates*, by Plato.
   b. *Don Quixote*, by Cervantes.
   c. *Great Expectations*, by Dickens.
   d. *The Sorrows of the Young Werther*, by Goethe.
      ANSWER: d (p. 389)

43. The romantic movement can be viewed as a(n)
   a. reaction against the Enlightenment's preoccupation with reason.
   b. continuation of Enlightenment ideals and practices.
   c. attempt to create a socialist society.
   d. movement of lower-class, less literate people.
      ANSWER: a (p. 389)

44. The American romantic author of *The Fall of the House of Usher* was
   a. Mary Shelley.
   b. Thomas Carlyle.
   c. Edgar Allan Poe.
   d. Hans Christian Anderson.
      ANSWER: c (p. 390)

45. The most important form of literary expression for the romantics was
   a. the educational treatise.
   b. poetry.
   c. the novel.
   d. the play.
      ANSWER: b (p. 389)

46. Which of the following were major themes/subjects of Romantic artists?
   a. portraits
   b. Madonnas and religious scenes
   c. landscapes and depictions of nature
   d. scenes from aristocratic family life
      ANSWER: c (p. 390)

47. Romanticism in art and music was well characterized by
   a. Chateaubriand, whose many paintings anticipated the Impressionist movement.
   b. Beethoven, whose dramatic compositions bridged the gap between classicism and Romanticism.
   c. Delacroix, who broke classical conventions by using only blacks and whites in his paintings.
   d. Friedrich, whose "program" music played upon the listeners' emotions.
      ANSWER: b (p. 391)

48. The German Romantic painter of landscapes and nature was
a. Eugene Delacroix.
b. Johann Wolfgang von Goethe.
c. Casper David Friedrich.
d. Hector Berlioz.
ANSWER: c (pp. 390-391)

49. All of the following are major Romantic poets except
a. Hector Berlioz.
b. Percy Bysshe Shelley.
c. Lord Byron.
d. William Wordsworth.
ANSWER: a (p. 389)

50. By 1850, it was apparent that
a. liberalism had triumphed.
b. the days of conservatism and the old order were numbered.
c. nationalism had declined as a force for change.
d. socialism had no attraction for any segment of society.
ANSWER: b (p. 377)

RELEVANT WORLD-WIDE WEB SITES/RESOURCES

1. Documents of the Revolution of 1848 in France:
http://history.hanover.edu/texts/fr1848.htm
(Part of the Hanover College online History Project. Excellent collection of fine primary sources rarely included in standard textbooks or print readers.)

2. Encyclopedia of 1848 Revolutions:
http://cscwww.cats.ohiou.edu/~Chastain/index.html
(One of the best online encyclopedias with hundreds of relevant articles on revolutionary actors and actions before and after 1848 produced by the foremost scholars in the field.)

3. Pamphlets and Periodicals of the French Revolution of 1848:
http://humanities.uchicago.edu/ARTFL/projects/CRL/
(Great site with numerous online documents of the era.)

RELEVANT VIDEO RESOURCES

Civilisation, Public Media Video/BBC Television
(50 minutes each program). Program 11, "The Worship of Nature: Romantic Movements in Europe."

The Famous Composers Series, PBS Home Video, multiple programs (30 minutes each program). See the programs on Ludwig von Beethoven and Franz Schubert.

RELEVANT MUSICAL PERFORMANCES

Ludwig von Beethoven, Symphonies Nos. 5, 6, 7, and 9; Piano Sonatas (especially the sonatas entitled "Moonlight," "Appassionata," and "Waldstein;" or Piano Concerto No. 5, "The Emperor."

Hector Berlioz, Symphonie Fantastique or Harold in Italy: A Symphonic Poem.

Frederic Chopin, Nocturnes, Preludes, Etudes, or Waltzes for piano.

Felix Mendelssohn, A Midsummer Night's Dream; Violin Concerto in E Minor; Fingal's Cave Overture.

Franz Schubert, Piano Quintet in A Major "The Trout"; Piano Sonatas, (in C Minor, A Major, and B-flat Major, D. 958-960); or the song cycle "Winter Journey" (Die Winterreise).

SUGGESTED STUDENT ACTIVITIES

1. Have students do a close study of the work of the Congress of Vienna and the diplomatic maneuvering involved.

2. Students should pick out one of the early European socialists like Owen or Fourier and do a short biographical sketch. Does the term "utopian" rightfully apply to their subject?

3. Have students pick one of the later French revolutions and do a short essay. Why was their revolution not as successful as the French Revolution?

4. The Romantic period produced great artists and musicians. Have students do a short, oral report on one of these great people, pointing out their role in the overall Romantic movement.

CHAPTER 22
AN AGE OF NATIONALISM AND REALISM, 1850-1871

CHAPTER OUTLINE

I. The France of Napoleon III
- A. Louis Napoleon: Toward the Second Empire
- B. The Second Napoleonic Empire
- C. Foreign Policy: The Crimean War
  - 1. The Ottoman Empire
  - 2. The War

II. National Unification: Italy and Germany
- A. The Unification of Italy
- B. The Unification of Germany
  - 1. The Danish War (1864)
  - 2. The Austro-Prussian War (1866)
  - 3. The Franco-Prussian War (1870-1871)

III. Nation Building and Reform: The National State in the Mid-Century
- A. The Austrian Empire: Toward a Dual Monarchy
- B. Imperial Russia
- C. Great Britain: The Victorian Age
- D. The United States: Civil War and Reunion
- E. The Emergence of a Canadian Nation

IV. Industrialization and the Marxist Response
- A. Industrialization on the Continent
- B. Marx and Marxism

V. Science and Culture in an Age of Realism
- A. A New Age of Science
- B. Charles Darwin and the Theory of Organic Evolution
- C. A Revolution in Health Care
- D. Science and the Study of Society
- E. Realism in Literature and Art
  - 1. The Realistic Novel
  - 2. Realism in Art
- F. Music: The Twilight of Romanticism

VI. Conclusion

CHAPTER SUMMARY

Louis Napoleon was elected president of France's Second Republic in 1848, but when the National Assembly refused to sanction a second term, he led a coup d'etat against his own government, and, with the approval of the French voters, he became Emperor Napoleon III. Against the tide of laissez-faire liberalism, his regime took the economic lead, notably in the rebuilding of Paris. The decline of the Ottoman Empire sparked the Crimean War (1854-1856), the result of Britain and France's fear of Russian expansion. Russia was stalemated but it and Britain retreated from European affairs during the era of the unification of Germany and Italy.

Italian unification was headed by Count Camillo di Cavour (d.1861), prime minister of Piedmont-Sardinia. An alliance was made with France against Austria, and victories in 1859 enlarged Piedmont's territory. Giuseppe Garibaldi (d.1882) led an uprising against the Kingdom of the Two Sicilies, and in 1861 a kingdom of Italy under Piedmont's House of Savoy was realized except for Rome and Venetzia, which were taken over by 1870.

In 1862, Otto von Bismarck became Prussia's prime minister. A brilliant diplomat, in 1866 he maneuvered larger Austria into declaring war against Prussia. With its superior army, victorious Prussia united the northern states into the North German Confederation. In 1870, Bismarck edited an exchange between a French envoy and the Prussian king to make it appear that the king had insulted France. In the subsequent war, France was defeated, and the Second German Empire was the result. Under Bismarck, nationalism was allied with conservatism, whereas earlier in the century nationalism had been associated with liberalism.

Austria compromised with Hungarian nationalists, creating the dual monarchy of Austria-Hungary. Russia's defeat in the Crimean War led to reforms under Alexander II (r.1855-1881), including the freeing of millions of serfs. Conservatives feared the tsar went too far, but others wanted more reform, which led to the tsar's assassination in 1881. Britain escaped disruption because of economic growth and Parliament's willingness to make necessary reforms. The American Civil War (1861-1865) ended with the Union preserved and slavery abolished, and in 1867, Britain gave Canada dominion status, including the right to rule itself in domestic matters.

Karl Marx (d.1883), with Friedrich Engels (d.1895), published *The Communist Manifesto* in 1848, but initially it passed unnoticed. According the Marx, "the history of all hitherto existing society is the history of class struggles." In the modern world it was the middle-class, or the bourgeoisie, which controlled the means of production, but, Marx predicted, the proletariat would rise up, reorganize society on a socialist model, and create a classless society.

In science, the laws of thermodynamics, the germ theory of disease, electromagnetic induction, and chemistry's periodic law changed the world, as did Charles Darwin's *On the Origin of Species* (1859) with its theory of the struggle for existence, the survival of the fittest, and the emergence of new species. In health care, Louis Pasteur and others developed vaccines against specific diseases, the antiseptic principle reduced infections, and the discovery of chloroform lessened surgery's pain. Medical schools and medical associations were established, although initially closed to women. In the arts, it was the the age of realism, exemplified in the novels of Gustave Flaubert and the works of Charles Dickens. Gustave Courbet painted scenes of everyday life as exemplified in his *The Stonebreakers*..

LECTURE AND DISCUSSION TOPICS

1. Discuss the unification of Germany in the light of twentieth-century Germany history.

2. Compare and contrast Napoleon Bonaparte with Napoleon III, and France under its first emperor with France during the years of the Second Empire.

3. In a slide lecture, illustrate Napoleon III's modernization of Paris.

4. Compare and contrast the unification of Germany and the unification of Italy, noting both the differences and the similarities.

5. Explore the possible reasons why twentieth century fascism evolved from the two countries of Europe which only achieved nationhood in the nineteenth-century.

6. Discuss the causes and the issues involved in the Crimean War, and the war as a prelude to the twentieth-century.

7. Examine the possible explanations how the Austrian Empire managed to survive the nineteenth-century age of nationalism.

8. Analyze the nineteenth-century European state conflicts, geopolitics, and utilitarian conceptions of war.

9. Assess what was "Victorian" about Victorian Britain.

10. Discuss Karl Marx and Marxism and Charles Darwin and Darwinism as products of the nineteenth-century and as prophets of the twentieth-century.

11. Present a slide lecture in Realism in the arts.

MAP EXERCISES

1. The Unification of Italy. MAP 22.1. From the map, what challenges or difficulties did Piedmont face in eventually unifying Italy under its control? Was any other Italian state any better positioned to unify the peninsula? Why or why not? (page 396)

2. The Unification of Germany. MAP 22.2 How essential was Prussia and its territories to Bismarck's plan to unify the Germanies? Could he have succeeded if he came from another German state? Why or why not? What might be the different geographical, and thus political, relationships differ between northern and southern Germany? (page 400)

3. Europe in 1871. MAP 22.3. Did the unification of Germany make the Germanies more or less secure from their neighbors? Why or why not? Did their neighbors insecurities increase? If so, why? (page 401)

4. Ethnic Groups in the Dual Monarchy, 1867. MAP 22.4. In an age of nationalism, what was the likely future of the Austro-Hungarian Empire, and why? Why did Austria concede to Hungarian demands in 1867 but not to the other ethnic groups making up its empire? (page 402)

DISCUSSION QUESTIONS FOR THE PRIMARY SOURCES (BOXED DOCUMENTS)

1. "Bismarck `Goads' France into War": What did Bismarck do the Ems telegraph? What does this affair tell us about Bismarck's motives and his concept of politics? In your opinion, was the Ems dispatch really the final justification for the Franco-Prussian War? Why or why not? (page 399)

2. "Emancipation: Serfs and Slaves": Compare contrast the "emancipation proclamations" of Alexander II and President Lincoln. Were both equally effective? What are the differences between them? In which society, Imperial Russia or the United States, would the proclamations be easiest to implement, and why? (page 403)

3. "The Classless Society": What steps did Marx believe would lead to a classless society? Although

Marx criticized early socialists as utopian and considered his own socialism scientific, why does his own socialism appear equally utopian? What made Marx's ideas as expressed in this excerpt of *The Communist Manifesto* so appealing to so many in the nineteenth and twentieth centuries? (page 406)

4. "Realism: Charles Dickens and an Image of Hell on Earth": What image of Birmingham do you get from this selection of Dickens? Why is it so powerful? How does this excerpt reflect the traumas in western civilization brought about by the Industrial Revolution? What does it reveal about Dickens himself and the roles European writers took in the reform of nineteenth-century European society? (page 408)

STUDENT RESEARCH AND PROJECT TOPICS

1. Assess the accomplishments and failures of Louis Napoleon's regime in terms of the impact his policies had on France.

2. What was Napoleon III's most positive and most negative legacies to France's future, and why?

3. Evaluate the unification of Italy and Germany. How were the roles of Cavour and Bismarck in the unification of their countries similar? How were they different? What role did war and diplomacy play in the two unification movements?

4. Compare the aims and accomplishments of Bismarck and Cavour. Which statesman faced the greatest challenges and who was most successful? Be specific.

5. "Despite the defeat of the revolutions of 1848, the forces of liberalism and nationalism triumphed after 1850." Discuss to what extent is this true in the Austrian Empire, Russia, and Great Britain?

6. What reasons does the author give to convince the reader that continental industrialization came of age between 1850 and 1871? How did continental industrialization differ from England's?

7. What were the chief ideas of Marxism? Despite Marx's claim for its scientific basis and timelessness, why can Marxism be viewed primarily as a product of its age?

8. How did the expansion of scientific knowledge affect the Western world-view and the everyday lives of Europeans during the mid-nineteenth century? How does this expansion of scientific knowledge differ from that in the sixteenth and seventeenth centuries?

9. How did Realism differ from Romanticism? How did Realism reflect the economic and social realities of Europe during the middle decades of the nineteenth century?

10. In your opinion, what force or forces played the most important role in reviving the progress of European social and political reform in the later nineteenth century?

IDENTIFICATIONS

1. Napoleon III
2. Crimean War
3. Ottoman Empire
4. battle of Savastopol
5. Piedmont and the House of Savoy
6. Count Camillo di Cavour
7. Giuseppe Garibaldi and the Red Shirts
8. Count Otto von Bismarck
9. "iron and blood"
10. Austro-Prussian War
11. North German Confederation
12. Franco-Prussian War
13. battle of Sedan
14. Second German Empire
15. Dual Monarchy
16. *Ausgleich*
17. Alexander II and the serfs
18. *zemstvos*
19. Benjamin Disraeli and the Reform Bill of 1867
20. Lincoln's Emancipation Proclamation
21. Dominion of Canada
22. Karl Marx
23. *The Communist Manifesto*
24. bourgeoisie v. proletariat
25. First International
26. Louis Pasteur
27. Dmitri Mendeleyev
28. Michael Faraday
29. Charles Darwin
30. *On the Origin of Species*
31. "survival of the fit"
32. Realism
33. Gustave Flaubert's *Madame Bovary*
34. Charles Dickens
35. Gustave Courbet's *The Stonebreakers*

MULTIPLE CHOICE QUESTIONS

1. In establishing the Second Empire, Napoleon III
   a. received the overwhelming electoral support of the people.
   b. granted the National Assembly stronger legislative powers.
   c. rescinded universal male suffrage.
   d. cared little about public opinion.
      ANSWER: a (page 395)

2. Under the "liberal empire" of Napoleon III in the 1860's
   a. tariffs on foreign goods were raised.
   b. the legislature was permitted little say in affairs of state.
   c. trade unions and the right to strike were legalized.
   d. Jews were given complete freedom of worship.
      ANSWER: c (p. 396)

3. Among Napoleon III's great domestic projects was
   a. the building of the Eiffel Tower.
   b. the rededication of the Cathedral of Notre Dame.
   c. a reconstruction of Paris with broad boulevards, public squares, and municipal utilities.
   d. the damming of the Seine River for flood control.
      ANSWER: c (p. 396)

4. In economic matters, Napoleon III
   a. had a laissez-faire attitude.
   b. used government resources to stimulate the national economy and industrial growth.
   c. strove to diminish the power of great industrialists.
   d. worked diligently to establish monopolies for foreign firms possessing more business experience and capital than French firms.
      ANSWER: b (p. 396)

5. In the opinion of senior British politicians, the proclamation of a newly unified German state ruled by an emperor in 1871
   a. could only bode well for stable future European state relations.
   b. required immediate embargoes against all German manufactures.
   c. implied British renunciation of all existing treaties.
   d. entirely destroyed the previous European balance of power.
      ANSWER: d (p. 395)

6. The immediate origins of the Crimean War involved
   a. French expansionism in the Black Sea.
   b. Austrian expansionism in the Balkans.
   c. Russia's right to protect Christian shrines in Palestine.
   d. the Turks' assassination of a British diplomat.
      ANSWER: c (p. 396)

7. An overall result of the Crimean War was
   a. the reinforcement of the Concert of Europe until World War I.
   b. continued Russian expansionism in Europe for the next two decades.
   c. increased involvement for Great Britain in continental affairs.
   d. destruction of the Concert of Europe
      ANSWER: d (p. 396)

8. In seeking unification, many Italian nationalists in the 1850's looked for leadership from
   a. the Pope.
   b. the kingdom of Piedmont.
   c. the house of Habsburg.
   d. the kingdom of the Two Sicilies.
      ANSWER: b (p. 397)

9. The prime minister of Piedmont who organized the Italian unification movement was
   a. Giuseppe Mazzini.
   b. Giuseppe Garibaldi.
   c. Camillo di Cavour.
   d. Victor Emmanuel.
      ANSWER: c (p. 397)

10. The dominant foreign power in Italy prior to unification was
   a. France.
   b. Austria.
   c. Papal States.
   d. Savoy.
      ANSWER: b (p. 397)

11. Cavour's key strategy to free Italy from Austrian domination required the military and diplomatic support of
   a. England.
   b. Russia.
   c. France.
   d. Prussia.
      ANSWER: c (p. 397)

12. The leader of the Red Shirts who helped to unify Italy through his military command was
   a. Prince Napoleon.
   b. Giuseppe Garibaldi.
   c. Victor Emmanuel II.
   d. Camillo di Cavour.
      ANSWER: b (p. 397)

13. Giuseppe Garibaldi
   a. was an ally of Cavour in Italian unification from the beginning of that campaign.
   b. helped subdue the two Sicilies in the unification movement.
   c. put together a revolutionary army called the "Black Shirts."
   d. was a self-centered hindrance to the broader unification movement.
      ANSWER: b (p. 397)

14. The final act of Italian unification occurred in 1870 when
   a. Garibaldi's Red Shirts defeated the kingdom of the Two Sicilies.
   b. Savoy was defeated with the aid of Prussian troops.
   c. Rome became the capital city following the withdrawal of French troops.
   d. Piedmont took control of Lombardy as a result of French abandonment of Venice.
      ANSWER: c (p. 398)

15. Among the key motives prompting England and France to fight Russia in the Crimean War must be counted
   a. the French emperor's ambition to humble the tsar.
   b. Britain's great concern over disruption of the existing balance of power by a Russia victorious over the Turks.
   c. Prussian demands that the allies attack Russia at any cost.
   d. Russian efforts to promote revolution in western European nations.
      ANSWER: b (p. 396)

16. Otto von Bismarck, the Prussian-born leader of German unification,
   a. instituted the *Zollverein*, the German customs union that drove industrial development.
   b. followed a rigid plan for national unification at all costs.
   c. was a liberal from lower class origins who used politics to achieve his reform goals.
   d. practiced *Realpolitik* in conducting domestic and foreign policy.
      ANSWER: d (p. 398)

17. The emergence of a true parliamentary system in Prussia was blocked by
   a. the king's overwhelming executive power.
   b. the political divisions of the industrial middle class.
   c. opposition from the Catholic Church.
   d. a tradition of highly decentralized governmental authority in Germany.
      ANSWER: a (p. 398)

18. At the battle of Sadowa,
   a. Napoleon III was captured by the Prussians.
   b. the Russians were forced to retreat in the face of a British-French assault.
   c. Prussia defeated the Austrian army.
   d. Bismarck forced the surrender of Schleswig-Holstein.
      ANSWER: c (p. 398)

19. Otto von Bismarck
   a. as chancellor of Prussia instituted vital liberal land reforms.
   b. largely bypassed the Prussian parliament in pursuing his political goals of military modernization.
   c. was totally dependent on the Prussian military.
   d. was extremely unpopular among ordinary Germans.
      ANSWER: b (p. 398)

20. A result of Bismarck's Austro-Prussian War was
   a. the incorporation of Austria into the North German Confederation.
   b. a harsh treaty against Austria that reduced it to a second-rate power.
   c. the Prussian liberals' disgust over Bismarck's unscrupulous policies.
   d. the exclusion of Austria from the North German Confederation.
      ANSWER: d (p. 398)

21. As a statesman, Bismarck can best be appreciated as
   a. a determined nationalist who planned every move toward German unification.
   b. a conservative but a traitor to his aristocratic class.
   c. a consummate politician and opportunist capitalizing on unexpected events and manipulating affairs to his favor.
   d. a narrow-minded tyrant incapable of mastering the art of negotiation vital to modern European diplomacy.
      ANSWER: c (p. 398)

22. The immediate origins of the Franco-Prussian War concerned
   a. the control of the Spanish throne by a French prince.
   b. Bismarck's devious editing of a telegram from King William I.
   c. the French invasion of Alsace and Lorraine.
   d. Napoleon III's annexation of Schleswig and Holstein
      ANSWER: b (p. 399)

23. During the Franco-Prussian War
   a. Napoleon III successfully defended the French homeland.
   b. the French were decisively defeated at the Battle of Sedan.
   c. Bismarck allowed the Prussian army to fall into a chaotic condition.
   d. a military standoff resulted between the two great armies.
      ANSWER: b (p. 399)

24. As a consequence of her defeat in the Franco-Prussian War, France had to
   a. cede Normandy to Prussia.
   b. abandon Nice.
   c. give the eastern frontier provinces of Alsace and Lorraine to Prussia, a loss leaving the French set on revenge.
   d. try Napoleon III for war crimes before a Prussian tribunal.
      ANSWER: c (p. 399)

25. Prussian leadership of German unification meant that
   a. a new era of peaceful European interstate relations had begun.
   b. the triumph of authoritarian and dangerous militaristic values over liberal and constitutional values in the development of the new German state.
   c. Austrian bureaucrats would have new opportunities to shape the political culture of the new German Empire.
   d. true parliamentary democracy would triumph in the new German state.
      ANSWER: b (p. 400)

26. The Second German Empire was proclaimed at
   a. Berlin.
   b. Versailles.
   c. Vienna.
   d. Munich.
      ANSWER: b (p. 399)

27. The *Ausgleich* or Compromise of 1867

a. created a loose federation of ethnic states within the Austrian Empire.
b. freed the serfs and eliminated compulsory labor services with the Austrian Empire.
c. made Austria part of the North German Confederation.
d. created the dual monarchy of Austria-Hungary.
ANSWER: d (p. 401)

28. The creation of the dual monarchy of Austria-Hungary

a. allowed the Magyars and German-speaking Austrians to dominate the other ethnic minorities.
b. enabled Alexander von Bach to become an absolute ruler.
c. left Hungary an independent nation in domestic affairs.
d. overturned the *Ausgleich* (Compromise) of 1867.
ANSWER: a (p. 402)

29. The reforms of Tsar Alexander II centered around

a. government sponsorship of popular societies like the Bolsheviks.
b. improvements in the military.
c. the abolition of serfdom.
d. the formation of local, self-governing assemblies called "dumas."
ANSWER: c (p. 402)

30. The Russian *Zemstvos* were

a. radical, populist societies that supported all revolutionary causes.
b. local assemblies with regional self-governing powers.
c. agreements between peasants and landlords concerning work rules.
d. the emancipation proclamations that set groups of serfs free.
ANSWER: b (p. 403)

31. The British Conservative responsible for expanding the suffrage in the Reform Act of 1867 was

a. Henry John Temple.
b. Lord Palmerston.
c. William Gladstone.
d. Benjamin Disraeli.
ANSWER: d (p. 404)

32. Among the key political consequences of Disraeli's Reform Act of 1867 was

a. the outbreak of mass strikes by industrial workers in Britain.
b. a large increase in the number of voters.
c. the emergence of female suffrage movements in other European countries inspired by extension of the vote to British women.
d. the freeing of the last British serfs on northern landed estates.
ANSWER: b (p. 404)

33. The American Civil War of 1861-65

a. was ended by the Missouri Compromise.
b. was highly destructive due to the equal balance of forces between North and South.
c. led to the death of 600,000 soldiers.
d. did not completely eradicate slavery in all of the states due to local referendums on the question.
ANSWER: c (p. 404)

34. The issue which most threatened American unity in the mid-nineteenth century was

a. British tariffs.
b. serfdom.
c. slavery.
d. Manifest Destiny.

ANSWER: c (p. 404)

35. *The Communist Manifesto* of Marx and Engels

a. was a guidebook for the European workers in their revolutions of 1848.
b. viewed the bourgeoisie as leading the proletariat in the destruction of the aristocracy.
c. saw the successful realization of its ideas in the First International.
d. based all historical development on class struggle.

ANSWER: d (pp. 405-406)

36. Karl Marx stated that the final battle of history would be between

a. right and wrong.
b. Christianity and Islam.
c. the bourgeoisie and the proletariat.
d. industry and agriculture.

ANSWER: a (pp. 405-406)

37. According to Karl Marx, the final product of the struggle between bourgeoisie and proletariat would be

a. a classless society.
b. the dictatorship of the proletariat.
c. all political power transferred to the proletariat.
d. a utopian society.

ANSWER: a (p. 406)

38. The First International

a. failed due to Marx's preoccupation with *Das Kapital.*
b. became the largest working-class organization in Europe in the nineteenth century.
c. was rejected by Marx as a "bourgeois-dominated institution."
d. served as a type of umbrella organization for all European labor interests.

ANSWER: d (p. 406)

39. The theoretical discoveries in science in the nineteenth century led to all of the following except

a. a renewal of spiritual belief.
b. a belief in material reality as the only reality.
c. great advances in mathematics and thermodynamics.
d. technological improvements that affected all Europeans.

ANSWER: a (p. 407)

40. Which of the following statements best applies to Charles Darwin and his evolutionary theory?
   a. His ideas were readily accepted by religious extremists and cultural conservatives.
   b. His works were truly revolutionary in that they were the first to propose a theory of evolution.
   c. His theory emphasized the idea of the "survival of the fit" in which advantageous natural variants and environmental adaptations in organisms determine their survival.
   d. His *On the Origin of Species* described man's evolution from animal origins through natural selection.
   ANSWER: c (pp. 407-408)

41. Charles Darwin's *The Descent of Man*
   a. is filled with expressions of doubt and hesitancy over the new evolutionary theory.
   b. expressed the first theory of genetic mutations.
   c. argued for the animal origins of human beings and emphasized their survival through myriad adaptations to their environment over time.
   d. placed humans in the center of a rational universe.
   ANSWER: c (p. 408)

42. Louis Pasteur
   a. classified the material elements on the basis of their atomic weights.
   b. postulated the germ theory of disease.
   c. discovered the phenomenon of electromagnetic induction.
   d. wrote *The Descent of Man.*
   ANSWER: b (p. 407)

43. The discoverer of the primitive generator that laid the groundwork for the use of electricity was
   a. Joseph Lister.
   b. Samuel Morse.
   c. Michael Faraday.
   d. Dmitri Mendeleyev.
   ANSWER: c (p. 407)

44. Which popular author, even though he realistically portrayed the social and psychological milieu of his time, still included an element of Romanticism in his novels, was
   a. Charles Dickens.
   b. Gustave Flaubert.
   c. Edgar Allan Poe.
   d. William Thackeray.
   ANSWER: a (p. 408)

45. The dominant literary and artistic movement in the 1850's and 1860's was
   a. Romanticism.
   b. Realism.
   c. Positivism.
   d. Modernism.
   ANSWER: b (p. 409)

46. The leading realistic novelist of the nineteenth century was
a. Edgar Allan Poe.
b. Gustave Flaubert.
c. Jane Austin.
d. Gustave Courbet.
ANSWER: b (p. 409)

47. In addition to examining everyday life, the literary realists of the mid-nineteenth century were also interested in
a. completely avoiding romantic imagery, as shown in the works of Charles Dickens.
b. employing emotional and poetic language to cause social reform.
c. using careful observation and accurate description.
d. showing the positive values of middle-class life.
ANSWER: c (p. 409)

48. Realist art in the mid-nineteenth-century
a. was praised by critics for showing the beauty of ordinary people.
b. was best characterized by the urban scenes of Jean-François Millet.
c. still contained an element of romantic sentimentality, best shown in Gustave Courbet's paintings.
d. was particularly interested in the natural environment and in showing scenes from everyday life.
ANSWER: d (p. 409)

49. "Nature red in tooth and claw" is associated with
a. Gustave Flaubert.
b. Karl Marx.
c. Charles Darwin.
d. Friedrich Engels.
ANSWER: c (p. 409)

50. The most famous artist of the Realist school was
a. Wagner.
b. Courbet.
c. Liszt.
d. Flaubert.
ANSWER: b (p. 409)

RELEVANT WORLD-WIDE WEB SITES/RESOURCES

1. Nationalism in Historical and Global Context:
http://kennedy.soc.surrey.ac.uk/socresonline/2/1/natlinks.html
(A remarkable site with source texts, media articles, journal pieces, and multiple links to other sites related to European and global nationalisms in historical context.)

2. The Victoria and Albert Museum:
http://www.vam.ac.uk/
The venerable "Vic" online with news and virtual tours of the collection. Best subsection here is "Object in Focus," a regularly updated analysis of some evocative piece from the museum's peerless collections in English material culture and decorative arts. Excellent site for analysis of the effects of social and political change on contemporaneous English patterns of consumption, interior decoration, and adornment.)

3. The Victorian Web (at Brown University):
http://www.stg.brown.edu/projects/hypertext/landow/victorian/victov.html
(A superb site with information on literature, visual arts, science, technology, gender issues, and politics of the era. Fine links to other relevant sites and detailed time lines here listing notable accomplishments of Victorian culture.)

RELEVANT VIDEO RESOURCES

The Europeans: The Nationalists, Films for the Humanities and Sciences, (60 minutes).
(Available through Wadsworth Publishing.)

SUGGESTED STUDENT ACTIVITIES

1. Have students do a comparative study of Cavour and Bismark–their personalities and the methods by which they unified their countries.

2. Numerous books and web sites discuss Queen Victoria and the Victorian era. Encourage students to use these sources in reporting on a major aspect of English urban society and culture of the period.

3. Have students do a paper on the ideas of Karl Marx and the degree to which key elements of his thought have either failed to or continued to influence current political systems.

4. Have students do a comparative study of realism and romanticism in art, music, and literature.

CHAPTER 23
MASS SOCIETY IN AN "AGE OF PROGRESS," 1871-1894

CHAPTER OUTLINE

- I. The Growth of Industrial Prosperity
    - A. New Products
    - B. New Markets
    - C. New Patterns in an Industrial Economy
        - 1. German Industrial Leadership
        - 2. European Economic Zones
        - 3. A World Economy
    - D. Women and Work: New Job Opportunities
        - 1. White-Collar Jobs
        - 2. Prostitution and Lower-Class Women
    - E. Organizing the Working Classes
        - 1. Socialist Parties
        - 2. Revision and Nationalism
        - 3. The Role of Trade Unions
        - 4. The Anarchist Alternative
- II. The Emergence of Mass Society
    - A. Population Growth
    - B. Transformation of the Urban Environment
        - 1. Improving Living Conditions
        - 2. Housing Needs
        - 3. Redesigning the Cities
    - C. The Social Structure of Mass Society
        - 1. The Elite
        - 2. The Middle Classes
        - 3. The Lower Classes
    - D. The "Woman Question": The Role of Women
        - 1. The Middle-Class Family
        - 2. The Working-Class Family
    - E. Education and Leisure in an Age of Mass Society
        - 1. Mass Leisure
- III. The National State
    - A. Western Europe: The Growth of Political Democracy
        - 1. Reform in Britain
        - 2. The Third Republic in France
        - 3. Spain and Italy
    - B. Central and Eastern Europe: Persistence of the Old Order
        - 1. Germany
        - 2. Austria-Hungary
        - 3. Russia
- IV. Conclusion

CHAPTER SUMMARY

A Second Industrial Revolution occurred in the latter nineteenth century, a revolution of steel, chemicals, electricity, and the internal combustion engine. Higher wages fueled internal markets. Tariffs replaced free trade and cartels monopolized production. Germany became the industrial leader as Britain was overly cautious in adopting new technologies. Europe was divided into a industrialized north and a poorer south and east, and, world-wide, European manufactured goods and investment capital was exported abroad in exchange for raw materials.

The status of women improved somewhat in service and white-color jobs as typists and clerks. Prostitution remained an avenue for survival for many women. Working-class political parties, such as Germany's Social Democratic Party, were established. The Second International, 1889, hoped to coordinate Marxist socialist parties, but unity floundered on the shoals of nationalism as well as disagreements between the advocates of the revolutionary class struggle and those who envisioned socialism being achieved democratically. Trade unions were most successful in Britain. The anarchist movement was another response to industrial capitalism.

Europe's population reached to 460 million by 1910. Many migrated from the poorer east and south to industrialized northern Europe and abroad, often for economic reasons, but also to escape ethnic and religious persecution. In the industrial north, urban populations constituted up to 80 percent of the total. Urban conditions improved because of building codes and better housing, cleaner water, and new sewage systems. Governments often took the lead in contrast to earlier laissez-faire, but wealthy reformer-philanthropists also established model houses and new garden towns. Old city walls were torn down and workers commuted by trains and streetcars to the new suburbs. In redesigned cities, such as Paris and Vienna, parks and wide roads were built.

The standard of living generally improved. The elite were 5 percent of the population but controlled 30-40 percent of the wealth, as old landed wealth merged with the new industrial wealth. The middle classes, with their values of hard work and propriety, encompassed the upper middle class professionals down to the lower middle class white-collar clerks and bank tellers. Family togetherness was the aim, with a new focus upon the child. The lower classes made up 80 percent of the population, but with rising wages many workers adopted middle class values. Industrialism re-enforced traditional female inferiorly: women stayed at home while men went out to work. The birthrate dropped as families limited the number of children.

Because of expanding voting rights and the need to have an electorate educated in national values, most states assumed responsibility for mass compulsory education up to the age of twelve. Literacy rates reached almost 100 percent in northern Europe, leading to a demand for mass newspapers, filled with sports and sensationalism. New leisure hours, including the weekend, led to new mass entertainment; the music hall and dance halls were popular, as was organized tourism for the middle classes.

By the end of the century most British males had the vote. In France, the Third Republic was established in spite of opposition from monarchists, army officers, and the Catholic clergy. Italy was troubled by regional differences, political corruption, and ever-changing governments. The traditional order lasted longer in central and eastern Europe. In Germany, where the popularly elected Reichstag lacked power, Bismarck implemented social welfare programs to seduce the workers away from socialism. After the assassination of Russia's Alexander II, the reactionary Alexander III (r.1881-189) and Nicholas II (r.1894-1917) opposed all reforms.

LECTURE AND DISCUSSION TOPICS

1. Discuss the impact of the Second Industrial Revolution upon the transformation of Europe in the latter half of the nineteenth-century.

2. Explore the role of women in urban society in the late nineteenth-century.

3. Compare and contrast the middle classes and the working classes in nineteenth-century European society.

4. Examine the role of mass politics in the age of mass society.

5. Discuss the "women's question" and the new (and old) role of women in the second half of the nineteenth-century.

6. Compare and contrast late nineteenth-century "mass society" with earlier "societies" in the West before industrialization and urbanization.

7. Explore the evolving and changing concept of "leisure" in the mass society of the late nineteenth-century.

8. Assess the relationship between the emergence of mass society and the increasing democratization of Western society.

9. Using urbanization and the mass society as organizing concepts, discuss the differences between western Europe and central and eastern Europe by the end of the nineteenth-century.

10. Compare and contrast several of the socialist (Marxist and non-Marxist) movements of the nineteenth-century.

MAP EXERCISES

1. The Industrial Regions of Europe at the End of the Nineteenth Century. MAP 23.1. Which parts of Europe were the most industrially developed by 1900 and what areas were the least developed industrially. How do you account for the differences? Are the causes political, cultural, social, resource availability, or others? (page 416)

2. Population Growth in Europe, 1820-1900. MAP 23.2. Compare the two maps, one representing the year 1820 and the other the year 1900. Which regions experienced the greatest population growth? What are the factors which might explain the growth differences between areas? (page 421)

DISCUSSION QUESTIONS FOR THE PRIMARY SOURCES (BOXED DOCUMENTS)

1. "The Department Store and the Beginnings of Mass Consumerism": What does this document tell us about the growth of a new mass consumerism? Who were these new consumers and how had their habits of buying and selling changed over time? What were the broader socioeconomic repercussions of nineteenth-century changes in the sites and scale of European retail trade? Does the excerpt seem "modern"? Why and or why not? (page 415)

2. "The Housing Venture of Octavia Hill": Discuss the housing venture of Octavia Hill. What did she hope to achieve? Was she successful? What does this document tell you about the new ambitions and civic responsibilities of private philanthropists in modern European urban society? (page 420)

3. "Advice to Women: Be Dependent": According to Elizabeth Sanford, what is the proper role of women? What forces in late nineteenth-century European society do you believe merged to shape Sanford's understanding of "proper" gender roles? Among women only, do you believe that most would have agreed with Sanford? Why and/or why not? Which women might have disagreed with her position? (page 423)

4. "A Leader of the Paris Commune": What does this excerpt from the memoirs of the Parisian radical feminist Louise Michel tell you about new opportunities for political engagement available to female and male residents of great European nineteenth-century capital cities during the latter half of the nineteenth century? (page 427)

STUDENT RESEARCH AND PROJECT TOPICS

1. Explain what is meant by the "Second Industrial Revolution" and how it differed from the first revolution in industry. Discuss its impact on European society.

2. What do we mean by the phrase "mass society" and how was the growth of this mass society related to changes in the urban environment?

3. To what extent did the emergence and development of socialist parties and trade unions meet the needs of the working classes between 1871 and the end of the century?

4. Discuss the structure of European society between 1870 and 1894. Why do historians focus so much attention on the middle class during this period?

5. What was the position of women during the second half of the nineteenth century? Had women's positions and opportunities for self-expression changed any since the previous century? How?

6. Compare and contrast middle-class and working-class families. How do you explain the similarities and the differences?

7. How were the promises and problems of the new mass society reflected in education and leisure?

8. Between 1871 and 1894, two major domestic political issues involved the achievement of liberal practices and the growth of political democracy. To what extent were these realized in Great Britain, France, Spain, and Italy?

9. Was nineteenth century liberalism a hindrance or a help to the development of political democracy in western civilization? Be specific.

10. How and why did the old order continue to persist in central and eastern Europe?

IDENTIFICATIONS

1. the "weekend"
2. Coney Island and Blackpool
3. "day-trippers"
4. Thomas Edison and Joseph Swan
5. Graham Bell
6. Guglielmo Marconi
7. internal combustion engine
8. Henry Ford
9. the Wright brothers
10. cartels
11. the assembly line
12. Second Industrial Revolution
13. sweatshops
14. white-collar jobs
15. Wilhelm Liebknect and August Bebel
16. Germany's Social Democratic Party
17. May Day
18. Marxist "revisionism"
19. Eduard Bernstein
20. Britain's Public Health Act of 1875
21. V.A. Huber and Octavia Hill
22. domestic servants
23. Lord Tennyson's *The Princess*
24. "family planning"
25. amusement parks and dance halls
26. Thomas Cook
27. English Football Association
28. Britain's Reform Act of 1884
29. France's Third Republic
30. the Commune
31. Italy and Ethiopia
32. the Reichstadt
33. *Kulturkampf*
34. Bismarck's welfare legislation
35. Nicholas II and "the principle of autocracy"

MULTIPLE CHOICE QUESTIONS

1. In late nineteenth-century Europe, human progress was increasingly identified with
   a. war.
   b. economic inequality.
   c. material progress or greater consumption of material goods.
   d. sport.
      ANSWER: c (page 412)

2. By 1871, the focus of Europeans' lives had become
   a. their weekends.
   b. their schools.
   c. their favorite sports teams.
   d. the national state.
      ANSWER: d (p. 413)

3. The "Second Industrial Revolution" saw the advent of what new product?
   a. textiles
   b. steel
   c. coal
   d. railroads
      ANSWER: b (p. 413)

4. What type of new energy source powered the second industrial revolution?
   a. coal
   b. hydro-electric
   c. natural gas
   d. electricity
      ANSWER: d (p. 413)

5. Between 1860 and 1913, European steel production went from
   a. 5000 tons to 1 million tons.
   b. 35,000 tons to 2 million tons.
   c. 50,000 tons to 15 million tons.
   d. 125,000 tons to 32 million tons.
      ANSWER: d (p. 413)

6. Air transportation began with the
   a. Hamburg-Amerika Airships in 1897.
   b. Zeppelin in 1900.
   c. the Wright Brothers in 1903.
   d. Ford Trimotor in 1911.
      ANSWER: b (p. 413)

7. The development of markets after 1870 was best characterized by
   a. decreased competition through free trade agreements.
   b. the dismantling of the cartels that hindered free trade.
   c. urban consumers in Europe who desired a growing number of consumer products.
   d. an abandonment of overseas markets, especially by Britain, due to their small profit potential.
      ANSWER: c (p. 414)

8. Germany began to replace Britain as Europe's industrial leader by the early twentieth century largely due to
   a. Britain's careless and radical changes made to its industries.
   b. Germany's cautious approach and doctrine of "sticking to what works" in industry.
   c. Britain's reliance on cartels to invest large sums of money in new industries.
   d. Germany's development of new areas of manufacturing including chemicals and heavy electric machinery.
      ANSWER: d (p. 415)

9. By 1900, which of the following nations was <u>not</u> advanced industrially
   a. Britain.
   b. Germany.
   c. France.
   d. Spain.
      ANSWER: d (p. 415)

10. In late nineteenth-century Europe, increased competition for foreign markets and the growing importance of domestic demand for economic development led to
   a. the elimination of trade restrictions like tariffs.
   b. a strong reaction against free trade and imposition of steep protective tariffs by most nations.
   c. greater economic instability and a sequence of ever deeper economic depressions.
   d. closer economic cooperation among the great powers.
      ANSWER: b (p. 414)

11. One of the chief results of the Second Industrial Revolution concerning agriculture was
   a. a drop in agricultural prices.
   b. the shift from a three-field to a two-field crop rotation system due to better chemical fertilizers.
   c. the emergence of a new class of agricultural production leaders called <u>coloni</u>.
   d. a sharp increase in agricultural prices.
      ANSWER: a (p. 415)

12. Employment opportunities for women during the Second Industrial Revolution
   a. changed in quality and quantity with the expansion of the service sector.
   b. declined dramatically as prostitution became illegal.
   c. increased greatly with working-class men pushing their wives to work outside the home.
   d. declined when piece-work was abandoned as inefficient and "sweatshops" were outlawed.
      ANSWER: a (p. 417)

13. When not able to find work in the factories, many lower class European women
   a. became housewives.
   b. turned to prostitution.
   c. joined socialist movements.
   d. took jobs as clerks, shop assistants, and nurses.
      ANSWER: d (p. 417)

14. The consumer-driven department store was pioneered in
   a. London.
   b. Paris.
   c. New York City.
   d. Berlin.
      ANSWER: b (p. 415)

15. In 1900, the "backward and little industrialized" parts of Europe included
   a. Russia.
   b. Germany.
   c. France.
   d. Belgium.
      ANSWER: a (p. 415)

16. An issue that brought socialists together in the nineteenth century was
   a. nationalism.
   b. revisionism.
   c. the need for military action.
   d. improvement of working and living conditions for most workers.
      ANSWER: d (p. 417)

17. The Marxist revisionist Eduard Bernstein stressed the need for
   a. violent overthrow of capitalist governments.
   b. the extermination of all individualists.
   c. working through democratic politics to create socialism.
   d. totally disregarding *The Communist Manifesto*.
      ANSWER: c (p. 418)

18. The trade union movement prior to World War I
   a. was strongest in France after the dissolution of the Second International in 1890.
   b. occurred despite trade unions being banned by most state governments.
   c. varied from state to state, but was generally allied with socialist parties.
   d. was primarily for unskilled laborers, especially the New Model unions.
      ANSWER: c (p. 417)

19. Trade unions in the nineteenth century were shaped by all of the following <u>except</u>
   a. fusions of nationalism and socialism.
   b. the liberalism of Russian rulers.
   c. the rise of the labor movement in Britain.
   d. the development of evolutionary socialism.
      ANSWER: b (p. 418)

20. Who said that "Working men have no country"?
   a. Wilhelm Liebknecht and August Bebel.
   b. Karl Marx and Friedrich Engels.
   c. Eduard Bernstein.
   d. Benjamin Disraeli and William Gladstone.
      ANSWER: b (p. 417)

21. Some of the most powerful of the nineteenth-century labor unions were to be found in
   a. England.
   b. Germany.
   c. France.
   d. Italy.
      ANSWER: b (p. 417)

22. During the Second German Empire, the German parliament was the
   a. Landstag.
   b. Diet.
   c. Reichstag.
   d. Cortes.
      ANSWER: c (p. 417)

23. Between 1850 and 1910, European population
   a. increased by 190 million to 460 million.
   b. actually decreased slightly.
   c. increased from 45 to 60 million.
   d. stagnated, causing severe problems for the development of leisure industries.
      ANSWER: a (p. 418)

24. The chief cause of rising European populations between 1850 and 1880 was
   a. a rising birthrate.
   b. a declining mortality rate.
   c. better childhood immunization programs.
   d. better human diet in a consumer economy.
      ANSWER: b (p. 418)

25. The driving force behind immigration to the cities was
   a. job opportunities.
   b. a desire for culture.
   c. curiosity.
   d. masochism.
      ANSWER: a (p. 419)

26. Reforms in urban living included all of the following <u>except</u>
   a. the development of pure water and sewerage systems.
   b. model homes built for the poor by wealthy philanthropists.
   c. the demolition of old, unneeded defensive walls, replaced by wide avenues.
   d. a concerted effort to clean up all polluted rivers and lakes.
      ANSWER: d (pp. 419-420)

27. Octavia Hill's housing venture was designed to
   a. give the poor an environment they could use to improve themselves.
   b. give the poor charity since they could never help themselves.
   c. let the wealthy know what it was like to be poor.
   d. break down class barriers in London.
      ANSWER: a (p. 420)

28. The middle classes of nineteenth-century Europe
   a. were composed mostly of shopkeepers and manufacturers who barely lived above the poverty line.
   b. offered little opportunity for women in improving their lot.
   c. were very concerned with propriety and shared values of hard work and Christian morality.
   d. viewed progress with distrust as they did not wish to lose their economic gains.
   ANSWER: c (p. 422)

29. The largest segment of European society in the nineteenth century was composed of
   a. skilled artisans such as winemakers and cabinet makers.
   b. peasant landholders, unskilled day laborers, and domestic servants who worked for very low wages.
   c. semi-skilled laborers such as carpenters and bricklayers.
   d. urban workers in eastern Europe and peasants in western Europe.
   ANSWER: b (p. 422)

30. For Elizabeth Poole Sanford, women should
   a. avoid being self-sufficient.
   b. strive to become equal to men.
   c. accept their roles at home until a new government was elected.
   d. make it known to their husbands that they were dissatisfied.
   ANSWER: a (p. 423)

31. European middle-class families during the late nineteenth century
   a. were more concerned with displaying the work ethic than in displaying wealth and following proper decorum.
   b. stressed functional knowledge for their children to prepare them for their future roles.
   c. prided themselves on doing the housework and cooking for their families.
   d. increasingly became less cohesive as togetherness was no longer an important value.
   ANSWER: b (p. 424)

32. The domestic ideal of the nineteenth-century middle-class family was
   a. everyone working outside the home for the common good.
   b. togetherness with leisure time being very important.
   c. an almost military environment with the husband as commander.
   d. for girls and boys to grow up to be merchants and bankers.
   ANSWER: b (pp. 424, 426)

33. Changes in the standard of living from 1890 to 1914 in Europe affected the working-classes
   a. as more children were produced, which provided more family income.
   b. negligibly, since most families could not afford consumer goods beyond necessities.
   c. due to the severe reduction in real wages.
   d. by allowing working-class parents to devote more attention to their children.
   ANSWER: d (p. 424)

34. Daughters in European working-class families
   a. were fully expected to work until marriage.
   b. by long custom, were kept at home until of age to marry.
   c. were barred from working by state law in many countries.
   d. had traditionally never shown an interest in working either before or after marriage.
   ANSWER: a (p. 424)

35. By 1900, most European educational systems

a. were free and compulsory at least at the primary level.

b. were expensive to operate, and charged high tuition.

c. were backward and lacked good teachers.

d. still taught a "medieval" variety of subjects.

ANSWER: a (p. 424)

36. Although several motives drove European states to develop systems of mass public education for their citizens, the chief reason for which they did this was

a. economic, to produce a more educated workforce.

b. military, to produce better trained army conscripts capable using modern weapons.

c. political, to produce more informed voters in expanding electorates and to heighten patriotism producing more integrated nations.

d. religious, so as to teach the poor obedience to authority.

ANSWER: c (p. 425)

37. In regard to mass leisure and entertainment in the nineteenth century

a. amusement parks and dance halls became very popular.

b. cockfights and bull baitings remained very popular.

c. the working classes of Europe still liked baseball.

d. gambling and dicing were still popular among the rich and poor alike.

ANSWER: a (p. 426)

38. The "father" of tourism in England was

a. David Lloyd-George.

b. Thomas Cook.

c. John Boothe.

d. Frederick Cartwright.

ANSWER: b (p. 426)

39. Which of the following was a major development in British politics before 1914?

a. the continual growth of political democracy

b. the peaceful and successful settlement of the "Irish question"

c. the transformation of the Fabians into the Conservatives

d. the reduction of the House of Commons' power

ANSWER: a (p. 426)

40. Which of the following national groups had realized nationhood by 1871?

a. Irish

b. Slovenes.

c. Czechs

d. Germans

ANSWER: d (p. 428)

41. In 1911, the British Parliament passed legislation
   a. paying salaries to members of the House of Commons thus opening Parliament to those other than the wealthy.
   b. granting Home Rule to Ireland.
   c. increasing the size of the British navy by construction of "Dreadnought" battleships.
   d. split the Liberal party in Parliament and diminished the national importance of British political parties.
   ANSWER: a (p. 426)

42. The English Reform Bill of 1884
   a. enfranchised women.
   b. gave English agricultural workers the right to vote.
   c. did not dramatically increase the size of the electorate.
   d. increased the total number of members in the House of Commons.
   ANSWER: b (p. 426)

43. Louis Napoleon's Second Empire was brought to an end by
   a. France's defeat in the Franco-Prussian War.
   b. the emperor's financial policies.
   c. his choice of poor administrators.
   d. his defeat by the Austrians.
   ANSWER: a (p. 426)

44. Splits between the French working and middle class
   a. were largely solved by the liberal reforms of the Third Republic.
   b. enabled the Third Republic to elect a new monarch in 1875.
   c. led to a strong parliamentary system of government.
   d. were further widened by the brutal suppression of the Paris Commune in 1871.
   ANSWER: d (pp. 426-427)

45. All of the following are correct about France's Third Republic <u>except</u>
   a. it lasted for sixty-five years.
   b. it was thought to be only a stopgap and temporary solution.
   c. it soon gave way to a restored monarchy under the Bourbon dynasty.
   d. the Chamber of Deputies achieved a position of supremacy.
   ANSWER: c (p. 427)

46. Which of the following statements best applies to Italy in the late nineteenth century?
   a. Italy had achieved the status of a great power.
   b. Italy's unification was vigorously supported by the pope.
   c. Italy acquired a large empire in Africa.
   d. Italy remained a second-rate European power, less transformed by the economic and cultural innovations of the age.
   ANSWER: d (pp.427-428)

47. In 1867 Austria-Hungary was theoretically a constitutional government; in reality it was a/an
   a. autocracy.
   b. democracy.
   c. government similar to Great Britain.
   d. very corrupt and inefficient.
   ANSWER: a (p. 429)

48. Under the chancellorship of Bismarck, Germany

a. realized the growth of a real democracy through universal male suffrage.
b. passed social welfare legislation to woo workers away from the Social Democrats.
c. engaged in the *Kulturkampf* or crusade to make Catholicism Germany's national religion.
d. maintained a military second only to that of France on the Continent.

ANSWER: b (p. 428)

49. Which statement best applies to the Germany under chancellor Otto von Bismarck?

a. Prussia lost much of its influence on state politics.
b. Coalitions were used by Bismarck to get what he wanted and then he dropped them.
c. Socialism was almost completely stamped out by the Prussian army.
d. Almost all regional differences disappeared under the charismatic leadership of Bismarck.

ANSWER: b (p. 428)

50. Which of the following statements best applies to the Dual Monarchy of Austria-Hungary before World War I?

a. Both Austria and Hungary had working parliamentary systems.
b. The Magyars dominated politics in Austria under Emperor William II.
c. The nationality problem remained unresolved and led to strong German as well as other nationalist movements.
d. Prime minister Count Edward von Taafe was ousted in 1893 by the Slavic minorities for his failure to make concessions to them.

ANSWER: c (p. 429)

RELEVANT WORLD-WIDE WEB SITES/RESOURCES

1. Spanish Museum of Decorative Art:
http://www.mus-kim.dk/kim.htm
(An excellent museum site especially rich in online objects of decorative art and interior design analyzed in the context of socioeconomic history before and after 1900. Highly recommended.)

2. Internet Modern History Sourcebook
http://www.fordham.edu/halsall//mod/modsbook.html
(See in particular the subsection here on "The Long Nineteenth Century." Excellent online selection of relevant documents.)

RELEVANT VIDEO RESOURCES

Industry and Empire 1870-1914, Landmark Films (60 minutes). (Available through Wadsworth Publishing.)

The Aristocracy, PBS Home Video, 4 programs on 4 cassettes (55 minutes each program). (Series offers comprehensive view of the British nobility and gentry from 1875 to 1997, focusing on the declining fortunes and political influence of this elite under the effects of socioeconomic and socio-political change brought about by industrialization and the rise of mass society.)

SUGGESTED STUDENT ACTIVITIES

1. Have students do a comparison and contrast paper on socialism and communism.

2. Have students choose a large European city of the nineteenth century, prepare a graph of the city's population growth over the course of the century, and then write an essay on the socio-cultural and socio-political changes that occurred in this city related to population shifts.

3. Have students do some research on the early socialist movements, the different leaders and ideas that started those movements.

CHAPTER 24
AN AGE OF MODERNITY, ANXIETY, AND IMPERIALISM, 1894-1914

CHAPTER OUTLINE

I. Toward the Modern Consciousness: Intellectual and Cultural Developments
  - A. Developments in the Sciences: The Emergence of a New Physics
  - B. Toward a New Understanding of the Irrational
  - C. Sigmund Freud and Psychoanalysis
  - D. The Impact of Darwin: Social Darwinism and Racism
  - E. The Attack on Christianity and the Response of the Churches
  - F. The Culture of Modernity
    - 1. Naturalism and Symbolism in Literature
    - 2. Modernism in the Arts
    - 3. Modernism in Music

II. Politics: New Directions and New Uncertainties
  - A. The Movement for Women's Rights
    - 1. The New Woman
  - B. Jews within the European Nation-State
  - C. The Transformation of Liberalism: Great Britain and Italy
  - D. Growing Tensions in Germany
  - E. Industrialization and Revolution in Imperial Russia
    - 1. The Revolution of 1905
  - F. The Rise of the United States
  - G. The Growth of Canada

III. The New Imperialism
  - A. Causes of the New Imperialism
  - B. The Creation of Empires
    - 1. The Scramble for Africa
    - 2. Asia in an Age of Imperialism
  - C. Responses to Imperialism
    - 1. Africa
    - 2. China
    - 3. Japan
    - 4. India

IV. International Rivalry and the Coming of War
  - A. The Bismarckian System
    - 1. The Balkans: Decline of Ottoman Power
    - 2. New Alliances
  - B. New Directions and New Crises
    - 1. Crises in the Balkans,1908-1913

V. Conclusion

CHAPTER SUMMARY

By the end of the nineteenth century, faith in reason, progress, and science was being subverted by a new modernity about the physical universe, the human mind, and in the arts. The anxieties about old certainties were seemingly confirmed by the Great War, which began in 1914.

The Newtonian mechanistic universe was challenged by the discovery of radiation and the randomness of subatomic particles. Max Planck said that energy is radiated in packets, or quanta. Albert Einstein claimed that time and space were relative to the observer, and that matter was a form of energy (E = mc2.). Friedrich Nietzsche lauded the instinctive irrational and blamed Christianity for its "slave morality"; Supermen would transcend mass democracy and equality. Sigmund Freud argued that human behavior was governed by the unconscious, that childhood memories were repressed, and that the mind was a battleground between the pleasure-seeking id, the reason of the ego, and the conscience of the superego.

Social Darwinists, arguing that society was also a survival of the fittest, justified laissez-faire government, but it was also used by nationalists and racists as a justification for war and inequality as did the German general, Friedrich von Bernhardi, and Houston Stewart Chamberlain, in his *The Foundations of the Nineteenth Century*.

In literature, Naturalism exhibited a mechanistic attitude toward human freedom, exemplified in the novels of Emile Zola. Symbolists denied objective reality; it was only symbols in the mind of the poet, as in the poem of William Butler Yeats and Rainer Maria Rilke. Art Impressionism stressed the changing effects of light in the paintings of Camille Pissarro and Berthe Morisot. In Post-impressionism, Vincent van Gogh emphasized light but also structure in portraying subjective reality (photography mirrored objective reality). Pablo Picasso's Cubism reconstructed subjects according to geometric forms and Vasily Kandinsky's Abstract Expressionism abandoned representational images. In music, the rhythms and dissonances of Igor Stravinsky's *The Rite of Spring* caused a riot at its Paris debut.

Many women demanded equal rights, including political equality; British suffragettes broke windows and went on hunger strikes to gain attention. Anti-Semitism revived in the pseudo-scientific racism of the late century, and there were anti-Semitic political parties in Germany and Austria. In Russia, pogroms led many Jews to emigrate. Theodor Herzl claimed that Jews should have their own state in Palestine. British Liberals enacted social welfare legislation. Germany's Social Democratic Party was opposed by the emperor and right-wing parties. In Russia, socialists turned to revolution; after the 1905 Revolution, Nicholas II accepted a weak Duma. By 1900, the United States was the world's leading industrial nation.

National rivalry, Social Darwinism, religious and humanitarian concerns, and economic demands of raw materials and overseas markets contributed to the New Imperialism. By 1914, Africa had been colonized. Britain occupied Australia and New Zealand and took over India from the East India Company. France colonized Indochina and Russia expanded to the Pacific. China was unable to resist Western pressures, and Japan was forced to open its borders, but modernized by borrowing from the West. An imperial United States emerged after 1898.

After the unification of Germany, Bismarck formed the Triple Alliance of Germany, Italy, and Austria-Hungary. Russia turned to France, and Britain, fearing Germany's ambitions, joined them in the Triple Entente. Austrian annexations in the Balkans were resented by Serbia. With Germany backing Austria and Russia supporting Serbia, a spark could set off a conflagration.

LECTURE AND DISCUSSION TOPICS

1. An introduction to the emergence of Modernism in the visual arts could be presented through a slide lecture.

2. A general introduction to or overview of Modernism in its many manifestations would be a useful background to an understanding of the twentieth-century.

3. Analyze the New Imperialism, and its causes and consequences, particularly in Africa but also in Asia.

4. Survey the diplomatic background to the Great War/World War I, posing the question as to whether the war was inevitable.

5. Discuss the impact of the New Physics, both within the world of science, but also its implications in non-scientific areas of western society.

6. A survey of the psychological concepts of Sigmund Freud could be enlightening, particularly the impact of Freudianism in literature, the arts, and on popular culture generally.

7. Discuss the changing (and unchanging) role of women at the beginning of the twentieth-century, including the quest for women's rights and the emergence of the "New Woman."

8. Survey the several possible causes for the changing role of government in Germany, Britain, the United States, and elsewhere, and the seeming abandonment of nineteenth century laissez-faire liberalism.

9. Examine the impact of the West on China and Japan in the late nineteenth century.

10. Analyze the "problem of the Balkans," both historical, as a cause of World War I, and even today.

MAP EXERCISES

1. Africa in 1914. MAP 24.1. What parts of Africa were still independent in 1914? Why? Which European nations controlled the largest territories in Africa? Can one ascertain from the map which areas would be of greatest value? Why and or why not? Which of the European powers were the "have-nots" in Africa? Could that be a cause for war in Europe? Why and or why not? (page 444)

2. Asia in 1914. MAP 24.2. From a geographical perspective, why was China more subject to the foreign pressures of the New Imperialism than Japan? Compare and contrast Britain's Asian empire with that of Germany? How can the differences be explained? (page 446)

3. The Balkans in 1878. MAP 24.3. Compare the maps of the Balkans both before and after the Congress of Berlin. Who won and who lost territory, and what might have been the reasons? What role did the long-term weaknesses of the Ottoman Empire play in the history of the Balkan peoples before 1914? (page 450)

DISCUSSION QUESTIONS FOR THE PRIMARY SOURCES (BOXED DOCUMENTS)

1. "Freud and the Concept of Repression:" What did Freud mean by the concept of "repression"? What forces in modern European society would have contributed to force individuals into repressive modes of thinking and acting? What, according to Freud, was the function of the "unconsciousness"? (page 434)

2. "Advice to Women: Be Independent": How do you explain the differences between this approach to the role of women and the one found in the selection by Elizabeth Sanford on page 423? What developments in the social, political, and cultural histories of Europe in the period between the two documents may explain the differences you detect within them? Would Henrik Ibsen's play have been controversial when first performed, and if so, why? (page 439)

3. "The White Man's Burden": What arguments did Rudyard Kipling present to justify European expansion in Africa and Asia? What imperialist motives were not expressed in Kipling's famous poem? How might an Asian or African respond to Kipling's concepts? Why? (page 443)

4. "The Emperor's 'Big Mouth'": What did Emperor William II mean to say? What did he actually say? What does this interview with William II reveal about the emperor's attitudes and character? Might another German monarch have avoided war in 1914? How? (page 449)

STUDENT RESEARCH AND PROJECT TOPICS

1. Discuss philosophical thinking at the end of the nineteenth century. How did it differ from the philosophy of the Romantics?

2. Define Social Darwinism. How did this interpretation of human existence shape late nineteenth- and early twentieth-century European society? In what sections of modern society today do we see the persistence of this philosophy?

3. Define Modernism. What are its intellectual and aesthetic preoccupations? How did this movement affect literature? Art? Music?

4. What did the New Physics and concepts of psychoanalysis contributed to Modernism?

5. What did women hope to achieve in the feminist movement? To what extent were they successful by 1914? Today?

6. Describe the situation of and attitudes toward European Jews in the nineteenth century?

7. Evaluate the Russian Revolution of 1905, as to its causes, course of events, and results.

8. What were the causes of the "New Imperialism" of the late nineteenth century? What were some of the arguments to justify this imperialism? What were the results or consequences of this imperialism?

9. What were some of the underlying causes for the Great War that broke out in 1914?

10. How did "bearing the white man's burden" affect European society in modern times?

IDENTIFICATIONS

1. Max Planck and quanta
2. Albert Einstein's $E=mc^2$
3. Friedrich Nietzsche's "slave morality"
4. Sigmund Freud and psychoanalysis
5. the ego, the id, and the superego
6. Social Darwinism
7. Houston Stewart Chamberlain
8. Emile Zola
9. the Symbolists
10. Impressionism and Camille Pissarro
11. Post-Impressionism and Vincent van Gogh
12. George Eastman
13. Pablo Picasso and Cubism
14. Igor Stravinsky's *The Rite of Spring*
15. the Pankhursts and the "suffragettes"
16. the "new woman"
17. Maria Montessori
18. Theodore Herzl and Zionism
19. Fabian Socialists
20. David Lloyd George
21. Pan-German League
22. New Imperialism
23. "white man's burden"
24. Cecil Rhodes
25. Boer War
26. Hong Kong
27. Commodore Matthew Perry
28. Boxer Rebellion
29. Meiji Restoration
30. Indian National Congress
31. Bismarckian System
32. Triple Alliance
33. Emperor William II
34. Triple Entente
35. Balkans' Crises

MULTIPLE CHOICE QUESTIONS

1. Who was responsible for the Theory of Relativity?
    a. Planck
    b. Rhodes
    c. Einstein
    d. Nietzsche
        ANSWER: c (p. 432)

2. Just prior to World War I, the European intellectual community was marked by
    a. boundless enthusiasm, confidence, and optimism about the future.
    b. a sense of confusion and anxiety leading to feelings of imminent catastrophe.
    c. total complacency on the part of a self-satisfied mass public.
    d. grim determination among nationalists to adopt and enforce international peace treaties.
        ANSWER: b (p. 432)

3. The experimental work of early twentieth-century physicists challenged and ultimately invalidated
    a. the geocentric theories of Copernicus.
    b. the mechanical conception of the universe posited by Newton.
    c. the heliocentric theory of Galileo.
    d. Harvey's claims regarding circulation.
        ANSWER: b (p. 432)

4. Inquiry into the disintegrative processes within atoms became a central theme in the new physics in part due to the experimental work of
    a. Einstein on cosmic rays and gravity.
    b. Marie and Pierre Curie on radium and radiation.
    c. Planck on Quanta.
    d. Pasteur on microbes and infection.
        ANSWER: b (p. 432)

5. The quantum theory of energy developed by Max Planck raised fundamental questions about the
    a. structure of stars.
    b. accepted renaissance theories of chemical reaction.
    c. subatomic realm of the atom and the basic building blocks of the material world.
    d. safe transmission of electrical energy for powering modern mechanical economies.
        ANSWER: c (432)

6. Friedrich Nietzsche
    a. Supported the theory of relativity.
    b. felt reform was needed to save religion and God from unbelief.
    c. believed that Christianity was a scourge and had deeply undermined the creative power of western civilization.
    d. was an advocate of Darwin's theories.
        ANSWER: c (p. 433)

7. The claim that “God is dead” was made by
   a. Charles Darwin.
   b. Karl Marx.
   c. Friedrich Nietzsche
   d. Albert Einstein.
      ANSWER: c (p. 433)

8. According to Sigmund Freud, behavior was
   a. largely determined by genetics.
   b. shaped by one's environment.
   c. determined by one's unconscious and by inner drives of which people were generally unaware.
   d. shaped by one's socio-economic status as Marx had argued.
      ANSWER: c (p. 433)

9. Freud maintained that a human being's inner life was a battleground between all of the following <u>except</u>
   a. id.
   b. ego.
   c. alterego.
   d. superego.
      ANSWER: c (p. 433)

10. According to Freud, the superego
   a. was the locus of conscience and represented the inhibitions and moral values society in general and parents in particular impose upon people.
   b. was the chief attribute of the superman and generated all creativity in one's psychology.
   c. encouraged people always to go beyond what they thought best or practical.
   d. accounted for the growing selfishness and violence of European society.
      ANSWER: a (pp. 433-434)

11. Social Darwinism was
   a. applying the ideas of Darwin to society.
   b. an effort to explain the problems of society by psychological means.
   c. an explanation, sociologically, of Darwin's biological ideas.
   d. advocated by Nietzsche.
      ANSWER: a (p. 434)

12. According to Houston Stewart Chamberlain, the Aryans were
   a. the degenerates of Western Civilization exemplifying the vicious German combination of social Darwinism, nationalism, and racism.
   b. the real creators of western culture.
   c. the "fit" who would "survive" Darwin's world.
   d. a fictitious people who were destined to rule the Slavic people of the east.
      ANSWER: b (p. 435)

33. Psychoanalysis is
   a. a method to unlearn tragic events.
   b. a method to delve into one’s memory and retrace the chain of repression back into childhood.
   c. associated with the analytic movement founded by Max Planck.
   d. practiced through individual self-meditation.
      ANSWER: b (p. 434)

14. The person who argued “war is a biological necessity” and that “war is the father of all things” was
   a. Charles Darwin.
   b. Friedrich Nietzsche.
   c. Friedrich von Bernhardi.
   d. Houston Stewart Chamberlain.
      ANSWER: b (p. 434)

15. The greatest difference between naturalism and realism in literature was
   a. realism dealt more with themes like human suffering.
   b. naturalism was more popular than realism.
   c. in general, naturalism was more pessimistic than realism.
   d. realism was simply a continuation of naturalism.
      ANSWER: c (p. 435)

16. The best example of naturalistic literature can be found in the novels of
   a. Victor Hugo.
   b. Charles Dickens.
   c. Albert Camus.
   d. Emile Zola.
      ANSWER: d (p. 435)

17. Explaining his use of naturalism in his novels and his depiction of characters, Emile Zola said
   a. "I have never given up on nature and the uplifting lessons it can teach us."
   b. "I have simply done on living bodies the work of analysis which surgeons perform on corpses."
   c. "People are naturally bad and all my fictions are truths."
   d. "My stories tell of a new Enlightenment."
      ANSWER: b (p. 435)

18. The Symbolist poets believed
   a. that objective knowledge of the world was possible.
   b. art should attempt to serve or understand society.
   c. that the external world was only a collection of symbols.
   d. agreed with the Realists in having a pessimistic world view.
      ANSWER: c (p. 435)

19. Postimpressionism differed from Impressionism by
   a. denying the importance of light and color.
   b. abandoning any interest in structural representation.
   c. shifting from objective reality to subjective reality.
   d. attempting in painting to replicate the pictures of George Eastman’s Kodak camera.
      ANSWER: c (p. 435)

20. Which of the following pairings is <u>incorrect</u>:
   a. Impressionism and Pissaro
   b. Picasso and Cubism
   c. Van Gogh and non-objective art
   d. Kandinsky and non-objective art
      ANSWER: c (pp. 435-436)

21. In art, modernism found its beginnings in the work of Pissarro called
    a. surrealism.
    b. abstract realism.
    c. baroque.
    d. impressionism.
        ANSWER: d (p. 435)

22. Modernism in music included all of the following elements except
    a. attraction to the exotic and the primitive.
    b. the exclusive use of stringed instruments to make soft sounds.
    c. sharp dissonances.
    d. unusual dancing.
        ANSWER: b (pp. 436-437)

23. The original performance of Igor Stravinsky's *Rite of Spring*
    a. was inspired by Napoleon's defeat in Russia.
    b. inspired many authors to write poems using the music.
    c. caused a great riot at the theater by audience members fighting over the music's heavy beat, sharp dissonance, and blatant sensuality.
    d. restored audiences' faith in music as a rational and soothing art.
        ANSWER: c (pp. 436-437)

24. The first professional occupation to be opened up to women was
    a. teaching.
    b. the legal profession.
    c. business management.
    d. engineering.
        ANSWER: a (p. 438)

25. Which of the following was not a pioneer in the field of nursing?
    a. Clara Barton
    b. Florence Nightingale
    c. Amalie Sieveking
    d. Emmeline Pankhurst
        ANSWER: d (p. 438)

26. The leader of the women's suffrage movement in England was
    a. Louise Michel.
    b. Babette Josephs.
    c. Emmeline Pankhurst.
    d. Octavia Hill.
        ANSWER: c (p. 438)

27. To advance the cause of women's suffrage, the Women's Social and Political Union founded by Emmeline Pankhurst and her daughters

a. took a moderate approach to the problem seeking to demonstrate first that women were intelligent and could use political power wisely if given the vote.
b. took a conservative approach to the problem and strongly recommended that only upper-class and educated women be considered as potential voters.
c. took a radical, public, and well publicized approach to the movement, employing different media and provocative public actions, like pelting male politicians with eggs, to demand the vote for women.
d. considered the political situation of women in Europe to be hopeless and advised women seeking the vote to move to other countries, like the U.S., where the chances of gaining political equality were greater.

ANSWER: c (p. 438)

28. During the nineteenth century, Jews

a. were persecuted in almost every European country.
b. received complete emancipation in France and Germany.
c. were emancipated in most western countries, but still faced restrictions
d. were not allowed into certain professions.

ANSWER: c (p. 439)

29. In general, by the late nineteenth century, the worst treatment of the Jews occurred in

a. Italy.
b. Germany.
c. eastern Europe.
d. Scandinavia.

ANSWER: c (p. 440)

30. Maria Montessori exemplifies the "new woman" of modern times in that she

a. became a leading advocate of the vote for women.
b. entered Italian politics as a liberal.
c. created the International Women's League for Peace and Freedom.
d. successfully studied for a professional degree and worked independently to apply her expertise to new fields of inquiry like early childhood development.

ANSWER: d (pp. 438-439)

31. Theodor Herzl, the leader of the Zionist movement

a. advocated the creation of a Jewish state in Palestine.
b. advocated the development of separate Jewish communities European cities.
c. argued that Jewish assimilation into western European society would only be complete when Jews renounced their religious beliefs.
d. argued that living conditions for Jews were better in eastern Europe than in western Europe.

ANSWER: a (p. 440)

32. The great English political liberal of the early twentieth century was
   a. David Lloyd George.
   b. Winston Churchill.
   c. Neville Chamberlain.
   d. Benjamin Disraeli.
      ANSWER: a (p. 440)

33. Among the notable achievements of the British Liberals under Lloyd George was
   a. unilateral British disarmament and world peace proposals.
   b. passage of the National Insurance Act of 1911 providing sickness and unemployment benefits to workers with state aid.
   c. the nationalization of all private industry in Britain.
   d. reductions in the size of the British colonial empire.
      ANSWER: b (p. 440)

34. Growing tensions in modern German society were exemplified by
   a. rapidly rising suicide rates especially in cities.
   b. refusals by German leaders to enact new welfare legislation.
   c. the use of military forces to put down urban riots.
   d. the proliferation of ultra-nationalist right-wing political pressure groups with anti-Semitic, racist, and imperialist beliefs.
      ANSWER: d (p. 440)

35. The Pan-German League advocated
   a. German withdrawal from world affairs and concentration on internal political reforms.
   b. anti-Semitic and anti-liberal policies including the development of a global German colonial empire to unite all different classes of citizens at home.
   c. German leadership in the development of international pacifist organizations.
   d. strict limitations on development of German industry including far heavier corporate taxation to pay for new state social welfare programs deemed essential by the group.
      ANSWER: b (p. 440)

36. The Fabian Socialists in Britain advocated
   a. class war and the immediate revolutionary destruction of parliamentary government following Marxist principles.
   b. the use of political terrorism to win concessions from wealthy political leaders.
   c. the necessity of workers using their new voting rights to progressively to elect a new House of Commons wherein legislation favorable to the working classes could be passed in democratic fashion.
   d. the formation of pan-European working class parties to bring democratic reforms to all states especially through disarmament and higher taxation of the rich.
      ANSWER: c (p. 440)

37. By 1900, the world's richest nation was
   a. Great Britain.
   b. the United States.
   c. Germany.
   d. Japan.
      ANSWER: b (p. 441)

38. Russia's disastrous defeat in the Russo-Japanese war indirectly led to
   a. the dismissal of Count Witte.
   b. the Revolution of 1905.
   c. the enlargement of the Duma.
   d. an unsuccessful coup by the Tsar.
   ANSWER: b (p. 441)

39. Which of the following was not an argument to justify imperialism at the turn of the century?
   a. the argument of "the white man's burden"
   b. Social Darwinism
   c. the need for military bases
   d. the argument to lessen the burden of excess European population, especially criminals and other "undesirables"
   ANSWER: d (p. 442)

40. All of the following areas were part of the British empire in the Far East except
   a. India.
   b. Australia.
   c. New Zealand.
   d. Mozambique.
   ANSWER: d (p. 443)

41. The Boer War was fought by the British in
   a. Australia.
   b. China.
   c. South Africa.
   d. Botswana.
   ANSWER: c (pp. 442-443)

42. The mid-Pacific islands became a sphere of influence of
   a. Great Britain.
   b. United States.
   c. Germany.
   d. China.
   ANSWER: b (p. 445)

43. The "Boxers"
   a. were nationalist revolutionaries in Korea.
   b. were Americans who advocated Chinese independence.
   c. were Dutch who sought to monopolize Chinese trade, especially in opium.
   d. were nationalist Chinese who attempted to expel all foreigners from the country through armed rebellion.
   ANSWER: d (p. 447)

44. The Meiji Restoration in Japan
   a. successfully accomplished the expulsion of all foreigners from the country.
   b. created a political system democratic in form but rigidly authoritarian in practice.
   c. concentrated on the reestablishment of feudal principles of decentralized government and native Japanese values.
   d. sent many Japanese to China to be educated in the ways of Confucius.
   ANSWER: b (p. 447)

45. The basis of the Bismarckian System was
   a. the acquisition of a huge overseas empire.
   b. the isolation of France through a series of military alliances.
   c. an enhanced civil service.
   d. the creation of a German war college.
      ANSWER: b (p. 448)

46. The Triple Alliance included which of the following countries?
   a. England, Germany, Italy
   b. Russia, England, France
   c. Italy, Turkey, England
   d. Germany, Italy, Austria
      ANSWER: d (p. 448)

47. The Bismarckian System had the ultimate result of
   a. bringing peace to Europe for over fifty years.
   b. creating friendship between Germany and England.
   c. easing tensions between France and Germany.
   d. dividing Europe into two opposing groups of nations making war more likely.
      ANSWER: d (p. 448)

48. The Triple Entente included which of the following countries?
   a. Great Britain, France, Russia
   b. Austria, Germany, Italy
   c. Turkey, Russia, Germany
   d. France, Spain, Great Britain
      ANSWER: a (p. 448)

49. The struggle for control of the remnants of what empire led to the First World War?
   a. Russian empire
   b. Ottoman empire
   c. Austrian empire
   d. Spanish empire
      ANSWER: b (p. 448)

50. The primary antagonists in the Balkans region were
   a. Serbs, Austrians.
   b. Russians, French.
   c. English, Germans.
   d. Serbs, Croats.
      ANSWER: a (p. 448)

RELEVANT WORLD-WIDE WEB SITES/RESOURCES

1. The Metropolitan Museum of Art, New York:
http://www.metmuseum.org/
(Site offers virtual tours of world-class nineteenth- and twentieth-century art collections.)

2. Museo Picasso (Pablo Picasso Museum Online):
http://www.tamu.edu/mocl/picasso/
(Excellent site with paintings by the modernist master arranged in virtual rooms by date of creation. One of the best web sites dedicated to the work of a single artist.)

3. The Rodin Museum, Paris:
http://www.musee-rodin.fr/welcome.htm
(Fine site in English with excellent examples of Rodin's modern French sculpture and other art works. Includes chronology of artist's life and links to other resources on the art and history of the era.)

4. Monet Gallery:
http://webpages.marshall.edu/~smith82/monet.html
(Excellent online collection of Monet's works.)

5. Musée Marmottan Monet
http://www,marmottan.com/uk/sommaire/index.html
(Superb site of a small museum in Paris housing one of the foremost collections of Monet's Impressionist works in the world—gorgeous online images and history of the museum's collections and benefactors over time. Highly recommended.)

6. WebMuseum, Paris (on the works of Edouard Manet):
http://metalab.unc.edu/wm/paint/auth/manet/

RELEVANT VIDEO SOURCES

The End of the Old Order: 1900-1929, Landmark Films, (60 minutes).
(Available through Wadsworth Publishing).

Friedrich Nietzsche, Insight Media, (30 minutes).
(Program offers simulated interview with the philosopher who explains key concepts such as "will to power," "superman," and "heroic morality" of the modern man.)

Is Time Real, Insight Media, (30 minutes).
(Investigation of Einstein's theory of relativity and the effects of modern philosophical and scientific inquiry on fundamental human conceptions of the world.)

Masters of Impressionism, PBS Home Video, 3 programs on
3 cassettes (50 minutes each).

SUGGESTED STUDENT ACTIVITIES

1. Students should do an essay comparing the Modernistic movement in art, music, and literature with other cultural movements like Baroque or Surrealism.

2. Have students do an essay on Darwinism, bringing out the influence it had not only on society, but in other areas of human endeavor like politics and the arts.

3. Have students do a comparative essay on liberalism and how it has changed over the last two centuries.

4. If you have a small class, divide it into teams and have the teams debate the pros and cons of imperialism.

CHAPTER 25
THE BEGINNING OF THE TWENTIETH-CENTURY CRISIS: WAR AND REVOLUTION

CHAPTER OUTLINE

I. The Road to World War I
- A. Nationalism and Internal Dissent
- B. Militarism
- C. The Outbreak of War: The Summer of 1914

II. The War
- A. 1914-1915: Illusions and Stalemate
- B. 1916-1917: The Great Slaughter
  - 1. Daily Life in the Trenches
- C. The Widening of the War
  - 1. Entry of the United States
- D. The Home Front: The Impact of Total War
  - 1. Total War: Political Centralization and Economic Regimentation
  - 2. Public Order and Public Opinion
  - 3. The Social Impact of Total War

III. War and Revolution
- A. The Russian Revolution
  - 1. The March Revolution
  - 2. The Bolshevik Revolution
  - 3. Civil War
- B. The Last Year of the War
- C. Revolutionary Upheavals in Germany and Austria-Hungary

IV. The Peace Settlement
- A. The Treaty of Versailles
- B. The Other Peace Treaties

V. Conclusion

CHAPTER SUMMARY

The text rightly calls World War I the defining event of the twentieth century. The June 28, 1914, assassination of Archduke Francis Ferdinand, heir to the Austro-Hungarian Empire, by a Serbian terrorist, was the final spark. National rivalries were compounded by ethnic groups who had yet to secure their own "nation." Social and class conflict led politicians to engage in foreign adventures to distract the masses. Conscript armies were ready. Perennial conflict in the Balkans threatened a wider war, given the tight-knit alliance systems. Austria, after receiving a "blank check" by Germany, declared war against Serbia on July 28. Germany declared war on Russia after the latter's military mobilization. Germany's Schlieffen Plan was to attack France through neutral Belgium. By August 4, the Great War had begun. Initially there was great enthusiasm. War gave excitement to ordinary lives and most assumed that it would soon be over. The Germans drove the Russians back in the east, but in the west a stalemate developed, with trenches extending from the Swiss border to the English Channel, defended by barbed wire and machine guns. Attacking troops had to cross "no man's land": 21,000 British died on the first day of the Battle of the Somme. Artillery, poison gas, seasonal mud, and ever-present rats and decaying corpses added to the carnage.

The Ottoman Empire joined Germany and Italy adhered to the Entente. After German submarine attacks, the United States entered the war in 1917. Conscription ensured a steady supply of soldiers. Governments took the economic lead, especially in producing munitions, and wage and price controls were instituted. Propaganda was employed to keep up morale and newspapers were censored. Many women entered the labor force, and after the war were given the vote in the United States and Britain. Fortunes were made by some, but inflation hurt many.

Russia was unprepared for war, lacking a large industrial base or adequate leadership, and public support waned because of military losses. When bread rationing was introduced in March 1917, women demonstrated in the streets of St. Petersburg/Petrograd. The Duma established a Provisional Government and Nicholas abdicated on March 15. But socialist soviets, or workers' councils, challenged the new government's legitimacy. A faction of the Marxist Social Democrats were the revolutionary Bolsheviks of V.I. Lenin, who returned to Petrograd in April, where he campaigned for "Peace, Land, and Bread" and "All Power to the Soviets." The war was increasingly unpopular, and in November the Bolsheviks seized power. Lenin established a dictatorship and signed a costly peace with Germany. Civil war broke out between the Bolshevik Reds and the Whites, who were unable to agree politically and militarily. Able military leaders, interior lines of defense, and "revolutionary terror" led the Bolsheviks to victory by 1921.

After Russia's withdrawal from the war, Germany launched a massive attack in the west. However, the war had taken its toll in Germany, and in the fall, after American troops entered the conflict, the German government collapsed. On November 11, 1918, an armistice was signed. Riots occurred in Germany, but an attempted Bolshevik revolution failed. The peace delegates gathered at Paris in January 1919. Some, like America's Woodrow Wilson, had idealistic hopes, including an association of nations to preserve the peace. Others wanted to punish Germany. The most important of five separate treaties was the Treaty of Versailles; Article 231 required Germany to accept guilt for causing the war and pay reparations. Its army was reduced to 100,000 and it lost territory to France and Poland. The Austrian and Ottoman empires were casualties of the war and the subsequent treaties. The United States refused to ratify the Treaty of Versailles and did not join the League of Nations, the institution that was to guarantee permanent peace.

LECTURE AND DISCUSSION TOPICS

1. Discuss the unending controversy among historians and others regarding the causes of World War I.

2. Analyze the various military strategies of World War I and the relationships between the generals, the general staffs, and military advisors with the civilian politicians and government officials.

3. Examine the trenches of No-Man's-Land as historical fact and as symbolic image of the Great War.

4. Survey the impact of "total war" on various home fronts in World War I.

5. Assess the impact of World War I on the several "isms" of the nineteenth century, including liberalism, nationalism, and the various socialisms.

6. A class discussion: "Why did the soldiers continue to fight?"

7. Compare and contrast the significances of the dates, 1914 and 1917, as to which year had the greatest impact upon the twentieth-century.

8. Survey the various causes of the Bolshevik Revolution of 1917.

9. Discuss the question of whether the 1917 Revolution was inevitable, including a consideration of the roles and responsibilities of such figures as Lenin, Nicholas and Alexander, Kerensky, et.al.

10. Explore the significance of the Versailles Treaty. Were there alternatives, was it a *diktat* to Germany, and was it a major cause of World War II.

11. "World War I: The Greatest Catastrophe to Befall Mankind in the Twentieth Century."

12. Discuss the twentieth-century as a war beginning in 1914 and only "ending" in 1990.

MAP EXERCISES

1. Europe in 1914. MAP 25.1. What were the geographical locations of the two contending alliances in 1914, and what strategic military challenges did both sides face? Who were the major contending powers in the Balkans, and why did the Ottoman Empire ultimately join Germany and Austria-Hungary in World War I? (page 454)

2. The Western Front, 1914-1918. MAP 25.2. What factors might explain the extent of the German advances in the west in 1914 and again in 1918? Why is it that the actions on Western Front are so much better known than those of the Eastern Front? (page 456)

3. The Eastern Front. MAP, 1914-1918. 25.3. Note the sites of the major battles on the Eastern Front. What is the geographical explanation for those several battles? What geographical advantages and what disadvantages did each side face on the Eastern Front? (page 457)

4. Europe in 1919. MAP 25.4. Compare MAP 25.4 with MAP 25.1. Who were the winners and who were the losers, and where? What impact did these geopolitical changes have on the period from 1919 to 1939? (page 468)

DISCUSSION QUESTIONS FOR THE PRIMARY SOURCES (BOXED DOCUMENTS)

1."The Reality of War: Trench Warfare": What does this excerpt from Erich Maria Remarque's famous novel reveal about the realities of trench warfare? What is there in the passage quoted that could give support to the idea that World War I was both the end of the nineteenth century and the beginning of the twentieth century? Do you think it would ever be possible for the surviving frontline victims of the war to describe or explain their experiences there to those left behind on the home front? What subsequent tensions in post-war European society might be attributable to this disjuncture? (page 459)

2. "Women in the Factories": How did work in a munitions factory broaden the outlook of an upper-middle-class woman? What can one say about the effects of total war on European women? Can it be argued that many women benefited from the Great War? If so, how? (page 461)

3 "Ten Days That Shook the World: Lenin and the Bolshevik Seizure of Power": What impressions does John Reed give of Lenin? Is Reed's reporting "objective"? If not, how and why not? What do you believe may have been the broader effects of such political reporting on the culture of modern Europe, modern Europeans, and particularly the European governments in 1917? (page 464)

4. "Two Voices of Peacemaking: Woodrow Wilson and Georges Clemenceau": How did the peacemaking aims of Wilson and Clemenceau differ? How did their different views affect the deliberations of the Paris Peace Conference and the nature of the final peace settlement? Did their differences lead to World War II? If so, how, and if not, why not? (page 466)

STUDENT RESEARCH AND PROJECT TOPICS

1. Discuss the causes of World War I: What were the major long-term causes of the war? How important were the decisions made by European statesmen during the summer of 1914 in causing the war?

2. What nation, if any, played the biggest role in the start of World War I? Base your answer on the actual events that preceded the conflict.

3. Discuss the course of the first two years of World War I: Why did many people expect a short war? Why was it not a short war? Why did World War I become a "war of attrition"? Why did the warring nations, worn out by the end of 1916, not make peace?

4. Why can 1917 be viewed as the year that witnessed the decisive turning point of World War I?

5. How did wartime governments maintain public order and mobilize public opinion during the course of the war? Compare these actions with those taken by governments in previous wars.

6. Discuss the effects of World War I on political life, economic affairs, the social classes, and women.

7. Why is World War I the defining event of the twentieth century?

8. Write a brief history of the Russian Revolution by discussing the following questions: What caused the Russian Revolution? How did Lenin and the Bolsheviks manage to seize and hold power despite their small numbers? How did the Bolsheviks secure their power during the civil war?

9. What were the chief aims of the Paris Peace Conference? To what extent were these aims incorporated into the actual peace treaties?

10. Can the Treaty of Versailles be viewed as a successful settlement of the war? Why or why not?

IDENTIFICATIONS

1. No Man's Land
2. Black Hand
3. Sarajevo
4. the Schlieffen Plan
5. First Battle of the Marne
6. Battles of Tannenberg and Masurian Lakes
7. trench warfare
8. Verdun
9. the Somme
10. the machine gun and poison gas
11. Central Powers
12. Lawrence of Arabia
13. the *Lusitania*
14. "unrestricted submarine warfare"
15. Hindenburg and Ludendorf
16. Georges Clemenceau
17. DORA
18. the Nineteenth Amendment
19. Nicholas II and Alexandra
20. Rasputin
21. Petrograd
22. "Peace, Land, and Bread"
23. soviets
24. Bolsheviks
25. V.I. Lenin
26. Treaty of Brest-Litovsk
27. Reds and Whites
28. Leon Trotsky
29. "war communism"
30. the Cheka
31. Second Battle of the Marne
32. November 11, 1918
33. Woodrow Wilson
34. Treaty of Versailles
35. League of Nations
36. Article 231
37. reparations
38. Yugoslavia
39. League of Nations' mandates
40. the Great War

MULTIPLE CHOICE QUESTIONS

1. Which of the following trends helped lead to the outbreak of the Great War?
   a. conservative leaders hoped to crush internal communist movements through war
   b. European generals adopted new military policies
   c. European states felt they had to uphold the power of their allies for their own internal security
   d. the downward spiral of European economies
      ANSWER: c (pages 454-455)

2. The First World War not only killed millions of human beings, it also destroyed one of the basic intellectual precepts upon which recent Western Civilization had been founded:
   a. the concept of a benevolent God
   b. the belief in progress
   c. the conviction of the enlightened spirit of man
   d. the belief in justice for all
      ANSWER: b (p. 453)

3. Before the outbreak of World War I in 1914, the general outlook for the future by most Europeans was
   a. highly optimistic with material progress expected to create an earthly paradise.
   b. one of extreme indifference and reckless abandon.
   c. extremely negative, with most people believing that Armageddon was near.
   d. largely determined by state agencies.
      ANSWER: a (p. 453)

4. The immediate cause of World War I was
   a. an uprising of Catholic peasants in Bavaria.
   b. the assassination of Austrian Archduke Francis Ferdinand in Bosnia.
   c. the German invasion of Poland.
   d. the German naval blockage of Britain.
      ANSWER: b (p. 454)

5. Among nineteenth-century European political movements, the one most responsible for triggering World War I was
   a. nationalism.
   b. liberalism.
   c. conservatism.
   d. Marxism.
      ANSWER: a (p. 453)

6. Between 1890 and 1914, in part through conscription, European military forces had
   a. increased ten times.
   b. quadrupled in size.
   c. tripled in size.
   d. doubled in size.
      ANSWER: d (p. 453)

7. The outbreak of the Great War was greatly accelerated by the Schlieffen Plan, which was
a. Germany's promise of full-fledged support for Austrian military actions against Serbia.
b. the Black Hand's plan for the assassination of Archduke Ferdinand of Austria.
c. Germany's military plan to invade France rapidly through neutral Belgium before attacking Russia.
d. Russia's mobilization plan against both Germany and Austria-Hungary.
ANSWER: c (p. 455)

8. The rivalry between which states for domination of southeastern Europe helped create serious tensions before World War I?
a. Germany and Italy
b. Russia and Italy
c. Austria-Hungary and Russia
d. Britain and France
ANSWER: c (p. 454)

9. What was the state that was a thorn in Austria-Hungary's side and a primary cause of World War I?
a. Serbia
b. Bulgaria
c. Greece
d. Italy
ANSWER: a (p. 454)

10. On the eve of the outbreak of war in Europe in 1914, William II of Germany
a. was plotting the overthrow of Nicholas II in Russia.
b. was intentionally provoking the Russians to attack Austria and set off a world war.
c. gave full support to Austria-Hungary in dispute with Serbia.
d. sent ultimatums to England and France that were so clumsy and insulting as to make war inevitable.
ANSWER: c (p. 454)

11. Austrian ultimatums to Serbia, hastening the outbreak of World War I, came, in part, because
a. the Austrians had received a "blank check" of German support and military backing in their dispute with the Serbs.
b. England had refused to guarantee Serbian territorial integrity.
c. the French did nothing to suggest that they might cancel their alliance with the Habsburgs.
d. the Italians renewed their military alliance with Austria.
ANSWER: a (p. 454)

12. In August 1914, the perception of the upcoming war among Europeans was that
a. it would be the dawn of a new socialist Europe.
b. the war would be very short, possibly only weeks in duration.
c. it would mark the end of European civilization.
d. its long-term nature would revive Europe's suffering economy.
ANSWER: b (p. 455)

13. As early as July 28, 1914, European diplomats were becoming incapable of slowing a rush toward war mainly because
a. European kings, tsars, and emperors were too bent on war to heed their advice.
b. the complex, rigid, and demanding mobilization plans devised by European army generals made immediate military action essential.
c. ordinary people everywhere went to the polls and voted for immediate opening of the war on all fronts.
d. European industrialists, seeking to profit from mass destruction, induced the politicians they owned through bribery to push declarations of war through all European legislatures.
ANSWER: b (p. 455)

14. Most Europeans believed that the Great War would
a. be much like the American Civil War in length.
b. be an exciting, emotional release from the otherwise dull and boring existence of mass society.
c. last for years creating a rousing state of perpetual heroics as proclaimed by Nietzsche in his writings on the "superman."
d. ultimately bring about the unification of Europe in one centralized and highly militarized government.
ANSWER: b (p. 455)

15. The most important consequence of the first year of World War I was
a deadly stalemate on the western front as a result of the failure of German war plans at the First Battle of the Marne.
b. Italy's decision to switch sides to the German-Austrian alliance.
c. the collapse of German armies on the Russian front.
d. Serbia's rapid advance into Austria-Hungary.
ANSWER: a (p. 455)

16. The development of trench warfare in France was characterized by
a. quick advances and seizures of enemy trenches.
b. fewer casualties due to thick fortifications.
c. long periods of dreary boredom broken by murderous artillery barrages and terrifying frontal assaults by enemy troops.
d. high morale and assurance of victory among the troops whose use of modern weapons reduced casualty rates.
ANSWER: c (pp. 457-458)

17. The First World War in the east was characterized by
a. more mobility than the trench warfare on the Western Front.
b. relatively little loss of life and small skirmishes.
c. trench warfare as in France.
d. the overwhelming superiority of Russian forces.
ANSWER: a (p. 455)

18. The usual tactic of trench warfare was to
a. surround the enemy and starve him into submission.
b. use heavy artillery bombardments and then launch direct frontal infantry assaults on well-defended enemy positions.
c. attempt to outflank the enemy through rapid and mobile deployment of troops and cavalry.
d. meet the opposing force on the "field of honor" between the trenches for hand-to-hand combat.
ANSWER: b (p. 457)

19. Desperate for any innovations in battle that might bring some success in terrible trench fighting, all sides in the conflict employed new weapons perfected by European science, such as
a. air-to-air missiles.
b. poison gas.
c. jet aircraft.
d. steam-driven tanks.
ANSWER: b (p. 458)

20. As fought in the World War I, trench warfare
a. became a senseless slaughter of troops on all sides with hundreds of thousands of men dying for battlefield gains of a few miles at best.
b. increased the morale of soldiers who fought well and came to obey promptly the orders of their superiors.
c. quickly led to the use of tanks and missiles which ended the trench stalemate.
d. brought great innovations to military tactics as the long conflict forced generals to devise novel tactics.
ANSWER: a (pp. 457-458)

21. As soldiers on both sides realized that no one could gain an advantage in trench warfare
a. savage treatment of prisoners became commonplace.
b. new weapons were developed to kill rather than overrun the enemy.
c. daily life for the soldier became increasingly squalid, regimented, and miserable in filthy, rat-infested trenches.
d. they were increasingly encouraged by their officers not to fight and to await a peace treaty ending the war.
ANSWER: c (p. 458)

22. At the Battle of the Somme,
a. the French casualties numbered 700,000.
b. the British lost 21,000 dead on the first day of the battle.
c. America joined World War I just in time to assist the French in defeating the Germans.
d. V.I. Lenin led the Bolsheviks to victory over the Whites.
ANSWER: b (p. 458)

23. The entry of the United States into World War I in April 1917
a. gave the nearly-defeated allies a psychological boost.
b. was greatly feared by the German naval staff.
c. was a response to Turkey's entrance into the war on the side of the Central Powers.
d. put an end to Germany's use of unlimited submarine warfare.
ANSWER: a (p. 460)

24. The chief reason for the United States' entry into World War I was
a. the success of British propaganda.
b. blatant German violations of the principles of neutrality and freedom of the seas.
c. the expulsion of the American consul from Berlin.
d. diplomatic chicanery on the part of the Austrians.
ANSWER: b (p. 460)

25. Economically, World War I
a. saw European governments adopt a "hands off" policy toward their economies.
b. saw European governments all take control of only war-related industries.
c. witnessed European governments gradually take full control of all aspects of their economies.
d. did little to affect the domestic industries of European nations.
ANSWER: c (p. 460)

26. In World War I, the Turkish Ottoman Empire fought on the side of
a. Austria and Germany.
b. Russia.
c. Italy.
d. France and Britain.
ANSWER: a (p. 458)

27. The fact that European states fighting in World War I had to effectively organize masses of men and material for years of deadly combat led to
a. increased centralization and expansion of government powers.
b. economic regimentation of entire countries.
c. manipulation of public opinion through mass propaganda and government control of information.
d. all the above
ANSWER: d (p. 460)

28. As public morale and support for the war ebbed
a. workers' strikes became less frequent as they were brutally repressed.
b. the liberal French government under Clemenceau found it impossible to end internal dissent.
c. propaganda posters and weapons became less important.
d. police powers were widely expanded to include the arrest of all dissenters as traitors to the state.
ANSWER: d (p. 460)

29. The most famous novelist of World War I was
a. Herman Hesse.
b. Vladimir Ulyanov.
c. Erich Maria Remarque.
d. Robert Graves.
ANSWER: c (p. 459)

30. The empire which collapsed in World War I and whose fall led to the emergence of the modern Middle East was the
a. Iranian empire.
b. Ottoman empire.
c. Egyptian empire.
d. Austro-Hungarian empire.
ANSWER: b (pp. 458-459)

31. The women workers of World War I played an important role in
   a. winning women the right to vote immediately following the war.
   b. gaining equal industrial wages with men by the end of the war.
   c. achieving permanent job security in the once male-dominated workplace.
   d. all work areas except the textile industry.
      ANSWER: a (p. 462)

32. Britain's DORA
   a. gave women the vote in 1918.
   b. ended military conscription in favor of a volunteer army.
   c. gave government the authority to arrest dissenters to the war as traitors.
   d. established the Department of Munitions, administered by Winston Churchill.
      ANSWER: c (p. 460)

33. "Daddy, what did YOU do in the Great War?" was
   a. a poem written by anti-war activists in protest to the carnage of the trenches.
   b. a propaganda poster to inspire Britons to support the war.
   c. an attempt to shame fathers into doing their share of housework while their wives worked in armament factories.
   d. a popular song, sung in vaudeville and in dance halls.
      ANSWER: b (p. 460)

34. The collapse of Russia's tsarist regime in March 1917 was aided by all of the following <u>except</u>
   a. the leadership of the Mensheviks in forming the new Provisional Government.
   b. a general strike in Petrograd.
   c. the wartime casualties due to incompetent leadership and poor equipment.
   d. strife in the ruling dynasty as evidenced by the influence of Rasputin, "the mad monk."
      ANSWER: a (p. 462)

35. The Russian army's woes during World War I included all of the following <u>except</u>
   a. not enough manpower.
   b. poor leadership.
   c. lack of modern armaments.
   d. great losses of men in battle.
      ANSWER: a (p. 462)

36. Which of the following statements best applies to Nicholas II's tsarist regime?
   a. Rasputin, an alleged holy man, ran a very efficient government.
   b. Alexandra, Nicholas' wife, kept him isolated from the reality of domestic disturbances.
   c. It was patriotically supported by ordinary Russians throughout the war.
   d. Many reforms were made to keep the peasants content.
      ANSWER: b (p. 462)

37. V.I. Lenin
   a. was a central figure in the establishment of a provisional government.
   b. denounced the use of revolutionary violence in his "April Theses."
   c. with strong middle-class support, led the formation of a new, democratic labor party.
   d. as a leader of the anti-democratic Bolsheviks, promised "land, peace, and bread" and a quick Russian withdrawal from the war.
      ANSWER: d (p. 463)

38. When Lenin returned to Russia in April 1917, he
  a. outlined a specifically Russian movement toward socialism to be led by soviets of soldiers, workers, peasants.
  b. contained his proposals to continue Russian participation in World War I.
  c. listed the conditions under which the Bolsheviks would accept a new republican form of government.
  d. argued that revolution was an impractical means of establishing a new government for Russia.
    ANSWER: a (p. 463)

39. Following the Bolshevik seizure of power in November 1917, Lenin
  a. accelerated the war effort against Germany.
  b. returned the control of factories to their rightful owners.
  c. signed the treaty of Brest-Litovsk with Germany.
  d. successfully managed to reestablish the Duma under socialist control.
    ANSWER: c (p. 464)

40. Even though facing tremendous odds against a successful seizure of power, the Bolsheviks prevailed in the end due to
  a. poor discipline among the Mensheviks.
  b. aid from the French and British.
  c. poor leadership among the socialists.
  d. ruthless discipline and leadership in part due to the efforts of Leon Trotsky.
    ANSWER: d (p. 463)

41. The Cheka was a
  a. Serbian terrorist group.
  b. Slovak nationalist organization.
  c. Bolshevik secret police unit used to murder and terrorize opponents.
  d. Tsarist military reform agency.
    ANSWER: c (p. 465)

42. The Second Battle of the Marne was
  a. the end of Germany's final, futile effort to win the war.
  b. the decisive victory Germans had long sought.
  c. a disaster for the French.
  d. decided by the entry of Australia into the war.
    ANSWER: a (p. 465)

43. The series of revolutionary upheavals in central Europe following Germany's defeat led to
  a. the successful creation of a new socialist state in Germany led by Karl Liebknecht.
  b. a military dictatorship in Austria headed by the Free Corps.
  c. the creation of several independent republics within the old Austro-Hungarian Empire.
  d. a strong communist influence among most of the German populace.
    ANSWER: c (p. 469)

44. The German November revolution of 1918 resulted in
  a. a parliamentary democracy dominated by the Republicans.
  b. the division of Germany among the victorious allies.
  c. the creation of a communist state similar to the Soviet Union.
  d. the creation of a German Republic with the socialists in power.
    ANSWER: d (p. 466)

45. All of the following states were created out of the Austro-Hungarian Empire following World War I <u>except</u>

a. Austria.
b. Hungary.
c. Poland.
d. Czechoslovakia.
ANSWER: c (p. 468)

46. For Woodrow Wilson, the most important thing after the war was to

a. punish Germany severely.
b. assure acceptance of his "general association of nations."
c. deepen America's isolationism from European affairs.
d. bring about the disintegration of the Soviet Union.
ANSWER: b (p. 466)

47. The chief motivation of Georges Clemenceau's terms of armistice was to

a. punish Germany and gain security for France.
b. help Germany become a democracy.
c. maintain a demilitarized Europe.
d. limit Britain's influence on the continent.
ANSWER: a (pp. 466-467)

48. The Treaty of Versailles

a. absolved the Central Powers of full guilt in causing the war.
b. created Wilson's United Nations.
c. forced Germany to acknowledge "war guilt" and to pay massive reparations for its alleged wartime aggression.
d. created a system by which the old Turkish Empire could be safely dismantled.
ANSWER: c (pp. 467-468)

49. The feature of the Versailles Treaty that most Germans found very hard to accept was

a. the loss of land that reduced the nation by half.
b. the reductions imposed in the size of the German military.
c. Article 231, the "War Guilt Clause" which imposed heavy war reparations on Germany.
d. the loss of all political sovereignty for a period of twenty years.
ANSWER: c (pp. 467-468)

50. As a result of World War I, eastern Europe

a. experienced little or no real change.
b. fell subject to the new Russian communist state.
c. witnessed the emergence of many new nation-states.
d. quickly overtook western Europe economically.
ANSWER: c (p. 469)

RELEVANT WORLD-WIDE WEB SITES/RESOURCES

1. The Great War (PBS Television Series Site):
http://www.pbs.org/greatwar/
(One of the very finest web sites developed to complement a television broadcast--in this case the multi-part PBS documentary on World War One. Fine maps, documents, time lines, and maps. See video reference below.)

2. History of the Battle of the Somme:
http://www.somme.com/
(Site dedicated to analysis of the war's single greatest, catastrophic day of human slaughter. Site is also superb for a general overview of the genesis and course of the war with excellent online documentation stretching back to the mid-nineteenth century. Components of this site highly relevant to themes of nationalism, militarism, and great power rivalry treated in earlier chapters of this text.)

3. Military Plans of the Great War:
http://hsc.csu.edu.au/modhist/courses/2unit/corestud/74/page83.htm
(A superb site offering online detailed excerpts from and analysis of the grand war plans of all combatants in World War One. Australian university site.)

4. Trenches on the Web: Photo Archive, The Somme 1916:
http://www.worldwar1.com/pharc001.htm
(Fine site offering graphic evidence of the destruction and terror of trench warfare. Excellent on material culture and imagery of modern war with extensive links to other relevant sites offering analyses of battles on Western and Eastern Fronts, memoirs of ordinary soldiers, war museum collections, and veterans groups.

5. World War One Document Archive:
http://www.lib.byu.edu/~rdh/wwi/
(One of the most comprehensive collections online of documents relevant to all phases and aspects of the Great War. Comes complete with images, extensive original document quotations, and a suite of links to other relevant web pages. Highly recommended.)

RELEVANT VIDEO RESOURCES

The Great War and the Shaping of the Twentieth Century, PBS Home Video, 4 cassettes, multiple chronological programs, (55 minutes each).

SUGGESTED STUDENT ACTIVITIES

1. Have students read as an outside assignment classic texts on the "Great War" such as Remarque's *All Quiet on the Western Front* or Paul Fussell's *The Great War and Modern Memory* and then prepare reports on the realities and long-term effects of trench warfare in Europe.

2. Have students write an essay on "World War I as the First Modern War," focusing on the new weapons employed, innovative propaganda campaigns, and developments on the home front.

3. Have students read and analyze the text of the Versailles Treaty (complete editions of the Treaty are frequently to be found in older, post-war encyclopedias and can easily be located in online document collections available through the World-Wide Web). What are the global implications of the Treaty and its various clauses? How does the document virtually guarantee the outbreak of World War II and prefigure the state rivalries of 1939-45?

CHAPTER 26
THE FUTILE SEARCH FOR A NEW STABILITY: EUROPE BETWEEN THE WARS, 1919-1939

CHAPTER OUTLINE

I. An Uncertain Peace: The Search for Security
- A. The Great Depression

II. The Democratic States

III. The Retreat from Democracy: The Authoritarian and Totalitarian States
- A. Fascist Italy
  - 1. Mussolini and the Italian Fascist State
- B. Hitler and Nazi Germany
  - 1. Weimar Germany and the Rise of the Nazis
  - 2. The Nazi State, 1933-1939
- C. The Soviet Union
  - 1. The Stalin Era (1929-1939)
- D. Authoritarian States

IV. The Expansion of Mass Culture and Mass Leisure
- A. Radio and Movies
- B. Mass Leisure

V. Cultural and Intellectual Trends in the Interwar Years
- A. Nightmares and New Visions: Art and Music
- B. The Search for the Unconscious
- C. The "Heroic Age of Physics"

VI. Conclusion

CHAPTER SUMMARY

The treaties ending World War I did not assure peace as the League of Nations had little power. France, fearing Germany, formed the Little Entente with the militarily weak states of eastern Europe. Occupying the Ruhr when Germany failed to pay reparations, France gained little other than a disastrous fall in the German mark. By 1924, the Dawes Plan established a realistic reparations schedule. The Treaty of Locarno made permanent Germany's western borders, but not the east. Germany joined the League, and in 1928, sixty-three nations signed the Kellogg-Briand pact, renouncing war, but it lacked any enforcement provisions.

European prosperity, largely the result of American loans and investments, ended with the Great Depression. The economist John Maynard Keynes favored increased government spending and deficit financing rather than deflation and balanced budgets, but had little support. Britain's unemployment remained at 10 percent during the 1920s and rose rapidly in the depression. France was governed by frequent coalition governments; its far-right was attracted to fascism and many on the left by Soviet Marxism. The United States' New Deal was more successful in providing relief than in recovery, and unemployment remained high until World War II.

Totalitarian governments, which required the active commitment of their citizens, came power in Germany, Italy and the Soviet Union. Italian fascism resulted from Italy's losses in the Great War, economic failure, and incompetent politicians. In 1919, Benito Mussolini organized the *Fascio di Combattimento.* Threatening "to march on Rome," he was chosen prime minister in 1922. Legal due process was abandoned and rival parties were outlawed, but totalitarianism in Italy was never as effective as in Nazi Germany or Soviet Russia.

In Germany, the depression brought the political extremes to the forefront. Adolph Hitler headed the National Socialist German Workers' Party (Nazis). A powerful orator, Hitler published his beliefs in *Mein Kampf,* and created a private army of storm troopers (SA), but it was not until the depression that the Nazis received wide support. Hitler became chancellor in 1933, and a compliant Reichstag passed the Enabling Act, giving him dictatorial power. In his quest to dominate Europe, Hitler rearmed Germany, abolished labor unions, and created a new terrorist police force, the SS. The Nuremberg laws excluded Jews from citizenship, and in the 1938 *Kristallnacht*, Jewish businesses and synagogues were burned and Jews beaten and killed. After Lenin's death in 1924, Joseph Stalin assumed leadership in the Soviet Union. In 1928, he announced his first five-year plan to turn the Soviet Union into an industrial society by emphasizing oil and coal production and steel manufacturing. Giant collective farms were created, and in the process 10 million lives were lost. Stalin's opponents were sent to Siberia, sentenced to labor camps, or liquidated. With the exception of Czechoslovakia, authoritarian governments appeared in eastern Europe as well as in Portugal and Spain. In the Spanish Civil War, the fascist states aided Francisco Franco and the Soviet Union backed the Popular Front.

Radio and movies become widely popular, as did professional sports. Automobiles and trains made travel accessible to all. Issues of sexuality became more public and psychology became more popular. In art, Dada focused upon the absurd and Surrealism upon the unconscious. The unconscious "stream of consciousness" technique was used in the novels of James Joyce and Virginia Woolf. The Bauhaus movement emphasized the functional in architecture. It was also the "the heroic age of physics." The discovery of subatomic particles indicated that splitting the atom could release massive energies, and Werner Heisenberg's "uncertainty principle" had implications far beyond the study of physics.

LECTURE AND DISCUSSION TOPICS

1. Survey the Italian origins of fascism and how it influenced, and how it differed, from fascism in Germany.

2. Discuss the search for security and peace during the interwar years.

3. "The Shadow of Versailles"—the West during interwar decades.

4. Examine the polarities of ideology and opportunism in the dualistic nature of Adolf Hitler's policies.

5. Discuss the significance of propaganda in the totalitarian societies of the first half of the twentieth-century, using the example of Nazi Germany.

6. A class discussion: How did Hitler come to power?

7. Compare and contrast the totalitarian states of Nazi Germany and the Soviet Union.

8. Assess the career of Stalin, and whether he fulfilled Lenin's goals or whether he perverted those hopes --or were there any fundamental differences between the two Soviet leaders.

9. Discuss the influence and the significance of radio and the movies during the Great Depression of the 1930s.

10. Present a slide lecture on the arts during the interwar years, an era of uncertainty.

DISCUSSION QUESTIONS FOR THE PRIMARY SOURCES (BOXED DOCUMENTS)

1. "The Great Depression: Unemployed and Homeless in Germany": Discuss the plight of the homeless in Germany in 1932. How did the growing misery of many ordinary Germans promote the rise of extremist political parties like the Nazis and facilitate seizure of political power in Germany by racist and anti-democratic forces. (page 474)

2. "Propaganda and Mass Meetings in Nazi Germany": How did Hitler envision the role of propaganda and mass meetings in the totalitarian state? How do you believe the stage- management of Nazi spectacles contributed to the acceptance of corrupt and inhuman Nazi ideology by many ordinary Germans, such as the teacher quoted? Would the same propaganda techniques be effective in the twenty-first century? Why or why not? (page 479)

3. "The Formation of Collective Farms": What is a collective farm and how was it created? What traditions of Russian life and character did this novel unit of agricultural production attack? What social and economic costs were involved in the formation of the collectives? (page 482)

4. "Hesse and the Unconscious": How might the German Nazis have capitalized on the psychic uncertainties and confusion among ordinary people that Hesse describes here afflicting a central character in one of the author's most popular novels? What are the political dangers inherent in a populace comprised of too many people vulnerable to the problems of Hesse's literary character? Are the uncertainties and confusions discussed by Hesse unique to a particular time and place or are they timeless? (page 487)

STUDENT RESEARCH AND PROJECT TOPICS

1. The decade of the 1920s has been characterized as both an "age of anxiety" and a "period of hope." Why?

2. What were the causes of the Great Depression? How did the European states respond to the Great Depression?

3. How did America cope with the Depression? Why was the depression in the United States so long-lasting and what finally ended unemployment?

4. What are the chief characteristics of totalitarianism? To what extent was Fascist Italy a totalitarian state?

5. Compare and contrast fascism in Italy with Nazism in Germany. What were the similarities and what were the differences between the two regimes?

6. What were Hitler's core ideas or assumptions? What were the methods used to implement them once he and the Nazis had established the Nazi state in Germany?

7. Why does the author state that the Stalinist era inaugurated an "economic, social, and political revolution that was more sweeping in its results than the revolutions of 1917"?

8. How were the totalitarian revolutions in the Soviet Union, Italy, and Germany similar? How were they different?

9. What impact did the growth of mass culture and mass leisure have upon European society in the 1920s and 1930s?

10. How do the cultural and intellectual trends of the 1920s and 1930s reflect a crisis of confidence in Western Civilization?

IDENTIFICATIONS

1. League of Nations
2. Dawes Plan
3. Treaty of Locarno
4. Great Depression
5. John Maynard Keynes
6. Popular Front
7. the New Deal
8. Benito Mussolini
9. *Fascio di Combattimento*
10. *squadristi*
11. *Il Duce*
12. Weimar Republic
13. Adolph Hitler
14. *Mein Kampf*
15. NSDAP/Nazis
16. *Lebensraum*
17. *Fuhrer*
18. Aryanism
19. *Hitler Jugend*
20. Nuremberg laws
21. *Kristallnacht*
22. New Economic Policy
23. Joseph Stalin
24. five-year plan
25. collective farms
26. General Francisco Franco
27. Spanish Civil War
28. “wireless” and the BBC
29. *Birth of a Nation* and *The Blue Angel*
30. *Kraft durch Freude*
31. Dadaism and Surrealism

32. Bauhaus School and Walter Gropius
33. "degenerate art"
34. Arnold Schoenberg and atonal music
35. Herman Hesse
36. Carl Jung
39. Werner Heisenberg
38. Ernest Rutherford

MULTIPLE CHOICE QUESTIONS

1. French policy toward a defeated Germany following World War I was guided by all of the following except

    a. a strict enforcement of the Treaty of Versailles.
    b. occupation of German industries in the Ruhr Valley.
    c. a strict collection of Germany's war reparations.
    d. a policy of passive resistance under Raymond Poincaré.
        ANSWER: d (page 472)

2. Which of the following nations did not join the League of Nations?

    a. Great Britain
    b. France
    c. the United States
    d. Italy
        ANSWER: c (p. 472)

3. Efforts to maintain European peace following World War I included

    a. a three-way alliance between Great Britain, France, and the Weimar Republic.
    b. the addition of an armed international security force to the League of Nations.
    c. the Treaty of Locarno.
    d. increased intervention by the United States in European political affairs.
        ANSWER: c (p. 472)

4. Following Germany's failure to pay its war reparations, France occupied Germany's Ruhr valley, resulting in

    a. policy of passive resistance by the German government and German resort to printing money to pay war debts—a move that ruined the economy through inflation.
    b. an alliance concluded between Germany and Russia.
    c. the election of Raymond Poincaré's French government in 1924.
    d. an increase in the size of the German military.
        ANSWER: a (p. 472)

5. The period of 1924-1929 in Europe witnessed

    a. a growing feeling of optimism for a peaceful future.
    b. the Great Depression destroy Europe's economy.
    c. a direct occupation of Germany by World War I's victorious powers.
    d. the western powers cut off all ties with Communist Russia.
        ANSWER: a (p. 472)

6. The treaty of 1925 that guaranteed France and Belgium's postwar boundaries was called the
 a. Locarno Pact.
 b. Kellogg-Briand Treaty.
 c. the Dawes Plan.
 d. the Milan treaty.
 ANSWER: a (p. 472)

7. A major cause of the Great Depression was
 a. European governments were too involved in their own economies.
 b. the recall of American loans from European markets.
 c. the underproduction and high prices of agricultural goods in eastern and central Europe.
 d. the inability of the League of Nations to set complementary economic policies in different global markets.
 ANSWER: b (p. 473)

8. An overall effect of the Great Depression in Europe was
 a. the complete destruction of Communist parties.
 b. huge unemployment rates in all nations but Great Britain.
 c. the strengthening of liberal, democratic movements in the 1930s.
 d. the rise of authoritarian movements in many areas of Europe.
 ANSWER: d (pp. 473-474)

9. After 1924, American financial investment in Europe
 a. decreased rapidly.
 b. increased rapidly but soon came to crisis.
 c. stagnated as American banks preferred to invest at home.
 d. slowly declined as American capital flowed to more lucrative new markets in Asia and South America.
 ANSWER: b (p. 473)

10. Great Britain came out of the worst stages of the Great Depression under
 a. John Maynard Keynes.
 b. the National Socialist Government.
 c. David Lloyd George.
 d. the coalition of Liberal, Conservative, and Labour party members.
 ANSWER: d (p. 474)

11. The first Popular Front government in France
 a. solved the depression by eliminating workers' benefits.
 b. gave ordinary workers new rights and benefits including a minimum wage.
 c. was responsible for solving the problems of the depression.
 d. collapsed in 1926, allowing Raymond Poincaré's Cartel of the Left to take power.
 ANSWER: b (p. 475)

12. The economist who condemned the view that depressions should be left to work themselves out was
 a. Karl Marx.
 b. Adam Smith.
 c. Warner Heisenberg.
 d. John Maynard Keynes.
 ANSWER: d (pp. 472-473)

13. Franklin Roosevelt's New Deal policies in the United States
    a. were successful by 1933.
    b. virtually eliminated unemployment.
    c brought about government ownership of most industries.
    d. brought about limited employment through greater government intervention in the economy.
        ANSWER: d (p. 475)

14. The totalitarian regimes of Germany, Italy, and the Soviet Union
    a. pursued vastly different foreign policies.
    b. held each other in disdain.
    c. hoped to control every aspect of their citizens' lives.
    d. retained power due to the charisma of their leaders.
        ANSWER: c (p. 475)

15. The first Fascist state in Europe was
    a. Italy.
    b. Germany.
    c. Russia.
    d. Spain.
        ANSWER: a (p. 475)

16. The growth of Mussolini's Fascist movement was aided by
    a. the inability of the parliamentary parties to conduct an adequate foreign policy.
    b. popular, nationalistic resentment toward Italy's treatment following World War I.
    c. crop failures in 1920 and 1921.
    d. economic cooperation between Italy, Germany, and the Soviet Union.
        ANSWER: b (p. 476)

17. *Squadristi* were
    a. the closest advisors of Mussolini.
    b. armed bands of fascists who used violence to intimidate enemies.
    c. elite soldiers of the Fascist state.
    d. officers in the Italian military.
        ANSWER: b (p. 475)

18. The state established in Germany after World War I was known as the
    a. Second Reich.
    b. Third Reich.
    c. Weimar Republic.
    d. Bavarian Republic.
        ANSWER: c (p. 477)

19. The institutional framework of Mussolini's Fascist dictatorship
    a. lacked a secret police force.
    b. included highly popular and well attended Fascists youth organizations.
    c. was primarily aimed at aiding the workers and peasants.
    d. never created the degree of totalitarian control found in Russia and Germany in the 1930s.
        ANSWER: d (p. 477)

20. Women in Mussolini's Fascist Italy
  a. were coerced into factory work to aid industrial production.
  b. were regarded as equal to men in social status.
  c. were largely forced through government legislation to become homemakers.
  d. were aided by the government's emphasis on birth control.
    ANSWER: c (p. 476)

21. The Lateran Accords of 1929
  a. nationalized all church property.
  b. recognized Catholicism as the sole religion of Italy.
  c. marked the Catholic church's official condemnation of the Fascist state.
  d. eliminated government support for the Catholic church.
    ANSWER: b (p. 477)

22. The city in which Hitler spent his formative years and developed his fundamental ideas was
  a. Berlin.
  b. Munich.
  c. Vienna.
  d. Hamburg.
    ANSWER: c (p. 477)

23. During World War I, Adolf Hitler
  a. served four years in the German army.
  b. reached the rank of general.
  c. was conscripted into the army against his will and came close to execution for cowardice and insubordination.
  d. opposed the war from the beginning and fled to neutral Switzerland to escape the draft.
    ANSWER: a (p. 477)

24. *Mein Kampf*
  a. depicted Hitler's plan to take power through a massive rebellion.
  b. was autobiographical, but set forth Hitler's twisted ideology of racism, Aryan supremacy, and anti-Semitism.
  c. excluded any trace of Hitler's anti-Semitism.
  d. was immediately seen by German politicians as the dangerous work of a madman.
    ANSWER: b (p. 478)

25. The German president at the time of Hitler's maneuvers to gain sole political power over Germany was
  a. Heinrich Bruning.
  b. Paul von Hindenberg.
  c. Franz von Papen.
  d. Herman Göring.
    ANSWER: b (p. 478)

26. The Nazis proved to be effective in the realm of politics by
   a. securing many small donations from large German corporations.
   b. making the Nazi program appeal to every segment of German society.
   c. persuading the average German that their program was the only alternative to the inept Weimar regime.
   d. forcing the poorer Germans to vote for Nazi candidates through intimidation.
      ANSWER: b (p. 478)

27. The *Gleichschaltung* was
   a. the coordination of all institutions under Nazi control.
   b. the purge of the SA leadership in June of 1934.
   c. the subordination of the German army to the Nazi Party under Hitler.
   d. Hitler's plan for securing "living space" from other nations.
      ANSWER: a (p. 478)

28. The most famous and spectacular of the Nazi mass demonstrations were held in the city of
   a. Berlin.
   b. Munich.
   c. Augsburg.
   d. Nuremberg.
      ANSWER: d (p. 479)

29. Economic and labor conditions in Nazi Germany were characterized by
   a. nationalization of all major industries.
   b. a confused and chaotic effort to create Nazi trade unions.
   c. persistently high rates of unemployment until the outbreak of World War Two.
   d. the use of rearmament to solve the unemployment problem.
      ANSWER: d (p. 479)

30. The Nazi leader Heinrich Himmler was responsible for
   a. forming Nazi professional organizations for civil servants, doctors, and teachers.
   b. carrying out the racial and terrorism policies of the SS, fanatical bands of Nazis devoted to Hitler's ideas.
   c. guiding the German Labor Front.
   d. the indoctrination of Nazi ideals into Hitler Youth organizations.
      ANSWER: b (pp. 478-480)

31. Hitler's anti-Semitic policies in the 1930s
   a. included the Nuremberg laws, which centered on the forced emigration of most Jews from Germany.
   b. reached their most violent phase during the events of *Kristallnacht* with attacks on Jewish homes, businesses, and synagogues.
   c. did not exclude Jews from legal, medical, and teaching positions.
   d. would remain minimal and unorganized until World War II.
      ANSWER: b (p. 480)

32. The Nazi policies toward women
  a. differed fundamentally from those of Fascist Italy.
  b. eliminated females from all professional occupations.
  c. were aimed at bridging the differences between the sexes.
  d. were geared toward the idea that through childbearing and service in the home women would bring about the triumph of the Aryan race.
    ANSWER: d (p. 480)

33. The only eastern European nation to maintain political democracy throughout the 1930's was
  a. Bulgaria.
  b. Czechoslovakia.
  c. Poland.
  d. Hungary.
    ANSWER: b (p. 483)

34. The dominant form of government in eastern Europe in the 1920's and 1930's was
  a. authoritarianism.
  b. Russian Soviet-style Communism.
  c. parliamentary democracy.
  d. totalitarian.
    ANSWER: a (p. 483)

35. The Spanish Civil War ended with the victory of
  a. King Alfonso XIII and General Miguel Primo de Rivera.
  b. an antifascist coalition, aided by Soviet troops and supplies.
  c. the National Front, aided by Italian and German arms and money.
  d. General Francisco Franco, who established a conservative, authoritarian, and anti-democratic regime with the strong backing of the reactionary Spanish Catholic Church.
    ANSWER: d (p. 481)

36. Lenin's New Economic Policy in the early 1920s
  a. put Russia on the path of rapid industrialization at the expense of the peasantry.
  b. was a modified form of the capitalist system.
  c. forced Communism to move forward as both industry and agriculture were nationalized.
  d. failed to reverse the patterns of famine and industrial collapse that began in 1921.
    ANSWER: b (p. 481)

37. Joseph Stalin's emergence as leader of the Communist party was aided by
  a. Lenin's recommendation that he become sole leader.
  b. his alliance with Trotsky and the Right in the Politburo.
  c. his position as general secretary of the Bolshevik party.
  d. strong support of the left in the Politburo, which favored the spread of Communism abroad.
    ANSWER: c (p. 481)

38. The Stalinist era in the 1930's witnessed
  a. the decline of industrialization in favor of the collectivization of agriculture.
  b. real wages and social conditions for the industrial labor force improve dramatically.
  c. millions of ordinary citizens arrested and sent into force labor camps.
  d. an abundance of permissive social legislation.
    ANSWER: c (p. 481)

39. The collectivization of agriculture under Stalin was characterized by
   a. widespread famine due to peasant hoarding and slaughter of livestock.
   b. the cooperation of kulaks.
   c. the destruction of the collective farms.
   d. the immediate financial benefits for most of the peasants.
   ANSWER: a (p. 481)

40. The new forms of mass communication and leisure created between the wars
   a. saw cinema become an increasingly popular form of entertainment.
   b. were used by Fascist nations for propaganda purposes.
   c. witnessed radio production and broadcasting companies increase dramatically.
   d. all the above
   ANSWER: d (pp.484-485)

41. *Kfraft durch Freude* was
   a. a Spanish anti-Republican military formation.
   b. a cultural club begun in England during the inter-war years.
   c. a Nazi program to coordinate the free time of the working class.
   d. a French radical political party advocating anarchy as the only solution to the corrupt government practices of the era.
   ANSWER: c (p. 484)

42. "Strength through Joy"
   a. was one of the most effective Nazi propaganda films to be made by German actors, producers, and directors corrupted by Hitler's ideology.
   b. was Fascist Italy's most popular national recreation agency.
   c. attempted to monitor and homogenize the leisure time of the German workers, building public support for Nazi policies.
   d. failed miserably in its attempts to draw German workers to vacation package tours.
   ANSWER: c (p. 484)

43. Artistic and intellectual trends in the inter-war years were concerned with
   a. a rejection of the avant-garde.
   b. a sense of disillusionment with Western Civilization provoked by the horrors of World War I.
   c. realistic forms of art, as with the Dadaists.
   d. an acceptance of modern art forms, especially in Germany and Russia.
   ANSWER: b (p. 484)

44. The most famous of the Surrealistic painters was
   a. Arnold Schonberg.
   b. Salvador Dali.
   c. Walter Gropius.
   d. Hans Holbein.
   ANSWER: b (p. 485)

45. The Dada movement in art was known for all of the following except

a. an expressed contempt for Western culture.
b. an effort to put a clear sense of purpose and ambition back into art and life.
c. "anti-art" and the mockery of all known, traditional forms of artistic expression.
d. a celebration of chaos and the absurd often expressed in bizarre performances and collages of unrelated objects.

ANSWER: b (p. 485)

46. Walter Gropius was best known for his

a. "socialist realism" paintings.
b. atonal, experimental music.
c. revolutionary directions in theater.
d. ideas of functionalism and useful in architecture.

ANSWER: d (p. 485)

47. Culture in Nazi Germany centered around

a. the use of modern, abstract forms to reflect Germany's "new order."
b. the functionalism of the Bauhaus school.
c. the Hitler loved, with sentimental and realistic scenes glorifying strong, heroic Aryans.
d. religious scenes influenced by Catholic dogma.

ANSWER: c (p. 486)

48. Not associated with the new literary techniques of the 1920's was

a. the "stream of consciousness."
b. James Joyce.
c. Herman Hesse.
d. Ernest Rutherford.

ANSWER: d (pp. 486-487)

49. The physicist Walter Heisenberg was most noted for

a. proposing that uncertainty was at the bottom of all physical laws.
b. being among the first team to split the atom.
c. resurrecting the scientific predictability of classical physics.
d. the development of the atomic bomb.

ANSWER: a (p. 487)

50. All of the following concepts were central to the psychological theories of Carl Jung except

a. the collective unconscious.
b. the process of individuation.
c. the uncertainty principle.
d. universal archetypes.

ANSWER: c (p. 486)

RELEVANT WORLD-WIDE WEB SITES/RESOURCES

1. Versailles Treaty Online:
http://ac.acusd.edu/History/text/versaillestreaty/vercontents.html
(Complete text of this epoch-making diplomatic document permitting students to study closely its finer points and geo-political implications.)

2. Soviet Archives Online:
http://metalab.unc.edu/expo/soviet.exhibit/entrance.html
(Superb online collection of Soviet internal administrative documents, police files, and diplomatic material, arranged by era from the U.S. Library of Congress. Excellent original documentation on the consolidation of Russian totalitarianism including sections on internal workings of Soviet system, rise of the secret police, repression and terror, and the human cost of collectivization.)

3. Albert Einstein: Image & Impact:
http://www.aip.org/history/einstein
(Site at the American Institute of Physics with extensive information on Einstein, the development of atomic weapons, and modern physics.)

RELEVANT VIDEO RESOURCES

Degenerate Art, PBS Home Video, (60 minutes). (Excellent video Documentary on the infamous 1937 Nazi exhibition of "Entartete Kunst"—allegedly degrading artworks by the German and international avant-garde. Reveals terrible effects of the Nazi regime on German and European artistic expression.)

The Europeans: Between the Wars: The Economic Seeds of World War II, Films for the Humanities and Sciences, (55 minutes). (Available through Wadsworth Publishing.)

The Fatal Attraction of Adolf Hitler, Films for the Humanities and Sciences (55 minutes). (Available through Wadsworth Publishing.)

How Wars End: World War I Armistice, and The Peace Conference, Films for the Humanities and Sciences, (55 minutes). (Available through Wadsworth Publishing.)

Lenin and His Legacy, Films for the Humanities and Sciences, (55 minutes). (Available through Wadsworth Publishing.)

RELEVANT MUSICAL PERFORMANCES

Anton Berg, Wozzeck.

Leos Janacek, Symphonetta.

Anton Webern, chamber music works, especially his string quartets.

Kurt Weill, The Threepenny Opera

SUGGESTED STUDENT ACTIVITIES

1. Have students write an essay validating the statement: "The seeds of World War II were planted in the peace of World War I."

2. Have students do a comparative essay, discussing the similarities and differences in Fascism in Italy and Nazism in Germany.
and Nazism.

3. Have students compare the economic philosophies and practices of Fascist Italy, Nazi Germany, and Communist Russia. Ask them to determine if any were successful. Is so, which one(s) and why?

4. Have students compare the twentieth-century artistic movements (Dadaism, Surrealism) with those of previous centuries (Renaissance, Baroque, etc.). How were they different in theme and application?

CHAPTER 27
THE DEEPENING OF THE EUROPEAN CRISIS: WORLD WAR II

CHAPTER OUTLINE

I. Prelude to War (1933-1939)
- A. The "Diplomatic Revolution," 1933-1936
- B. The Path to War, 1937-1939

II. The Course of World War II
- A. Victory and Stalemate
- B. The War in Asia
- C. The Turning Point of the War, 1942-1943
- D. The Last Years of the War

III. The Nazi New Order
- A. The Nazi Empire
- B. The Holocaust

IV. The Home Front
- A. The Mobilization of Peoples: Three Examples
- B. Civilians on the Frontline: The Bombing of Cities

V. Aftermath: The Emergence of the Cold War
- A. The Conferences at Teheran, Yalta, and Potsdam

VI. Conclusion

CHAPTER SUMMARY

Of the causes of World War II, Adolph Hitler's ambitions loom large, including his beliefs in Aryan racial supremacy and the need for Germany to have living space in the east (*Lebensraum*). Posing as a man of peace, Hitler claimed that the Treaty of Versailles was unfair; and when he stated that Germany would rearm and when German troops occupied the demilitarized Rhineland, there was little reaction by Britain and France. Criticized for invading Ethiopia, Mussolini joined Hitler in forming the Rome-Berlin Axis.

Hitler annexed Austria in March 1938. Czechoslovakia's Sudentenland, home of three million ethnic Germans, was next. In late 1938, Britain and France agreed to Hitler's demands, believing it meant "peace in our times," but Hitler soon seized the rest of Czechoslovakia. Western distrust of the Soviets played into his hands, and in August 1939 Germany signed a non-aggression pact with the Soviet Union, and Germany launched the *Blitzkrieg* against Poland on September 1, 1939. In April 1940, the Nazis successfully attacked in the west. Under Winston Churchill's leadership, Britain survived Germany's air assault in the Battle of Britain. Hitler invaded Russia in June 1941, but Soviet resistance and winter conditions led to stalemate. Imperial ambitions and economic concerns propelled Japan to attack the United States at Pearl Harbor on December 7, 1941. America fought back, forming the Grand Alliance with Britain and the Soviet Union. The Japanese advance was ended at the naval battles of the Coral Sea and Midway in 1942. By mid-1943 the Axis was driven out of North Africa, German submarine attacks were thwarted in the Atlantic, and a German army was defeated at Stalingrad. In June 1944, Rome fell to the Allies and Normandy was invaded. The Soviets linked up with the western Allies in April 1945, and on April 30, 1945, Hitler committed suicide. Atomic bombs were dropped on Hiroshima and Nagasaki in August. The war had ended, but at the cost of 50 million dead.

In the Nazi empire racial assumptions were paramount, with Nordics deemed superior, Latins less so, and Slavs were to be replaced by Aryan Germans. Millions of slave laborers fueled the Nazi war machine. Resistance movements had only mixed results. Anti-Semitism was central to Nazism. In the 1930s, Jewish emigration was encouraged, but ultimately the Final Solution was annihilation, first at the hands of German troops, and then in extermination camps where millions died in gas chambers. Up to six million Jews died in the Holocaust, along with Gypsies, homosexuals, and others.

In Britain, 55 percent of the population engaged in war work, and women played a major role in all the combatant nations. The mainland of the United States was never endangered, and because of its industrial wealth, the United States became the chief arsenal for the Allies. War brought population movements, social problems of shifting morals, and racial conflict, and 110,000 Japanese-Americans were placed in relocation camps. Both sides bombed civilian populations; the Allied bombing of Dresden in February 1945 killed 100,000 persons, and. Japanese cities suffered from widespread bombing even before the use of the atomic bomb.

By the Yalta conference of February 1945, the Soviet Union controlled most of Eastern Europe. Germany was to be divided into zones of occupation. However, Stalin soon showed he would not allow free elections which might be anti-Soviet. The West feared Soviet expansion, the Soviets believed their actions were necessary to their future security. An ideological struggle had emerged, pitting totalitarian communism against democratic capitalism. In 1946, Churchill gave a label to the new Cold War reality: Europe was divided by "an iron curtain."

LECTURE AND DISCUSSION TOPICS

1. Discuss Hitler's "successes" between 1933 and 1939, and the possible explanations for those successes.

2. Compare and contrast the military strategies and technologies of World War I and World War II.

3. Compare and contrast the roles of the United States and the Soviet Union which resulted in the defeat of Nazi Germany and Imperial Japan.

4. Locate the importance and significance of World War II in the context of the "Twentieth-Century Crisis of Western Civilization."

5. Assess Hitler's war on the innocents, or the Holocaust, and compare it with other twentieth-century holocausts or genocides.

6. Discuss the possible complicity of "ordinary Germans" in all phases of the Holocaust, comparing the German response to the populations of other genocidal regimes.

7. Compare and contrast the home fronts of World War I and World War II, considering in particular the use of air power against civilian populations.

8. Assess the War in the Pacific and its relationship to the war against fascism in the European theater.

9. Discuss the personalities involved as well as the significance of the several war-time conferences.

10. Consider the proposition that the defeat of the Axis powers guaranteed a Cold War.

MAP EXERCISES

1. Changes in Central Europe. MAP 27.1. What difficulties did the expansion of Germany and Italy in Central Europe pose to possible British and French aid to the victims? Which areas, if any, were the most accessible to western assistance? Trace Germany's territorial seizures chronologically and give the Nazi justification for each. (page 493)

2. World War II in Europe and North Africa. MAP 27.2. Geographically, what were Germany's greatest weaknesses? Which were the neutral states in Europe, and what role did they play in the war, if any? Given their geographical position, was complete neutrality possible? (page 495)

3. World War II in Asia and the Pacific. MAP 27.3. Geographically, what were Japan's strengths and what were its weakness in waging war in Asia and the Pacific? Was Japan's invasion of China a mistake? Why or why not? What role did the Pacific islands play in America's ultimate victory over Japan/? (page 496)

4. The Holocaust. MAP 27.4. From what states did most of the Holocaust victims come from? Did most come from Germany? What is the explanation? Where were most of the extermination camps located? Is there a correlation between the victims' nations and the location of the camps? (page 502)

5. Territorial Changes after World War II. MAP 27.5. Who gained the most territory as the result of World War II? Which German territories were lost and which states gained those lands? What were the explanations or justifications for those gains? Given the accomplishments of the Soviet armies, was a pro-Soviet Eastern Europe inevitable? Why and or why not? (page 506)

DISCUSSION QUESTIONS FOR THE PRIMARY SOURCES (BOXED DOCUMENTS)

1. "The Munich Conference": Compare the responses of Churchill and Chamberlain to the Munich Conference appeasement agreement. What arguments and claims did each make? Why did they disagree so much? Is Chamberlain to be "blamed" for the aftermath of Munich? Why or why not? (page 491)

2. "A German Soldier at Stalingrad": What does this excerpt tell you about the attitude of German soldiers prior to the battle of Stalingrad and the degree to which ordinary soldiers understood the realities of modern urban warfare. Why do you think the author here is so surprised at determined and effective Russian resistance? (page 497)

3. "The Holocaust: The Camp Commandant and the Camp Victims": What death camp procedures in mass murder did the Germans create for the extermination of people who were Jewish? Why do you think that the Germans were so meticulous in these procedures? What do you think induced German killers to produce so many documents about the construction and conduct of the Holocaust later so valuable in the many war crimes trials of these criminals? (page 501)

4. "The Bombing of Civilians": What common elements do you find in these different descriptions of bombing raids? What effect did aerial bombing of cities and civilians have on the nature of modern warfare? Were the bombings justified militarily? Why or why not? Politically? Morally? (page 504)

STUDENT RESEARCH AND PROJECT TOPICS

1. Discuss the major steps taken by Hitler from 1933 to 1939 that ultimately led to war. Could Hitler have been prevented from plunging Europe into war? When and how?

2. How do you account for the early successes of the Germans from 1939 to 1941? To what degree did Blitzkrieg play a role in these successes?

3. When and why did the initiative in World War II pass out of Germany's hands?

4. Compare in your text the maps of the fighting fronts in World War I and World War II and discuss what this comparison reveals about the nature of fighting in the two wars. How do you explain the differences you find?

5. Why did Germany lose the war? Was it a foregone conclusion?

6. How did the Nazis attempt to establish a new Order in Europe after their military victories? What were the results of their efforts?

7. Discuss the "Final Solution." What was it? Who was responsible for it? How did it work? How committed was the entire German war machine to this murderous campaign? If so many ordinary Germans took part in this crime, can its perpetration merely be attributed only to the evil (and aberrant) mind of Hitler?

8. Compare the home fronts of Great Britain, the Soviet Union, the United States, and Germany. What differences and similarities do you find? How did the organization of each home front affect the outcome of the war?

9. How did the attempt to arrive at a peace settlement after World War II lead to the beginning of the new conflict known as the Cold War?

10. What, in essence, was the Cold War?

IDENTIFICATIONS

1. Aryans
2."diplomatic revolution"
3. Rhineland
4. Rome-Berlin Axis
5. appeasement
6. Neville Chamberlain
7. Sudentenland
8. Munich Conference
9. “peace in our time”
10. 1939 non-aggression pact
11. *Blitzkrieg*
12. Dunkirk
13. Winston Churchill

14. Battle of Britain
15. Pearl Harbor
16. Great East Asia Co-Prosperity Sphere
17. Grand Alliance
18. El Alamein
19. Stalingrad
20. Normandy
21. Battle of Kursk
22. New Order
23. the Holocaust
24. Madagascar Plan
25. Final Solution
26. *Einsatzgruppen*
27. Auschwitz
28. gas chambers
29. Great Patriotic War
30. "Night Witches"
31. Albert Speer
32. *Luftwaffe*
33. the Blitz
34. Arthur Harris
35. Dresden
36. Allied Strategic Bombing Survey
37. Hiroshima and Nagasaki
38. Big Three
39. Yalta and Potsdam
40. "an iron curtain"

MULTIPLE CHOICE QUESTIONS

1. World War II was largely made possible by
   a. Great Britain's aggressive plans on Europe.
   b. the failure of Britain and France to strongly oppose flagrant German violations of the Versailles treaty.
   c. Soviet expansionism and interference in western Europe's affairs.
   d. the League of Nations.
   ANSWER: b (pages 490-491)

2. The "diplomatic revolution" refers to the
   a. formation of the Grand Alliance against Fascism.
   b. Nazi-Soviet pact of 1939.
   c. scrapping of the Versailles Treaty and the restoration of Germany to a world power.
   d. onset of the Cold War.
   ANSWER: c (p. 490)

3. For Hitler to achieve his goals, he thought
   a. he must follow a strict time schedule and order of events.
   b. he must gain the confidence of the United States.
   c. careful consideration must be given to the desires of the nationalists.
   d. his basic plan of racial supremacy and empire over "inferior" peoples was most critical.
      ANSWER: d (p. 490)

4. Hitler settled on acquiring German "living space" in the east in Russian territory in part because of his racist belief that
   a. the Slavs were an "inferior" people now governed by impotent Jews among the Bolsheviks and worthy of enslavement.
   b. the weakened Aryan "race" could only be rejuvenated and made better through war against the ancient enemies of the Fatherland.
   c. the Anglo-Saxons were now a decadent race and would never come to the aid of Eastern Europeans.
   d. Germany must rapidly conquer all of Europe before the great American race dominated the globe.
      ANSWER: a (p. 490)

5. The British policy of appeasement was based on
   a. Britain's cowardly nature in world politics.
   b. a general admiration of the Germans and their accomplishments.
   c. a hatred and distrust of France.
   d. a belief that it would maintain peace and stability in Europe, avoiding another catastrophic conflict like World War I.
      ANSWER: d (p. 491)

6. Hitler's first act of aggression took place in 1936 when the Germans occupied what area?
   a. Austria
   b. Sudetenland
   c. Bavaria
   d. the Rhineland
      ANSWER: d (p. 490)

7. By 1938, Neville Chamberlain, the British prime minister, was
   a. a strong advocate of appeasement.
   b. calling for Britain to declare war on Germany.
   c. working with Hitler to divide Europe into spheres of influence.
   d. busy denouncing all changes in the status of central Europe.
      ANSWER: a (p. 491)

8. The Munich Conference was
   a. applauded by Winston Churchill as a "wise and noble agreement."
   b. formulated with the idea that if Germany wanted the Sudentenland war with the western powers was inevitable.
   c. criticized by Winston Churchill as a tragic outcome of appeasement.
   d. a severe setback for Hitler.
      ANSWER: c (p. 491)

9. Following the Munich Conference, Hitler soon
   a. had Germany relinquish its claims to Czechoslovakia.
   b. systematically took the rest of Czechoslovakia.
   c. attacked France.
   d. launched an attach on the Soviet Union.
      ANSWER: b (p. 491)

10. Hitler's first dramatic acts as head of the German state was/were
   a. a failed attack on Hungary and obedience to sanctions imposed by the League.
   b. unilateral repudiation of the Treaty of Versailles.
   c. legal action before the World Court in the Hague to revoke key provisions of the Versailles Treaty and bribery of the judges involved.
   d. fanatical decrees outlawing the marriage of Jews and the internment of Jewish orphans in death camps.
      ANSWER: b (p. 490)

11. Hitler took Poland in 1939
   a. despite interference by the Soviet Union.
   b. in a long protracted struggle that cost Germany dearly.
   c. upon Poland's request for a restructured government.
   d. using *Blitzkrieg* or "lightening war" tactics and with active support from Joseph Stalin.
      ANSWER: d (p. 492)

12. Immediately following the fall of Poland
   a. France and Britain declared war and started an offensive against Germany.
   b. France and Britain decided to continue to appease Hitler.
   c. France and Britain declared war, but remained relatively inactive militarily.
   d. Germany turned on its Russian allies.
      ANSWER: c (p. 492)

13. The successful British retreat from the European continent in 1940 was from
   a. the Rhineland.
   b. Dunkirk.
   c. Dover.
   d. Normandy.
      ANSWER: b (p. 493)

14. Following the Allied evacuation at Dunkirk, France
   a. soon surrendered and the Vichy government was set up as a puppet state collaborating in German war crimes.
   b. went on the offensive and bogged Germany down in Normandy.
   c. benefited when Italian forces assisted Allied defenses, giving France time to regroup.
   d. benefited when the United States declared war on Germany.
      ANSWER: a (p. 493)

15. Hitler's plan for defeating Britain relied on
   a. the support of Soviet troops in a massive amphibious invasion.
   b. Germany's *Luftwaffe* gaining control of the skies.
   c. V-2 rockets to destroy British industrial power.
   d. a giant tunnel under the English channel.
      ANSWER: b (pp. 493-494)

16. The war in North Africa was best characterized by
   a. the overwhelming superiority of the Italian troops.
   b. Hitler's lack of the total commitment needed to secure the region.
   c. Hitler's easy lines of supply that allowed the war to drag on.
   d. the intense fighting due to the strategic importance of its rubber supplies.
      ANSWER: b (p. 494)

17. Serious conflict in Asia contributing to the outbreak of World War Two in the Pacific began with Japan's 1937 attack on
   a. the Philippines.
   b. Korea.
   c. China.
   d. Malaysia.
      ANSWER: c (p. 496)

18. Among the motives for Japan's attack on the United States was
   a. America's refusal to sign a treaty of alliance with Japan against Communist China.
   b. the American embargo of oil and iron.
   c. a feeling of inferiority regarding American cultural superiority.
   d. a belief that a *kamikaze* ("divine wind") would quickly blow away the American military.
      ANSWER: b (p. 496)

19. The Grand Alliance included all of the following countries <u>except</u>
   a. Britain.
   b. the Soviet Union.
   c. France.
   d. the United States.
      ANSWER: c (p. 495)

20. After the attack on Pearl Harbor, the main priority for the United States was
   a. defeating Japan as quickly as possible.
   b. recovering the Hawaiian Islands.
   c. defeating Germany first and then turning its great naval war machine against Japan.
   d. to remain neutral, while buying time to build up industrial and military supplies.
      ANSWER: c (p. 495)

21. It can be argued that this key decision early in the war by Adolf Hitler made the defeat of Germany inevitable:
   a. abandoning the Battle of Britain
   b. dividing France into a zone of German occupation and a French national puppet government at Vichy
   c. immediately declaring war on the United States after the Japanese sneak-attack on Pearl Harbor
   d. snubbing British proposals for an armistice in 1941
      ANSWER: c (p. 494)

22. The turning point of the North African campaign came
   a. at El Alamein where the British stopped Rommel in the summer of 1942.
   b. when South African troops crossed the Sahara and overwhelmed Rommel.
   c. with the revolt of the Vichy French in North Africa.
   d. when the Italians joined the Allied cause in 1942.
      ANSWER: a (p. 496)

23. The decisive Battle of Stalingrad was best characterized by

a. the Russians fighting to the last man until an exhausted German army took the city.

b. gradual breakdown in German morale until the Germans were surrounded and forced to surrender by a resurgent Red Army.

c. the lack of conviction on the part of the Russians to defend their city.

d. the decisive role that the Soviet air force played in halting the German advance.

ANSWER: b (pp. 496-497)

24. The naval battle in the Pacific that is considered the turning point of the war and established U.S. naval supremacy in the area was

a. Guadalcanal.

b. Coral Sea.

c. Siam.

d. Midway.

ANSWER: d (p. 497)

25. In order to open up a "second front" in western Europe, the Allies

a. quickly advanced through Italy into France in 1943.

b. invaded Normandy in June 1944, successfully carrying out the greatest naval invasion in history.

c. landed on the Iberian peninsula and advanced through southern France.

d. lured German forces south to Italy and invaded the north German coast.

ANSWER: b (p. 498)

26. In pursuing the war against the Axis powers, the Grand Alliance demanded of its opponents

a. unconditional surrender.

b. the maintenance of diplomatic contacts for the earliest arrangement of an armistice.

c. the exchange of promises regarding post-war spheres of influence around the globe.

d. careful accounting of all sums spent on armaments so that war reparations from the guilty parties could be more accurately determined once the war was over.

ANSWER: a (pp. 495-496)

27. The final human death toll of world War II may have numbered as high as

a. 3.5 million.

b. 5 million.

c. 23.5 million.

d. 50 million.

ANSWER: d (p. 498)

28. The Nazi Empire was

a. strictly organized into efficient states that paid tribute to Germany.

b. never much larger than the size of present-day Germany and Austria.

c. never organized systematically or governed efficiently despite German claims to the contrary.

d. for the most part composed of independent states that collaborated with Hitler.

ANSWER: c (pp. 498-499)

29. The Nazi rule of Europe was most ruthless in
- a. eastern Europe because the Slavs were considered racially inferior.
- b. France due to the long rivalry between France and Germany.
- c. Norway, Denmark, and the Netherlands due to their close proximity to Germany.
- d. Italy because the Italians were generally considered to be disloyal.

ANSWER: a (p. 499)

30. Demonstrating again that ever-higher military technology was crucial to the conduct and outcome of World War Two, the greatest tank battle of all time was fought in this conflict at
- a. Stalingrad.
- b. Moscow.
- c. Leningrad.
- d. Kursk.

ANSWER: d (p. 498)

31. Germany's policy of forced labor of conquered people
- a. helped cause more resistance to the Nazis.
- b. crushed the morale of peoples so they could not revolt.
- c. gave Germany a critical advantage in industrial production.
- d. was really quite exaggerated and was no more brutal than Allied practices.

ANSWER: a (p. 499)

32. The head of the SS and the person responsible for German resettlement in the east was
- a. Joseph Goering.
- b. Heinrich Himmler.
- c. Reinhard Heydrich.
- d. Albert Speer.

ANSWER: b (p. 499)

33. Which of the officers in the feared German SS was given administrative responsibility for the "Final Solution"?
- a. Himmler
- b. Goering
- c. Bormann
- d. Heydrich

ANSWER: d (pp. 499-500)

34. Hitler's "Final Solution" to the Jewish problem called for
- a. the extermination of all European Jews.
- b. the forced deportation of the Jews to Madagascar.
- c. the resettlement of Jews in ghettos, isolated from other Europeans.
- d. breeding "Jewish genes" out of the Jewish population itself.

ANSWER: a (p. 499)

35. In the Holocaust, the Germans killed six million or more people who were Jewish as well as other victims deemed "undesirable." To murder so many innocent civilians in so short a time, the Germans

a, used specially trained naval units to round up "undesirables" and execute them by machine gun fire.

b. sent opponents to prison and then starved them to death.

c. created vast death camps where victims, including young children, women, and the elderly, were systematically murdered in gas chambers and their bodies burned in huge ovens.

d. circulated the plague and other diseases in Europe to kill as many as possible.

ANSWER: c (p. 500)

36. Besides the Jews, another group singled out by the Nazis for extermination were the

a. Poles.

b. Ukrainians.

c. Gypsies.

d. Swedes.

ANSWER: c (p. 501)

37. The Nazi *Einsatzgruppen* were

a. corrupt German journalists who worked to fill European newspapers with pro-Nazi propaganda.

b. special commando units sent to infiltrate Britain.

c. special strike forces used in eastern Europe that proceeded to round up and kill by shooting Jewish men, women, and children.

d. highly mobile tank forces used to fight against Russian tank armies.

ANSWER: c (p. 500)

38. The only country to use women as combatants in World War II was

a. Germany.

b. the Soviet Union.

c. Japan.

d. Britain.

ANSWER: b (p. 502)

39. The "Great Patriotic War" was

a. the Cold War of the United States vs. the Soviet Union.

b. Nazi Germany's reoccupation of the Sudentenland.

c. Soviet Russia's battle against Nazi Germany.

d. the French resistance to the Nazi occupation.

ANSWER: c (p. 501)

40. The mobilization of the United States for war included all of the following <u>except</u>

a. full employment by December 1941.

b. substantial internal migration of the population.

c. the racially motivated internment of Japanese-Americans in guarded camps.

d. a breakdown in social mores.

ANSWER: a (pp. 502-503)

41. In the Soviet Union, the pressures of mobilization for total war produced
   a. a nearly complete breakdown in the supply of munitions.
   b. the "super-centralization" of government authority and planning in the hands of Stalin and the Communist bureaucracy.
   c. essential decentralization of planning by region so that local resources could be more efficiently used.
   d. no significant internal migration of workers or peasants.
      ANSWER: b (p. 501)

42. When Germany went to war in 1939
   a. the populace was euphoric as in 1914.
   b. the populace feared that it would spell disaster for Germany.
   c. consumer goods were cut in favor of war materials.
   d. war production was tripled.
      ANSWER: b (p. 503)

43. Civilian bombing was done mainly
   a. to reduce the number of people available to participate in war.
   b. to exact revenge on the people.
   c. to break the will of a people to resist.
   d. by the Germans and was never an Allied strategy.
      ANSWER: c (p. 504)

44. The first atomic bombs were dropped on the Japanese cities of
   a. Osaka and Kyoto.
   b. Kyoto and Tokyo.
   c. Hiroshima and Nagasaki.
   d. Osaka and Kobe.
      ANSWER: c (p. 504)

45. In the Allied bombing strategy, Americans participated
   a. primarily in the nighttime saturation bombing of civilian populations.
   b. only when British bomber wings needed reinforcements.
   c. primarily in daytime, precision bombing of German strategic targets.
   d. primarily as fighter pilots assigned to guard British bomber wings.
      ANSWER: c (p. 504)

46. Allied bombing raids on German civilians
   a. contrary to expectations, produced stubborn resistance from the German people.
   b. destroyed the average German's will to fight.
   c. were only done to retaliate for German bombing.
   d. occurred mostly by accident when bombing strategic targets.
      ANSWER: a (p. 504)

47. The official reason for dropping atomic bombs on Japan was
   a. to punish Japan for Pearl Harbor.
   b. to test out the new weapon to see how powerful it was.
   c. a shortage of conventional explosive materials in the United States.
   d. to save a million American casualties it was calculated that a U.S.-led invasion of Japan would cost.
      ANSWER: d (p. 504)

48. A chief concern of the Allies at the Tehran, Yalta, and Potsdam Conferences was
   a. how to end the war on favorable terms should any one of them be defeated.
   b. determining spheres of influence for the individual allied powers in post-war Europe.
   c. how to rebuild the German economy after the war so as to extract maximum war reparations.
   d. whether China and other lesser allies deserved any territorial rewards in any post-war settlement.
   ANSWER: b (p. 505)

49. Following the Second World War, Germany was
   a. divided into two zones of occupation: east and west.
   b. separated into twenty small security districts policed by the United Nations.
   c. divided into four zones of occupation under U.S., British, French, and Russian administration.
   d. dismembered and replaced by three new smaller states determined by the ethnicity of their inhabitants.
   ANSWER: c (p. 505)

50. The chief argument between Truman and Stalin at Potsdam in July of 1945 was over
   a. free elections in eastern Europe.
   b. the numbers of tanks Americans and Russians could keep in Europe.
   c. what to do with German prisoners of war.
   d. whether or not the Soviet Union would be in the United Nations.
   ANSWER: a (p. 507)

RELEVANT WORLD-WIDE WEB SITES/RESOURCES

Please note: the sites listed below are among the better locations on the Web for information on World War II. However, instructors should be especially vigilant in the selection and use of web sites on this topic for two reasons: 1) many web sites on the topic are maintained by war "buffs" of dubious "expertise" on their own home pages which are notoriously fluid, frequently going off line or being taken down with no follow up; and 2) numerous sites on this topic are maintained by ultra-rightist and neo-fascist organizations in the U.S. and abroad with the express purpose of spreading anti-Semitic bile, denials of the Holocaust, and crude racist propaganda. Undergraduates entering into this topic on the web should be apprized of these realities.

1. Cybrary of the Holocaust:
http://www.remember.org/
(Excellent site with numerous links to other pertinent online collections.)

2. World War Two: Online Archives (at Hanover College):
http://history.hanover.edu/20th/wwii.htm
(Broad selection of relevant documents, images, and maps with links to other germane web resources.)

3. U.S. Air Force Museum, Air War in Europe:
http://www.wpafb.af.mil/museum/tours/eto.htm
(A fine site on the scientific, aeronautical, and engineering developments spurred by the European air war. Excellent images of aircraft and the material culture of war.)

4. U.S. Memorial Holocaust Museum, Washington, D.C.:
http://www.ushmm.org/
(An excellent and sobering museum web site with virtual tours of the collections, scholarly information, and links to other Holocaust sites in the U.S. and abroad. Highly recommended.)

5. The Valour and the Horror: Canada at War:
http://www.valourandhorror.com/home.htm
(A superb Canadian site with many highly relevant subsections treating virtually every aspect of this global conflict. Subsections on subjects like the Home Front, the War at Sea, etc. can be accessed independently.)

6. The Winston Churchill Home Page:
http://www.winstonchurchill.org/index.html
(A fine site with many of the British war leader's finest and most rousing speeches online—see the subsection "Immortal Words" at this site for documentation on Churchill's public speaking before, during, and after the war. The famous "Iron Curtain" address is included. Site also includes excellent links and history material of all kinds relevant to the analysis of democratic government and leadership in wartime.)

RELEVANT VIDEO RESOURCES

Children of the Holocaust, Films for the Humanities and Sciences, (55 minutes). (Available through Wadsworth Publishing.)

Russia's War: Blood Upon the Snow, PBS Home Video, 10 programs on 5 cassettes, (55 minutes each). (Fine production bringing home the enormous human cost of Nazi-Soviet battles on the Eastern Front. Series shows clearly how wartime events powerfully affected post-war Soviet diplomacy and the origins of the Cold War.)

The Trial of Adolf Eichmann, PBS Home Video, (120 minutes). (Excellent production using original video footage, the testimony of trial participants, and dramatic re-enactments of the courtroom transcripts to convey the prosecution and conviction of one of the most heinous Nazi servants.)

The World at War, PBS Home Video, 26 programs on 26 cassettes, (50 minutes each). (Perhaps the finest and most comprehensive visual chronicle of the Second World War. Programs cover battles, tactics, alliances, and wartime diplomacy of all powers on all fronts. Highly effective use of authentic newsreels, still images of the era, and stunning maps.)

SUGGESTED STUDENT ACTIVITIES

1. Both Hitler and Churchill were excellent public speakers in their own ways. Have students write a paper comparing and contrasting their oratorical styles using their speeches as primary sources.

2. Have students do a short biographical essay on a great general of World War II, such as Patton, Rommel, Montgomery, Eisenhower, or Marshall.

3. Have students do research to determine the advantages and disadvantages of both sides in World War II.

4. Have students do an essay on the various ways that countries dealt with the war on the home front; for example, victory gardens, rationing, scrap metal drives, war bond drives, etc.

5. Have students report on D-Day – its strategic role, the careful planning (and what went awry), the military consequences of the invasion, and the impact on the lives of people who participated as combatants and as civilians.

6. Have students research the Free French Army and the French Resistance. Compare and contrast the tactics of these two movements with those of the armies of the Axis and Allied powers. Argue for or against the position that the FFA and the French Resistance were significant in changing the outcome of the European war.

7. Much recent controversy has been generated over the role of ordinary Germans in the conduct of the Holocaust, especially by Christopher Browning's *Ordinary Men* and Daniel Goldhagen's controversial *Hitler's Willing Executioners*. Have students read some or all of these texts along with scholarly and popular critiques of these works and then ask them to evaluate in a paper the accuracy and persuasive power of the arguments made regarding the capacity of many ordinary Germans to indulge in atrocities for years.

CHAPTER 28
COLD WAR AND A NEW WESTERN WORLD, 1945-1970

CHAPTER OUTLINE

I. Development of the Cold War
- A. Confrontation of the Superpowers
- B. New Sources of Contention
- C. The Cuban Missile Crisis and the Move toward Detente

II. The End of European Colonies
- A. Africa: The Struggle for Independence
- B. Conflict in The Middle East
- C. Asia: Nationalism and Communism
    1. China under Communism

III. Recovery and Renewal in Europe
- A. The Soviet Union: From Stalin to Khrushchev
- B. Eastern Europe: Behind the Iron Curtain
- C. Western Europe: The Revival of Democracy and the Economy
    1. France: The Domination of De Gaulle
    2. West Germany: A New Nation?
    3. Great Britain: The Welfare State
- D. Western Europe: The Move toward Unity

IV. The United States and Canada: A New Era
- A. American Politics and Society in the 1950s
- B. An Age of Upheaval: America in the 1960s
- C. The Development of Canada

V. The Emergence of a New Society
- A. The Structure of European Society
- B. Patterns New and Old: Women in the Postwar Western World
    1. The Feminist Movement: The Quest for Liberation
- C. The Permissive Society
- D. Education and Student Revolt

VI. Conclusion

CHAPTER SUMMARY

The Cold War began in the aftermath of World War II. The United States and the Soviet Union had different philosophies and conflicting ambitions and fears. The West saw the pro-Soviet regimes in Eastern Europe as the result of Soviet aggression; the Soviets said they were a defensive buffer. The Truman Doctrine promised to aid nations threatened by communism, and the Marshall Plan, which provided $13 billion to rebuild Europe, was rejected by the Soviets. Germany and Berlin were divided into zones. When the Americans, British, and French unified their zones, the Soviets blocked access to Berlin, leading to a year-long Berlin Air Lift. A western German Federal Republic and an eastern German Democratic Republic were established.

In 1949, the North Atlantic Treaty Organization (NATO) was created as a defensive alliance against Soviet aggression, one of a series of military alliances. North Korea invaded South Korea in 1950, and the West claimed it was instigated by the Soviets. The Berlin Wall was built in 1961, a major Cold War symbol. The 1962 Cuban Missile Crisis almost led to nuclear holocaust until the Soviets backed down. In Vietnam, the United States feared a communist victory would result in the fall of all of Asia, like a row of dominoes. The communists achieved victory in 1975, but the dominos did not fall. Tension between the Soviet Union and Communist China improved Chinese and American relations, and detente occurred between the Soviets and America.

By the end of the 1960s, most of Africa had achieved independence. In the Middle East, Israel was founded in 1948 amidst war with the Arab states; the 1967 Six Day War brought the Palestinian West Bank under Israeli control. The Philippines became independent, and British India, with its Hindu majority and Muslim minority, was partitioned into Pakistan and India, but at the cost of a million dead. In China, Mao Zedong's Communists forced Chiang Kai-Shek's Nationalists to Taiwan. Mao's Great Leap Forward failed in its attempt to surpass the West industrially, and in 1966, his Great Proletarian Cultural Revolution sought to eliminate all vestiges of the past, often through violence. Soviet emphasis on heavy industry left little for consumers, and when their satellite states pursued independent paths the Soviets cracked down.

The Western European economy boomed. Charles de Gaulle's Fifth Republic saw France leave NATO and develop an atomic bomb. The Federal Republic of Germany experienced an "economic miracle," as did Italy in spite of its many coalition governments. Britain's Labour Party created a welfare state, but unrealistic union demands and a lack of business investment slowed the economy. European integration began with the 1951 European Coal and Steel Community, the 1957 establishment of the European Atomic Energy Community and the European Economic Community (EEC), or Common Market. The New Deal continued to guide the United States domestic policy, the economy boomed, but Cold War fears led to a "Red Scare." The 1960s was a time of upheaval, with the civil rights movement, race riots, and the Vietnam anti-war movement. Canadian events often mirrored those in the United States.

A new society, with its own challenges, resulted from economic growth and new technologies. White-collar workers increased, and installment plan buying fueled a consumer society. The welfare state provided pensions and health care. Birth control led to smaller families, and more women joined the work force. A significant feminist or women's liberation movement emerged. Greater sexual freedom and recreational drug use were part of the new "permissive society." Complaints about authoritarian administrators and irrelevant curricula compounded by opposition to the Vietnam War led to numerous student revolts.

LECTURE AND DISCUSSION TOPICS

1. Survey the causes of the Cold War as interpreted by historians.

2. Discuss the major events of the Cold War and their significance in the period 1945-1970.

3. Attempt to recreate the climate of fear and concern which existed in the general populations of the United States and elsewhere during the 1950s when, like the sword of Damocles, nuclear weapons seemed poised to annihilate civilization and even life itself.

4. Explore the decade of the 1960s in the context of the Cold War as well as various domestic issues in the United States and Western Europe.

5. Survey "the winds of change" which blew away the western empires in the two decades after the end of World War II.

6. Analyze the development of nuclear weapons and the doctrine of Mutual Assured Destruction (MAD) as an effective balance of power mechanism during the Cold War years.

7. Discuss China under Mao Zedong and the significance of Communist China upon the events of the Cold War, including its impact on Soviet and United States policies.

8. Compare and contrast the political and economic systems of Soviet Russia and the People's Republic of China.

9. Survey the resurgence of Western Europe and the stagnation of Eastern Europe during the 1950s and 1960s.

10. Discuss Modernity and its discontents in the post-World War II world, or "Are sex, drugs, and rock and roll good for you?"

MAP EXERCISES

1. Decolonization in Africa. MAP 28.1. During which decade did most of the African states gain independence? Why in that decade? What impact did World War II and what impact did the Cold War have upon the process of African decolonization? (page 516)

2. Decolonization in the Middle East. MAP 28.2. Is there any relationship between the date of independence of the Middle Eastern states and the region's oil reserves? Which nations gained their independence after World War I and which after World War II? Did the Cold War have any significance in the timing of Middle Eastern decolonization? (page 517)

3. Decolonization in Asia. MAP 28.3. What was the relationship of World War II to Asian decolonization and the impact of the Cold War on decolonization? What, if any, was the geographical significance of Korea and Vietnam, the sites of two Cold War wars? (page 518)

DISCUSSION QUESTIONS FOR THE PRIMARY SOURCES (BOXED DOCUMENTS)

1. "The Truman Doctrine": What attitudes or themes about America and Russia does Truman express in this section? What, in essence, is the "Truman Doctrine?" How did Truman justify his request for aid? How might a Russian react to these statements? Does Truman himself bear some responsibility for beginning or aggravating the Cold War? (page 511)

2. "The Cuban Missile Crisis: Khrushchev's Perspective": How does Khrushchev's account differ from America's version? From his perspective, can it be argued that he was correct in his claim? What did each side "lose" and what did each side "win" in the Cuban Missile Crisis? Was the resolution of the crisis a highpoint in Khrushchev's career obvious in 1962 or was it merely a later rationalization? (page 514)

3. "Soviet Repression in Eastern Europe: Hungary, 1956": Based on this selection , what was Soviet policy in the 1950s toward its Eastern European satellite states? Compare this policy to Soviet policy in Eastern Europe in the late 1980s. What accounts for the difference? What impact did this change of policy have on Eastern Europe in the late 1980s? (page 520)

4. "The Times They Are A-Changin'. The Music of Youthful Protest." In your opinion, what is this song about? Who are its protagonists and antagonists? What do the lyrics tell you about the roles of popular culture and popular entertainment in American and Western Civilization after 1945? Are Dylan's lyrics still relevant today or do they seem dated? If so, why? (page 528)

STUDENT RESEARCH AND PROJECT TOPICS

1. What was the Cold War? What were the major turning points in its development through 1970?

2. Discuss how the balance of power moved from Europe to the United States and the Soviet Union between 1945 and 1970.

3. Discuss the events that divided the world into two heavily armed camps capable of obliterating one another with nuclear weapons carried by intercontinental missile systems.

4. Trace the development and history of the U.S. and NATO policy of "containment of Communism" from Truman's presidency through Vietnam.

5. What were the major political developments in the history of the Soviet Union from 1945 to 1970? How did Soviet policies affect the history of Eastern Europe?

6. Compare and contrast Stalin's policies with those of Khrushchev's.

7. What were the major developments in domestic politics in Western Europe and how were they expressed in France, West Germany, and Great Britain? What efforts toward unity were made by Western European states? How did the policies of the United States affect those efforts?

8. Compare and contrast the political, social, and economic histories of Eastern Europe and Western Europe.

9. Discuss the major social changes affecting the status, expectations, and ambitions of women that occurred in Western society form 1945 to 1970.

10. On balance, was the decade of the 1960s "constructive" or "destructive" or both? Discuss with examples.

IDENTIFICATIONS

1. Superpowers
2. Truman Doctrine
3. Marshall Plan
4. "containment"
5. Berlin blockade
6. NATO
7. Korean War
8. CENTO and SEATO
9. Nikita Khrushchev
10. Berlin Wall

11. Bay of Pigs
12. Cuban Missile Crisis
13. Vietnam War
14. domino theory
15. Détente
16. African National Congress
17. Arab League
18. state of Israel
19. PLO
20. Six-Day War
21. Mahatma Gandhi
22. Mao Zedong
23. Great Leap Forward
24. Great Proletarian Cultural Revolution
25. Hungarian uprising
26. "Prague Spring"
27. Charles de Gaulle's Fifth Republic
28. Konrad Adenauer
29. Germany's "economic miracle"
30. welfare state
31. Suez Crisis
32. European Coal and Steel Community
33. EEC/Common Market
34. War on Poverty
35. Martin Luther King
36. "consumer society"
37. women's liberation movement
38. Simone de Beauvoir
39. birth-control pill
40. student protests

MULTIPLE CHOICE QUESTIONS

1. World War Two not only devastated the countries, cities, peoples, and cultures of Europe, but also destroyed

   a. American commitment to globalism in foreign policy.
   b. European supremacy in world affairs.
   c. any commitment of old and new nations around the globe to supranational bodies of diplomacy and conflict resolution.
   d. the capacity of western European nations to forge lasting economic and cultural ties in the post-war world.

   ANSWER: b (page 510)

2. Essentially, the Cold war was
   a. a clash of Soviet and American ideologies over the most secure geopolitical arrangement of peoples and nations in the aftermath of World War II.
   b. a non-shooting war that developed over socioeconomic differences between the two superpowers.
   c. a clash of political objectives in post-war Poland.
   d. differences over how Western Europe nations should be aligned with clear borders after World War II.
   ANSWER: a (p. 510)

3. The first area of conflict in the unfolding of the Cold War was
   a. Scandinavia.
   b. Western Europe.
   c. North Africa.
   d. Eastern Europe.
   ANSWER: d (p. 510)

4. A key factor contributing to the development of the Cold War in Eastern Europe was
   a. the withdrawal of victorious Russian armies from lands conquered during the campaign against Nazism.
   b. raids by American troops pursuing German Nazi war criminals into areas of the former Third Reich under Russian control.
   c. Stalin's desire to establish pro-Soviet governments in the countries of Eastern Europe to serve as a buffer zone against possible western attacks on the Soviet Union.
   d. the domination of Austrian and Italian politics by popular pro-Communist parties.
   ANSWER: c (p. 510)

5. The Truman Doctrine was a consequence of a civil war in
   a. Yugoslavia.
   b. Greece.
   c. Italy.
   d. Czechoslovakia.
   ANSWER: b (p. 510)

6. The Truman Doctrine did all of the following <u>except</u>
   a. condemn the victory of the Communists in the Chinese civil war.
   b. call for $400 million in aid for the defense of Greece and Turkey.
   c. express America's fear of Communist expansion in Europe.
   d. announce the United States' intention to support "free peoples" throughout the world.
   ANSWER: a (p. 510)

7 . The Marshall Plan
   a. intended to rebuild European prosperity and stability.
   b. was viewed by Western Europe as Capitalist imperialism.
   c. excluded Soviet Union and Eastern Europe from participation.
   d. was not considered a success.
   ANSWER: a (p. 510)

8. In 1948, the Soviets blocked western access to
   a. Vienna.
   b. Warsaw.
   c. Berlin.
   d. Munich.
   ANSWER: c (p. 511)

9. The battle between East and West over Germany in the Cold War resulted in
   a. the creation of an independent west German state under Walter Ulbricht.
   b. a successful plan of industrial and economic revitalization.
   c. a successful blockade of West Berlin by the Soviet Union.
   d. the creation of two separate German states by 1949.
   ANSWER: d (p. 511)

10. A critical event causing the development of the Cold War outside of Europe was
   a. the popularity of Communism in the Middle East.
   b. the overthrow of the Japanese government by pro-Soviet radicals in 1951.
   c. the victory in 1949 of Communist forces in the Chinese Civil War.
   d. the defeat of Fidel Castro's pro-Communist forces in Cuba.
   ANSWER: c (p. 511)

11. The Communist response to the formation of NATO was the
   a. Moscow Alliance.
   b. Warsaw Pact.
   c. Eastern European Community.
   d. Stalin Plan.
   ANSWER: b (p. 512)

12. An overall effect of the Korean War on the Cold War was
   a. the Soviet Union's domination over all of Southeast Asia.
   b. the end of American and Soviet involvement in Asian political affairs.
   c. the reinforcement of the American determination to "contain" Soviet power.
   d. a decrease in American defense spending since the capacity of the West to win the conflict outright on the battlefield demonstrated the superiority of modern weapons systems and no need to develop new war machines.
   ANSWER: c (p. 512)

13. The United States played a dominant role in all of the following alliances <u>except</u>
   a. NATO.
   b. COMECON.
   c. CENTO.
   d. SEATO.
   ANSWER: b (p. 512)

14. The Warsaw Pact included all of the following nations <u>except</u>
   a. Poland.
   b. Czechoslovakia.
   c. Yugoslavia.
   d. Hungary.
   ANSWER: c (p. 512)

15. The policy used by the Americans against Communism was called
- a. massive retaliation.
- b. containment.
- c. appeasement.
- d. curtailment.

ANSWER: b (p. 512)

16. The event which immediately preceded and sparked the Cuban Missile Crisis was
- a. the Berlin Wall.
- b. *Sputnik*.
- c. the death of Stalin.
- d. the Bay of Pigs.

ANSWER: d (p. 513)

17. The Cuban Missile Crisis of 1962 concluded with
- a. improved communications between the United States and the Soviet Union essential to prevent nuclear war.
- b. the installation of Soviet missiles in Cuba.
- c. the United States overthrowing Cuba's Soviet-supported government.
- d. John Kennedy backing down to the threats of Nikita Khrushchev.

ANSWER: a (p. 513)

18. An event which disproved the domino theory threat of communism was the
- a. decline and fall of the People's Republic of China.
- b. rupture between the Soviet Union and Communist China.
- c. successful testing of the Cruise Missile by the United States.
- d. fall of the Berlin Wall.

ANSWER: a (p. 513)

19. During the Vietnam War, the Communist/national leader was
- a. Ngo Dihm.
- b. Nguyan Ho.
- c. Ho Chi Minh.
- d. Mekong Delti.

ANSWER: c (p. 517)

20. The Vietnam War
- a. was resolved in 1975 with the Helsinki Agreements.
- b. ended in 1973 with the defeat of North Korea.
- c. showed the limitations of American power, leading to improved Soviet-American relations.
- d. marked the beginning of the total domination of Southeast Asia by the Soviet Union.

ANSWER: c (p. 513)

21. The process of global decolonization was accelerated by
- a. the Japanese humiliation of Western nations by overrunning their empires at the beginning of World War II.
- b. World War II, which had exhausted and destroyed the power of the colonial powers.
- c. political independence movements which had arisen in the West's colonies.
- d. all the above

ANSWER: d (p. 514)

22. The European nation which most willingly gave up its colonial possessions was
   a. France.
   b. Great Britain.
   c. the Netherlands.
   d. Portugal.
      ANSWER: b (p. 515)

23. In South Africa, the transition to independence was complicated by
   a. a Soviet-inspired guerilla movement.
   b. the practice of racial apartheid by the black minority.
   c. apartheid laws enforced by the white minority.
   d. the assassination of Nelson Mandela.
      ANSWER: c (p. 515)

24. The one issue on which the Arab states were united was
   a. the Suez Canal.
   b. equal sharing in oil revenues.
   c. Palestine.
   d. a sympathy for Communism.
      ANSWER: c (p. 515)

25. In Asia, the process of decolonization began with the granting of independence to
   a. the Philippines by the United States.
   b. India and Pakistan by Great Britain.
   c. Taiwan by Nationalist China.
   d. Indonesia by the Dutch.
      ANSWER: a (pp. 516-517)

26. The Great Leap Forward was
   a. Stalin's stated philosophy for his last five-year plan.
   b. the radicalization of the feminist movement.
   c. Mao Zedong's effort to achieve a classless society and the final stage of communism.
   d. the missile race between the United States and the Soviet Union.
      ANSWER: c P. 517)

27. The economic policies of Stalin
   a. emphasized the development of heavy industry and the production of modern weapons and space vehicles.
   b. completely overtaxed a war-damaged industrial plant as production of material goods.
   c. were unrealistic since Russia lacked readily accessible natural resources and fossil fuels.
   d. managed to produce both "guns and butter," that is rearmed the Soviet military while providing cheap and plentiful consumer goods.
      ANSWER: a (p. 518)

28. The economic policies of Nikita Khrushchev in the 1950s and early 1960s
   a. were basically a continuation of Stalinist policies.
   b. were a great success.
   c. failed to significantly improve the Soviet economy and industry.
   d. focused on building the economy on luxury goods.
      ANSWER: c (p. 519)

29. An example of the relaxation of repressive Stalinism during Khrushchev's regime was the publication of

a. his autobiography.
b. Stalin's *Last Will and Testament.*
c. Trotsky's *Dr. Zhivago.*
d. Solzhenitsyn's *A Day in the Life of Ivan Denisovich.*
ANSWER: d (p. 519)

30. Yugoslavia from World War II through the 1970s was characterized by
a. its close alliance with the West in the Cold War.
b. a strict adherence to Stalinist-style Communism.
c. the dominant leadership of Tito, who asserted Yugoslavia's independence from the Soviet Union.
d. its adoption of a Maoist rather than the Stalinist model of communism.
ANSWER: c (p. 519)

31. The independence movement in Hungary in 1956 resulted in
a. the end of Communist rule in Hungary.
b. the leadership of Imry Nagy for the next thirty years.
c. armed Soviet intervention and reassertion of Communist leadership.
d. the creation of a federal republic.
ANSWER: c (p. 520)

32. Due to its strong democratic traditions, the last Eastern European country to fall under Soviet, one-party domination after World War II was
a. Bulgaria.
b. Poland.
c. Hungary.
d. Czechoslovakia.
ANSWER: d (p. 510)

33. The "Prague Spring" in Czechoslovakia in 1968
a. was triggered by the reforms of Alexander Dubcek.
b. led to the presidency of Vaclav Havel in 1970.
c. witnessed Czechoslovakia's successful withdrawal from the Soviet bloc.
d. brought about the resignation of President Gustav Husak.
ANSWER: a (p. 521)

34. In general, Western European states in the post-war world have witnessed
a. the growing electoral success of Communist parties.
b. the hegemonic power of socialist parties.
c. a continual decline in industrial production due to war-damaged factories.
d. successful mixed economies combining state planning and market forces producing technological development and greater prosperity.
ANSWER: d (p. 521)

35. As president of France, Charles de Gaulle's position in the Cold War was to
a. closely align France with the Warsaw Pact nations.
b. make France the "third" nuclear power and pursue a largely independent political course.
c. let American policy guide France and other European nations.
d. make France the leading European power in NATO.
ANSWER: b (p. 521)

36. The French economy under de Gaulle
   a. witnessed increased deficits, in part due to the nationalization of key industries.
   b. became the second leading producer of steel in the world.
   c. saw the GNP shrink to one-half that of Great Britain.
   d. advanced rapidly in traditional areas like railroads and steel.
      ANSWER: a (p. 522)

37. The first chancellor and "founding hero" of the West German Federal Republic was
   a. Helmut Kohl.
   b. Helmut Schmidt.
   c. Willy Brandt.
   d. Konrad Adenauer.
      ANSWER: d (p. 522)

38. Which of the following statement concerning postwar Great Britain is <u>false</u>?
   a. The National Insurance Act and National Health Service Act made Britain a welfare state in the 1940s.
   b. The Conservative party in the 1950s and 1960s revoked nearly all of the welfare legislation passed by the Labour party in the 1940s.
   c. Britain suffered from losing its pre-war colonial revenues.
   d. By the Suez Canal debacle, Britain was no longer a superpower.
      ANSWER: b (pp. 516, 522-523)

39. Problems faced by Great Britain in the 195s and 1960s included all of the following <u>except</u> the
   a. demands of trade unions for wages which rose faster than productivity.
   b. unwillingness of the British to invest in modern industrial technology.
   c. debt from its many international commitments.
   d. rapid rise and fall of Socialist coalition governments.
      ANSWER: d (p. 523)

40. The Common Market was
   a. primarily a military alliance of certain European countries.
   b. a forum of European nations founded to solve social problems.
   c. founded for economic reasons, one of which was to promote free trade among member nations.
   d. started for cultural reasons to combat American materialism.
      ANSWER: c (p. 523)

41. The student upheavals in the United States in the 1960s included all of the following <u>except</u>:
   a. demands for civil rights for African-Americans.
   b. a desire to adopt Soviet Communism as an alternative to rapacious capitalism.
   c. protests against the Vietnam War.
   d. increased sexual permissiveness.
      ANSWER: b (p. 524)

42. The social structure of the postwar European society has been greatly affected by a dramatic increase in the number of
   a. white-collar management and administrative personnel.
   b. the number of industrial workers.
   c. rural, agricultural workers.
   d. government workers, especially in the military.
      ANSWER: a (p. 525)

43. After the 1950s the ratio of blue-collar and industrial workers to the rest of the work in Western society
a. decreased..
b. increased.
c. remained the same.
d. led to a renewed interest in socialism.
ANSWER: a (p. 525)

44. For women, the end of World War Two brought
a. their greater integration in recovering European national economies.
b. their removal from the workforce and the war-time jobs they held to make way for returning male soldiers in search of work.
c. an immediate decline in birthrates due to the large numbers of men killed in the conflict.
d. greater opportunities for self-expression outside of the home.
ANSWER: b (p. 525)

45. In her path-breaking text, *The Second Sex*, the influential French feminist author Simone de Beauvoir argued that
a. women should renounce all contact with men and set up their own self-governing communes.
b. as a result of male-dominated societies, women were always and wrongly defined by their differences from men and consequently seen as second-class beings.
c. the Second World War had legitimated the political advantages and hegemonic power of males.
d. a "sexual revolution" was impossible and discouraged women outside of France from taking up her ideas.
ANSWER: b (p. 527)

46. One of the major accomplishments of women as the result of World Wars I and II was
a. the right to an abortion.
b. the right to vote.
c. equal pay for equal work.
d. equal quotas in job hiring.
ANSWER: b (p. 526)

47. One of the most revolutionary contributions of the sexual revolution was
a. no-fault divorce.
b. serial monogamy.
c. the birth control pill.
d. MTV.
ANSWER: c (p. 527)

48. The "permissive society" is characterized by all of the following <u>except</u>
a. sexual freedom.
b. experimentation with drugs.
c. declining rates of divorce.
d. decriminalization of homosexuality.
ANSWER: c (p. 527)

49. The outburst of student revolts in the late 1960s was instigated in part by
a. the Korean War.
b. overcrowded classrooms and lack of attention from professors.
c. discontent with government efforts to establish a welfare state.
d. a belief that the governments were becoming too sympathetic to communism.
ANSWER: b (p. 528)

50. The most violent student revolts took place in
   a. France, where students successfully encouraged unionized workers to back their protests.
   b. Britain, where conservative governments attempted to use military force against demonstrators.
   c. Germany, where young Nazi sympathizers attempted to reestablish the Third Reich.
   d. Italy, where anti-church demonstrations led to the burning of Cathedrals.
   ANSWER: a (p. 528)

RELEVANT WORLD-WIDE WEB SITES/RESOURCES

1. Cold War Hot Links (at St. Martin's College):
http://www.stmartin.edu/~dprice/cold.war.html
(A fine and quirky site with many links to other highly relevant sites on the subject. A great place to begin online document searches.)

2. Cold War International History Project:
http://cwihp.si.edu/default.htm
(Site maintained by the Woodrow Wilson International Center for Scholars. Very comprehensive online collection of original and translated primary documents in such areas as Cold War Origins, Leaders, Stalin Era, Reagan Era, etc. Highly recommended site.)

3. Cold War Policies Online:
http://ac.acusd.edu/History/20th/Coldwar0.html
(An excellent site including original documents, time lines, and fine maps which can be enlarged to chart the geopolitics of the conflict. The maps alone are accessible at their own site: http://ac.acusd.edu/History/20th/coldwarmaps.html)

4. Cold War: Soviet and Related History:
http://www.csusm.edu/public/guests/history/websites/coldwar.html
(Site maintained at California State University San Marcos. Contains fine translated primary diplomatic documents and memoirs presenting Soviet views on genesis and course of Cold War.)

5. Korean War:
http://www.koreanwar.org/
(A fine site devoted to all aspects of a "forgotten" conflict. Site is most notable for memoirs of American soldiers in the conflict posted online. Excellent material here for appreciation of oral history and memoirs as historical sources.)

RELEVANT VIDEO RESOURCES

The Berlin Airlift: The Most Dramatic Rescue, PBS Home Video, (60 minutes).(A new production documenting with original newsreels and interviews one of the signal events (1948) in the conduct of the Cold War.)

The Berlin Wall. Films for the Humanities and Sciences, (60 minutes).
(Available through Wadsworth Publishing.)

Birth of the Cold War, PBS Home Video, 2 cassettes (55 minutes each).

The G.I. Bill: The Law that Changed America, PBS Home Video, (60 minutes). (An excellent video source particularly appropriate for undergraduate instruction since it details the dramatic expansion of American higher education as millions of veterans (the parents and grandparents of today's students) used their benefits to pursue college and university degrees, often to the distaste of the WASP administrative elite and professorate at those institutions.)

Korea: The Forgotten War, PBS Home Video, 5 Programs, (55 minutes each). (One of the finest documentaries on all military and geopolitical aspects of this conflict.)

SUGGESTED STUDENT ACTIVITIES

1. One historian has maintained that the Cold War was "inevitable." Have students, using specific incidents and people, prove or disprove this statement.

2. Have students pick a European country and trace the development of the welfare state after World War II.

3. Have students do a comparative study of the Soviet Union under Lenin, Stalin, and Khrushchev. Were there any real differences in their rule? Which of the leaders was the most effective?

4. Have students do an essay on a modern day European educational system and determine how that system was influenced by the events of the 1960s.

CHAPTER 29
THE CONTEMPORARY WESTERN WORLD (SINCE 1970)

CHAPTER OUTLINE

I. Moving Beyond the Cold War: A New World Order?
  - A. The End of the Cold War

II. Toward a New Western Order
  - A. The Revolutionary Era in the Soviet Union
    1. The Gorbachev Era
    2. The End of the Soviet Union
  - B. Eastern Europe: The Collapse of the Communist Order
  - C. The Reunification of Germany
  - D. The Disintegration of Yugoslavia
    1. The War in Kosovo
  - E. Western Europe: The Winds of Change
    1. Germany Restored
    2. Great Britain: Thatcher and Thatcherism
    3. Uncertainties in France
  - F. The United States: The American Domestic Scene
  - G. Contemporary Canada

III. New Directions and New Problems in Western Society
  - A. Transformation in Women's Lives
    1. The Women's Movement
  - B. The Growth of Terrorism
    1. Terrorist Attack on the United States
  - C. The Environment and the Green Movements

IV. The World of Western Culture
  - A. Trends in Art and Literature
  - B. The Revival of Religion
  - C. The New World of Science and Technology
  - D. The Explosion of Popular Culture
    1. Popular Culture and the Americanization of the World

V. Toward a Global Civilization?

CHAPTER SUMMARY

With the Anti-Ballistic Missiles Treaty (1972), the United States and the Soviet Union believed they had reached a balance, or "equivalence," which would assure peace. The 1975 Helsinki Accords guaranteed human rights. However, detente declined with the Soviet invasion of Afghanistan in 1979. President Ronald Reagan introduced the cruise missile and began the development the Strategic Defense Initiative (SDI), or "Star Wars." However, by the early 1990s the Cold War had ended. Coming to power in 1985, Mikhail Gorbachev proposed radical reforms through *perestroika* (restructuring) and *glasnost* (openness), but his reforms had other results and at the end of 1991, several Soviet republics including Russia became independent and the Soviet Union was no more. Boris Yeltsin was elected

Russia's first president, but its quest for a free-market economy was complicated by organized crime and radical nationalists.

In Poland, Hungary, Bulgaria, Albania, Romania, and Czechoslovakia, Communist regimes collapsed. The Berlin Wall was torn down, and Germany was unified. Ethnic demands shook multi-ethnic Yugoslavia, and Slovenia became independent in 1991, but war resulted when Croatia declared its independence. "Ethnic cleansing" occurred in Bosnia-Herzegovina, and the province was divided between Serbs and Muslims-Croats, but only a bombing campaign by NATO brought autonomy to Kosovo with its ethnic Albanian majority.

In 1994 the EC (European Community) became the European Union, with a common currency, the *euro* (2002). German reunification came at considerable economic cost given the east's bankrupt economy. Britain's Margaret Thatcher curbed the labor unions, reduced welfare, and lowered taxes, but at a social cost. The Labour Party moved to the political center and was elected in 1997. Socialism failed to work in France, but economic problems continued under conservatives. Italy's economy rebounded during the 1980s, where political corruption was endemic. The United States suffered from economic problems and the Watergate scandal in the 1970s. Stagflation–inflation and unemployment–along with Iranian radicals holding American hostages brought the conservative Reagan to the presidency. The 1990s saw renewed economic growth under Bill Clinton, but scandals dogged his personal life. Canadians were divided over centralization vs. provincial rule and French-speaking Quebec's demand for autonomy.

Families became smaller and women's lives more diverse. The women's movement grew with "consciousness raising" groups, demands for abortion and contraception, and women's studies at universities. Terrorism increased. On September 11, 2001, a militant Islamic group hijacked four jetliners, crashing two into New York's World Trade Center. In response, President George W. Bush declared war on terrorism. Filling a labor shortage, many "guest workers" emigrated to Western Europe, but their presence often led to social tensions. Ecological problems led to the growth of Green Parties.

Abstract Expressionism and Pop Art were post-war art movements, and Modernism gave way to Postmodernism. In music, serialism and minimalism were influential. The "theatre of the absurd" and "magical realism" were significant literary movements. Existentialism reflected the meaningless of modern society: the world is absurd, there is no God, and man stands alone. A revival of religion was another response to the anxieties of the times. The transistor and the computer radically changed the modern world. "Pop culture"–much of it American–had a world-wide impact. Some claim that cultural differences will diminish, creating a new "global village," but globalization could also have negative ramifications, such as invasive pollution, multi-national corporate business abuses, and religiously-inspired violence.

LECTURE AND DISCUSSION TOPICS

1. Discuss the causes, consequences, and implications of a New World Order--if there is a New World Order.

2. Examine the causes and consequences of the decline, fall, and breakup of the Soviet Union.

3. Reagan v. Gorbachev, who ended the Cold War?

4. Compare and contrast the Balkans in 1914 and the Balkans at the beginning of the twenty-first century.

5. Assess the possible relationships between "Big Science" and "Big Environmental Problems," and the emergence of the Green movement.

6. Survey the promises and problems of the women's movement.

7. Compare and contrast the Cold War decades with era since the collapse of the Soviet Union, or is the world a safer or a more dangerous place?

8. Discuss the relationships between religion and nationalism in the post-Cold War world.

9. Examine today's world as a possible "clash of civilizations," including an assessment of the "new terrorism" and its causes and consequences.

10. Examine Modernism and Post-Modernism in the arts and literature, perhaps including a slide presentation for the visual arts.

MAP EXERCISES

1. The New Europe. MAP 29.1. What new nations resulted from the breakup of the Soviet Union? Which of those states might be scenes of future unrest and conflict, and why? How did the demise of the Soviet Union complicate the geopolitical world? (534)

2. The Lands of Former Yugoslavia. MAP 29.2. Did nationalism or religion play the major role in the breakup of Yugoslavia? Was Yugoslavia doomed from its post-World War I creation? Why and or why not? Why have the Balkans been a flashpoint of violence for so long? Does geography give at least a partial answer or explanation? (page 540)

DISCUSSION QUESTIONS FOR THE PRIMARY SOURCES (BOXED DOCUMENTS)

1. "Gorbachev and Perestroika": How revolutionary was Gorbachev's rejection of nuclear war? What impact did his idea of restructuring have on Communism and the Soviet state's capacity to reform itself? Did Gorbachev cause "the fall" of the Soviet Union? Why and/or why not? (page 535)

2. "Vaclav Havel: The Call for a New Politics": How different is Havel's view of politics than the mainstream politicians' views? What broader forces working in modern European society do you believe shape Havel's thinking? How can Havel's emphasis on our common humanity and responsibility to conscience nullify the selfishness of modern consumer society and contribute to a political and moral revitalization of Western Civilization? (page 538)

3. "Margaret Thatcher: Entering a Man's World": From this document, what appears to be Thatcher's greatest strength as a highly successful British politician at the national level? How does her evident and articulate ability to succeed in a "man's world" evoke the broader forces enabling women to have greater opportunities for political participation and self-expression in modern Western society? (page 541)

4. "Small is Beautiful: The Limits of Modern Technology": What is Schumacher's critique of modern technology? To what extent has this critique been substantiated by developments since 1975? What broader forces in Western Civilization active after 1939 may have contributed to the criticism of industrial technology in which Schumacher participates? (page 549)

STUDENT RESEARCH AND PROJECT TOPICS

1. How and why did the Cold War end? Did anyone "win" this conflict? Who? Why?

2. When, how, and why did the Soviet Union collapse?

3. In what ways have the former Soviet satellite nations handled the demise of Russian Communism as a ruling system? Have these countries been successful? Which countries have made the transition from totalitarianism to freedom most effectively? Why?

4. What are the basic problems and antagonisms between Serbia and the other countries that once made up Yugoslavia — Bosnia-Herzegovina, Croatia, Kosovo, Macedonia, and Slovenia? What forces in the post-Cold War world enabled this dangerous and bloody conflict to escalate so terribly?

5. What major economic problems have plagued the West during the 1970s, 1980s, and 1990s?

6. In what ways does the post-war feminist movement resemble the feminist movement of the nineteenth century? In what ways is it different?

7. What are Modernism and Postmodernism and how have they been expressed in art, music, and literature since 1945?

8. In what ways were the movements of existentialism and the revival of religion responses to the "despair generated by the apparent collapse of civilized values in the twentieth century"?

9. What was the role of science and technology in the post-war Western world? What fundamental critiques have been made of science? Why do you think the mass public is now both ignorant of and wary of science and scientists?

10. What role has popular culture played in the Western world since World War II?

11. What forces have conspired to cause the return of racism, war crimes, and genocide in the Balkans? How did the reformations or reformulations of society, politics, and culture in the region after World War II lay the groundwork for current upheavals there?

12. Does the world face a "clash of civilizations" in the near future? Why and or why not?

IDENTIFICATIONS

1. Helsinki Agreements
2. the "evil empire"
3. Mikhail Gorbachev
4. Persian Gulf War
5. Leonid Brezhnev
6. *perestroika*
7. *glasnost*

8. Boris Yeltsin
9. Solidarity
10. Lech Walesa
11. Vaclav Havel
12. Czech Republic and Slovakia
13. Erich Honecker
14. Slobodan Milosevic
15. Bosnia
16. Kosovo
17. the EC
18. *Ostpolitik*
19. Helmut Kohl
20. Margaret Thatcher
21. Thatcherism
22. Tony Blair
23. Francois Mitterrand
24. Watergate
25. OPEC
26. Ayatollah Khomeini
27. Pierre Trudeau
28. the IRA
29. World Trade Center
30. Green parties
31. Abstract Expressionism
32. Postmodernism
33. Theater of the Absurd
34. *Waiting for Godot*
35. Existentialism
36. Albert Camus and Jean Paul Sartre
37. Popes John XXIII and John Paul II
38. computers
39. MTV
40. NGOs

MULTIPLE CHOICE QUESTIONS

1. Between 1950 and the early 1970s, Western Europeans
    a. suffered deep economic depression because of the Cold War struggle.
    b. became accustomed to the East-West divisions and economic prosperity.
    c. demanded that the Untied States leave Europe.
    d. pursued a policy of neutralism.
        ANSWER: b (page 531)

2. One of the underlying causes for the end of the Cold War was
   a. the fall of Khrushchev in the Soviet Union and election of Reagan in the United States.
   b. financial difficulties for both the superpowers and the unbearable expenses of the arms race.
   c. peace movements in both countries.
   d. the end of the Afghan War.
      ANSWER: b (p. 532)

3. The 1975 Helsinki Agreements
   a. established American military dominance in Europe.
   b. accorded the Soviet Union the right to intervene in western European political affairs.
   c. recognized all borders in central and eastern Europe established since World War II thereby acknowledging a Soviet sphere of influence in Eastern Europe.
   d. provided for the transfer of American nuclear weapons and submarines to Europe.
      ANSWER: c (p. 532)

4. An appropriate symbol of détente between Russia and America was the ABM Treaty of 1972 that
   a. guaranteed massive American financial aid to the Russians.
   b. allowed the Russians to export more luxury commodities to the U.S. without paying import taxes.
   c enabled both countries to trade freely in aircraft, bonds, and minerals.
   d. pledged the two nations to limit their development of anti-ballistic missile systems thus avoiding a new arms race.
      ANSWER: d (p. 532)

5. Under the U.S. presidency of Jimmy Carter, a major goal of American foreign policy was
   a. new efforts to contain Communism around the globe.
   b. the protection of human rights globally.
   c. American withdrawal from European defensive alliances to counter Soviet power.
   d. the emplacement of new nuclear weapons systems in Europe for possible use against Russia.
      ANSWER: b (p. 532)

6. The American President who referred to the Soviet Union as the "evil empire" was
   a. Richard Nixon.
   b. Jimmy Carter.
   c. Ronald Reagan.
   d. Bill Clinton.
      ANSWER: c (p. 532)

7. The ruling policies of Mikhail Gorbachev in the Soviet Union
   a. included the forcible exportation of Russian Communism to Central and South America.
   b. evoked a "New Thinking" about world affairs and the balance of power leading to new arms limitation treaties and greater autonomy for Communist regimes in Eastern Europe.
   c. only increased political repression in Russia and did little to increase the political freedoms of eastern Europeans.
   d. grew out of Russian misperceptions of United States strengths and failed to appreciate that American military spending and tax reductions under Ronald Reagan had greatly increased American budget deficits.
      ANSWER: b (p. 532)

8. "Small" wars like the ones in Vietnam and Afghanistan demonstrated that
   a. the superpowers could never be at peace.
   b. there would always be a sphere of influence in the world where the superpowers would be in conflict.
   c. there would be wars that the superpowers could not win against a strong nationalist and guerilla type opposition.
   d. warfare in the world would be incessant.
      ANSWER: c (p. 532)

9. The first opportunity for testing the new relationship between the United States and the Soviet Union in the post-Cold War era was
   a. the Chinese-Vietnamese War.
   b. the Arab-Israeli War.
   c. the war in Angola.
   d. the Persian Gulf War.
      ANSWER: d (p. 532)

10. The Soviet Union under Leonid Brezhnev
   a. was completely shut off from Western influences.
   b. stressed worker incentives and increased efficiency in industrial production.
   c. saw heavy industry decline with improvement in agriculture.
   d. was static and calm, although it threatened Soviet intervention when socialism was threatened in eastern European nations.
      ANSWER: d (p. 533)

11. The problem of the Soviet Union in the 1970's and 1980's was the lack of vigorous leadership and reform under
   a. Brezhnev.
   b. Yeltsin.
   c. Gorbachev.
   d. Khrushchev.
      ANSWER: a (p. 534)

12. Mikhail Gorbachev's radical reforms under *perestroika* included all of the following except
   a. the demise of the office of president.
   b. the creation of a new Soviet Parliament.
   c. the creation of a market economy with limited free enterprise and private property.
   d. the open discussion of Soviet weaknesses in public.
      ANSWER: a (pp. 534-535)

13. One of the most successful independence movements among the Soviet republics during Gorbachev's rule occurred in the Baltic area of
   a. Afghanistan.
   b. Azerbaijan.
   c. Lithuania.
   d. Georgia.
      ANSWER: c (p. 536)

14. After the breakup of the Soviet Union, the leader of Russia became
  a. Boris Yeltsin.
  b. Andrei Sakharov.
  c. Leonid Brezhnev.
  d. Josif Venediktov.
    ANSWER: a (p. 536)

15. After the fall of the Soviet Union, Russia struggled with all of the following <u>except</u>:
  a. a renewed Communist Party majority which took over the government.
  b. organized crime.
  c. an uprising in largely Muslim Chechnia.
  d. economic hardships.
    ANSWER: a (p. 536)

16. Boris Yeltsin was succeeded as president of Russia by
  a. Lech Walesa.
  b. Mikhail Gorbachev.
  c. Vladimir Putin.
  d. Yuri Andropov.
    ANSWER: c (p. 536)

17. The Solidarity movement in Poland
  a. was temporarily crushed by General Lech Walesa in 1981.
  b. failed to gain massive support due to stiff opposition from the politically conservative Polish Catholic church.
  c. ended the Communist monopoly of power in 1988.
  d. was formed by Wladyslaw Gomulka in 1956.
    ANSWER: c (p. 536)

18. In 1990, the Communists lost power in Hungary to the political party known as the
  a. Round Table.
  b. Hungarian Socialists.
  c. Democratic Forum.
  d. Kadar Party.
    ANSWER: c (p. 537)

19. The leader of Czechoslovakia in 1990 who replaced the Communist government was the former dissident writer and philosopher
  a. Janos Kádár.
  b. Gustav Husák.
  c. Alexander Dubcek.
  d. Vaclav Havel.
    ANSWER: d (p. 537)

20. The brutal dictatorial Communist government of Nicolae Ceausecu occurred form 1965 to 1989 in
  a. Czechoslovakia.
  b. Bulgaria.
  c. East Germany.
  d. Romania.
    ANSWER: d (p. 537)

21. In 1988, the first free parliamentary elections to occur in Eastern Europe for forty years took place in
   a. Hungary.
   b. Austria.
   c. Poland.
   d. Estonia.
      ANSWER: c (p. 536)

22. The East German leader Erich Honecker was most noted for
   a. building the Berlin Wall in 1961.
   b. establishing a virtual dictatorship with the help of the Stasi or secret police in the 1970s and 1980s.
   c. urging the political unification of West and East Germany in the late 1980s.
   d. leading an unsuccessful independence movement from the Soviet Union in 1953.
      ANSWER: b (p. 538)

23. Yugoslavia was divided into warring factions because of
   a. demands for ethnic separatism.
   b. differences of political goals.
   c. support of the Serbs.
   d. lack of cultural diversity.
      ANSWER: a (p. 539)

24. After World War II, Yugoslavia was successfully held together by the efforts of
   a. Vaclav Havel.
   b. Marshal Tito.
   c. Slobodan Milosivik.
   d. Janos Kadar.
      ANSWER: b (p. 539)

25. The tactic of "ethnic cleansing," murdering or forcibly removing ethnic minorities from their lands in the former Yugoslavia, is a savage strategy of modern political terror practiced most brutally by
   a. Serbs.
   b. Croatians.
   c. Bosnians.
   d. Herzgovenians.
      ANSWER: a (p. 539)

26. The Treaty on European Union
   a. resulted in the unification of Germany.
   b. eased the path for Eastern European nations to become members of NATO.
   c. committed the states of the European Community to achieving a true economic and monetary union.
   d. established the tribunal to try those accused of committing war crimes in Bosnia and Kosovo.
      ANSWER: c (p. 540)

27. The common currency which was initially adopted by eleven member states of the European Union is the

a. continental.
b. euro.
c. maastricht.
c. francmark.
ANSWER: b (p. 540)

28. The reunification of Germany was accomplished under the leadership of

a. Willy Brandt.
b. Conrad Adenauer.
c. Helmut Kohl.
d. Eric Hindenburg.
ANSWER: c (pp. 540-541)

29. All of the following occurred in Great Britain under Margaret Thatcher except

a. a popular victory against Argentina in the Falklands War.
b. improved industrial production in the Midlands.
c. serious cutbacks in education.
d. a large military buildup and hard-line approach against Communism.
ANSWER: b (pp. 541-542)

30. In 1992, when Margaret Thatcher was forced to resign, her government was replaced by one led by

a. Clement Atlee.
b. John Finian.
c. John Major.
d. Ramsey McDonald.
ANSWER: c (p. 542)

31. The Red Brigades, a radical political terrorist group, complicated post-Cold War national politics and reform in

a. France.
b. Italy.
c. Austria.
d. Germany.
ANSWER: b (p. 545)

32. The economic problems of the United States in the 1970s are referred to as

a. inflation.
b. deflation.
c. stagflation.
d. hyperism
ANSWER: c (p. 543)

33. In Canada, the Parti Québécois, headed by René Lévesque has as its main political objective
   a. Canadian withdrawal from NATO.
   b. Canadian withdrawal from the United Nations.
   c. the secession of the French-speaking province of Quebec from the union of all Canadian provinces.
   d. the establishment of higher tariffs on manufactures to protect the Canadian economy from complete U.S. domination.
   ANSWER: c (p. 544)

34. A dramatic social development affecting the status and expectations of women in western Europe since the 1960's has been
   a. a persistent decline in birth rates across Europe with Italy's becoming the lowest in the world.
   b. moves by conservative governments to pass legislation making it far more difficult for women to work outside the home.
   c. the effective lobbying of the European Catholic churches to outlaw abortion and restrict the sale of contraceptives.
   d. the collapse of European social welfare states under the burden of rapidly aging populations.
   ANSWER: a (p. 544)

35. An example of "nationalist terrorism" is the
   a. Baader-Meinhof gang in Germany.
   b. IRA in Northern Ireland.
   c. New Order in Italy.
   d. Charles Martel Club in France.
   ANSWER: b (p. 545)

36. Terrorist acts in the late twentieth and early twenty-first centuries included all of the following <u>except</u>:
   a. the murder of eleven Israeli athletes at the 1972 Munich Olympic Games.
   b. the destruction of the Twin Towers in New York City.
   c. the assassination of the United States Secretary of State.
   d. the attacks on the ruling government and civilians in Northern Ireland.
   ANSWER: c (p. 545)

37. European Green movements
   a. won notable political successes in most European countries.
   b. were not very successful in most cases.
   c. made average people aware of severe environmental problems and gained a variety of local and national political offices.
   d. were primarily involved with the anti-nuclear movements in Europe.
   ANSWER: c (p. 546)

38. The post-World War II art world has been mostly dominated by
   a. New York City.
   b. Paris.
   c. Berlin.
   d. London.
   ANSWER: a (p. 546)

39. The American artist Jackson Pollock was most noted for
  a. a return to extreme realism in his paintings.
  b. Postmodernist sculptures.
  c. Pop Art, which celebrated the whims of popular culture.
  d. Abstract Expressionist paintings.
    ANSWER: d (p. 547)

40. The most famous of the practitioners of Pop Art was
  a. Jackson Pollock.
  b. Andy Warhol.
  c. Samuel Beckett.
  d. Albert Camus.
    ANSWER: b (p. 547)

41. Postmodernism differs from Modernism in
  a. abandoning tradition and the past in favor of "futurism.
  b. attempted to restore the Baroque and Rocco of the eighteenth century.
  c. favoring tradition rather than the future's "cutting edge."
  d. following the dictates of Herman Hesse.
    ANSWER: c (p. 547)

42. The "Theater of the Absurd"
  a. is well exemplified in Samuel Beckett's *Waiting for Godot*.
  b. reflected the postwar disillusionment with fixed religious and political ideologies.
  c. left the audience to wonder not about what is going to happen next but what is happening now.
  d. all the above
    ANSWER: d (p. 547)

43. Postmodernism in literature is exemplified in the writings of
  a. Albert Camus.
  b. James Joyce.
  c. Milan Kundera.
  d. Karl Barth.
    ANSWER: c (p. 547)

44. The philosophical doctrine of existentialism, with its emphasis on God as a fiction, no preordained human destiny, and the human creation of all values
  a. was dominant in the universities of Great Britain and the United States.
  b. concentrated on logic and a theory of knowledge.
  c. was totally at odds with the confidence and prosperity of the post-war world.
  d. was best expressed in the works of the French writers Albert Camus and Jean-Paul Sartre.
    ANSWER: d (p. 547)

45. The philosophical doctrine of existentialism stressed
  a. the need for people to create their own values and give their lives meaning.
  b. a return of God to the universe.
  c. the human need to find the sole and true meaning and purpose of the world.
  d. a complete withdrawal from an active, involved life.
    ANSWER: a (p. 547)

46. The most famous product of World War II scientific research was
- a. the jet airplane.
- b. radar.
- c. the atomic bomb.
- d. the theory of relativity.

ANSWER: c (p. 548)

47. A fundamental critique of the destructive nature of Big Science and modern technology was offered in *Small is Beautiful* written by
- a. Robert Oppenheimer.
- b. E.F. Schumacher.
- c. Ludwig Wittgenstein.
- d. Michael Goric.

ANSWER: b (p. 548)

48. The horrors of two world wars, the Cold War, and attendant socio-cultural upheavals have also stimulated a late twentieth-century religious revival exemplified in the works of Karl Barth, who has argued that
- a. the Bible, although not inherently true, still gives the best instruction for moral behavior.
- b. the sinful and imperfect nature of humans means that they can know religious truth not through reason but only through the grace of God.
- c. the mystery religions of Asia and the Middle East give humans a more transcendent sense of the divine and should come to replace Christian bigotry.
- d. a diversity of religious beliefs, including such "New Age" practices as witchcraft, the worship of healing rock crystals, and devotion to Gaia the Earth Mother, is a healthy sign of a new spiritualism in Western Civilization.

ANSWER: b (p. 548)

49. American motion pictures in the post-war years have
- a. been the primary vehicle for the diffusion of American popular culture throughout the world.
- b. completely destroyed the avant-garde expressions of Europe's "national cinemas."
- c. proven to be unpopular among European audiences.
- d. done little to reflect the changing sentiments of contemporary society.

ANSWER: a (p. 549)

50. Which of the following statements regarding popular culture since World War II is <u>false</u>?
- a. The politicization of sports and nationalistic sentiments were virtually eliminated by global telecasting.
- b. The United States has exerted the most dominant influence on worldwide cultural expressions.
- c. Advancements in mass communications technology have led to the emergence of global cultures in the 1960s and 1980s.
- d. MTV changed the music scene by making image as important as sound.

ANSWER: a (pp. 549-550)

RELEVANT WORLD-WIDE WEB SITES/RESOURCES

1. The Bureau of Atomic Tourism:
http://www.oz.net/~chrisp/atomic.html
(A prize-winning site containing links and information on a host of places around the world directly affected by the use, development, sighting, and storage of atomic weapons and the industrial infrastructure necessary for the creation of weaponry of mass destruction. An idiosyncratic and insightful tour of missile bases, reactors, obliterated cities, ruined Pacific atolls, and neighborhood fallout shelters. Excellent site for the study of the material culture accompanying "life with the Bomb.")

2. Centre Georges Pompidou (Pompidou Center), Paris
http://www.cnac-gp.fr/
(Foremost museum of modern art in France and one of the finest in Europe. Excellent online images from the museum's extensive collections of modern French and European art. Site includes fine lists of relevant links to other modern art resources on the Internet.)

3. MOMA, Museum of Modern Art, New York:
http://www.moma.org/
(Premier modern art collection in the world with outstanding selections online from the galleries. Superb for modern interior and industrial design. From the menu page, check "Online Projects" screen for highly accessible artistic material for students.)

4. The Andy Warhol Museum, Pittsburgh, Pa.
http://www.clpgh.org/warhol/
(Excellent site for a museum dedicated to the works of one modern artist. Good online materials for study of contemporary art trends including op-art, hyper realism, celebrity portraiture, and the effects of mass market advertising on modes of modern artistic expression.)

RELEVANT VIDEO RESOURCES

Solidarity. Films for the Humanities and Sciences, (60 minutes).
(Available through Wadsworth Publishing.) (Good video documentary on the rise of the Polish trade union clearly responsible for initiating Poland's break with Russian tyranny and the bankrupt ideology of communism.)

Soviet Disunion. Films for the Humanities and Sciences, (60 minutes).
(Available through Wadsworth Publishing).

Vietnam: The Ten Thousand Day War. PBS Home Video, Multi-part documentary on 6 cassettes, (Approx. 60 minutes each segment). (One of the most comprehensive documentaries on the subject, covering all military, social, cultural, and diplomatic aspects of the conflict—excellent use of contemporary television broadcasts and print media investigations. European anti-war protests covered effectively.)

RELEVANT MUSICAL PERFORMANCE

Ask your students.

SUGGESTED STUDENT ACTIVITIES

1. Have students pick an ex-Communist Bloc country and trace its development since the end of Communism in that country.

2. Have students do a post project showing the before and after maps of Europe with the demise of Communism.

3. Have students do a hypothetical essay dealing with the potential future problems of Europe and Western Civilization.

4. Students should know the various reasons for worldwide terrorism. How has the practice of modern terrorism changed over the course of the last several years? What do terrorists now seek to achieve and how are their motives and techniques different from the terrorist organizations of the 1970s and 1980s?